"Human Pot

Studien zu Aldous Huxley & zeitgenössischer Kultur
Studies in Aldous Huxley & Contemporary Culture

herausgegeben von

Prof. Dr. Bernfried Nugel
(Englisches Seminar der
Westfälischen Wilhelms-Universität Münster)

und

Prof. Dr. Lothar Fietz
(Seminar für Englische Philologie,
Eberhard-Karls-Universität Tübingen)

Band 9

LIT

Aldous Huxley
(drawing by Uwe Rasch)

Aldous Huxley, Man of Letters: Thinker, Critic and Artist

Proceedings of the
Third International Aldous Huxley Symposium
Riga 2004

edited by

Bernfried Nugel, Uwe Rasch
and Gerhard Wagner

LIT

Gedruckt auf alterungsbeständigem Werkdruckpapier entsprechend
ANSI Z3948   DIN ISO 9706

Cover Picture: Erwin J. Löhr

Printed with the support of Deutscher Akademischer Austauschdienst (DAAD),
Gesellschaft zur Förderung der Westfälischen Wilhelms-Universität zu Münster
e.V., and Aldous Huxley Society

Bibliographic information published by the Deutsche Nationalbibliothek
The Deutsche Nationalbibliothek lists this publication in the Deutsche
Nationalbibliografie; detailed bibliographic data are available in the Internet at
http://dnb.d-nb.de.

ISBN 978-3-8258-9034-6

A catalogue record for this book is available from the British Library

© LIT VERLAG Dr. W. Hopf Berlin 2007
Auslieferung/Verlagskontakt:
Fresnostr. 2   48159 Münster
Tel. +49 (0)251–62 03 20   Fax +49 (0)251–23 19 72
e-Mail: lit@lit-verlag.de   http://www.lit-verlag.de

Distributed in the UK by: Global Book Marketing, 99B Wallis Rd, London, E9 5LN
Phone: +44 (0) 20 8533 5800 – Fax: +44 (0) 1600 775 663
http://www.centralbooks.co.uk/acatalog/search.html

Distributed in North America by:

Transaction Publishers
Rutgers University
35 Berrue Circle
Piscataway, NJ 08854

Phone: +1 (732) 445 - 2280
Fax: + 1 (732) 445 - 3138
for orders (U. S. only):
toll free (888) 999 - 6778
e-mail:
orders@transactionspub.com

Transaction Publishers
New Brunswick (U.S.A.) and London (U.K.)

"HUMAN POTENTIALITIES":
STUDIEN ZU ALDOUS HUXLEY & ZEITGENÖSSISCHER KULTUR /
STUDIES IN ALDOUS HUXLEY & CONTEMPORARY CULTURE

is a series focused on the writings of Aldous Huxley, his ideas and their cultural context. Throughout his works he confronts us with the limits and possibilities of man's development. It is particularly in his later writings that the term "human potentialities" assumes a key-position. The individual, he maintains, should actualize his potential in relation to society and culture. Huxley's spectrum of ideas is culled from a wide range of different fields. He draws on the natural sciences and comparative religion, on economics and philosophy, art, politics, psychology, ecology, history, sociology, not to mention mysticism and critique of utopian thought. Hence the series is not confined to monographs on the literary significance of Aldous Huxley, but also presents a forum that aims to establish a dialogue between literary scholarship and other disciplines. The term "contemporary culture" refers not only to Huxley's standpoint but also to the views of the present-day reader.

We welcome dissertations, *Habilitationsschriften* and other monographs in German or English. As to their layout, they should follow the latest edition of the *MLA Handbook for Writers of Research Papers*. A special style sheet is available on request. Please send all inquiries to: Prof Dr Bernfried Nugel, Westfälische Wilhelms-Universität, Englisches Seminar, Centre for Aldous Huxley Studies, Johannisstr. 12–20, 48143 Münster, Germany; phone +49-251-83-24828; fax +49-251-83-24827, or e-mail: <nugel@uni-muenster.de>.

Die Reihe "HUMAN POTENTIALITIES": STUDIEN ZU ALDOUS HUXLEY & ZEITGENÖSSISCHER KULTUR / STUDIES IN ALDOUS HUXLEY & CONTEMPORARY CULTURE umfasst Arbeiten über den Schriftsteller und Denker Aldous Huxley und sein kulturelles Umfeld. In seinem gesamten Oeuvre hat Huxley durchgängig die Frage nach den Entfaltungsmöglichkeiten des Menschen aufgeworfen und mit dem Begriff "human potentialities" vor allem in seinem Spätwerk Überlegungen verbunden, die die Fähigkeit des Menschen betreffen, sein eigenes Potential besser auszuschöpfen und es als Individuum und gesellschaftliches Wesen kulturschaffend einzusetzen. Hierbei bezog Huxley prinzipiell Erkenntnisse und Vorstellungsweisen aus einem breiten Spektrum unterschiedlicher Gebiete ein, so aus Naturwissenschaft und Religion, aus Wirtschaft und Philosophie, aus Kunst, Politik, Psychologie, Geschichte, Soziologie, Mystik, Utopiekritik u. a. m. In diesem Sinne nimmt die Reihe nicht nur literaturwissenschaftliche Studien zu Huxley und seinem literarhistorischen Kontext auf, sondern steht als Forum auch solchen Arbeiten offen, die einen Dialog zwischen Literaturwissenschaft und anderen Disziplinen anstreben. Der Begriff „zeitgenössische Kultur" bezieht sich dabei sowohl auf Huxleys eigene Position als auch auf die des heutigen Lesers.

Willkommen sind Dissertationen, Habilitationsschriften und andere Monographien in deutscher oder englischer Sprache. Für die formale Gestaltung sei auf das *MLA Handbook for Writers of Research Papers* verwiesen. Auf Wunsch wird ein besonderes *style sheet* zugesandt. Alle Anfragen bitte an: Prof. Dr. Bernfried Nugel, Westfälische Wilhelms-Universität, Englisches Seminar, Aldous-Huxley-Forschungsstelle, Johannisstr. 12–20, 48143 Münster; Telefon +49-251-83-24828; Fax +49-251-83-24827, oder E-mail: <nugel@uni-muenster.de>.

For Ingo

(11.12.1976–25.3.2007)

Contents

V. Workshops

The Third International Aldous Huxley Symposium, organized by the Aldous Huxley Society and the Faculty of Modern Languages at the University of Latvia and held in Riga from 25 to 29 July 2004, served two main purposes, namely to ascertain Aldous Huxley's reputation in Eastern Europe and to stimulate wider interest in his thought and writings. Almost four years earlier, at the turn of the millennium, the Second Aldous Huxley Symposium in Singapore had tried to achieve something similar for South-East Asia, and the First Aldous Huxley Symposium, held as Centenary Symposium at the University of Münster, Germany, in 1994, had brought together Huxleyans from all over the world for the first time and paved the way for the foundation of the Aldous Huxley Society and the Centre for Aldous Huxley Studies at Münster in 1998. Thus the Riga Symposium was the third in a line of attempts to explore the contemporary significance and worldwide attraction of Huxley's thought beyond the confines of established literary scholarship. In this respect, also from Huxley's own point of view, the fact that a number of experts from other disciplines as well as many young scholars took part in the conference cannot be too highly appreciated.

As regards Huxley's reputation in Eastern Europe, a simple question arises: was he ever in Riga? Quite certainly not in person—but in spirit he has left his mark on the study of English literature at the University of Latvia, as the work of Prof Tamara Zalite in the 1960s to 1980s and the activities of her students, now on the staff of the Faculty of Modern Languages, clearly attest. Or, to ask the same question on a larger scale, did Huxley ever visit other parts of Eastern Europe? No again, but there is evidence that at a late point in his life he seriously planned to go to Leningrad (now St Petersburg again), which in the age of the Cold War surely was a difficult enterprise.

Writing to his wife Laura from London in July 1961, he mentioned that he had met a certain "Professor Tolstoy, son of the novelist Alexy (a distant relative of the great Tolstoy). He tells me that I am very popular in Russia among people of his generation and urged me to visit the country. So what about going on to Russia after Copenhagen for ten days or so. We would see everything we wanted under the best possible circumstances—for Tolstoy is an important man and knows everybody. [...] My own feeling is that we should go to Russia. I have never been anxious to go; but Tolstoy's extreme cordiality and obvious desire to be helpful have changed my feelings, and I think we ought to take the opportunity that is being presented to us." But the practical conditions of travelling to Russia in those days stymied Huxley's plans. After a visit to the Soviet consulate, he stated somewhat despairingly: "It seems that unless one is travelling in one of those Intourist Groups, one has to have an official invitation to go. Of course I could get such an invitation from the Writers' Group there: but (a) there is not much time for this and (b) I don't want to go officially. A letter from Professor Tolstoy would also get me a visa; but I hesitate to ask him—[...] meanwhile there is the problem of hotels, about which the consul was gloomy."[1]

If, because of these difficulties, Huxley could not make up his mind to travel eastward, the political situation in Europe had changed by 2004 to such a degree as to make it rewarding to belatedly take him to Eastern Europe by organizing our Third Aldous Huxley Symposium there. For various reasons, Riga promised to be an excellent venue: officially, the University of Latvia and the University of Münster, where the Centre for Aldous Huxley Studies is based, offered support as partner universities, and personally, the close acquaintance between Robin Hull, Curator of the Aldous Huxley Society, and Prof Ingrīda Kramiņa, former Dean of the Faculty of Modern Languages at the University of Latvia, formed a solid basis for planning a conference in Riga, which was of course also attractive by its historical setting of an old Hansa city.

The organizing committee, consisting of Prof Bernfried Nugel (University of Münster), Prof Jerome Meckier (University of Kentucky), Dr Claudia Olk (Humboldt University, Berlin), Dr Gerhard Wagner (University of Münster) on behalf of the Aldous Huxley Society, and Prof Ingrīda Kramiņa, Prof Viktors Freibergs, Lecturer Ilona Goldmane on behalf of the Faculty of Modern Languages, quickly agreed to choose "Aldous Huxley, Man of Letters: Thinker, Critic and Artist" as the general theme of the conference and accordingly arranged the main sections.[2] Basically, this overall arrangement has been retained in the present volume, even if a few papers were published elsewhere in the meantime.[3] In addition to the three sections devoted to Aldous Huxley, the thinker, the critic and the artist, the proceedings, as it was the case at the previous symposium, included a Panel for Young Huxley Scholars, from which five presentations have been chosen for this volume, and, as an entirely new Huxley conference item, a workshop section, which is here represented in full. Originally, the symposium programme offered 27 lectures, 14 panel presentations and 4 workshops, of which, unfortunately, 3 lectures and 3 panel presentations had to be cancelled for various reasons. But with regard to the second general purpose of the conference, i.e., the stimulation of wider interest in Huxley in Eastern Europe, it was highly encouraging to see that 11 lectures and presentations came from Latvia (6), Russia (2), Poland (1), Romania (1), and Montenegro (1). One of these items, the lecture by Rodica Dimitriu ("Al. I. Cuza" University of Iasi), was kindly read out by Prof Evelyn S. Firchow (University of Minnesota) to give the conference a Romanian perspective.

As the willingness to hold the conference in Riga was a great credit to the Latvian convenors, so they deserve most cordial thanks from all Huxleyans and participants. It is particularly to Prof Ingrīda Kramiņa, Prof Viktors

Freibergs and their friendly helpers that the Aldous Huxley Society is grateful for their indefatigable efforts to act as Huxley pioneers in Latvia and make the conference a success. But thanks are also due to the University of Latvia and the University of Münster (particularly Vice-Chancellor Claus Dapper) for their respective contributions to the costs of the conference.

To recapture the stimulating atmosphere at the symposium,[4] the editors have thought fit not only to present the main proceedings but also to include the addresses from Mrs Laura Huxley, the late Mr Matthew Huxley and the President of the University of Münster, Prof Jürgen Schmidt, as well as a brief memoir of Huxley studies at the University of Latvia, written by Prof Viktors Freibergs and printed in the conference brochure. By adding an index compiled by Uwe Rasch, M.A., the editors hope to make the present volume particularly useful for future research.

Finally, the editors wish to thank the Deutscher Akademischer Austauschdienst (DAAD), the Gesellschaft zur Förderung der Westfälischen Wilhelms-Universität zu Münster e.V., and the Aldous Huxley Society for generous subventions towards the printing costs of this volume, and the Centre for Aldous Huxley Studies for including the Riga proceedings in its series "Human Potentialities."

Münster, November 2007   Bernfried Nugel
Uwe Rasch
Gerhard Wagner
(University of Münster)

---

[1] Laura Huxley, *This Timeless Moment* (New York, 1968), 94, 97–98, 101.

[2] For the detailed symposium programme as well as notes on the speakers and abstracts of their papers see the Riga Symposium brochure accessible via <www.anglistik.uni-muenster.de/Huxley/RigaBrochure.pdf>.

[3] See Peter Firchow (University of Minnesota), "Aldous and Julian: Men of Science, Men of Letters," *Aldous Huxley Annual*, 4 (2005), 205–230; Jerome Meckier (University of Kentucky), "*Crome Yellow*: The Georgian Poet Orders His Tomb," *Aldous Huxley Annual*, 5 (2005), 69–96. Four papers were included in: *The Perennial Satirist: Essays in Honour of Bernfried Nugel*, ed. Peter E. Firchow and Hermann J. Real (Münster, 2005): David King Dunaway (University of New Mexico), "Broadcasting Aldous Huxley" (201–210); Sanford Marovitz (Kent State University), "*Brave New World*: A Drama of 1938" (211–220); Guin A. Nance (Auburn University at Montgomery), "Psyche and Soma: Aldous Huxley and the Mind-Body Connection" (277–290); James Sexton (Camosun College, Victoria, B.C.), "Aldous Huxley's Letters to Mary Hutchinson: A Partial

Preview to a Coming Collection" (313–325). David Bradshaw (Oxford University) plans to incorporate his lecture "The Odour of the Goat: Huxley, Prudery and Censorship" in a book of his own.

[4] For an overall report on the Riga Symposium see Sanford E. Marovitz (Kent State University, Ohio), "Aldous Huxley in Riga: The Third Aldous Huxley Symposium, Riga, July 2004," *The European English Messenger*, 14.1 (Spring 2005), 91–92.

LOOKING BACK ON THE ALDOUS HUXLEY SYMPOSIUM IN RIGA

With the appearance of this volume we proudly remember the Third International Aldous Huxley Symposium, entitled "Aldous Huxley, Man of Letters: Thinker, Critic and Artist," which was held at the University of Latvia in Riga in 2004.

When I say 'we,' I do not solely mean the academic community of Latvia who despite the 'iron curtain' managed to get acquainted with the ideas of Huxley, Kafka, Lawrence and other western writers, thanks to the individual efforts of university professors in those days. The pronoun 'we' also encompasses the students of today who not only study the English language but, doing so, also appropriate all the cultural values the newly acquired language opens up to them.

Thus we, staff as well as students, gladly recall the opportunity the summer of 2004 granted us.

Our deep gratitude goes to the convenors of the symposium, particularly to the International Aldous Huxley Society and the Faculty of Modern Languages at the University of Latvia. It was due to their mutual engagement and sustained efforts that the conference came true and presented a rare opportunity for Huxleyans in Latvia to experience Huxley's intellectual mobility and spirit of exploration in the numerous valuable presentations at the symposium.

On behalf of the Latvian convenors,

Ingrīda Kramiņa
Head of the Department of English Studies
Faculty of Modern Languages,
University of Latvia, Riga

ADDRESSES

All my best wishes for a richly promising conference. It is my loss not to be able to attend. I look forward to the report on your literary and public success.

With gratitude, Laura Huxley

I appreciate the opportunity to send a few words to participants at the Symposium "Aldous Huxley Man of Letters: Thinker, Critic and Artist."

Clearly, reviewing the list of contributors, Aldous attracts scholars from many countries and many cultures. He traveled the world encountering the diversity of cultures that enriched his life and work.

I think that he would be pleased that his writing is being widely read. Translations of *Brave New World* abound in many languages and most recently from countries formerly behind the Iron Curtain and China. How prescient the test tube babies and hatchery seem today in light of recent developments in the fields of genetics and cloning! Young people and students everywhere read *Brave New World*; one can only hope that these young people read and reflect.

I am gratified that Aldous' work is being studied by scholars. Much of the Huxley œuvre remains in print and even some of the more obscure writing has found publishers. I believe scholarship has led to the focusing of attention on the breath of ideas he explored especially in his essays. The publication of Aldous Huxley's *Complete Essays* in six volumes brings me great satisfaction and is clearly the result of the efforts of many scholars.

Matthew Huxley

To the Participants of the
Third International Aldous Huxley Symposium in Riga

Ladies and Gentlemen,

in my capacity as President of the biggest German partner university of the
University of Latvia I am highly pleased that the Centre for Aldous Huxley
Studies at the English Department of the University of Münster, in
cooperation with the International Aldous Huxley Society and the Faculty of
Modern Languages at the University of Latvia, contributes to the planning and
materialization of the Third International Aldous Huxley Symposium in Riga
and thus helps to strengthen the scholarly connections between both
universities. The world-famous writer Aldous Huxley, who once called
himself a bridge-builder between the humanities and the natural sciences, is
himself—multi-faceted as his interests as thinker, critic and artist are—an
impressive example of the fact that philosophy, literature and art have the
power to integrate different perspectives and mentalities. To test this
integrative potential of the liberal arts also in Eastern Europe is—all the more
so in the context of the current expansion of the European Union—one of the
main objectives of the Symposium: this is clearly reflected, among other
things, in the two Panels for Young Huxley Scholars, which comprise, in
almost equal number, presenters from Western and Eastern Europe and thus
form an outstanding component of the conference. It is particularly in this
spirit that I wish all participants a fruitful exchange of ideas and a successful
Symposium!

Professor Dr Jürgen Schmidt
President of the Westfälische Wilhelms-Universität Münster

Aldous Huxley's name in Latvia during the Soviet rule was not propagated or widely known among what one might call the general public, and yet there was a strong interest in his writing and ideas among quite a few scholars and students. The irony of the censorship in the old days was that it could, at least to some extent, be by-passed by individual initiative: although such authors as Huxley, Kafka, Lawrence, Proust and others were not included in many of the university syllabuses, their creative activities could be presented through individual efforts of university professors.

One of such names was Tamara Zalite, who not only had a deep personal interest in the writings of Huxley but who also devoted many sessions to discussing his works with her students. She also wrote a study of British modernist fiction entitled *Polyphony of Four Voices*, in which one of the voices was that of Aldous Huxley. Owing to Tamara Zalite's deep and insightful knowledge of British and American, and indeed also of world, literature and her ability to inspire enthusiasm among students and young scholars, Huxley's writing was very widely known at least among the students of the Modern Languages Faculty at the University of Latvia, where Tamara Zalite taught literature for many years. I myself had the opportunity to write my graduation thesis on Shakespeare quotations in Huxley's writing, and on the initiative of Tamara Zalite there were regular seminars and even reports in local (mainly university) publications and some also in the Transactions of Tartu University, with which she had very active links).

Tamara Zalite was not only a Professor of English (despite the fact that she was never officially granted the title she can be referred to as such without any reservations) but also a literary critic and a translator of Latvian literature into English as well as a member of the Shakespeare Society whose seat was Weimar.

Tamara's life was as complex and intense as her academic preoccupations. In 1938 she went to England to improve her English and attended various language courses, including those offered by the London Polytechnic and London Institute of Linguistics. After that she entered Birkbeck College at the University of London, where she did not finish her studies but embarked on her dream of a visit to Mexico, which, however, never came true because of the war. She returned to London and devoted her time to reading and the passion of her youth—ballet. Back to Latvia after the war, she began her teaching career, which was interrupted by deportation to Siberia. She survived and continued working as a teacher. Most of her career was spent at the University of Latvia, where she also defended her doctoral thesis. Tamara Zalite was the author of many books, among which are studies of Marcel Proust, John Fowles, Iris Murdoch, and Muriel Spark. One of her greatest literary passions always was Shakespeare, culminating in a book called *My Shakespeare*.

Venturing to be sentimental, I would say that the Third International Huxley Symposium held in Riga could have been one of the unformulated dreams of Tamara Zalite.

On behalf of the Latvian convenors,
Viktors Freibergs

I.

Aldous Huxley, the Thinker

Dana Sawyer

(Maine College of Art)

"THE *ERSATZ* OF SUCHNESS":
ALDOUS HUXLEY AND THE SPIRITUAL IMPORTANCE OF ART

The word *philosopher* means literally 'lover of wisdom,' and as everyone at this symposium knows, Aldous Huxley was indeed a philosopher, for he loved wisdom above all else and was a lifelong seeker of it. As a philosopher, Huxley was specifically a pragmatist, striving for solutions to a wide array of maladies that plague humankind—including overpopulation, our increasing materialism and the dangers of environmental degradation. Sadly, his philosophical work is overlooked today and Huxley is chiefly remembered (at least in academic circles) as a novelist. Several things are to blame for this, including the facts that Huxley was not professionally trained as a philosopher and he rarely presented his ideas systematically—as academics believe is best. But the real 'kiss-of-death' for Huxley's philosophical work results from the fact that he focused his inquiry on metaphysics, which for more than two centuries has been very unpopular. Today, as a lingering repercussion of modernism, positivism and scientific materialism, academics generally believe that metaphysics is a vacuous sub-discipline of philosophy, and the general public, following their lead, seems to accept this idea. But Huxley, whom I say again was a pragmatist, sagaciously studied metaphysics because he believed (like Plato, Hegel, and many others) that it is fundamental to a workable and useful philosophy.

Today, even after the postmodern revolution, philosophers continue to consider frivolous and irrelevant what cannot be quantified—including any idea of a metaphysical reality like Huxley's "absolute Ground" (or Plato's 'Pure Form' realm, the Hindu postulate of *brahman*, or the Buddhists' *dharmakaya)*. But Huxley pointed out repeatedly that we need not look beyond the physical world to find phenomena that science cannot quantify. He argued that most of what we find meaningful in life—including love and beauty—lies beyond science's ability to prove or even definitively describe. So are these phenomena also sophistries that we should dismiss from consideration when forming our philosophies? Are love and beauty irrelevant because science cannot prove their existence? Huxley found this an absurd notion and thought it more reasonable to simply admit that the scientific method has limitations for describing such things.[1] And so, if we consider the issue of metaphysics with reference to epistemology rather than ontology (i.e., relative to the problem of knowing instead of being), we realize that most of what we find meaningful in life is arguably metaphysical—transcendental to science's ability either to know or quantify it.

In this short lecture I will focus on the issue of beauty and look into how Huxley's theory of aesthetics is based in his metaphysics. I will do this for two reasons. First, because of all the philosophical sub-disciplines Huxley spends the least amount of time discussing aesthetics,[2] so this analysis may add something to our understanding of his overall viewpoint. The second reason for this analysis is in the spirit of Huxley himself, for it focuses on the more broadly practical. We live in a time when art has been increasingly pushed to the periphery by a culture preoccupied with physical comfort and pleasure. Today, when science programmes and even sports programmes receive an integral multiple of the public funding available to the arts, Huxley's theory gives cogent support for why we should, as individuals and as a society, reconsider our relationship to art.

The thesis of this lecture is that Huxley believed that art is a vehicle of truth and therefore of tremendous benefit to humanity. The truth to which it leads is synonymous with beauty and likewise absolute, timeless, and trans-cultural. But art itself is not, strictly speaking, timeless or trans-cultural, nor is it synonymous with beauty; art is a means of connecting the human mind with a Beauty and Truth transcendental to the physical world—including the forms and images of art. Art leads us to truth but it is not the truth; art is a means to an end and should not be considered an end in itself. There is no 'art for art's sake' in Huxley's thinking. Art is a spiritual tool that can facilitate an awakening into the "unitive knowledege" (a secular version of Hindu or Buddhist enlightenment), and since enlightenment is Huxley's ultimate goal, this is art's ultimate value and purpose. He agrees with Plotinus that "he who beholds beauty becomes beautiful,"[3] and wishes to activate that connection.

The best expression of Huxley's mature outlook is found in *The Perennial Philosophy* (1945).[4] He drew this position from many sources (believing, as he did, that there is one spiritual insight at the heart of the world's religions) but his synthesis is closest to the Advaitin (non-dual) branch of Vedanta philosophy,[5] an Indian viewpoint that more than a century earlier had influenced such German philosophers as Schelling and Schopenhauer. Advaita Vedanta, based on the Upanishads, maintains that all reality emerges from one infinite, unmanifest source of spiritual energy called *Brahman*— capitalized here to signify its absolute nature. Of course, some of the things that emerge are human beings—and so we too are connected to *Brahman*, and in essence non-different from it. *Brahman*, which Huxley more often referred to as the "divine Ground of being," after Meister Eckhart's terminology, is in fact the essence of everything—or as the famous Upanishadic dictum states, "I am That, you are That, all this is That, and That alone is."[6]

Huxley had first learned about Vedanta in the early nineteen-thirties from his friend Gerald Heard, and he quickly became intrigued by its possibilities for interpreting and improving the human condition. When the Hindu scripture states "Tat Tvam asi", "you are That," it is issuing us a wake-up call to stop thinking of ourselves as only physical beings muddling through the work-a-day world. We may think of ourselves as only a man or a woman, but in reality we are also the infinite, unchanging, timeless oneness of *Brahman*, an absolute field of pure energy and intelligence at the root of our being. Waves on the ocean, so the analogy goes (an analogy Huxley often used), are not ultimately individual entities; they are, at their source, the ocean itself. Unfortunately, we are prevented from realizing our 'ocean' side, according to both Vedantists and Huxley, because without refinement of our consciousness, we mistake the realm of change and multiplicity, including our bodies and minds, for the whole story of our existence and the whole possibility of our experience.

Huxley saw this as lamentable because without knowing the experience of our complete nature, we in some sense know nothing about ourselves at all. The value of all knowledge and experience is relative to the knower and, to put it simply, without knowing who we really are, how can we know what we really like, want, or need? Without knowing itself as ocean, the wave lacks perspective and so flounders in its appreciation of life: "It is because we don't know who we are, because we are unaware that the Kingdom of Heaven is within us, that we behave in the generally silly, the often insane, the sometimes criminal ways that are so characteristically human" (*PP*, 14).

Huxley was convinced that there exists (or, at least, there could exist) a trans-rational, trans-cultural truth underlying the material universe—an absolute Being underlying all discrete beings. And since it is trans-cultural (dependent upon no humanly created values or ideals), it is also pan-cultural, available everywhere to everyone, and therefore a potential means of uniting human beings one to the other through a mutual apprehension of their singular essence, as all waves are a part of one ocean. Here Huxley was arguing in agreement with his character Anthony Beavis, who observes at the end of *Eyeless in Gaza*: "United at the depths with other lives, with the rest of being. United in peace. [...] For beneath all being, beneath the countless identical but separate patterns, beneath the attractions and repulsions, lies peace. [...] Peace from pride and hatred and anger, peace from cravings and aversions, peace from all the separating frenzies. [...] Peace in the depths, under the storm, far down below the leaping of the waves, the frantically flying spray."[7]

If this sounded too good to be true, Huxley only asked that his readers consider his logic and explain where it failed. He was not advocating with this metaphysics a return to religious supernaturalism. If anything, he wanted to embrace supra-naturalism, contact with a Truth beyond the physical level of existence. Of course, since this absolute level of Being was, in essence and by nature, beyond the physical world, science could never verify it—in fact, could never either prove or disprove its existence. But the postulate of this "Ground," this *Brahman*, Huxley believed, contradicts no scientific fact, and that it cannot be verified by science does not mean that it cannot be experienced. Perhaps it is simply another unquantifiable phenomenon like love or beauty. And certainly investigation should not be avoided just because we have a philosophical bias against metaphysics.

Huxley advocated that whether the Ground exists or not should be found out by stringent effort to experience it, and enlightenment (an ongoing experience of the Ground) should not be dismissed out of hand because it cannot be quantified. Scientists, he said, may disclaim this as mysticism, as "subjective and illusory," but should remember that any direct intuition must seem subjective and illusory to those who have not yet experienced it. As an analogy, he pointed out that it is impossible for the "deaf to form any idea of the nature or significance of music" (*EM*, 287). He suggested that his critics should be more empirical about the possibility. He cast the burden of proof back into their court, asking of the scientists and materialist philosophers the same open-mindedness his grandfather, the famous scientist Thomas Henry Huxley, had once asked of the Church. He wanted them to remember, as they doubted, those "Pisan professors who denied, on *a priori* grounds, the validity of Galileo's direct intuition (made possible by the telescope) of the fact that Jupiter has several moons."(*EM*, 289)

Even in this brief overview of Huxley's philosophy we have laid out both his ontology and epistemology. His ontology is clear because he includes a truth claim about the nature of existence and our place in it. He argues for a non-dual position, believing that Reality is ultimately a Oneness whose essence is transcendental and non-different from our own. And his epistemology, too, is clear because he tells us that the ultimate nature of Truth and Knowing is found in directly experiencing this essence. And here we see another reason why Huxley's position is often disliked, for in his mysticism we find a refutation of the Western philosophical tradition's starting point.

In the West we have assumed axiomatically that ultimate truth is a product of thinking and can be grasped directly by the rational mind via a system of ideas. Truth is the province of thinkers and so philosophers can get directly at it. Huxley believed that this reveals an epistemological assumption about the nature of Truth that is no less grandiose or presumptuous than his own mystical leanings (especially since ultimate truth remains a Holy Grail that no thinker has ever definitively discovered). In his system, the mind can only grasp an intellectual analogue of Truth, and this analogue differs as much from the direct experience of *Brahman*, the absolute Truth, as a cake recipe differs from a cake. He offered logical reasons for why we should go beyond logic to seek an experience of the "unitive knowledge," a direct cognition of our oneness with *Brahman*. Huxley believed that the Truth could be, at least to some extent, described in words (which is why he wrote *The Perennial Philosophy*), but he made it clear that all descriptions are ultimately inferior to Truth: "The subject matter of the Perennial Philosophy is the nature of eternal, spiritual Reality: but the language in which it must be formulated was developed for the purpose of dealing with phenomena in time. [...] The nature of Truth-the-Fact cannot be described by means of verbal symbols that do not adequately correspond to it" (*PP*, 128).

Description and argument offer rational support for seeking the experience but only the experience is an apprehension of Truth. Truth is trans-rational and beyond the senses; it is ultimately something that we must know ontically—by *being* it. In that experience, Huxley contended, "we not only have, but are, the unitive knowledge of the divine Ground" (*PP*, 29). In his last published article he described his philosophy as a variety of 'mystical existentialism,'[8] for he believed human consciousness has the potential to experience a hierarchy of existential states—including, at its apex, a breakthrough into a continuous embrace of the unitive knowledge. Truth then is a state of existence, a condition of Buddha-like awakening.

But how can this unitive knowledge be gained? If rational thought can only point out its possibility, what method of knowing can directly reveal it? Huxley, in agreement with Schiller, Coleridge, and Emerson before him (and for very similar philosophical reasons), argued that art provides such a method. Huxley believed that art gives us a glimpse of absolute Truth. In fact, that is what makes it beautiful; it leads us to the experience of Beauty itself—which, "along with Goodness and Truth, takes its place in the trinity of manifested Godhead."[9] In this quote Huxley equates the Ground of Being with "Godhead" and he contends in his philosophy that art is one way of touching it: "The aesthetic experience is in some sort an analogue of the mystical experience. By coming to know perfection in a work of art, we gain a kind of knowledge of the ultimate nature of things" (*TV*, 120). And so art can do what logic cannot; it can open us ontically to Truth, and this is valuable to Huxley specifically because it transforms and elevates us.

But in Huxley's system art, though extremely valuable, like rational discourse, has its epistemic limitations; and these are significant, for they reveal the nuances of how art works for him. Specifically, art is limited because it cannot guarantee a glimpse of the unitive knowledge. We can be drenched in art and not necessarily get wet. Fans of Huxley's novels—and there are many here today—will remember Jo Stoyte, the consummate Philistine of *After Many a Summer*, who owns a beautiful painting by Vermeer (which he keeps in his elevator!) only to boost his social prestige. Even in the presence of such a great work of art, Stoyte is not edified in the least. So art can uplift us but it will not do so necessarily.

Secondly, even when art does edify, it is limited in that the experience it gives is generally inferior to the unitive knowledge in both kind and quantity. Sometimes art provides a breakthrough into pure Beauty, an aesthetic apprehension of the absolute Ground, but too often it conveys only a shadow of Beauty—a vague, imperfect, more relative experience that Huxley classifies as "visionary experience." Visionary experience is uplifting and valuable but it is a step down from the highest insight.[10] And even when art does give a glimpse of pure insight, it is just that—a glimpse only, a temporary experience of what ideally we will make permanent in enlightenment. Huxley argued this point as early as 1936 and we find this bitter summation in *Eyeless in Gaza*. After Mr Croyland observes, "'The great artists carry you up to *heaven*,'" Mark Staithes objects: "'But they never allow you to stay there [...]. They give you just a taste of the next world, then you fall back, flop, into the mud. Marvellous while it lasts. But the time's so short. And even while they've actually got me in heaven, I catch myself asking: Is that all?'" (*EG*, 302).

A third reason why aesthetic experience is limited is simply that it is not an exclusive or necessary means for awakening. Appreciating art objects is not the only way to ontically know the Truth. Huxley sees art as a kind of yoga— and there are other yogas that work at least as well. The word yoga derives from the Sanskrit verb root *yuj,* meaning 'to unite.' *Yoga* is a participle meaning 'union,' and in Indian philosophy it refers to any practice, including meditation and breathing exercises, that results in uniting our relative consciousness with our essential self. Appreciation of art is simply one type of yoga, one way to achieve the "unitive knowledge," and since it is neither necessary nor generally enough, Huxley believed it should not be confused for an ultimate end or otherwise thought irreplaceable.

To understand these limitations better, let us look further into the mechanics of how art works for Huxley. Art is a phenomenon of the physical world, and therefore it has implicit shortcomings for apprehending Beauty and Truth. In *The Perennial Philosophy,* Huxley points out that the absolute Ground has no relative qualities because it is essentially transcendental to time and space. It is, as the Upanishads put it, larger than the largest and smaller than the smallest. It is simultaneously at the heart of the atom and out beyond the rim of the universe. And consequently, it cannot be directly conveyed or captured by words, sounds, or images—all of which are bound by time and space. Huxley believed that no work of art can directly reveal the Ground because as a physical phenomenon art can only depict what can be seen, the things of relative existence.

Huxley believed that in a work of art, consciously or unconsciously, the artist is trying to capture pure Beauty, trying to bind what is by its very nature boundless: "The aim of art in all cases is to give form to the essentially formless" (*Vedanta*, 120). And, of course, this is quite impossible. For art, even when brilliant, cannot hold the Ground directly—as a bucket holds a volume of water. And so artists must find ways to suggest the formless Truth, to conjure and invoke Beauty. In their work, they use lines, forms, and tones to nudge us beyond the world of relative phenomena into an experience of the Ground.[11] In Huxley's view, this principle holds true for other arts as well, including literature: "Verbalized thought points the way to the wordless not-thought which is the ground of our being. Self-knowledge is the awareness of this wordless ground; but the road to wordlessness runs through the realm of words."[12] Or as T. S. Eliot, a friend of Huxley's, once put it, "only by the form, the pattern, can words or music reach the stillness."[13]

In summary, Huxley argues that we should appreciate art much more than we do, for it is a doorway into Truth, and an epistemic tool superior to rational thought in many ways. The great artists—and in this category Huxley put Paolo Uccello, Michelangelo, Vermeer, Rembrandt, Vuillard, and a few others[14]—are geniuses of using physical forms to conjure eternal Beauty. But still, in light of its inherent limitations, we must be careful not to over-value art, or sacralize it by making it an end in itself: "By itself, art can never be completely redemptive. It can only point in the direction from which redemption comes; it can only indicate at one remove the nature of the primordial and ineffable Fact" (*TV*, 120).

Art is a means for accessing Beauty but if it cannot contain Beauty directly—and since it cannot—we must not overly glorify it. If the artist or aesthete "persists in worshipping the beauty in art and nature without going on to make himself capable [...] of apprehending Beauty as it is in the divine Ground, then he is only an idolater" (*PP*, 138).

No object or form can function perfectly as a springboard into the unitive knowledge, and no springboard will work for everyone. Forms, formats, and styles are relative entities. They have different significance in different cultures, and so objects of art that work enormously well in one culture can be closed doorways for people from another: "An Indian, for example, finds European orchestral music intolerably noisy, complicated, over-intellectual, inhuman. It seems incredible to him that anyone should be able to perceive beauty and meaning, to recognize an expression of the deepest and subtlest emotions, in this elaborate cacophony" (*EM*, 287). Today we find significant the paintings of the Impressionists but in their own time they were generally thought ugly. Max Nordau, a German psychologist writing a few years after the Impressionists, even argued that their paintings were proof of psychosis.[15] No object, Huxley believed, is sufficient in and of itself, everywhere, always.

Today, we continue to stockpile pieces of art as though they implicitly contain Beauty. We have even tried to quantify art's value by putting price tags on its relative worth as investment property. But if Huxley is right, then worshipping art objects is a kind of idolatry—in many ways like confusing a faucet for water, or an airplane for where it takes us. A particular work of art can have profound value as an efficient means for experiencing Beauty in a particular culture at a particular time, and so it should be respected and cared for, but Beauty alone should be worshipped and Beauty alone is the goal. We say that great art is timeless but from Huxley's perspective that is only true when and if art transcends itself, transporting us into the Timelessness, and this depends upon conditions that cannot be guaranteed for any particular art object.[16] Of course, the plus side of this is that since beauty is not contained in the object directly, virtually any object can become—for someone somewhere—a significant springboard into Beauty. Under the right conditions, a person could be transfigured not only by a sunset or a symphony but even the movement of a bug or the shape of a bit of beach glass. This may actually explain why hip-hop music and certain postmodern artists are able to find a fan base.

Having sketched out his view of aesthetics one sees that Huxley greatly respected and endorsed the world of art but he did so provisionally. And when *The Doors of Perception* came out, critics jumped on him for presenting art as a vehicle for Beauty rather than as inherently beautiful. "I rather think that the people who were most angry," Sybille Bedford writes, "were the aesthetes who were really outraged by Aldous' attempt to put art in its place."[17]

Artists and their appreciators were appalled at Huxley's claim that true mystical experience seemed to make art obsolete. In *The Doors of Perception* he had written: "I strongly suspect that most of the great knowers of Suchness [a Buddhist term for ultimate Truth] paid very little attention to art."[18] And also: "Art, I suppose, is only for beginners, or else for those resolute dead-enders, who have made up their minds to be content with the *ersatz* of Suchness, with symbols rather than with what they signify, with the elegantly composed recipe in lieu of actual dinner"(*DP*, 29–30). But Huxley was not criticizing art in and of itself; his point was that for an enlightened person, whom he believed experiences every moment with consummate richness and significance, art objects would be no more valuable than any other phenomena, for example, "the hedge at the bottom of the garden" (*DP*, 19).

Huxley was not saying that art is uniformly worthless. He was saying that it is of much less value to someone who has become a living Buddha—that the human mind, if properly awake, can see all the world as a continuous masterpiece of unsurpassed beauty and not require humanly created art for its edification. But it seems doubtful that his position constitutes much of a threat to museums and galleries since most people are likely to fall short of being Buddhas and could, after all, use a bit of upliftment. For the unenlightened person, Huxley avidly recommended art—writing forty-five articles on visual art alone. He believed that great art, when enjoyed by a capable aesthete, performs a miracle of transubstantiation, converting crude consciousness into an ontic appreciation of Beauty. And, like his great-uncle, Matthew Arnold, Huxley argued that our culture is falling into a state of materialism and spiritual destitution partially from lack of that miracle. Art is, or can be, a great spiritual medicine. And passing it off as nothing more than entertainment or decoration—as our society generally does—is dead wrong. We think art frivolous only because we wrongly appraise its potential. In his introduction to *Texts and Pretexts*, an anthology of poetry compiled during the Great Depression, Huxley wrote: "An anthology compiled in mid-slump?

Fiddling, you protest indignantly, while Rome burns. But perhaps Rome would not now be burning if the Romans had taken more intelligent interest in their fiddlers."[19] For anyone who is less than enlightened—which after all is the vast majority—Huxley urged a much greater embracing of art. He wanted more museums, not fewer.

Huxley's viewpoint is certainly anomalous to the mainstream philosophical tradition, but, as a way of closing, it is interesting to point out that Huxley does not stand alone. Huxley claimed that there is a "perennial philosophy," a natural and eternal religion, implicit within reality. But whether this is true or not there has been a persistent trend in Western philosophy for more than two hundred years to think so. For instance, we find in Friedrich Schelling's *The System of Transcendental Idealism*, published in 1800, an almost perfect correlate to Huxley's position, and we find agreement with Huxley's general world-view and aesthetic theory in the writings of Schiller, Coleridge, Emerson, Kandinsky, Mondrian, and Ananda Coomaraswamy.[20] This tradition, which arguably has its Western classical roots in the philosophy of Parmenides, is based in metaphysics but carries a set of recessive memes that continue to resurface in our culture. Today we find this viewpoint in the writings of Ken Wilber, Huston Smith, Andrew Harvey, and Pico Iyer, and in the aesthetic theory of the painter Alex Grey, to give but one example.[21]

Psychology has taken over these memes to the greatest extent—first picked up by the transpersonalists, including Rollo May, Gordon Allport, and Abraham Maslow, and currently evident in the work of Stanislav Grof,[22] all of whom were deeply influenced by Huxley. This viewpoint acts as a possible antidote to materialism, posing what Maslow termed "self-actualization" as an alternative conception of wealth, and on those grounds alone we should be willing to investigate its possibilities.

Today, we in the West live in an era of abject materialism. We live in a time of rampant consumption and rampant waste, a time when 'citizen' has become synonymous with 'consumer' and avarice has been elevated to a virtue. Huxley worried about this direction of our culture and wrote *Brave New World* as a warning against it. Today environmentalists buttress Huxley's position by arguing that if we do not back off from our present course, we may soon exhaust the world's natural resources and cause a degree of environmental degradation that disallows our very existence. To avoid this tragedy, Thom Hartmann, Bill McKibben, Amory Lovins, Lester Milbrath, and many others advise that we reconceive 'affluence' as something other than material goods. In their lists of possibilities (including 'wealth' as leisure time, health and fitness, and stronger relationships with our families, friends and communities), these writers uniformly cite the value of spiritual growth and aesthetic development. For Huxley, as we have seen, these two were in some sense synonymous, and certainly his theory of aesthetics offers a compelling rationale for how and why art might help lead us beyond what

Paul Wachtel has called our current "poverty of affluence."[23] This is the practical goal of Huxley's aesthetics—and Huxley, as was pointed out, wished above all else to be of use. In the final analysis, whether we agree with his theory or not, Huxley poses provocative questions deserving of further exploration. Is there such a thing as self-actualization and enlightenment? Is self-actualization the highest form of knowledge? Is art a means for knowing and self-actualizing? And if we wish for art to help us reach beyond materialism, does it make sense that we constantly commodify it?

---

[1] See, e.g., Aldous Huxley, *Ends and Means* (London, 1937; hereafter, *EM*), 267: "Science did not and still does not possess intellectual instruments with which to deal with these aspects of reality."

[2] For example, note that in *The Perennial Philosophy* (New York, 1945; hereafter, *PP*) there is only one reference to 'beauty,' and all references to 'art' and 'artist' in the index appear on just four pages.

[3] Cited in Huston Smith, *The Soul of Christianity* (San Francisco, 2005), xxii.

[4] Further articulation of its details, with special reference to his mature theory of art and aesthetics, is found in *Themes and Variations* (1950), *The Doors of Perception* (1954), *Heaven and Hell* (1956), *Adonis and the Alphabet* (1956), *The Human Situation* (published posthumously, 1978), and his essays for *Vedanta for the Western World* (1945), *Vedanta for Modern Man* (1945), and Gerald Heard's interesting little book *Prayers and Meditations* (1949).

[5] See Dana Sawyer, "What Kind of a Mystic was Aldous Huxley Anyway?" *Aldous Huxley Annual,* 2 (2003), 207–218.

[6] "Tat Tvam Asi" is a famous Advaitin *mahavakya* (great saying) from Chandogya Upanishad. For an excellent explanation of it, see Eliot Deutsch, *Advaita Vedanta: A Philosophical Reconstruction* (Hawaii, 1973), 49.

[7] Aldous Huxley, *Eyeless in Gaza* (New York, 1936), 618–619. Hereafter, *EG*.

[8] See Aldous Huxley, "Shakespeare and Religion," in: *Aldous Huxley: A Memorial Volume*, ed. Julian Huxley (New York, 1965). The next to last line reads: "We are well on the way to an existential religion of mysticism" (175). And note that in *Themes and Variations* (New York, 1950; hereafter, *TV*), 122, he applauds Maine de Biran as a "mystical existentialist."

[9] Aldous Huxley, "Some Reflections on Time," *Vedanta for Modern Man*, ed. Christopher Isherwood (Hollywood, 1945), 119. Hereafter, *Vedanta*.

[10] See Aldous Huxley, *Heaven and Hell* (New York, 1956; hereafter, *HH*), 56: "Visionary experience is not the same as mystical experience. Mystical experience is beyond the realm of opposites. Visionary experience is still within that realm. [...] [It] is merely a vantage point, from which the divine Ground can be more clearly seen than on the level of ordinary individualized existence."

[11] See *PP*, 138: "The poet is born with the capacity of arranging words in such a way that something of the quality of the graces and inspirations he has received can make itself felt to other human beings in the white spaces, so to speak, between the lines of his verse."

[12] Aldous Huxley, "Literature and Modern Life," *Aldous Huxley: Complete Essays*, ed. Robert S. Baker and James Sexton (Chicago, 2002), VI, 337.

[13] T. S. Eliot, *Four Quartets* (New York, 1943), 19.

[14] One of the best descriptions of Huxley's favorite visual artists, along with his reasons why, appears in *HH*, 30–44.

[15] See Max Nordau, *Degeneration* (New York, 1895), e.g., 15, 27.

[16] Huxley writes that "aesthetic goods are precious," but, "to regard any of these temporal goods as self-sufficient and final ends is to commit idolatry" (*Vedanta*, 118).

[17] Sybille Bedford, *Aldous Huxley: A Biography* (New York, 1974), 544.

[18] Aldous Huxley, *The Doors of Perception* (New York, 1954), 29. Hereafter, *DP*.

[19] Aldous Huxley, *Texts and Pretexts* (London, 1932), 1.

[20] Ananda Coomaraswamy was for thirty years a research fellow at the Boston Museum of Fine Art, and he wrote several books on art and aesthetics including *The Dance of Shiva* and *The Transformation of Nature in Art*. Huxley was familiar with and quoted from both these texts and others. Coomaraswamy's Advaitin viewpoint is very close to Huxley's and the former certainly influenced the latter—as he also influenced Rockwell Kent and many other intellectuals contemporaneous with Huxley.

[21] See Alex Grey, *The Mission of Art* (New York, 2001), especially 57–69.

[22] Abraham Maslow's *Toward a Psychology of Being* (New York, 1968), in which he lays out his view of the human psyche and how it may reach "self-actualization" via an accumulation of "peak experiences" (including those gained by enjoying works of art) is perhaps the most famous, but for a much more recent treatment, see Stanislav Grof, *Psychology of the Future* (New York, 2000).

[23] See Paul Wachtel, *The Poverty of Affluence* (New York, 1983).

Gerhard Wagner

(University of Münster)

ALDOUS HUXLEY AND THE WAYS TO KNOWLEDGE[1]

It is, to adapt a well-known phrase from the beginning of Jane Austen's *Pride and Prejudice*, "a truth universally acknowledged" that Aldous Huxley was an intellectual of the first order. Stemming from an academic family, he wanted to become a scientist, but his defective eyesight put an early end to his ambitions.[2] He became a literary artist, but this did not prevent him from stressing, in his 1925 essay "A Night at Pietramala," that if he was given the chance to become either a second Faraday or a new Shakespeare, he would prefer the scientist. And he adds in this essay: "I personally would rather be subdued to intellectual contemplation than to emotion, would rather use my soul professionally for knowing than for feeling."[3] This is a very important comment, opposing, as it apparently does, knowledge and emotion. In the essay "Views of Holland," also published in *Along the Road* in 1925, the traveller who preferred the *Encyclopedia Britannica* as his reading matter for the journey praises the geometrical landscape of Holland which so neatly corresponds to the clarity and sharpness of the human intellect. And in another essay, entitled "What, Exactly, Is Modern?" published roughly at the same time, Huxley stresses that what is characteristic of modern man is not so much his emotional qualities, which still link him up closely with his prehistoric ancestors, but his amazing intellectual achievements and potential.[4]

As has often been pointed out in Huxley criticism, his novels and essays abound with intellectual life, conversation and scientific or philosophical thought. Satire, a highly intellectual literary art, proved his appropriate field of occupation.[5] And even if he underlined that, philosophically speaking, he was a sceptic,[6] his Socratic decision to know that he did not know was, in the last resort, an intellectual one.

That he could later develop a mystical world-view, a perspective based on the assumption that immediate insight is superior to abstract reasoning, has led many critics to divide Huxley's career into two strictly separate parts, the first comprehending his satirical, intellectual period, which roughly corresponds to his time in Europe, the second his increasing occupation with mystical awareness, selflessness and timeless immediacy after his departure for the United States in 1937. The term 'conversion' is usually used to mark this transition.[7] My aim in this paper is to show, however, that as far as Huxley's opinion of the ways in which we gain knowledge is concerned, it is inappropriate and even misleading to talk of a conversion. I want to argue that the possibility of developing a mystical perspective was latent in Huxley's thought almost from the outset of his career. For this reason I will chiefly concentrate on his earlier writings.

In his collection of essays entitled *Do What You Will* (1929), Huxley touches on the question of man's intellectual powers and remarks:

> Abstracted from a mass of the most diverse sensations, the Idea is a sort of Lowest Common Measure of appearances. For the purposes of Man the remembering and foreseeing animal, of Man the exerciser of persistent and conscious action on the external world, the Idea or abstraction is truer than the immediate sensation. It is because we are predominantly purposeful beings that we are perpetually correcting our immediate sensations."[8]

What he calls "intellectual knowledge" (*DWYW*, 9) or "intellectual experiences of logical thought"[9] subjects the world to the human mind and thus makes it manageable and understandable. The power of abstraction enables us to "organize our experience profitably" (*DWYW*, 3). It is highly useful and helps us to survive. Furthermore, its great value consists in the fact that its results, just like the sense impressions that intellectual knowledge is based on, are, "if not identical for all human beings, at least sufficiently similar to make something like universal agreement possible" (*DWYW*, 297). Abstract knowledge, that is to say, is shareable and therefore generally convincing.

This raises the age-old question whether an act of abstraction singles out the essential core of the thing it abstracts from. Being a sceptic, Huxley does not venture an answer. He is merely interested in the utilitarian value of abstract knowledge. And, on the contrary, as far back as in 1927, he writes in his essay collection *Proper Studies*: "To abstract is to select certain aspects of reality regarded as being, for one reason or another, significant. The aspects of reality not selected do not thereby cease to exist, and the abstraction is therefore never a true, in the sense of a complete, picture of reality."[10] This remark, which clearly foreshadows his concept of comprehensiveness presented in the important essay "Tragedy and the Whole Truth" (*MN*, 3–18), stresses the negative, omissive element inherent in acts of abstraction. In this sense, the human intellect reduces, simplifies and thus, in the end, falsifies reality.

Accordingly, Huxley comments in his long essay from 1930, *Vulgarity in Literature*:

> Matter is incomparably subtler and more intricate than mind. Or, to put it a little more philosophically, the consciousness of events which we have immediately, through our senses and intuitions and feelings, is incomparably subtler than any idea we can subsequently form of that immediate consciousness. Our most refined theories, our most elaborate descriptions are but crude and barbarous simplifications of a reality that is, in every smallest sample, infinitely complex. (*MN*, 291)

Reality, for Huxley, is the total reality of our immediate consciousness, which does not only comprehend the sense data that our intellectual knowledge is based on, but also our feelings and intuitions. In other words, feelings and intuitions are just as real as sense impressions. In *Do What You Will* Huxley stresses: "Our psychological experiences are all equally facts. There is nothing to choose between them. No psychological experience is 'truer,' so far as we are concerned, than any other" (*DWYW*, 3). It is this insistence on the givenness and reality of 'immediate experience'—probably Huxley's most important philosophical term all in all—that accompanies him throughout his works.

As a consequence of his view that our immediate consciousness cannot be called into question, he actually does not hesitate to concede the epistemological value of direct, intuitive or emotional insights. In *Do What You Will* he uses the term "physical knowledge" and remarks: "Between the two kinds of knowledge—the direct physical knowledge [...] and the intellectual knowledge, abstracted and generalized out of this physical knowledge—is a difference analogous to that between food and an instrument. Knives and hammers are indispensable; but so, to an even higher degree, is bread" (*DWYW*, 9). And two years earlier, in *Proper Studies*, he defines 'intuition' as "the faculty of unconscious perception, the power of seeing beyond the immediate sensuous superficialities of here and now, of detecting realities behind masks, and dynamic possibilities latent in the stolid present" ("Personality and the Discontinuity of the Mind," *PS*, 254–255).

As a notable contemporary example of a person gifted with the power of intuition he mentions the Swiss psychologist Carl Gustav Jung, whom he calls an "intuitive knower of human nature" ("Varieties of Intelligence," *PS*, 42):

> Reading his books, you feel that here is a man who does genuinely understand human beings in the profound intuitive way in which a good novelist, like Tolstoi or Dostoievsky, understands them. I know of no other professional psychologist of whom one feels the same. Others know their business well enough; but Jung seems really to understand, not merely with the intellect, but with his whole being, intimately and intuitively. (*PS*, 42)

This passage not only hints at Huxley's concept of wholeness, the intellect being just one part of a greater whole. His wording strikingly anticipates his later distinction between verbalized, conceptualized 'knowledge' and unconceptualized, non-verbal 'understanding' in the essay "Knowledge and Understanding" from the 1956 collection *Adonis and the Alphabet*.[11]

A further example of intuitive power, this time mentioned in *Vulgarity in Literature*, is the French writer Balzac, of whom Huxley says: "He had a prodigious intuitive knowledge of man as a social animal, of man in his mundane relations with other men" (*MN*, 320). This intuitive knowledge helped him turn *The Human Comedy* into one of the greatest works of art. On the other hand, Huxley is sure that Balzac's novel *Séraphita*, in which the author tries to depict man as a solitary and religious being, is a hopeless failure:

> In *Séraphita* we see a terrifying example of the disaster which overtakes writers who succumb to the temptation of protesting too much about matters of which they know too little. (I use the word 'know' to signify, in this case, the immediate, first-hand knowledge that is born of feeling.) Balzac had a considerable abstract knowledge of mysticism; it was his crime that he also pretended to possess an intuitive, emotional knowledge from within. (*MN*, 326)

These examples show that at least since the mid-1920s Huxley had no difficulty in accepting ways to knowledge other than that based on intellectual abstraction. It is quite surprising how easily he fits the possibility of immediate understanding into his theory of knowledge. If he had not done so from the very start, his acknowledgment of the reality of feelings and intuitions must have been a great relief because it meant that the scientific materialism which had become the ruling philosophy during the nineteenth century[12] had been overcome and that the world was once again a valuable world. In his travel report from 1926, *Jesting Pilate*, he writes:

> Our belief that things possess value is due to an immediate sense or intuition; we feel, and feeling we know, that things have value. If men have doubted the real existence of values, that is because they have not trusted their own immediate and intuitive conviction. They have required an intellectual, a logical and 'scientific' proof of their existence. Now such a proof is not easily found at the best of times. But when you start your argumentation from the premises laid down by scientific materialism, it simply cannot be discovered. Indeed, any argument starting from these premises must infallibly end in a denial of the real existence of values.[13]

The scientific, quantified world-picture,[14] which is detached from immediate, subjective knowledge, requires to be supplemented by intuitions and feelings of value and quality.[15] Among these, quite obviously, religious intuitions—in *Music at Night* Huxley uses the term "numinous feelings" (*MN*, 77)[16]—are of particular importance for the experiencing human being. However, while what Huxley calls "the real existence of values" triggers optimism and gives new cause for enjoying life, the reinstatement of subjective experience in the world-picture complicates reality to an enormous degree. Like sense impressions, feelings and intuitions tend to be fleeting and elusive and to vary from individual to individual. Huxley describes them as being "diverse, occasional, and contradictory" (*DWYW*, 297). He uses the examples of Thomas Hardy, George Meredith, the mystic Jakob Boehme and Voltaire to underline the conflicting character of different direct insights and their rationalizations in terms of concepts:

> The psychological state called joy is no truer than the psychological
> state called melancholy [...]. Each is a primary fact of experience.
> And since one psychological state cannot be truer than another,
> since all are equally facts, it follows that the rationalization of one
> state cannot be truer than the rationalization of another. What Hardy
> says about the universe is no truer than what Meredith says; if the
> majority of contemporary readers prefer the world-view expressed
> in *Tess of the D'Urbervilles* to the optimism which forms the
> background to *Beauchamp's Career*, that is simply because they
> happen to live in a very depressing age and consequently suffer
> from a more or less chronic melancholy. [...] Both feelings are
> equally facts of experience, so are the facts called 'mystical ecstasy'
> and 'reasonableness.' Only a man whose life was rich in mystical
> experiences could have constructed a cosmogony like that of
> Boehme's; and the works of Voltaire could have been written only
> by one whose life was singularly poor in such experiences. (*DWYW*,
> 294–295)

And to make matters still more difficult, different and opposing intuitions
and feelings generally battle even within one single human being. To
rationalize them may, for example, mean: "A man may be a pessimistic
determinist before lunch and an optimistic believer in the will's freedom after
it" (*DWYW*, 297). In his essay "Beliefs and Actions," which is arguably
Huxley's most concise presentation of his philosophical thought, he
correspondingly says: "In our daily lives the most important immediate
realities are changing desires, emotions, moods" (*MN*, 117), and he adds that
he is "sceptical about everything except the immediate" (*MN*, 117). Truth,
accordingly, is not only a radically subjective, psychological, multifarious and
paradoxical affair. In the end, it is a matter of the moment, of the here and
now, of the fleeting contents of our "immediate consciousness."[17] Huxley
explicitly talks of the "chaos of immediate experience" (*DWYW*, 168).

Hence, searching for a more comprehensive truth—and man is helped in
this by what Huxley, in a later essay, calls a fundamental "urge to order and
[...] to meaning"[18]—makes it necessary to consider and include as many
truths and aspects of reality as possible, an impossible task. Huxley is not yet
ready to accept the all-embracing and therefore paradoxical character of the
mystical intuition. As the following quotation from *Do What You Will* clearly
shows, he regards it as just one intuition among others:

> True, the mystics are never tired of affirming that their direct
> perceptions of unity are intenser, of finer quality and intrinsically
> more convincing, more self-evident [...]. But they can speak only
> for themselves. Other people's direct intuitions of diverse
> 'appearances' may be just as intensely self-evident as *their* intuition
> of unique 'reality.' (*DWYW*, 38)

Similarly, he thinks that religious feelings cannot be ranked above their
opposite. Science, in Huxley's view, is certainly not sufficiently inclusive

either and "tells us nothing about the real nature of the world to which our experiences are supposed to refer. From the internal reality, by which I mean the totality of psychological experiences, it actually separates us" (*DWYW*, 3) because it "confines itself deliberately and by convention to the study of one very limited class of experiences—the experiences of sense" (*DWYW*, 3–4). It is true that science and the intellectual life in general are indispensable because they make possible a purposeful, useful, practical life. However, too much intellect tends to distort our immediate consciousness of the world and to literally cut us off from immediate experience and therefore from immediate truths: "Modern man's besetting temptation is to sacrifice his direct perceptions and spontaneous feelings to his reasoned reflections; to prefer in all circumstances the verdict of his intellect to that of his immediate intuitions" (*DWYW*, 123). The result is a neat and cosy world of abstractions, but at the same time a considerably impoverished life.[19]

Art, Huxley says, "deals with many more aspects of this internal reality than does science" (*DWYW*, 3). Indeed, it is mainly the arts that Huxley counts on to find ways of approaching something resembling the whole truth.[20] They are capable of including and integrating "diverse, occasional and contradictory" truths, of remaining much more faithful to our immediate consciousness. The ideal writer's ambition, according to Huxley, is therefore "to render, in literary terms, the quality of immediate experience—in other words, to express the finally inexpressible" (*MN*, 291–292). Huxley is convinced that the arts are a source of knowledge. In *Do What You Will* he remarks: "Science is no 'truer' [...] than art or religion" (*DWYW*, 3), and in *Ends and Means* he writes:

> The contents of literature, art, music—even in some measure of divinity and school metaphysics—are not sophistry and illusion, but simply those elements of experience which scientists chose to leave out of account, for the good reason that they had no intellectual methods for dealing with them. In the arts, in philosophy, in religion men are trying—doubtless, without complete success—to describe and explain the non-measurable, purely qualitative aspects of reality.[21]

It goes without saying that it is only with an open and receptive mind which gives free rein to the powers of intuition and feeling that we come into closer contact with these "qualitative aspects of reality." As has already been said, thought and preconceptions tend to overshadow our direct perceptions. The life we usually lead is a purposeful, self-dominated life and therefore dependent on our intellectual abilities. It generally takes a lot to change this state of things. Huxley comments in *Do What You Will*:

> Sickness transports a man from the battlefield where the struggle for existence is being waged, into a region of biological detachment; he sees something other than the merely useful. [...] But the revelation

is not the less credible for being accompanied by the fit; it is, on the contrary, more credible. For the fit detaches the mind from utilitarian reality and permits it to perceive, or create for itself, another reality, less superficial and tendencious than the normal utilitarian one of every day. (*DWYW*, 264–65)

He stresses, however, that there are people who are especially gifted with a more detached approach: "To be able to see things in the same disinterested way, with the eyes of a child, a god, a noble savage, is the mark and privilege of the artist. The artist is a man who has revelations without having to pay for them with epileptic fits" (*DWYW*, 265). It is, once again, the artist who is chiefly on Huxley's mind when it comes to experiencing the world of immediate reality. He has what Huxley, in *Texts and Pretexts*, calls the "gift of experience,"[22] which is, and this does not come as a surprise any longer, "a matter of sensibility and intuition, of seeing and hearing the significant things, of paying attention at the right moments, of understanding and co-ordinating" (*TP*, 5). The artist thus becomes a model for other people. He detects values and meanings ordinary people do not detect:

The world, like an ore-bearing mountain, is veined with every possible kind of significance. We are all miners and quarrymen, tunnelling, cutting, extracting. An artist is a man equipped with better tools than those of common men—sometimes, too, with a divining rod by whose aid he discovers, in the dark chaotic mass, veins of hitherto unsuspected treasure—new meanings and values. He opens our eyes for us, and we follow in a kind of gold rush. (*TP*, 49)

What this opening of our eyes really implies is also mentioned by Huxley in *Texts and Pretexts*:

Our immediate impressions of actuality, on the rare occasions when we contrive to see with the eyes of children or convalescents, of artists or lovers, seem to have a quality of supernaturalness. What we ordinarily call 'nature' and find duller than a witling's jest is in fact the system of generalizations and utilitarian symbols which we construct from our sensations. Sometimes, however, we are made directly and immediately aware of our sensations; it is an apocalypse; they seem supernatural. (*TP*, 22)

The wording of this passage from 1932 clearly foreshadows Huxley's later terminology after his acceptance of the transcendental character of the mystical intuition. He seems to be on the verge of accepting it already. The artist is a kind of aesthetic mystic—in a letter from 1945 Huxley actually uses the term "aesthetic mysticism"[23] to describe his earlier position. Artists order the world of immediate experience, i.e., they unify and co-ordinate what, from a strictly logical point of view, may resist unification and co-ordination.

It follows from Huxley's concept of the 'whole truth' that artists who manage to include and integrate a great deal of truths are greater than artists who fail to do so. The former reveal a more comprehensive understanding of immediate reality. Among Huxley's favourite authors was Chaucer, on whom he wrote an essay which first appeared in the *London Mercury* in 1920 and was later included in Huxley's first essay collection, *On the Margin* (1923). In the essay Huxley compares Chaucer with the French writer Anatole France and comes to the conclusion:

> But in at least one important respect Chaucer shows himself to be the greater, the completer spirit. He possesses, what Anatole France does not, an imaginative as well as an intellectual comprehension of things. Faced by the multitudinous variety of human character, Anatole France exhibits a curious impotence of imagination. He does not understand characters in the sense that, say, Tolstoy understands them; he cannot, by the power of imagination, get inside them, become what he contemplates. None of the persons of his creation are complete characters.[24]

If we now keep in mind that in other texts Huxley replaces the term 'imagination' by that of 'intuition' or 'feeling into somebody or something,'[25] it is quite safe to venture two assertions: not only his holistic concept was in the making from the very start of his career; his belief in, and acceptance of, immediate ways to knowledge was there from the outset, too.

---

[1] I would like to thank the Deutsche Forschungsgemeinschaft for a grant towards the costs of my journey to Riga.

[2] See Dana Sawyer, *Aldous Huxley: A Biography* (New York, 2002), 32–34.

[3] Aldous Huxley, *Along the Road* (London, 1925), 225.

[4] See Aldous Huxley, "What, Exactly, Is Modern?" *Vanity Fair*, 24 (May 1925), 73, 94.

[5] See Jerome Meckier, *Aldous Huxley: Satire and Structure* (London, 1969); Peter Firchow, *Aldous Huxley: Satirist and Novelist* (Minneapolis, 1972).

[6] See his essay "Beliefs and Actions" in *Music at Night* (London, 1931; hereafter, *MN*), 116f.

[7] A recent example is James Hull, *Aldous Huxley, Representative Man*, ed. Gerhard Wagner (Münster, 2004), 465. And yet Hull, who analyses Huxley's works from a psychologist's point of view, must be credited with detecting certain psychological determinants that link up Huxley's career and oeuvre to a whole.

[8] Aldous Huxley, *Do What You Will* (London, 1929), 9. Hereafter, *DWYW*.

[9] Aldous Huxley, *Literature and Science* (London, 1963), 7. Hereafter, *LS*.

[10] Aldous Huxley, "Varieties of Intelligence," *Proper Studies* (London, 1927; hereafter, *PS*), 35.

[11] See Aldous Huxley, "Knowledge and Understanding," *Adonis and the Alphabet* (London, 1956), 39–72.

[12] See Walter Houghton, *The Victorian Frame of Mind 1830–1870* (New Haven, 1957), 54ff.; Richard Altick, *Victorian People and Ideas* (London, 1973), 203ff.;

John A. Lester, *Journey Through Despair1880–1914: Transformations in British Literary Culture* (Princeton, 1968); C.E.M. Joad, *Guide to Modern Thought* (London, 1948), 32ff.; Gerhard Wagner, *The 'Beauty-Truths' of Literature: Elemente einer Dichtungstheorie in Aldous Huxleys Essayistik* (Münster, 2001), 9–26.

[13] Aldous Huxley, *Jesting Pilate* (London, 1926), 273.

[14] This world-picture is the result of what Huxley, in *Literature and Science*, calls "public experiences" (*LS*, 8).

[15] Important incentives for reconsidering the truth-value of feelings and intuitions were the discoveries of modern science, first and foremost those made by Einstein and Planck. For a concise account of the new ideas see C.B. Cox and A.E. Dyson, *The Twentieth-Century Mind: History, Ideas, and Literature in Britain* (2 vols., London, 1972), I, 248ff., and II, 196ff.; Joad, 80ff.; Wagner, 26–46. In his short story "Uncle Spencer," published in 1924, Huxley writes: "Now it is possible—it is, indeed, almost necessary—for a man of science to be also a mystic" (*Little Mexican* [London, 1924], 78).

[16] He borrows the term from the German philosopher and theologian Rudolf Otto (1869–1937); see Otto's *Das Heilige: Über das Irrationale in der Idee des Göttlichen und sein Verhältnis zum Rationalen* (Breslau, 1917).

[17] Useful analyses of the widespread and profound impact of the philosophy of the moment—which implies the loss of the self—on later Victorian and early modernist literature can be found in *Die Modernisierung des Ich: Studien zur Subjektkonstitution in der Vor- und Frühmoderne* (Passau, 1989), a collection of essays edited by Manfred Pfister. With regard to Huxley, see especially Lothar Fietz's study *Menschenbild und Romanstruktur in Aldous Huxleys Ideenromanen* (Tübingen, 1969), and his essay "The Fragmentariness of the Self: Continuity and Discontinuity in the Works of Aldous Huxley," in: *"Now More Than Ever": Proceedings of the Aldous Huxley Centenary Symposium Münster 1994*, ed. Bernfried Nugel (Frankfurt a.M., 1995), 347–358.

[18] Aldous Huxley, *The Human Situation*, ed. Piero Ferrucci (London, 1978), 182. In *Brave New World Revisited* (London, 1958), 37, Huxley makes a similar statement: "The wish to impose order upon confusion, to bring harmony out of dissonance and unity out of multiplicity, is a kind of intellectual instinct, a primary fundamental urge of the mind."

[19] The only solution to this problem Huxley sees at this stage is the life of a 'split personality': "The only satisfactory way of existing in the modern, highly specialized world is to live with two personalities. A Dr. Jekyll that does the metaphysical and scientific thinking, that transacts business in the city, adds up figures, designs machines, and so forth. And a natural, spontaneous Mr. Hyde to do the physical, instinctive living in the intervals of work. The two personalities should lead their unconnected lives apart, without poaching on one another's preserves or inquiring too closely into one another's activities" (*DWYW*, 125).

[20] For the following, see Wagner, 69–188.

[21] Aldous Huxley, *Ends and Means* (London, 1937), 268.

[22] Aldous Huxley, *Texts and Pretexts* (London, 1932), 5. Hereafter, *TP*.

[23] *Letters of Aldous Huxley*, ed. Grover Smith (London, 1969), 538.

[24] Aldous Huxley, *On the Margin* (London, 1923), 222–223.

[25] See *MN*, 336: "Why is *The Rosary* a less admirable novel than *The Brothers Karamazov*? Because the amount of experience of all kinds understood, 'felt into,' as the Germans would say, and artistically re-created by Mrs. Barclay is small in comparison with that which Dostoevsky feelingly comprehended and knew so consummately well how to re-create in terms of the novelist's art." In this passage Huxley probably refers to Theodor Lipps's *Einfühlungstheorie*, which the German philosopher and psychologist (1851–1914) propounded in his *Ästhetik: Psychologie des Schönen und der Kunst* (2 vols., Hamburg and Leipzig, 1903–1906).

Anita Eglīte

(University of Latvia)

ALDOUS HUXLEY'S PHILOSOPHICAL APPROACH TO LANGUAGE IN *MUSIC AT NIGHT*

As the general theme of the Third International Aldous Huxley Symposium clearly included, among other topics, Huxley's ideas on language and culture, one may more specifically argue that the conference aimed at the investigation of the potential of human consciousness with regard to knowledge, to the relationship between language and thought as well as to feeling and sensation.

Aldous Huxley's interests were not purely literary, but he stood out among his generation of men of letters as a philosopher of language, revealing his insight into the formation and fundamental processes of human understanding and communication both in his literary activities and his contemplative essays. As the philosophy of language was a newcomer on the contemporary philosophy scene, Huxley contributed to establishing the tradition of a philosophical investigation of language. He was among the first writers of the twentieth century to promote a specific intellectual attitude in men of letters towards their subtle ways of handling language. This attitude entails an intensity of interest in language similar to that of philosophers who, in earlier centuries, had investigated language within the framework of problems of human understanding and expression, like, for instance, John Locke in *An Essay Concerning Human Understanding*. In the twentieth century logical and cognitive theories of language, from Wittgenstein to Austin, Grice and others, tended to incorporate the fundamental categories of space and time into language philosophy. Language came to be treated as a constructed model of reality; genetic schemes of human languages were devised and linked with particular national languages.

Following such new concepts of reflecting on reality, writers like Huxley were free to create a rich and potent language of their own. Old literature was dependent on past language and past philosophy; modern literature required a new language in literary works to transport modern thoughts inseparably linked with their form.[1] Huxley was certainly well familiar with the logic and possibilities of language. As a language professional, he demonstrated its transparence to thought by actualizing rich semantic contents, by testing what can or cannot be expressed in language, and by treating language as something not finite and static, but infinitely flexible and vivid. This intellectual attitude towards language is clearly reflected in all genres of Huxley's writing, comprising poems, novels, biographies, travel books, essays and plays.

A writer is in a peculiar position when he works with language. He 'trusts' words and uses them for definite purposes of expressing two kinds of consciousness: the poetic and the argumentative. In both kinds the writer proceeds to express his 'second voice,' which is curious, doubtful, and interested in everything, eager to discover and recreate as far as language allows.

The real enemy of writing is talk—a paradox which still keeps true for the profession of writers. On the one hand, writing starts with silence. The writer works with language and ideas in the most imaginative way. He is a poet, and his business is discovery, not articulation or illustration. The process may be described as "groping through words towards something only vaguely grasped and which he [the writer] will recognize only when words have set it down on the page."[2] The second type of writing, on the other hand, is the product of a varied and vast consciousness extremely active and alert to question and challenge habits of thought. It is too broad to have a single name but is often referred to as essayistic writing.

The first type is essentially represented by the novel, which for the past hundred and fifty years has been a major literary form in our culture (see Malouf, 221). Gradually an essayistic quality has been integrated into the novel, which, at least in its modern form, displays a new mode of writing in the twentieth century, distinctly manifested in the writings of Thomas Mann, for example, who insists that the philosophical arguments and political exchanges in *The Magic Mountain* are a product of the poetic spirit.[3]

Similarly, Aldous Huxley's novels are closely linked with his essays. In fact, he himself is nowadays considered to be a specimen of the novelist of ideas that he describes in chapter XXII of *Point Counter Point*. His novels no longer possess a 'genuine' plot and present a prose of thoughts and ideas characterized by mistrust of classical form. As a novelist of ideas, Huxley gradually develops, instead of the sense of central emptiness and futility which goes under the label of 'modernism' with his contemporary fellow writers, a philosophical recognition of "ultimate reality."[4] For him, "the verbal expression of even a metaphysic or a system of ethics is very nearly as much of a work of art as a love poem" (*MN*, 46) and can be tentatively rendered in epigrams, verbal witticisms, maxims, and stimulating imagery. Since reality changes ideas, desires, moods and emotions, and since human beings communicate with people from other languages and cultures, an intellectual approach to language can help the writer to exploit words to their limits.

Yet, in his language philosophy, Huxley is not only concerned with examining the potential of linguistic expression, but he also takes into consideration the 'numinous.' As he notes in his essay "Meditation on the Moon," "the Universe throws down a challenge to the human spirit" (*MN*, 80). Like Aristotle, he argues that the essence of language can be approached not only by reason, but also by intuition. Analysing the category of divinity and the ways of describing it, his active mind and acute intelligence do not stop at the limitations of language. "The moon's divinity," he states, "[...] may be extracted from our own experiences, from the writings of the poets, and, in fragments, even from certain textbooks of physiology and medicine." It is manifest in "the peculiar kind of feeling which Professor Otto has called 'numinous' (from the Latin *numen*, a supernatural being). Numinous feelings are the original god-stuff, from which the theory-making mind extracts the individualized gods of the pantheons, the various attributes of the One" (*MN*, 76–77). Theology is based on numinous feelings and expresses them in theological writings. Men and women certainly have numinous feelings about the moon, but, Huxley emphasizes, also their physiology is in many ways governed by the lunar rhythm: "Touching the soul directly through the eyes and, indirectly, along the dark channels of the blood, the moon is doubly a divinity." It influences "the physiological and therefore the spiritual life" (*MN*, 78).

Continuing Huxley's line of thoughts, one may perhaps argue that poets and writers always are the first to develop a 'numinous' knowledge of language. Alongside with the philosophers, they add to an understanding of the ontology of language. Basically every talented writer forms his own 'numinous' style by creating neologisms and other innovations. Some writers develop a kind of language as distinctive as a fingerprint in the form of diction, syntax, rhythm, imagery, and metaphors. Huxley is meticulously careful about expressing the complex workings of the mind by adequate linguistic devices.[5] His wit and irony, his delicate sense of humour, his anti-utopian satire and his amusing but disquieting comments on the tendencies of the twentieth century distinguish his style as intellectual as well as 'numinous.'

For Huxley, the spiritual life of human beings is essentially concerned with numinous intuition, which can be tentatively expressed with the help of metaphors and symbols. Thus particular words of the writer's language receive a numinous sense and constitute a poetic language. Beyond that, there is only the numinous power of music, as Huxley argues in "The Rest Is Silence": "The man who wrote *Othello* and *The Winter's Tale* was capable of uttering in words whatever words can possibly be made to signify, [...] and yet, whenever something in the nature of a mystical emotion or intuition had to be communicated, Shakespeare regularly called upon music to help him to 'put it across'" (*MN*, 20–21).

It is difficult to render the numinous in words, because it exists in the imagination. Myths originate from empirical experience and from poetic imagination. The numinous code of a language is worked out in the course of its development when perceptions of hearing, vision, taste and touch are verbalised and a precise expression of sense becomes more and more important.

The numinous in thinking and expression has been described by the Latvian philosopher Roberts Mūks as a product of the poetic imagination, which does not deal with empirical reality or the facts of perception but is dynamic and spontaneous, possessing a mental vigour which holds everything together. Mūks believes that Aldous Huxley is among those who have most precisely reflected upon the psychological aspect of man's numinosity and argues that, according to Huxley, the numinous in human life may be characterized as the result of combining one's own highest resolution with obedience to the highest spiritual principles. Therefore, the numinous can be considered 'the culmination of a man's individualization in a profound intellectual sense.'[6]

Very often the numinous is associated with the words 'divine,' 'sacred' or 'archetypical' and may be interpreted as divine intuition, a 'feeling' of infinity. Poetic language has developed a specific style for the expression of the numinous, such as imagery, metaphors, and other devices.

Huxley, too, argues that the numinous in music and literary art helps to bring together time and space in human life: "This spatialization of time is achieved in poetry and music by the employment of recurrent rhythms and cadences, by the confinement of the material within conventional forms, such as that of the sonnet or the sonata, and by the imposition upon the chosen fragment of temporal indefiniteness of a beginning, a middle, and an end."[7]

Two sides of human thinking and expression, the sacred and the profane, have been discussed in the works of Lucien Lévy-Brühl, Nathan Söderblum, Mircea Eliade and Rudolf Otto (*The Idea of the Holy*, 1923). Looking for the essence of the numinous, they all deal with the process of expressing the world in language and therefore start from the oldest myths recorded in a particular language.

Myths and the numinous are not separable from the notions of soul, spirit, imagination, heart and human feeling. In this respect, one may refer to James Hillman, author of the *The Soul's Code*, who proposes a psychology with that perspective couched in the language of images and symbols.[8]

From the Middle Ages on, nominalism, an intellectual force attacking the notion of the world's reality, gained increasing influence. It considered universal laws and general types to be only names (*nomina*). Thus the word at the hands of philosophers like Descartes, Locke, Berkeley, Hume, Leibniz, Kant and Hegel changed from being a power of its own to being a tool of philosophy, as Hillman explains: "Words are labels given by the mind, with only subjective reality" (Hillman, 6). Invisibles, principles, generalities and universal powers (Time, Truth) were merely names; they had no substance, they were not real, the nominalists asserted, whereas a counter-position deriving from Plato still defended 'realism.' The battle between nominalism and realism, between fact and fiction, or reason and imagination, was also a struggle between nominalistic professions (e.g. law, medicine, theology) and realistic addressees.

In modern structural linguistics, words have no inherent sense—they can be reduced to mathematical signs: one cannot trust words of any sort as true carriers of meaning. People live in a world of slogans, jargon and press releases.

However, we nowadays need a numinous attitude towards words, we should once again have faith in at least some of them. Words signifying aspects of worth and powers of the soul should be used for communication in conversation, letters and books; they are personal presences possessing whole mythologies: "Words, like angels, are powers which have invisible power over us" (Hillman, 9). Words have genders, genealogies and etymologies which concern origins and creation, history and vogues. They evoke in our souls a universal resonance. Without the inherence of the soul in words, speech would not move us.

---

[1] See Aldous Huxley, "Music at Night," *Music at Night* (London, 1931), 21: "The substance of a work of art is inseparable from its form; its truth and its beauty are two and yet, mysteriously, one." Hereafter, *MN*.

[2] David Malouf, "When the writer speaks," talk given at the PEN (UK) International Writers Day on 28 March 1998, transcript published by PEN (UK), 220.

[3] See Malouf, 221: "[An] essayistic quality gets integrated into the main narrative, and Thomas Mann, for instance, goes to considerable lengths to insist that the philosophical arguments and political exchanges in *The Magic Mountain* are as much a product of the poetic spirit as the complex imagery of disease that makes the rest of the book so clearly a work of the imagination."

[4] See, e.g., *Ends and Means* (London, 1937), chs. I and XIII–XV.

[5] For some examples see, e.g., "Uncle Spencer," *Little Mexican & Other Stories* (London, 1924): "the obscure chambers of my mind" (11), "mental solitude," "the native eccentricity of his mind," "he would rush headlong down intellectual roads" (12), "knowledge of the universe" (15), "nameless things" (44), "[...] and there emerged, speck-like in the boundless blank ocean of her ignorance, a few little islands of strange knowledge" (47), "this man of another race, speaking in an unknown tongue words uttered out of obscure depths for no man's hearing and which even his own soul did not hear or understand" (132–133).

[6] See Roberts Mūks, *Mīts un iztēle* ['Essays and Poems'] (Riga, 2004), 91–92.

[7] Aldous Huxley, "Some Reflections on Time," *Vedanta for Modern Man*, ed. Christopher Isherwood (Hollywood, 1945), 119–120.

[8] See James Hillman, *Re-Visioning Psychology* (New York, 1976), 5–6.

Michel Weber

(Université catholique de Louvain)

PERENNIAL TRUTH AND PERPETUAL PERISHING:
ALDOUS HUXLEY'S WORLD-VIEW IN THE LIGHT OF A. N. WHITEHEAD'S
PROCESS PHILOSOPHY OF TIME[1]

Aldous Huxley was preoccupied with changing society for the better by reaching the general public, not only the intelligentsia. In order to define the meaning and significance of Huxley today, there are, from a philosophical point of view, two 'royal paths': Huxley's assessment of temporality and his understanding of consciousness. This paper argues that the key issue in the interpretation of Huxley's world-view—whatever its local instantiations are (political, religious, metaphysical etc.)—lies in his assessment of temporality, i.e., of historicity and destiny. Although Huxley's philosophical development has not been directly influenced by Alfred North Whitehead's (1861–1947) *magnum opus*, *Process and Reality* (1929),[2] it will be shown that its main categories are fully relevant in the context of this appraisal.

The following argument unfolds in four main points. First, a general heuristic is introduced with the help of William James' "radical empiricism" and David Griffin's distinction between "destructive" and "constructive" postmodernism. Second, Huxley's relevance is specified from the present historical standpoint, torn between early and late postmodernity. Third, Huxley's meaning is questioned with the help of Whitehead's concept of the "creative advance" of Nature. Fourth, by way of conclusion, the significance of Huxley is discussed, i.e., what is at stake in the assessment of his understanding of temporality from the perspective of the precarious socio-cultural situation introduced in section 1.

Before the argument itself can unfold, the nature of radical empiricism and the distinction between eliminative and revisionary postmodernism have to be clarified.

The attentive reader of Huxley's works is always struck by his capacity to suggest the interconnection between all epistemic fields, particularly philosophy, religion, science and politics. In other words, just like any fully fledged radical empiricist, Huxley acknowledges all experiences and their relationships at face value. "Radical empiricism"[3] is William James' term for the following position: when trying to frame a coherent and applicable world-view, it is advisable to accept all experiences and only experiences.

'All experiences' means not only the experiences conveyed by sense perception ("exteroception"), which constitute, so to speak, the tip of the experiential iceberg, but also the more subtle bodily experiences ("interoception" and "proprioception"[4]), which occur at the edges of the normal state of consciousness. In addition, 'all' includes experiences of altered—in the widest sense of the word—states of consciousness, or as Whitehead has it:

> Nothing can be omitted, experience drunk and experience sober, experience sleeping and experience waking, experience drowsy and experience wide-awake [...].[5]

It is on the same basis that Huxley formulates the goals of human action in his novel *Island*: "Nothing short of everything will really do."[6]

'Only experiences' means that what cannot be experienced is of no use in philosophy—it is even confusing to attempt to deal with such pure abstractions. Hence, since all and only experiences matter, religious 'facts' and scientific 'facts' have to receive a compatible status within the epistemological framework. This issue is at the core of postmodernity.

In 1988, Griffin proposed a useful distinction between "deconstructive or eliminative postmodernism" and "constructive or revisionary postmodern-ism"[7]: both positions claim that the modern world-view (basically the heir of techno-science vindicated by Cartesian dualism) has to be overcome, but whereas eliminative postmodernism does so through an anti-world-view (the notions of self, purpose, meaning, liberty, reality, truth and God are destroyed), constructive postmodernism attempts to give new meanings to these building blocks essential for any world-view. As a matter of fact, there are clear resemblances between the overall Whiteheadian vision promoted by Griffin and the synergy, depicted in *Island*, between science and ecological Buddhism. In other words, to peruse Huxley's works for "epistemological inconsistencies" is to entirely miss his point—all the more so since, as Whitehead himself, probably under the influence of Bradley, kept advocating, such a search reveals a total lack of speculative sophistication.[8]

Doubtless this distinction is mirrored in the current socio-political state of affairs: some people want to continue pushing the principles of modernity to the extreme and have neoliberalism destroy all forms of humanism—if not humanity itself and the planet with it; others venture to work on more holistic premises in order to create a better world.

1. The Relevance of Huxley: Between Early and Late Postmodernity

The present time seems to hold a vast choice of opportunities—for better and for worse. Corporate forces are now almost identical with political levers; they use techno-science on a vast scale to exploit and control a quasi-vegetative population and thereby to secure the highest profit in the shortest possible term. Even worse, the boundaries between techno-science and human nature are collapsing. A short overview of the present socio-political situation may serve to introduce Huxley's dystopia *Brave New World* and his positive utopia *Island* with a view to finding out what might occur in the near future. In order to sketch the spectrum of possibilities, it appears useful to distinguish between the early postmodern world (the current state of affairs) and the late postmodern world with two middle-term possibilities.

1.1. The Early Postmodern World

The current ideological striving for globalization is one of the most obvious signs of the fact that we are nowadays inhabiting an early postmodern world. Its major characteristics are twofold: commercialism and technoscientism. On the one hand—what for the Ancients was the most vulgar way of living— business now rules world-wide with a very simple motto: everything is for sale; if life is against profit, life has to be disciplined. There is, for instance, nothing more revolting to the contemporary promoters of GMO than the capacity of animals and plants to reproduce themselves by themselves, without the intervention of a specialist that could bill his/her mediation.

Three concepts are useful to differentiate this account, especially when contemplated through a Hobbesean lens: community, identity and stability. They receive further clarification when the main actor enters the scene: techno-science.

Nowadays, community no longer means family, union, nation or any other old-fashioned socio-political entity; it designates a global market usually imposed by persuasion (or, rather, a parody of persuasion: shameless rhetorical arguments and advertising), when possible by conviction (through a use of pure reason that systematically obliterates its ideological roots), and when necessary by coercion (the use of violence)[9]. Or as Hobbes says:

> In the nature of man, we find three principal causes of quarrel: first, competition; secondly, diffidence [distrust]; thirdly, glory. The first makes man invade for gain; the second, for safety; the third, for reputation.[10]

One fears that Hobbes' diagnosis is more valid than ever.

For its part, identity does not refer to persons belonging to a well-defined (but open) cultural sphere; it does not even apply to neurotic individuals (according to the obsolete Freudian thesis): identity, as becomes more and more obvious, refers to psychotics without an identity but the one that advertising imposes upon them. Or Hobbes again:

> During the time men live without a common power to keep them all in awe, they are in that condition which is called war; and such a war, as is of every man, against every man. [...] [there is] continual

> fear, and danger of violent death; and the life of man [is] solitary,
> poor, nasty, brutish, and short. (*Leviathan*, 186)

Now, it is true that mostly people in Third World countries live lives that are "solitary, poor, nasty, brutish, and short." At present, most Westerners still lead a life that is far more civilized: solitary, rich, nasty, brutish, and long. But the present social continuum is disintegrating rapidly.

Stability has always meant (i) the preservation of the *status quo* by those who benefit from it and (ii) the promotion of all 'changes' necessary to establish more firmly that same *status quo*, this double claim being only apparently a paradox. Thank God some things never change. Hobbes again:

> The notions of right and wrong, justice and injustice, have there [in
> the state of nature] no place. Where there is no common power,
> there is no law. (*Leviathan*, 188)

And hence, Hobbes concludes, a social contract is needed to create a commonwealth including some form of justice.

The engine of the present cultural decomposition—techno-science lured by the market—deserves a closer look. The sixteenth-century scientific revolution got a new boost at the end of the twentieth century: society is now indeed close to a new (Drexlerian)[11] break-through. A-bombs, H-bombs, nuclear power plants and the problematic propagation of nuclear fusion for civil purposes have already induced a significant ideological shift that some have called "eco-fascism": for their own safety, it is necessary to keep the citizens ignorant of the whereabouts of technological devices and to keep absolute control over the entire society. When the Human Genome Project, launched in 1990, produces all its effects, it will make the nuclear age and its eco-fascism look like a childish nightmare. Willing or unwilling, contraception and abortion have become common features of our world. Euthanasia—which has recently been legalised in some European countries—has, *de facto*, always been practised. Organ transplantation is bringing more and more hope to patients, and the purely commercial structure enveloping it seems still more or less under control at present (although under directive 98/44/CE, it is already possible to patent individual parts of the human body). But GMO technology (remember Terminator, the well-named necrotechnology), artificial insemination, in vitro fertilisation, the completion of the first phase of the Human Genome Project, the explosion of research on the pluripotent human stem cells and the concomitant prospects of cloning are taking us to the dawn of a new era that will most probably be ruled by bio-nano-technologies. This will simply mean the end of 'democracy' as the 'more advanced' countries know it.

Moreover, techno-science lured by the market maximises the destructive power of these two agents with a very simple synergy. On the one hand, techno-science is creating devices and producing waste that will keep their lethal virtues for hundreds of thousands of years. On the other hand, the leading financial tycoons are now taking decisions with a temporal horizon of the next ten minutes, as one of them proudly announced. That is their long-term thinking.

One last point should be kept in mind: the importance of what Whitehead refers to as the "medieval insistence on the rationality of God, conceived as with the personal energy of Jehovah and with the rationality of a Greek philosopher"[12] to bring forth Renaissance science. Whitehead's pioneering work can be interpreted as the first sign of the necessity to go past the dualistic world-view enforced by a transcendental reading of the Scriptures and to blend Christianity with Buddhism to achieve a healthier "world-loyalty."[13]

1.2. The Late Postmodern World

Now that the current state of affairs has been somewhat clarified, one can speculate on the two major roads that seem, right now, to lie open in front of us. On the one hand, the future postmodern world could, as most of the West seems to foresee—if not hope—, push its ruling principles to the hilt, and this would mean the destruction of the meagre achievements of the democratic systems (particularly in the fields of education and social security) and the enslavement of most of the world's population by a self-reproducing caste of technocrats that would, by the same token, destroy the ecosphere once and for all.[14] To them, this would not even constitute a catastrophy: it would only signal the happy emergence of new marketing possibilities. On the other hand, if the peaceful energies of those who are aware of the present dangers could be joined, they could work for the inversion of the ill-fated present trend and lead civilization towards a genuine democratic ideal.

The alternative described above can be readily illustrated with examples from *Brave New World* (1932)[15] and *Island* (1962). The former perfectly exemplifies the destructive-eliminative postmodernity of the present time, while the latter suggests the main features of a constructive-inclusive post-modernity that strives to make the best of all human potentialities. Four steps are expedient to sketch the two possible futures. The same pattern is used here for both works to provide a comparison which makes clear that the difference between the two utopias is very slight. Perhaps the key difference lies in the way hypnosis and eugenics (which had a strong impact on Western culture during Huxley's lifetime) are implemented in society: they both share a huge destructive potential as well as a remarkable civilizational one.[16]

The four relevant steps to sketch the 'ultramodern' landscape that *Brave New World* creates concern its motto, mass-production and mass-consumption as well as the 'savage' contrast.

First, the motto of the World State is the same as that which was already used to characterize early postmodernity: "COMMUNITY, IDENTITY,

STABILITY" (*BNW*, 1). Here, community basically means social utility, pure utilitarianism: "Everyone belongs to everyone else" (*BNW*, 38). Identity is a chief principle: thanks to biological and emotional engineering, each citizen is confined within a very precise social circle; there is (almost) no elbow room given to individual action. Stability is the *sine qua non* of civilization: total order is guaranteed by watertight structures. Even science has to be carefully monitored. Stability is the highest social virtue because it leads to lasting happiness.

Second, there are three major tools that guarantee the overall order of mass-production. Human beings are simple instruments for engineers that have been duly programmed themselves. Being artificial, everything belongs to the economic sphere: "a love of nature keeps no factories busy" (*BNW*, 19). Eugenics, here, appears in two guises: bio-engineering and contraception. Eupaedia, to coin a cover term, means emotional engineering (hypnopaedia) and (subliminal) conditioning. *Soma* is the omnipotent drug: besides all sorts of surrogates, omnipresent music, tap-TV, feelies (tactile talkies) and other overwhelming 'presences,' the state drug provides peace *ad libitum*—from a punctual stress-relief to a longer "*soma* holiday" from reality. Even first-hand religious experiences are destroyed or conditioned to suppress unwelcome emotions.

Third, there is mass-consumption and its three major consequences, obedient consumption, feverish ignorance and mindless promiscuity. Human beings are totally infantilized and thereby made "happy": they get what they want and want only what they can get; they love their servitude.

Fourth, at the edges of this sterilised and sterile paradise, one finds (i) islands populated with "alpha misfits" and (ii) savage reservations where marriage, natural birth, family life and religion are still common practice.

When applied to *Island*, the four steps lead to the following observations: First, a corresponding motto can be spelled out by using the same categories. Community now means that everyone and everything belongs to everyone and everything else, but not in a utilitarian way. "Elementary ecology leads straight to elementary Buddhism" (*Island*, 212)—and vice versa. Not means but ends have priority—the ultimate one being fundamental, global harmony. Identity refers to true individuals; maximum elbow room is provided for each person to find peace; however, no complete adjustment is expected: in a sane society that would not be sound. Stability means peacefulness, harmony, perfectly indifferent transience.

Second, there is a scientific culture of awareness: both Western science and Buddhist culture contribute to awareness through birth control to avoid a Malthusian explosion of misery (i.e., via contraception, artificial insemination and the yoga of love), through holistic education (on all fronts, verbal and non-verbal, with prevention and cure), through hypnosis ("psychological facts of applied metaphysics" [*Island*, 221; see also 76]) and spiritual exercises.

The State also provides a potent drug—*moksha*—as a way to liberation from the prison of the self and to an encounter with the Ultimate.

Third, there is a holistic culture of awareness: the goal is to provide the possibility for everyone to become a fully human being. Happiness here means awareness, spiritual growth, liberation, not just the satisfaction of bodily desires.

Fourth, at the edges of this utopian society, there is the international community as Huxley knew it in 1962: with mass consumption (e.g., oil-guzzling transport), mass communication, mass advertising, opiates, TV; in sum, militarism, ignorance and overpopulation.

2. Huxley's Meaning: Time as a Key

The meaning of Huxley's prose is now approached by contrasting Whitehead's radical process philosophy with Huxley's perennialism. As introduction, a few words on the historical context seem requisite.[17]

The nature and conditions of being and becoming are among the oldest philosophical puzzles. Although everyday experience testifies to both, reason has always had the greatest difficulties to articulate them coherently. Traditionally, philosophical systematization has started from being and has tried to understand becoming from that basis. This is the intuition lying behind Aristotle's substantialism (Aristotle being the traditional yardstick in these matters). Everything is made out of some underlying everlasting substance ('ousia') that can change only its qualities. This intuition is strongly supported by uncritical common sense and the linguistic subject-predicate pattern of Indo-European languages.

But nothing really decisive has been achieved by substantialism: there has always been the haunting challenge of Zeno's paradoxes, and lately science itself has completely processualized its understanding of the universe, with field physics, thermodynamics, quantum indeterminacy, and, more recently, with emergence, evolutionary epistemology, embodied cognition, autopoiesis, complexity, chaos and turbulence, non-linear dynamics and far-from-equilibrium systems, as well as biosemiotics. In other words, the Galilean vision inexorably gives way to the 'open universe' cherished by James. Thinkers like Peirce, James, Nietzsche, Boutroux, Bergson, Alexander, Dewey and Whitehead claim that there is no coherent and applicable theory starting from substantialistic premises and doing justice to becoming: from the unchanging one cannot generate any change. However, if one accepts becoming as the ultimate, it becomes possible to understand being by the same token. Flux, becoming, event, process (each author has a personal way of dealing with non-substantialism) can indeed locally suscitate islands of stability matching with individual experience.

One of the earliest tools devised to cope with being and becoming was the bipolar concept of actuality vs. potentiality. Aristotle (*Metaphysics*, Θ) systematised the actuality/potentiality contrast in order to answer the question of the conditions of being and becoming. According to him (and to Whitehead, too), actuality is primary and relative to potentiality. But the history of philosophy shows that thinkers promptly tended to go back to Plato and to advocate a 'two-world theory' according to which the given, i.e., actuality, is secondary and the potential structure primary and absolute. The ultimate ground is unmanifested, unchanging, eternal; the transient data are pure appearance. What is process-like, in the making, or temporal, is entirely devalued. In Plato's cave, one contemplates only shadows (of artefacts cast by the light of a fire).

Whitehead makes it very clear that what is actual, i.e., fully concrete, does not occur independently of a structure of possibility that precedes it and is modified by its occurrence. All events, all experiences (the two terms are synonymous for Whitehead) take place within a structure that brings them into, and sustains them in, existence, as it were (in a similar context, Plato spoke of a 'wet nurse'). In other words: in order to understand the given, one needs to posit a structural background that is not apparent—or at least not fully, not immediately apparent.

The concept of 'process' can adopt two main forms, both equating becoming and actuality. The weak concept—which thinks in terms of event, flux, instability and the like—puts becoming before being; accordingly, being is the surface effect of ever-changing underlying relationships. There is, in other words, a continuous stream of events, progressively disclosing new cosmic features by rearranging past features. One could use the image of the surface of the sea, neatly smooth whereas undersea waters are in perpetual movement. With the strong concept of 'process,' the question is bolder. In *Process and Reality*, Whitehead basically asks how genuine novelty can enter (so to speak, percolate) the world. His point is to make the emergence of the unexpected possible within the fabric of the universe. To secure an event ontology worthy of the name, i.e., to ground the possibility of true—unforeseeable—novelty, requires a strong concept of freedom, and the exercise of freedom necessitates privacy, i.e., ontological atomicity (epochality)—whose signature is duration.

2. 1. Whitehead's Creative Advance and Perpetual Perishing

According to process thinkers, the primordial feature of the Whole is its eventfulness. Totally new events—taking place at the edges of the world—are 'weaving' the world. This leads to a paradox: on the one hand, all experiences bring a new dimension to the picture (even possibly chaos)—one cannot bathe in the same river twice; on the other hand, we still live in a somewhat organized world, a cosmos. In other words, events continuously endanger the cosmos with the chaos of their novelty. Hence, the concept of chaosmos[18] aptly describes this double tension and helps one "to evoke, from the boundless chaos of night, rich island universes.[19] To introduce the concept of "creative advance" advocated by Whitehead's strong processualism with as few technicalities as possible, one may focus on his dialectic between actuality/becoming and potentiality/being from the perspective of its three functors difference, repetition and eschatological trend.

As to difference, actual occasions (also called "actual entities") manifest the ultimate; they are immediately given in experience-in-the-making: "What really exists is not 'things' made but 'things' in the making. Once made, they are dead."[20] Now, the process of becoming is, in itself, not temporal because it is not mundane. It is, to a certain extent, free to break old causal chains.

As to repetition, past events and what Whitehead calls "eternal objects" are potential. Actual events only last for a while, then they perish, topple into the past and become potential for further becomings: "Locke's notion of time hits the mark better: time is *perpetually perishing*. In the organic philosophy an actual entity has *perished* when it is complete" (*PR*, 81–82; see also 147, 210, 340).

As to trend, the dialectic between difference and repetition is furthermore lured towards the highest experiential value and intensity by God (who is in process as well). According to Whitehead, God locks the temporal trend inchoative in the prehension of the new present by the past.

In sum: process is all-embracing but time is not; it is structured by atemporal becomings. What matters most is the immediate event and its creativity; the potential structure is no doubt essential but continuously reframed as well. Actuality and potentiality are linked by transition (from potentiality to actuality) and perishing (toppling of completed actualities into potentiality). The normal state of consciousness does not allow us to notice that experience is bud-like; we are aware only of a stream of experience (that is, in fact, a contiguum of actual occasions).

2. 2. Huxley's Perennialism

The *Perennial Philosophy* (1946)[21] provides Huxley's most systematic account of the topic under consideration. It also adopts the bipolar structure actuality/potentiality, but in a more Platonic than Aristotelian fashion: being is the Ultimate; becoming is only apparent. More precisely, when looking for the immemorial and universal pattern at work in religious experiences, Huxley argues for a three-fold heuristic postulate—metaphysical, psychological and ethical—to understand the mundane manifold (*PP*, 1 and *passim*). First of all, a Divine/Ultimate Ground (Eckhart's "Godhead") is required: it designates the unmanifest principle of all manifestations; it is absolute, "spiritual," timeless, pure being. Second, human beings are endowed with a soul which is similar or even identical with the Ground. Third, the goal of human existence lies in the (unitive) knowledge of the Ground (see *PP*, 277,

337): it requires that one departs from the mundane "everlasting succession of events" to reach the "timeless now of the divine Spirit" (*PP*, 212).

In the normal state of consciousness, rationality distinguishes the Ground, the soul and the possible knowledge of the former by the latter. In the contemplative state of consciousness, all three merge together. The personal ego becomes what it always was implicitly: the eternal self or an explicit facet thereof. One sees at work here uncritical traces of dualism (Greek, Hindu) and of absolutism (Greek, Hindu, Hebrew). Being, the stable and eternal Ground, is prior to becoming, peculiar only to the accidental and apparent world. Of course, this two-world theory has some applicability in everyday life: it is strictly correlated to the normal state of consciousness and its construction of a 'mesocosm' (Reichenbach's "world of middle dimensions"). There is nothing much wrong with this 'theory' as long as one fully acknowledges that it embodies only an abstraction with a high pragmatic ('cash') value. But if, as will be seen below, time is an illusion—at best an unfortunate servitude and at worst a pure deviant idolatry (see *PP*, 63, 111)—action becomes illusory as well, and this raises two major difficulties: on the one hand, what becomes of the synergy Huxley proposes between a strong (Buddhist) spirituality and modern techno-science? On the other hand, can mankind be happy with the idea of personal salvation to the detriment of collective salvation?

3. The Significance of Huxley: Time and Late Postmodernity

Given the current state of affairs and especially its two possible futures depicted in the first section, and given the meanings of temporality treated in the second section, one can foresee the imperative conclusion. Nevertheless one last step seems expedient, viz. to complement the comparison by under-lining Whitehead's atemporalism and Huxley's processualism—and thereby to shed some light on the postmodern significance of Huxley.

3. 1. Process Perennialism: Active Optimism

Whitehead's radical processualism basically means that actuality as well as potentiality (with different modalities and pace) are not ultimately settled: process—not time—is all-embracing. Three further clarifications are required before one can reach a conclusion.

In the categoreal scheme of *Process and Reality*, the Ultimate is creativity, which is dipneumonous (i.e., it has two 'lungs'): God and the world are its two corresponding loci. There is no need here to spell out the various guises that awareness of the Ultimate can take; it is more directly relevant to consider the mapping that could be established between Whitehead and Eckhart (whose vision, together with Shankara's, obviously is of the highest importance to understand Huxley's). This mapping can be sketched as follows: on the one hand, there is the ultimacy of creativity—"the many become one, and are increased by one"—together with its mundane (many and one) and divine (one and many) co-processual instantiations; on the other hand, there is the timeless Godhead (pure formless One), together with the transient world (seat of becoming, i.e., of the many) and God who "becomes and disbecomes," who is one and many (see, e.g., *PP*, 37–38, 212).

Among the characteristics of actuality freedom/spontaneity and epochality were adduced without discussing duration. Genuine novelty is made possible by a structure of potentiality involving both the past world and God but actuality in the making is not in time, it belongs, as it were, to a dancing present that is perpendicular to ordinary time. More precisely, it is not in physical time, which is constructed by the consecution of the epochal events: "Time is sheer succession of epochal [i.e., atemporal] durations" (*SMW*, 125).[22]

The praxic consequences justify the 'active optimism' mentioned above. This becomes clear, for instance, for the issues of science and salvation. Since the future is truly open, since each individual can—actually ought to—make the difference, each of us is urged to work toward the best possible world, to liberate ourselves here and now and thereby to contribute to the salvation of all creatures. Personal and collective salvation cannot be separated from the *vita activa*. Neither can the different epistemic fields: science, theology, philosophy etc. are all interconnected. All necessary actions must be taken to contribute positively to the creative advance. Whitehead was an optimist.

3. 2. Classical Perennialism: Passivity if not Pessimism

It remains to be seen where a processual dimension can be found in Huxley.

The Perennial Philosophy makes it fairly clear that Huxley's basic ontology is Eckhartian and that his assessment of time is negative. There is no happiness or safety in time (see *PP*, 106); liberation is to go back solely to the atemporal Ground to celebrate the "adornment of the spiritual marriage."[23] Huxley's reflections may have been fuelled mainly by Otto's seminal *Mysticism East and West* (1929/1932)[24] and later by his personal drug-induced mystical experiences (1953–1963).

However, as Whiteheadian process philosophy makes plain, to posit an atemporal Ultimate does not necessarily imply a global deterministic *Weltanschauung* (James' "block universe"). The more far-reaching question consists in deciding whether what is actual has some degree of freedom or not and, consequently, whether it can change its own destiny or not. There is a sense in which we are, and have always been, one. If it is the goal of our existence to be (re)united with the eternal being, the sole nameless seat of existence—if transience is only deterministic—, then action is at best a mirage and at worst a karmic curse. The World Controller's view of the brave new world is quite straightforward:

> "Every change is a menace to stability. [...] Every discovery in pure science is potentially subversive; even science must sometimes be treated as a possible enemy. [...] Science is dangerous; we have to keep it most carefully chained and muzzled." (*BNW*, 205)

Happiness means changelessness. Of course, that sclerotic picture gets a bit processualized in *Island*, where social stability is used for individual liberation, i.e., spiritual progress, but it seems that solely the *Doors of Perception* proposes a definitively more dynamic version of the Eckhartian *Istigkeit* ("Is-ness"): Huxley here speaks—from his own experience (see James' essential distinction between second-hand and first-hand religious experiences[25])—of the necessity of gearing together being and becoming:

> The Being of Platonic philosophy—except that Plato seems to have made the enormous, the grotesque mistake of separating Being from becoming, and identifying it with the mathematical abstraction of the Idea. He could never, poor fellow, have seen a bunch of flowers shining with their own inner light and all but quivering under the pressure of the significance with which they were charged; could never have perceived that what rose and iris and carnation so intensely signified was nothing more, and nothing less, than what they were—a transience that was yet eternal life, a perpetual perishing that was at the same time pure Being [...].[26]

The chemical intoxication reveals the intricately dancing texture of the world, its creative rhythm. As Alan Watts beautifully claims in similar circumstances: "Everything gestures. Tables are tabling, pots are potting, walls are walling, fixtures are fixturing—a world of events instead of things."[27] When the percept swallows the concept (see *DP*, 42), it requires that eternity/everlastingness be reconciled with its bright and dark sides, i.e., with creativity and perishing. The Doors of Perception re-open the Universe.

What are the praxic consequences of these contrasting elements? As shown above, action is discarded if perfectly indifferent transience is the overall goal. Then only the *vita contemplativa* is worth living. This is an entirely coherent standpoint, but it is not applicable in most contexts, as the plot of the novel *Island* and the current socio-political state of affairs amply demonstrate. Huxley's novel indeed illustrates a fundamental historical pattern that has been well documented in Schmookler's *The Parable of the Tribes*:[28] No one is free to choose peace, but anyone can impose upon all the necessity for power. The author imagines a group of tribes living within reach of one another. If all choose the way of peace, then all may live in peace. But if all but one choose peace, the ways of power are spread throughout the system like a disease: there are four possible outcomes for the tribes threatened—destruction, absorption and transformation, withdrawal, and imitation—and in each case, peace is made irrelevant.

To adopt a purely deterministic view destroys the foundations of action and thereby of communal liberation. It is, moreover, incompatible with the promotion of science *qua* progressive tool (nothing much of the ancient 'theoria' remains in science nowadays). One could still argue for a certain limited meaning of the concept of destiny (although even for Plato a free decision initiates our mundane pilgrimage) but not of the concept of historicity.

To sum up: Huxley's works are susceptible of multiple interpretations. One of the basic hermeneutical decisions that have to be taken from the start is to adopt a clear strategy with regard to his (a)temporalism. Either his prose can sustain an interpretation that supports some form of combative attitude in adverse circumstances, and his work keeps a direct contemporary significance; or it does not justify such an interpretation, and its contemporary significance is rather limited. No doubt its relevance and meaning would remain impressive, but its revolutionary power would then be nil.

---

[1] The author wishes to thank the International Aldous Huxley Society for financial support which made it possible for him to attend the Riga Symposium.

[2] But Huxley occasionally discussed, or at least referred to, Whitehead, see Michel Weber, "On Religiousness and Religion: Huxley's Reading of Whitehead's *Religion in the Making* in the Light of James's *Varieties of Religious Experience*," *Aldous Huxley Annual*, 5 (2005), 117–132. Hereafter, Weber.

[3] See, e.g., his "A World of Pure Experience" (1904), reprinted in: William James, *Essays in Radical Empiricism* [posthumously published by Ralph Barton Perry] (New York, 1912).

[4] Three complementary sets of sensory receptors have to be distinguished. *Exteroception* (commonly called 'sense perception') is constituted by the five senses open to the external world. *Interoception* names the internal sensitivity complementing the exteroceptive one. Most of the time, its messages, coming from receptors housed in all organs and tissues, do not 'reach' consciousness: they are, through reflex action, the source of a harmonious bodily life. One can distinguish internal pains (cephalalgia, colic etc.), internal taste (chemical sensitivity ruling various reflex activities), and internal touch (sensitivity to variations of pressure, like distension of the bladder or the rectum, stomach contractions, antiperistaltic contractions of the œsophagus, determining the nausea feeling). *Proprioception* names the messages of position and movement allowing, with the help of the internal ear's semi-circular canals, a spatialisation —i.e., a full (ap)propriation—of the body. Proprioceptive perception grows from sensorial receptors delivering data about the position and the relative movements of the different parts of our body. Through reflex action, it regulates the muscular tone and helps us to localise ourselves in space and to create a sense of depth (stereognosy). Proprioception also includes the muscular sensitivity that complements exteroceptive touch in offering estimates on the weight and volume of the prehended and/or moved object. The structuration of our proprioceptive field provides for the fundamental organic anchorage of our sense of identity.

[5] Alfred North Whitehead, *Adventures of Ideas* [1933] (New York, 1969), 226.

[6] Aldous Huxley, *Island* (London, 1962), 132. Hereafter, *Island*.

[7] See *The Reenchantment of Science: Postmodern Proposals*, ed. David Ray Griffin (Albany, NY, 1988), x.

[8] See Christoph Bode, "Epistemological Inconsistencies in Aldous Huxley's Later Works," *"Now More than Ever": Proccedings of the Aldous Huxley Centenary Symposium, Münster 1994*, ed. Bernfried Nugel (Frankfurt a.M., 1995), 319–333; Francis Herbert Bradley, *Appearance and Reality: A Metaphysical Essay* [1893], (2nd rev. ed., London/New York, 1906); Alfred North Whitehead, *Process and Reality: An Essay in Cosmology* [1929], Gifford Lectures Delivered in the University of Edinburgh During the Session 1927–28, ed. David Ray Griffin and Donald W. Sherburne (New York, 1978); hereafter, *PR*.

[9] A recent and particularly edifying exemplification of this kind of cynicism can be found in John Perkins' *Confessions of an Economic Hit Man* (San Francisco, 2004).

[10] Thomas Hobbes, *Leviathan* [1651], ed. and with an introduction by C. B. Macpherson (Harmondsworth, 1968; hereafter, *Leviathan*), 185. All quotes are from Part I, Chap. 13.

[11] See K. Eric Drexler, *Engines of Creation: The Coming Era of Nanotechnology*, with a foreword by Marvin Minsky (Oxford, 1992).

[12] Alfred North Whitehead, *Science and the Modern World*, The Lowell Lectures, 1925 (New York, 1967; hereafter, *SMW*), 12.

[13] This expression comes from Josiah Royce, *The Philosophy of Loyalty* (New York, 1908); it means that our first duty is to accept and preserve our terrestrial roots, and not to argue or to hope for celestial ones (which are not, however, ruled out).

[14] See, e.g., Jean-Pierre Dupuy, *Pour un catastrophisme éclairé: quand l'impossible est certain* (Paris, 2002).

[15] Aldous Huxley, *Brave New World*, with an introduction by David Bradshaw (London, 1994). Hereafter, *BNW*.

[16] The term 'eugenics' was coined by Darwin's cousin Francis Galton in 1883; it describes any procedure that attempts to improve human genetic stock—by limiting the procreation of those with so-called 'undesirable/unfavourable' genetic qualities and/or by encouraging those with 'desirable/favourable' traits to breed. A 'weak' (and the quotation marks matter) form of eugenics was first systematically put into practice by the efficient and democratic American government in the State of Connecticut in 1896; outside any legal frame, it had actually occurred previously in Switzerland between 1880 and 1890). The 'stronger' form of eugenics, concentration camps, was actually instituted during the Boer War (1899–1902)—the 'Last of the Gentlemen's Wars,' as it is also called— by the very creative Lord Herbert Kitchener (1851–1916, the hero who went down stoically with his ship when torpedoed during the First World War). It was designed to ideally complement his scorched-earth policy. Needless to say that reliable statistics are quite scarce here.

[17] For a recent systematic and general introduction to Whitehead's development, see Michel Weber, "Alfred North Whitehead (1861–1947)," *Dictionary of Twentieth-Century British Philosophers*, ed. Stuart Brown (2 vols., Bristol, 2005). For a historico-speculative assessment of the notions of process, see Michel

Weber, "Introduction: Process Metaphysics in Context," *After Whitehead: Rescher on Process Metaphysics*, ed. Michel Weber, Process Thought, I (Frankfurt/Paris/Lancaster, 2004). For the overall background to this presentation, see Michel Weber, *La dialectique de l'intuition chez A. N. Whitehead: sensation pure, pancréativité et contiguïsme*, préface de Jean Ladrière, Chromatiques whiteheadiennes, I (Frankfurt/Paris/Lancaster, 2005) and *Whitehead's Pancreativism: The Basics*, with a foreword by Nicholas Rescher (Frankfurt / Paris, 2006).

[18] "Chaosmos" is of course Joyce's creation in *Finnegans Wake*. The concept of chaosmos has been particularly popularized by Gilles Deleuze and Félix Guattari.

[19] Aldous Huxley, *Heaven and Hell* (London, 1956), 69.

[20] William James, *A Pluralistic Universe*, Hibbert Lectures at Manchester College on the Present Situation in Philosophy (New York, 1909), 263.

[21] Aldous Huxley, *The Perennial Philosophy* (London, 1946). Hereafter, *PP*.

[22] See also (*SMW*, 126): "Thus time is atomic (i.e., epochal), though what is temporalised is divisible."

[23] Jan van Ruusbroec, *The Adornment of the Spiritual Marriage*, trans. C. A. Wynschenk, ed. Evelyn Underhill (London, 1916).

[24] Rudolf Otto, *West-östliche Mystik: Vergleich und Unterscheidung zur Wesensdeutung* (Gotha, 1929); *Mysticsm East and West: A Comparative Analysis of the Nature of Mysticism*, transl. Bertha L. Bracey and Richenda C. Payne (New York, 1932).

[25] See Weber, 117–118.

[26] Aldous Huxley, *The Doors of Perception* (London, 1954), 12. Hereafter, *DP*.

[27] Alan W. Watts, *The Joyous Cosmology: Adventures in the Chemistry of Consciousness* (New York, 1962), 69. Amazingly enough, Martin Heidegger adopts a similar oracular style in a lecture given on June 6, 1950 ("Das Ding," reprinted in *Vorträge und Aufsätze* [Pfullingen, 1954], and translated in *Poetry, Language, Thought*, transl. and with an introduction by Albert Hofstadter [New York, 1971]).

[28] Andrew Bard Schmookler, *The Parable of the Tribes: The Problem of Power in Social Evolution* (Boston, 1986 [1984]).

Bernfried Nugel

(University of Münster)

ALDOUS HUXLEY AS MORAL PHILOSOPHER: *ENDS AND MEANS* VIS-À-VIS GERALD HEARD'S *THE THIRD MORALITY*[1]

After the moral reflections that Aldous Huxley incorporated into his writings for the Peace Pledge Union,[2] into his novel *Eyeless in Gaza* and into his essay "Justifications," all published in 1936, *Ends and Means*, brought out in 1937, is his considered large-scale attempt to define his new-found metaphysics and to constitute, on this basis, a framework of modern ethics. How he arrived at his moral philosophy (a processs which is often misleadingly referred to as a conversion), I have discussed elsewhere, arguing that the change which can be noticed in his philosophical outlook from the beginning of the thirties onwards is a logical expansion of the agnostic position contained, for instance, in the exchange between the Savage and the World Controller at the end of *Brave New World*, an expansion that can conclusively be traced throughout Huxley's later works.[3] In addition, David Bradshaw and Paul Eros have pointed out the immense influence of Huxley's philosopher friend Gerald Heard, with whom he closely collaborated in the pacifist movement,[4] so closely in fact that, in July 1936, he even envisaged writing a book with him as "a kind of synthetic work on the whole problem" (Bradshaw, 18). In spite of this joint plan, however, the curious fact remains that Heard published a separate book on ethics, entitled *The Third Morality*, as early as in January 1937,[5] while Huxley was obviously still collecting notes for his own work, which he wrote up during his stay at Lawrence's ranch at Taos in the summer of 1937 and published in November under the title *Ends and Means*.[6] In view of these circumstances, the usual assumption in Huxley criticism that "the result of their collaboration was *Ends and Means*"[7] requires a re-examination and, since further information about the genesis of both books appears unavailable, calls for a close textual comparison.

The following analysis of *Ends and Means*, therefore, will first focus on Huxley's premises, scope and structure of argumentation and then compare these aspects with the make-up of Heard's book. Against this background, one may eventually venture a general appraisal of Huxley's capacity as moral philosopher.[8]

The almost universal scope of Huxley's approach to ethics is already clearly reflected in the detailed subtitle of *Ends and Means*: "*An Enquiry into the Nature of Ideals and into the Methods Employed for their Realization*:" "ends" are understood as "ideals," i.e., general goals of the highest order, and "means" as "methods" for the materialization of those general goals.

Accordingly, the first chapter carries the heading "Goals, Roads and Contemporary Starting-Point" and begins by formulating a premiss concerning the "ideal goal of human effort," followed by another concerning "the roads which lead to that goal" (*EM*, 1). As regards the first premiss, there exists, Huxley asserts, "a very general agreement" among the political and religious "prophets" of mankind: the "ideal goal of human effort" consists in "liberty, peace, justice and brotherly love" (1). As to the second premiss, which concerns the roads, he states a "clash of contradictory opinions, dogmatically held and acted upon with the violence of fanaticism" (1).

Obviously, by putting his two premisses into such a general and at the same time simple form, Huxley wants to gain the reader's assent from the outset, thus paving the way for a specific thesis with which he may open his argument. Indeed, in his overview of conflicting methods used to reach the ideal goal, he soon focuses on those social reformers who "believe that desirable social changes can be brought about most effectively by changing the individuals who compose society" (1) and not the other way round. This leads him to the discussion of several types of an ideal individual held up as models of behaviour by certain ages and classes in human history, such as the "chivalrous man" of the Middle Ages, and the "*honnête homme*," the "*philosophe*" as well as the "respectable man" of the seventeenth to nineteenth centuries respectively (2). Noting the fact that all ideals depend on the particular social context of their time, he nonetheless asserts that

> some thoughts and aspirations [...] are manifestly less dependent on particular social circumstances than others. And here a significant fact emerges: all the ideals of human behaviour formulated by those who have been most successful in freeing themselves from the prejudices of their time and place are singularly alike. Liberation from prevailing conventions of thought, feeling and behaviour is accomplished most effectively by the practice of disinterested virtues and through direct insight into the real nature of ultimate reality. (1–2)

This fundamental thesis is based on an inference arrived at inductively by an empirical observation of human behaviour in the course of history and contains two crucial components, first, an ethical assumption about the highest goal of human behaviour, viz "disinterested virtues," and, second, an epistemological assumption about the direct recognition of "ultimate reality." In the context of contemporary philosophy, this latter assumption looks extraordinary inasmuch as it seems to go beyond even Kant's idealist position, which claims that "ultimate reality," the so-called 'Ding an sich,' cannot be grasped by human reason. However, Huxley, in a parenthesis, links this assumption with the first by anchoring "direct insight into the nature of ultimate reality" in the sphere of morality:

(Such insight is a gift, inherent in the individual; but, though inherent, it cannot manifest itself completely except where certain conditions are fulfilled. The principal pre-condition of insight is, precisely, the practice of disinterested virtues.) (*EM*, 3)

This sounds very much like Kant's practical metaphysics, which postulates a categorical imperative inherent in man that directs his actions in accordance with absolute reality. Such a concept of autonomous morality entails an independence from religion inasmuch as man is solely guided by his practical reason and not by religious tenets. Considering Huxley's critical attitude towards established religions, this aspect is certainly desirable from his point of view. Huxley's affinity with Kant's ethical categories is further reflected in his use of the characteristically Kantian term "disinterested" and his mention of the human will, which, in Kant's sense, ought to 'will ethically':

> To some extent critical intellect is also a liberating force [i.e., besides the practice of disinterested virtues]. But the way in which intellect is used depends upon the will. Where the will is not disinterested, the intellect tends to be used [...] merely as an instrument for the rationalization of passion and prejudice, the justification of self-interest. That is why so few even of the acutest philosophers have succeeded in liberating themselves completely from the narrow prison of their age and country. (3)

So far Huxley has used Kantian notions of morality, with which an educated reader can be assumed to be familiar; his own innovative contribution, however, can be seen when he, referring to those "acutest philosophers," re-defines the categorical imperative as mystical insight:

> It is seldom indeed that they achieve as much freedom as the mystics and the founders of religion. The most nearly free men have always been those who combined virtue with insight. (3)

This indeed is the core of Huxley's fundamental thesis, from which he can step by step derive the main categories of his ethics. He goes on to define "the ideal man of the free philosphers, the mystics, the founders of religions" as the "non-attached man," naming as categories of non-attachment freedom from "bodily sensations and lusts," freedom from negative emotions, such as "craving for power and possesions" or "anger and hatred" as well as "exclusive loves," and freedom also from intellectual preoccupations, such as "science, art, speculation, philanthropy" (3–4). He is at the same time aware of the fact that such a catalogue of non-attachment or disinterested virtues dialectically entails "attachment to an ultimate reality greater and more significant than the self." And here he anticipates another cornerstone of his moral philosophy which he will deal with in the last chapters of his book, viz the necessary link between cosmology and ethics:

> [...] the ethic of non-attachment has always been correlated with cosmologies that affirm the existence of a spiritual reality

> underlying the phenomenal world and imparting to it whatever value
> or significance it possesses. (*EM*, 4)

There is no need here to follow Huxley's further remarks on the term "non-attached" or on the venerable age and wide distribution of this ethic in many cultures; what is more important is his intention to apply these categories to the developments in the society of his own time by asking the question: "In relation to these ideals, what are the relevant contemporary facts?" (6) and by assessing those facts in terms of the "progress in charity," one of the main disinterested virtues. He extensively argues that there is a general "regression in charity" (8) and announces that the main topic of his book will be the ways in which "existing society can be transformed into the ideal society described by the prophets" and in which men can be "transformed into those non-attached beings, who alone can create a society significantly better than our own" (8).

At this point the attentive reader can already anticipate the overall design of the book,[9] which Huxley later endorses in the concluding section of chapter I: the main middle part will be devoted to means, whereas the first and the three last chapters will discuss ends. More specifically, Huxley plans to present "a kind of cookery book of social reform" in chapters II to XII, beginning with a basic discussion of the multi-causal factors of human activity (II) and proceeding to "the most important of these fields of activity," first to "the political and economic and [then] to the fields of personal behaviour." The last three chapters (XIII–XV) are reserved for "a discussion of first principles" (*EM*, 9), i.e., the correlation between cosmology and ethics. While Huxley points out, with regard to the middle part, that his basic axiom will be the undeniable insight that ends can never justify means (see *EM*, 9), he even more emphatically praises the practical value of the last three chapters, inasmuch as "our metaphysical beliefs are the finally determining factor in all our actions" (10).

Looking back on the first chapter and its fundamental thesis, one may single out at least two conspicuous aspects: first, Huxley imperturbably holds a position of autonomous morality based on mystical insight, and second, he presents his argument with a tenor of complete conviction. It is particularly the first aspect that stands in sharp contrast to his agnosticism up to the beginning of the 1930s, which was characterized by a mainly empirical approach. What may have made his new idealist stance more palatable to himself, was perhaps the gratifying observation that his thesis about the ideal of non-attachment seemed to be borne out by empirical evidence from the last three thousand years.

As far as Huxley's discussion of means in the middle part of the book is concerned, one may—in the context of the present topic—disregard his more detailed arguments and rather concentrate on his character of a philosopher. In this respect, chapter II clearly sets the tone by discussing the "nature of expla-

Contents

Ends and Means: facsimile of contents page

nation" as the groundwork of Huxley's methodology, which, however, as he admits, is not his own but largely derives from Emile Meyerson's two books on the problem (see *EM*, 12). Whether the reader interprets this reference as modesty or inexperience, still Huxley's stance as philosopher cannot be overlooked. Quite consistently, the ensuing overtly systematic analysis of contemporary society enhances this first impression. He starts with general aspects, which he called "social machinery and large-scale organization" at the beginning of chapter I (*EM*, 1): these aspects cover chapters III to IX, ranging from "Large-Scale Social Reform" and "The Planned Society" to "The Nature of the Modern State," "Decentralization" and "War." Then he turns to the role of the individual, dealing with specific aspects in chapters X–XII, such as "Individual Work for Reform," "Inequality" and "Education."

What is more, in all these middle chapters Huxley regularly refers to the ideal of non-attachment as guideline for his disquisition, thus reinforcing his fundamental philosophical approach, which he calls that of a "rational idealist," in implicitly Kantian categories (*EM*, 68). In addition, he seems to be in his element not only as a social reformer but also as a satirist: he extensively draws on his socio-critical essays of the 1930s, in one instance , viz the chapter on "War", even directly acknowledging it (see *EM*, 89) as a little-altered reprint from his recently published *An Encyclopedia of Pacifism* (1937), and at the same time he freely employs his satirical talent in demolishing wrong policies and behaviour, and this with greater intensity than in his earlier publications since he now possesses the unquestionable norm of non-attachment as his main criterion of judgment. Characteristically, Huxley concludes his discussion of the educational uses of literature near the end of his chapter on "Education," which rounds off the middle part of the book, both with constructive hints for the literary representation of "non-attached men and women" (*EM*, 208) and with satirical remarks concerning the dilemma of "who will educate the educators" (210).[10]

But one must look at the last three chapters, which focus on "metaphysical beliefs," in order to understand how Huxley tries to lay the foundation for his ethics. In chapter XIII (on "Religious Practices") he again uses an empirical approach by discussing the forms of activity resulting from the metaphysical claims of institutionalized religion. He distinguishes between good, evil and "ethically neutral" effects and reinforces his position of a rational idealist:

> Towards the kind of religion whose fruits are moral evil and a darkening of the mind the rational idealist can only show an uncompromising hostility. Such things as persecution and the suppression or distortion of truth are intrinsically wrong, and he can have nothing to do with religious organizations which countenance such iniquities. (225)

From the effects of metaphysical beliefs Huxley turns to metaphysics proper in the next chapter entitled "Beliefs." Here he refers back to his thesis in the opening chapter and now proposes to cope in greater detail with "the social ideals of the prophets and the personal ideals of the founders of religions in the light of what we know about the world." In other words, Huxley postulates the necessity of a cosmology or, as he puts it, of "a good metaphysic [...], a metaphysic that corresponds reasonably closely with observed and inferred reality" (*EM*, 252). As for the overall arrangement of chapters, he is aware of a seeming inconsistency but explicitly justifies it:

> Logically, this discussion of the nature of the world should have preceded the discussion of the practical ways and means for modifying ourselves and the society in which we live. But the arrangement that is logically most correct is not always the most convenient. For various reasons it has seemed to be expedient to reserve this discussion of first principles to the last chapters. (252–253)

This remark reveals that, for Huxley, the moral philosopher, the appearance of systematicity is less essential than the intended effect on the reader, viz to persuade him of the high significance and importance of the last chapters, as he had announced in his opening chapter.

Accordingly, Huxley attempts to ground his metaphysic on a concise review of the state of knowledge achieved by contemporary science, particularly by physics, psychology and evolutionary biology. Though, to a great extent, he accepts the insights of these sciences into the nature of the world, he eventually cautions the reader against believing that "the scientific picture of the world [can] claim to be comprehensive" (*EM*, 266). On the contrary, he argues,

> in recent years, many men of science have come to realize that the scientific picture of the world is a partial one—the product of their special competence in mathematics and their special incompetence to deal systematically with aesthetic and moral values, religious experiences and intuitions of significance. (268–269)

Therefore, the crucial question, in contrast to any partial world-picture, ought to be, Huxley infers, the following: "Does the world as a whole possess the value and meaning that we constantly attribute to certain parts of it (such as human beings and their works); and, if so, what is the nature of that value and meaning?" (269). His answer is tentative but clear in its direction: he rejects "the philosophy of meaninglessness" (273), of which he himself, he frankly admits, had been guilty a few years before, and repeats his empirical argument from the opening chapter that so many philosophers and mystics who were convinced that "the world possesses meaning and value" (277) cannot have been wrong. Characteristically, Huxley at this point again assumes the attitude of a seemingly neutral philosopher who systematically reviews the most important proofs of the existence of God and refutes them, leaning heavily on Kant again. But then, having admitted that even the moral argument for theism may be wishful thinking, he introduces a surprising, because rather arbitrary, premiss: "there are certain circumstances in which wishes are a reliable source of information, not only about ourselves, but also about the outside world" (*EM*, 280). He substantiates this premiss by positing a general human "craving for explanation" and, analogously, also a fundamental "craving for righteousness, for meaning, for value" (281, 282). In his view, this assumption realistically bridges the gap that he had noted earlier, "the gulf between truth about the world on the one hand and practical goodness on the other"(275). In other words, Huxley here ventures to declare certain kinds of wishful thinking to be sound premisses of philosophy and even adds:

> Whether it will ever be possible to verify the theories of moral philosophers by direct observation and experiment seems doubtful. But that is no reason for denying the truth of such theories. Nor, as we have seen, is the fact that they originate in wishes. (281)

From here it is only a small step to Huxley's culminating conclusion that "final conviction can only come to those who make an act of faith" (285). Considered in their essence, all the world-pictures discussed before, Huxley argues, are grounded in acts of faith, and, in this respect, the act of faith necessary for moral philosophy is not intrinsically less respectable than those others. Reducing science and moral philosophy to this minimal common denominator may seem simplistic or even helpless but it is at the same time courageous: Huxley clearly demonstrates that he wishes, in Kant's sense, to 'will ethically,' since no reasoning will probably ever prove moral values. Thus the scene is set for the detailed discussion of the world-picture obtained by mystical meditation and of its relation to ethics. As he sums up, "goodness, meditation, the mystical experience and the ultimate impersonal reality discovered in mystical experience are organically related" (*EM*, 299). Rejecting Albert Schweitzer's argument that, though "mysticism is the correct world view, [...] the ultimate reality of the world is not moral ('God is not good')" and that, consequently, mysticism "is unsatisfactory in ethical content" (299), Huxley persuasively argues in favour of the practice of morality in the human sphere:

> It is impossible for the mystic to pay attention to his relation to God and to his fellows, unless he has previously detached his attention from his animal nature and the business of being socially successful. But he cannot detach his attention from these things except by the consistent and conscious practice of the highest morality. God is not good; but if I want to have even the slightest knowledge of God, I must be good at least in some slight measure; and if I want as full knowledge of God as it is possible for human beings to have, I must be as good as it is possible for human beings to be. Virtue is the essential preliminary to the mystical experience. (299)

Thus he at last substantiates his fundamental thesis of the opening chapter, which postulated that "the principal pre-condition of insight is, precisely, the practice of disinterested virtues" (*EM*, 3).

In addition, Huxley resorts again to his earlier analogical thinking and even theoretically finds no "incompatibility between an ultimate reality, which is impersonal and therefore not moral, and the existence of a moral order on the human level": as science has demonstrated that an identity of physical matter underlies the diversity of things, so "the mystical experience testifies to the existence of a spiritual unity underlying the diversity of separate consciousnesses" (*EM*, 300). Simultaneously he hopes to reinforce this notion through a counter argument by contending that "belief in a personal, moral God has led only too frequently to theoretical dogmatism and practical intolerance, [...] to the commission in the name of the divinely moral person of every kind of iniquity" (301). This statement directly ushers in the discussion of evil as opposed to the moral order of the world so conceived. With his extremely general definition of evil as "that which makes for separateness," a definition which clearly echoes Anthony Beavis' cosmological vision in the concluding chapter of *Eyeless in Gaza*,[11] Huxley eventually provides the link to his last chapter, entitled "Ethics."

The opening paragraph of this chapter can be considered the core of Huxley's moral philosophy and therefore deserves to be quoted in full:

> Every cosmology has its correlated ethic. The ethic that is correlated with the cosmology outlined in the preceding chapter, has, as its fundamental principles, these propositions: Good is that which makes for unity; Evil is that which makes for separateness. Relating these terms to the phraseology employed in the first chapters, we can say that separateness is attachment and that without non-attachment no individual can achieve unity either with God or, through God, with other individuals. (303)

In the rest of the chapter, which he has earlier on announced as the culmination of the whole book, Huxley tries "to illustrate the application of [these] ethical principles in life" (303). In his view, human life can be conveniently divided into the "plane of the body and its sensations [...], the plane of emotions, and [...] the plane of the intellect" (303), and he accordingly discusses the existence of good and evil on these three planes. Though thought-provoking in many details, Huxley's analysis, as a whole, does not significantly go beyond the philosophical position outlined in *Eyeless in Gaza*: as in the novel, he mentions evil in the form of a physical addiction to pleasure or suffering as well as in the shape of irresponsible sex, and enlarges on the evil emotions of anger, envy, fear, and the "lusts for power, social position and ownership" (319) resulting in pride, vanity, ambition, and avarice. He is particularly hard on sloth: "Sloth exists on all the planes, and can be physical, emotional or intellectual. In all its forms, sloth is a kind of negative malignity—a refusal to do what ought to be done" (319).

As for evil on the intellectual plane, Huxley detects it in any lack of intelligence, that is, in an unawareness of "things and events in the external world" as well as of "the phenomena of the inner world" (321). Here he stresses the necessity of forming a personality in order to later transcend it and castigates the Christian tendency to develop a personality preoccupied with sin as an obstacle to self-transcendence (see 327). To underscore the importance of non-attachment and self-transcendence, Huxley even contrasts the teachings of the mystics with those of the two main Christian denominations:

> The fruits of such doctrines as are taught by Eckhart, the author of *The Cloud* and the oriental mystics whom they so closely resemble, are peace, toleration and charity. The fruits of such doctrines as are taught by Luther and St. Augustine are war and the organized malice of religious persecution and the organized falsehood of dogmatism and censorship. On this point, it seems to me, the historical evidence is clear and explicit. Those who consider that the metaphysical theories of Luther and Augustine correspond more closely to the nature of ultimate reality than do the theories of Eckhart, Sankhara, or the Buddha must be ready to affirm the proposition that evil is the result of acting upon true beliefs about the universe and that good is the result of acting on false beliefs. All the evidence, however, supports the opposite conclusion—that false beliefs result in evil and that true beliefs have fruits that are good. (329)

Among the most dangerous kinds of intellectual evil, as Huxley points out emphatically, are the philosophical and theological beliefs that start from false premises and result in "war and the organized malice of religious persecution and the organized falsehood of dogmatism and censorship." What makes these activities so extremely evil is their being organized with the help of the human intellect as a vehicle for downright malice, and together with the strongest emotional evils, such as "the lust for power or the lust for possessions," the intellectual evils clearly occupy the top of Huxley's typology of moral evil. In other words, "these cravings are spiritual, therefore are unremittingly separative and evil; have no dependence on the body, therefore can assume almost any form" (320). And how can one detect those infinite forms of evil? As in this chapter, Huxley, the rational idealist, throughout *Ends and Means* repeatedly uses an empirical approach, viz the method of judging the tree by its fruits: in the last analysis, this method also underlies the overall make-up of the book inasmuch as Huxley in the main part focusses on the pernicious effects of wrong attitudes in the individual and of false policies in society but does not forget to relate these to "a theory of the ultimate reality" (330).

In contrast to *Ends and Means*, Gerald Heard's book *The Third Morality* has all the appearance of a thoroughly philosophical disquisition: it has a one-page foreword, in which the category used in the title is concisely explained as the conceptual framework of the book, it then offers a ten-page intro-duction, communicating the author's intention and reason for writing the book, and thereafter presents two large parts of nearly equal length, the first taking a survey of three main types of world-picture viewed against the state of the art in modern sciences, and the second applying the results as premises for moral conduct in human life.[12] Heard's working hypothesis is already spelt out in his foreword:

> This book is called *The Third Morality* because in man's history he has had three general ideas of conduct based on the three world-pictures he has so far made. The first world-picture, and its resultant morality, was Anthropomorphism, the belief that the universe was the expression of individual persons, and then of one such supreme person. The second world-picture was Mechanomorphism, the belief that the universe could be explained as a huge machine. [...] until this generation, [it] has been the accepted world-picture, even among the religious, [...] [the] attempt to act [according to it]— however inconsistent and however unethical—must then be classified as the Second Morality. [...] The Third Morality is the gradually defining impress which is to-day beginning to be made by the third world-picture [...] (*TM*, sig. [A7])

From the start this working hypothesis contains the axiom that governs the whole book, viz that there must be a logical progress from a world-picture to the system of moral conduct deduced from it, and thence to the acting out of that system, or in Heard's words, a progress from "a cosmology" to "an ethic", and thence to "an outline of training" (*TM*, 9). In the first two chapters of Part I Heard accordingly paves the way for his discussion of the new cosmology of his time by asking two seemingly simple rhetorical questions used as chapter headings: "Are Ethics Enough?" (the supposed answer being 'no' since one needs a cosmology first) and "Is There Evidence of Any Other Sanction?" (the supposed answer being 'yes' since one may use the new cosmology implied in the results of modern science). These methodical steps include the insight that "Means dictate ends," meaning that the new discoveries of science "compel the discovery of new ends" (4), i.e. of a third cosmology. Heard's reflections are generally couched in a vivid though often repetitive style, which clearly reflects Heard's basic concern for never losing the reader in his reasoning. The new cosmology is then presented in four chapters (III–VI), all headed with the general category "Evidence to Date" but subdivided into "Post-Mechanist Physics" (III), "Post-Mechanist Biology" (IV), "Post-Mechanist Psychology" (V), and, as a summary, "The Post-Mechanist Outlook" (VI). That Heard should think it apposite to re-number these four chapters as I to IV under the general heading "Evidence to Date"

CONTENTS

The Third Morality: facsimile of contents page

certainly demonstrates his methodicalness, though it may seem over-schematic to some readers. To understand what the philosopher Heard considers essential in his impressive survey of modern science, based as such on considerable philosophical as well as technical knowledge, one may conveniently turn to his own intermediate account:

> We must now sum up briefly the evidence for Mechanism transcended:
> In physics we see the universe is to-day realized to be fundamentally immaterial. All that matters takes place outside matter. [...]
> In physiology we see the body is an affair of the mind—but a mind vaster than our little surface minds. [...]
> In biology we see that the forces in evolution have not been blind and brute forces [...] On the contrary, the very powers which to-day [...] we value most highly—intelligence and devotion—it is these, primarily expressed in awareness, and sensitiveness, affection and sympathy, curiosity and gentleness, which have been the directive currents in our evolution.
> In psychology we see the mind is in its own right and cannot [...] be defined in terms of any lower or simpler activity. [...] Here then are the facts of telepathy, clairvoyance (or scrying) and even prevision. Here is the mind working on its own. (*TM*, 129–130)

This, then, for Heard, is the fundamental result of modern science: mind, and not matter, is the principle that constitutes the universe, in other words, the "case of idealism versus materialism" is "complet[ed]" in favour of the former (129). The delicate point in this thesis, however, is that Heard arrives at it by facile, because speculative, reasoning. Referring to the findings of the modern sciences just reviewed, he asks: "If [...] mind is proved on some occasions to be the *causa causans* [i.e., causing cause], why should it not be found to be underlying all phenomena?" (130) and concludes that "our every apprehension of the outer world is a psychological act of construction" (130). Thus, in his view, psychology is the master science of the third cosmology and also the third morality, as Part II of his book, entitled "The Actual Ethic," amply demonstrates.

The arrangement of chapters is equally methodical as in Part I. From a general discussion of the framework of the new ethic, called "The Outlook for Action"(VII), Heard proceeds to two chapters with the same heading "The Course Indicated" but distinguished into "The Attitude" (VIII) and "The Action" (IX), and via a chapter called "Training" (X) he eventually arrives at the last chapter entitled "Actual Exercises and Effects" (XI). Thus Heard becomes steadily more concrete and more practical along this way, focussing more and more—in fact, from chapter IX onwards—on ways of how to realize the new ethic. In the context of the present analysis, however, a brief look at the foundation of Heard's ethic must suffice. Three aspects are of particular importance here:

First, Heard posits a direct contact between "the individual mind" and "universal mind" (*TM*, 160) and thence deduces a psychological evolution from personal to "impersonal consciousness" (161), aspiring to the "apprehension of this profound uniting common life" (165). Second, he postulates survival after death inasmuch as the personal consciousness partakes of the immortal impersonal mind (169). Third, in his "super-personal cosmology" evil is "part of the condition of a transitional state" (172), i.e. a state in the evolution from the individual to the universal mind. Evil may exist as a negative force, as "simple failure of vitality or the wish to cease," or, more importantly, as a positive or active force, viz as "that vitality become, in its energy, somehow cut off, strangulated, only able to realize its life as something alien and hostile to all other lives, to the whole life" (176). Thus, in the last analysis, evils are aberrations in the evolution towards universal life in the cosmos.

It is certainly surprising how little space Heard devotes to the definition of evil, just seven pages to explain evil as anything that works against the unity of all life in the evolution of individual towards universal mind. Heard, it is true, acknowledges the fact of evil but restricts it to a transitional phase in the evolution of mind. It is clearly in this limited framework that he later discusses attitudes that hinder individuals from realizing their "unity with all life and being" (187), such as "physical addiction" (192), "possessiveness" in the social sphere (197) and "pretension" (201) on the "psychical" level. This, among other things, reveals Heard's overall tendency to become ever more confident, if not enthusiastic, in the course of his book as he appears to be whole-heartedly convinced of his fundamental thesis about the evolution of mind in the universe.

Comparing the scope and structure of argumentation in both books, one can easily see their common ground of basic assumptions: both Heard and Huxley postulate an idealist, i.e., distinctly anti-materialist philosophical approach supported by the findings of modern science, further a necessary correlation between cosmology and ethics, a direct interdependence of ends and means, and an autonomous morality based on the disinterested virtues of charity, intelligence (for both see *EM*, 4, 283; *TM*, 130), courage (*EM*, 4), devotion (*TM*, 130), generosity (*EM*, 4; *TM*, 187), and compassion (*TM*, 213), to name only a few. Hitherto overlooked in Huxley criticism but even more important are their differences: while Heard is at great pains to establish his new cosmology in the first place, and thence, smoothly and in regular steps, to deduce his ethic, with a progression from ends to means, Huxley frames his discussion of means in the middle part of his book with a statement of moral goals in the first and last chapters. Thus Heard, first and foremost, presents himself as a general philospher who also includes ethics in his outlook, whereas Huxley from the start tries to establish himself as a moral philosopher who is aware that he must ground his ethic in an idealist cosmology. Huxley, however, cautiously qualifies his idealism by the term "rational," while Heard somewhat deprecatingly connects this term with the "materialist-rationalist" ethic derived from Mechanomorphism (see *TM*, 49) and unconditionally pleads for an acknowledgement of universal mind. In addition, Huxley endeavours to be realistic and adduce empirical evidence, e.g. for his fundamental thesis about the validity of the ideal of non-attachment or in his concentration on observable effects when judging the tree by its fruits. Heard, on the contrary, constantly reiterates his unlimited belief in the universal evolution of mind, solely relying, as factual evidence, on his selective interpretation of the findings of modern science, and this mainly for the constitution of his cosmology, not directly for his ethic. All in all, the results of the above comparison of the two books—particularly the different logical arrangement of chapters—appear to support the conclusion that Huxley wished to give greater weight to a moral assessment of contemporary society than Heard. Looking back on their original plan for a joint book, which, according to Huxley, was "to start with metaphysics and proceed through psychology to a system of politics and economics—all being linked together as parts of a complete philosophy, theoretical and practical or applied, of life,"[13] one can see Heard focussing on the fundamental philosophical argument (Part I) and on the practical psychological teaching or training of the individual (Part II) and Huxley framing his central socio-political and economic analysis (chapters II–XII) with a presentation of his new cosmology and correlated ethic (chapters I and XIII–XV).

Their greatest difference, however, at least in my view, is an epistemological one and lies in the fact that Heard overtly rejects wishful thinking in earlier philosophers (see *TM*, 35 and 50, note, on Kant), not recognizing that his own position comes very close to wishful thinking, as his sweeping speculation about the universal validity of the mind-oriented findings of modern science implies.[14] Huxley, on the other hand, perhaps in deliberate reply to Heard, frankly admits that his similar position may be wishful thinking but nevertheless defends it as the necessary cosmological basis for his ethic. His demonstrative certainty notwithstanding, he clearly argues in terms of a working hypothesis which, at the time, appears to him to be the most convincing in the field of moral philosophy but has to be tested by applying it to contemporary behaviour in individual life and society. In this sense, though Heard asserts from the start that his work is "a practical book" (*TM*, 1), Huxley's is much more so, and even more persuasively so. And looking back from our present time, where we can see so many pernicious effects of the nowadays prevailing relativist ethics, are we not a little more inclined to wish for the realization of an autonomous morality as Heard and Huxley promoted it?

[1] I would like to thank the Deutsche Forschungsgemeinschaft for a grant towards the costs of my journey to Riga.

[2] See David Bradshaw, "The Flight from Gaza: Aldous Huxley's Involvement with the Peace Pledge Union in the Context of His Overall Intellectual Development," in: *"Now More Than Ever": Proceedings of the Aldous Huxley Centenary Symposium Münster 1994*, ed. Bernfried Nugel (Münster, 1995), 9–27.

[3] See Bernfried Nugel, "'A Kind of Early Christian Malignity': Aldous Huxley's Analysis of Evil in His Later Works," in: *"But to Vindicate the Ways of God to Man": Literature and Theodicy*, ed. Rudolf Freiburg and Susanne Gruss (Tübingen, 2004), 385–402.

[4] Besides Bradshaw see Paul Eros, "'A Sort of Mutt and Jeff': Gerald Heard, Aldous Huxley and the New Pacifism," *Aldous Huxley Annual*, 1 (2001), 85–115.

[5] Gerald Heard, *The Third Morality* (London, 1937). Hereafter, *TM*. See Bradshaw, 20. Heard's book was reviewed in *TLS* (Saturday, 6 February 1937), 84, under the heading "A Cure for Civilization: Outlines of Futurist Ethics."

[6] Aldous Huxley, *Ends and Means: An Enquiry Into the Nature of Ideals and Into the Methods Employed for Their Realization* (London, 1937). Hereafter, *EM*. See Sybille Bedford, *Aldous Huxley: A Biography* (2 vols., London, 1973–1974), I, 333–334, 348–349, and Bradshaw, 25. One of the first reviews appeared in *TLS* (Saturday, 20 November 1937), 880, under the heading "Mr Aldous Huxley as Mystic: A Cure for a Bad World."

[7] Eros, 87. As a matter of fact, there is only one explicit reference to Heard's book in *EM*, when, in chapter IX on "War," Huxley discusses "the apparent pointlessness of modern life": "[…] in the Western world at least, the prevailing cosmology is what Mr. Gerald Heard has called the 'mechanomorphic' cosmology of modern science" (123).

[8] An early—apparently the first extensive—critique of Huxley's book was published in 1938: K.S. Shelvankar, *Ends "Are" Means: A Critique of Social Values*, with an introduction by Professor H. Levy (London, 1938), [v]–xv, 146 pp. While conceding (with an ironic overtone) that Huxley's "socio-philosophical synthesis is an original intellectual creation" (v), Shelvankar rejects "the methods proposed by Mr Huxley for dealing with [war] and for bringing about large-scale social changes in general; and […] the fundamental beliefs concerning society and the world which govern Mr Huxley's approach" (vi). In his introduction, Prof. H. Levy pleads for "turning the searchlight of science on communal organisation" and concludes as follows: "Aldous Huxley, in his fictitious arguments in *Ends and Means* that science falsifies reality, adds his voice to those who would prevent us from dealing with this emergency by an informed socially scientific outlook, interlocked with direct and immediate political practice, and on a scale commensurate with the forces of reaction that have to be overcome. It is because Mr Shelvankar in this book seeks to nullify the damage done by Mr Huxley that I have added these words. It is an important task" (xv). I wish to thank Prof. A. A. Mutalik-Desai for drawing my attention to this book and for

donating a copy to the Centre for Aldous Huxley Studies at the Department of English, University of Münster, Germany.

[9] See the facsimile of the contents page below, 51.

[10] For Huxley's own definition of his method of argumentation see his later remark concerning the rational idealist's attitude towards the right use of religious practices: "[...] he will do all in his power to encourage their use for good purposes and, whether by argument, persuasion or satire, to prevent them from being used to further causes that are evil" (231).

[11] See *Eyeless in Gaza* (London, 1936), 614–615.

[12] See the facsimile of the contents page below, 58.

[13] Bradshaw, 18; see above, 47.

[14] See above, 59.

II.

Aldous Huxley, the Critic

Gerd Rohmann

(University of Kassel)

ALDOUS HUXLEY'S RESEARCH INTO THE FUTURE

Poets do not really care about science's working and underlying theories.
They only think about social and psychological consequences.

(Literature and Science)

The prophecies made in 1931 are coming true much sooner
than I thought they would.

(Brave New World Revisited)

Huxley's writing of *Brave New World* was clearly motivated by his humanism. With his world-famous[1] dystopian novel he begins the transition from the cynical intellectualism[2] of his early works, culminating in *Point Counter Point* (1928), towards the search for ways of saving humanitarian ideals in this world and beyond, starting with *Eyeless in Gaza* (1936).

Brave New World (1932) is the modernization of utopian novels by science fiction after H.G. Wells.[3] Huxley's dark science fiction represents the serious attempt to predict the world's future on the basis of the most probable development of its greatest power, the United States of America, projecting it into the year 632 after Henry Ford, which corresponds to the year 2.540.[4] In 1946, however, Huxley himself felt obliged to place the state of the nation which was to be reached 536 years ahead of the present point of time, into the much nearer future of 2.046 A.D.: "Today it seems quite possible that the horror may be upon us within a single century."[5]

What is the horror and how can it be avoided if mankind is able to escape from it at all? *Ape and Essence* (1948), *Brave New World Revisited* (1958), *Tomorrow and Tomorrow and Tomorrow* (1956), and *The Human Situation* (1959, published 1978) are further proofs that Huxley's interest in the future is motivated by his sense of responsibility for the defence and improvement of human potentialities. Following his main topics and including the context of our present knowledge I shall try to explain his thoughts on:
1. War and Peace, 2. The Population Explosion, 3. Human Nature, 4. History, 5. Art, 6. Science, 7. Religion, 8. Ecology, 9. Education, and 10. Human Potentialities.

1. War and Peace

In the important Chapters 16 and 17 of *Brave New World*, Mustapha Mond, Resident World Controller for Western Europe, offers his kind of *Mein Kampf* during the cross-examination of the dissidents Bernard Marx, Helmholtz Watson and the Savage. For the Cyprus experiment in A.F. 473 the island was re-colonized with 22.000 Alphas, who were left to manage their own affairs:

> "The land wasn't properly worked; there were strikes in all the factories; the laws were set at naught, orders disobeyed; all the people detailed for a spell of low-grade work were perpetually intriguing for high-grade jobs, and all the people with high-grade jobs were counter-intriguing at all costs to stay where they were. Within six years they were having a first-class civil war. When nineteen out of the twenty-two thousand had been killed, the survivors unanimously petitioned the World Controllers to resume the government of the island. Which they did. And that was the end of the only society of Alphas that the world has ever seen." (*BNW*, 175)

A *Gelehrtenrepublik* [6] does not work. The optimal society has to be modelled on the iceberg—with 10% Alphas above the waterline of intelligence and 90% of Betas, Gammas, Deltas and Epsilons in increasing underwater stupidity.

As the ideals of Liberté, Egalité, Fraternité of the French Revolution triggered more European and world wars than had been waged ever before, the romantic motto had to be reformulated as "COMMUNITY, IDENTITY, STABILITY" (*BNW*, 15). The total loss of liberty is the price. "Identity" has to be taken literally, like in "identical twins." And without absolute stability, which even excludes philosophical doubt, the emotional exaltations of great art and all change caused by new discoveries, there will be no peace.

Huxley was often reproached for not having predicted A-, H-, and Neutron bombs in *Brave New World*. He compensated for this in *Ape and Essence*, [7] which he wrote partly as a film script in order to invite Hollywood to show us the consequences of a nuclear holocaust, which he depicted as having occurred by the year 2.108. The film was never made because the policy of the United States favoured nuclear armament in the Cold War against the Soviet Union and the People's Republic of China. The consequences of an undoubtedly nuclear Third World War were considered to be too cruel to be shown. No democratic government would have been re-elected after the demonstration of effects produced by military toys of the devil. Moreover, *Brave New World*, published in 1932, could not have mentioned nuclear weapons, as Otto Hahn achieved the first nuclear fission only on 13 December 1938. World Controller Mustapha Mond, instead, refers to a Nine Years' War with biological weapons of mass destruction:

"What's the point of truth or beauty or knowledge when the anthrax bombs are popping all around you? [...] We've gone on controlling ever since. It hasn't been good for truth, of course. But it's been very good for happiness. One can't have something for nothing. Happiness has got to be paid for." (*BNW*, 179)

Mark the cynically jovial tone of Huxley's Big Brother figure. Happiness is peace eternal, but at an inhuman price. Huxley, due to his extraordinary erudition in biology and medicine, knew that, in contrast to the high explosives (dynamite and all kinds of nuclear bombs), bacteria and viruses, but also chemical weapons such as poison gas, will only destroy lives, leaving objects of material value entirely intact. Their effect makes war attractive to envious conquerors, whereas the rotting nuclear heritage of the Cold War will be dangerous only if radio-active waste gets into the hands of terrorists who aim at the largest possible random destruction rates and chaos within the hated capitalist system. The most powerful nation in this system is building new nuclear warheads instead of fighting terrorism and poverty with special police forces and foreign aid. War is not a convincing regulation system for peace.[8]

2. The Population Explosion

When Huxley wrote *Brave New World* in 1931, the earth had "two thousand million inhabitants" (*BNW*, 39).[9] This now corresponds to the populations of China and India together. At present we have six billion people on our planet in an extremely unbalanced distribution. The developing countries of Africa, Asia and South America are overpopulated whereas Europe and North America suffer under extremely low birth rates. The negative effect is more serious than the death rates during the two World Wars of the twentieth century. Fewer and fewer young people have to work for too many old, retired, and sick people. The social contract between the growing and the dying generations looks like a pyramid on its head. The broken generation contract is ruining the welfare states of the northern hemisphere. Soon there will be none left.

It took sixteen centuries for the population of the earth to double between Christ's birth and the death of Queen Elizabeth I. In the twentieth century, the number of people in the southern hemisphere doubled every twenty to thirty years. Huxley

> There are many roads to Brave New World; but perhaps the straightest and broadest of them [...] leads through gigantic numbers and accelerating increases. [...] Overpopulation leads to economic insecurity and social unrest. Unrest and insecurity lead to more control by central governments and an increase of their power. (*BNWR*, 19–21)

Huxley predicted that all the world's overpopulated and underdeveloped countries would be under totalitarian rule, probably by the Communist Party.

This was true until 1989, then pseudo-democracies like that of Russia and the global capitalism of the U.S. American Empire took over. DDT, penicillin, and the advancement of medical treatment lowered the death rate, which has not been accompanied by a corresponding fall in the birth rate. Racism, nationalism, religious fanaticism are killing millions in civil wars. A nuclear war will hopefully never take place, nor should AIDS or other pandemics stop the population explosion. As biochemical warfare would not offer any decent solution either, Huxley hoped for 'the pill,' which indeed became popular in the 'enlightened,' developed countries after 1968, although, paradoxically, they had falling birth rates anyway. In *The Human Situation* (1959) he analyses:

> The problem of control of the birth rate is infinitely complex. It is not merely a problem in medicine, in chemistry, in biochemistry, in physiology; it is also a problem in sociology, in psychology, in theology, and in education. [...] there has to be a great deal of fundamental research into biology [...] in the hope of producing some satisfactory oral contraceptive which can be distributed easily and cheaply to masses of people. [10]

Huxley correctly predicted the pill "within ten years" (*HS*, 52) but the cultural and religious problems causing overpopulation are still unsolved, as Fred Spier argues:

> Die rapide Zunahme der Erdbevölkerung und die Auswirkungen der anwachsenden Bedeutung des ökologischen Regulationssystems des Menschen einschließlich seiner Manipulation [...] beeinflussen [...] das gesamte Regulationssystem der Erde [...]. Zum ersten Mal in der Menschheitsgeschichte ist eine solche unvergleichliche Entwicklungsstufe erreicht. (Spier, 124–125)[11]

3. Human Nature

Huxley's concept of man's being is holistic. The mind-body dualism, unknown to Homer, was introduced by Plato and reinforced by St Paul in the Christian distinction between earthly flesh (the devil) and heavenly soul (the divine principle in human nature). As this one-sided view increases schizophrenia and destructive madness, Descartes' scientific *cogito ergo sum* should be compensated by *volo ergo sum* in the manner of Nietzsche's free will philosophy so that man,

> the self-conscious being who uses verbal symbols, who is able to employ reason, who looks before and after [...] is the creature who wills and who thinks. (*HS*, 137)

The extreme degree of genetic and psychological manipulation including the artificial production of standardized beings as envisaged in *Brave New*

World is even more inhuman, due to the fact that "the most highly variable species is homo sapiens" (*HS*, 140)—physically, psychologically and temperamentally.

The title of Huxley's University of California lectures was borrowed from Erich Fromm's *The Sane Society* (1955), chapter III, entitled "The Human Situation: Man's Needs—As they Stem from the Conditions of his Existence." Of course, our society is insane, but not yet as irreversibly half-witted and psychically crippled as the brave new worlders.

The virtual reality of advertising, films, propaganda, TV, and computers steadily increases the number of neurotics with a chronic lack of awareness. On the other hand, adaptation and uniformity are such outrages against human nature that, according to Huxley, quoting Fromm,

> "many [people] are normal because they are so well adjusted to our mode of existence, because their human voice has been silenced so early in their lives that they do not even struggle or suffer or develop symptoms as the neurotic does." (*BNWR*, 36)

And in *The Human Situation* Huxley explains:

> Neurosis is the failure of the conscious ego to deal with the events of the moment in terms appropriate to the moment. Instead of dealing with what is happening now, the neurotic person deals with events in terms of repressed feelings and hidden memories from the past which are totally irrelevant to what is happening at the present time. (*HS*, 156–157)

The horoscopes provided by our hidden persuaders are equally disastrous because they divert our potential to competently solve the problems of the present into speculations about the future. World-immanent ideologies such as communism, fascism, capitalism exhibit the same negative trend to avoid the real *hic et nunc* problems as the transcendental religions of Judaism, Christianity, and Islam. People identify themselves with the opium dreams of a classless society, of a Führer's providence, of speculation profits at the stock exchange, of going to Paradise instead of striving to know their highest human identity within themselves.

There is no way out, except for those who have learned how to go beyond all symbols to a direct experience of the basic fact of divine immanence.[12]

4. History

> "You know what Polish is [...]?"
> "A dead language."
> "Like French and German." (*BNW*, 30)

George Orwell's *Nineteen Eighty-Four* (1949) and Huxley's *Brave New World* have two things in common: the dictatorial attacks are concentrated on language and history. While in *Nineteen Eighty-Four* English is reduced to Newspeak and history falsified following communist and fascist practices, in the fully conditioned brave new world all languages, except *status quo* caste English, and history have simply been weeded out:

> "You all remember," said the Controller, [...] "that beautiful and inspired saying of Our Ford's: History is bunk." (*BNW*, 38)

"COMMUNITY, IDENTITY, STABILITY" cannot work if compared with the glory of the past—nor if there is a searching curiosity about the future. The Decemvirate of World Controllers has condemned everybody from Alpha to Epsilon to live in a flat communal, identical, and stable present, for ever:

> "People are happy; they get what they want, and they never want what they can't get. They're well off; they're safe; they're never ill; they're not afraid of death; they're blissfully ignorant of passion and old age; they're plagued with no mothers or fathers; they've got no wives, or children, or loves to feel strongly about; they're so conditioned that they practically can't help behaving as they ought to behave. And if anything should go wrong, there's *soma*." (*BNW*, 173)

Nineteen Eighty-Four with its wars, obvious propaganda lies, hate weeks, brain-washing and torture chambers is old-fashioned as compared with *Brave New World*, where history has come to an end through "non-stop distractions of the most fascinating nature" (*BNWR* 35): the feelies, orgy-porgy, sports, soaps, games, TV and extra rations of *soma* serve the Controllers' purpose of preventing people from paying attention to the realities of their social and political situation. He who has no past is uprooted in the present and will not understand the future:

> Distractions [...], in the West, are now threatening to drown in a sea of irrelevance the rational propaganda essential to the maintenance of individual liberty and the survival of democratic institutions. (*BNWR* 35)

5. Art

The general passions for truth and beauty have been sacrificed to flat comfort and shallow happiness. Heroism and noble passions make great tragedies; profound love, faithfulness and the threat of loss verging on tragedy are the essence of equally touching comedies. Man has an urge to order and meaning. The artist is, as Shelley asserts, an "Unacknowledged Legislator of the world"[13] because he gives ethical order and philosophical meaning in terms of "significant form" (*HS*, 183). The World Controller cynically admits:

"That's the price we have to pay for stability. You've got to choose between happiness and what people used to call high art. We've sacrificed the high art. We have the feelies and the scent organ instead." (*BNW*, 173)

Distractions have no deeper meaning than themselves. Many Americans spend five hours daily watching TV, other Western citizens follow closely. Chairs of literacy have been established. The International Reading Association confirms that the best pupils and students are readers.[14] The American government does not consider it worthwhile banning critical books, such as Browne's *The Da Vinci Code* (New York, 2003) because their effect, in contrast to Hollywood films, TV, smoking, alcohol or fast food, is irrelevant.

Modern economistic thinking is hostile to the humanities and to real art, as Ulrich Thielemann explains:

> Eine *Ökonomisierung des Denkens* [...] läuft [...] auf die Ablösung der Wahrheits- durch die Wettbewerbstheorie hinaus. Über die Gültigkeit wissenschaftlicher Aussagen entscheidet [...] nicht mehr [...] der [...] Diskurs der scientific community, sondern der [...] Markt.[15]

6. Science

Brave New World has become famous as a scientific dystopian novel. Artificial insemination, parentless test tube babies, cloning, genetic engineering, the discovery of the human genome, the growing of organs and other spare parts for the body on cell and tissue cultures, all those bio-medical opportunities seem to have come true in our time. Or as Mustapha Mond argues:

> "I see you don't like our Bokanovsky Groups; but, I assure you, they're the foundation on which everything else is built. They're the gyroscope that stabilizes the rocket plane of state on its unswerving course." (*BNW*, 174)

It is amazing but consequential that even scientific progress has to be checked in order to keep the *status quo* of conformity, identity, stability:

> "Every discovery in pure science is potentially subversive; even science must sometimes be treated as a possible enemy. [...] It isn't only art that's incompatible with happiness; it's also science. Science is dangerous; we have to keep it most carefully chained and muzzled." (*BNW*, 176–177.)

Mustapha Mond confesses this against all official propaganda. He himself has had a narrow escape from being exiled to a remote island for dealing individually and inquisitively with real science as a young man. Just compare George Orwell's *Nineteen Eighty-Four*:

> There was, indeed, no word for 'Science,' any meaning that it could possibly bear being already sufficiently covered by the word *Ingsoc*.[16]

The word 'Science' itself was made obsolete because it indicates that there is a huge field of well-educated people who could stand together. Such dystopian self-restriction of scientific research will be improbable before one mega power alone actually manages to get control of a World State. There is still competition, yet all nuclear powers have banned the proliferation of plutonium, and those who own biological and chemical weapons of mass destruction wage wars against countries who are suspected to have them.

7. Religion

In the contemporary brave new world of unsatisfying work, leisure, sex, games, drugs, and visual media man is reduced to materialism, consumerism and pleasure. Without a past and a future, without culture, he is reduced to less than himself. Complete and mature human beings, however, have a deeply felt need for religion. They want to give and receive love, joy, peace, and help. The inhabitants of *Brave New World* are flatly denied the chance to

> combine activity with relaxation, [...] [to] let go of the clutching personal self, in order to let this deeper self within [...] come through and perform its miracles. (*HS*, 214)

Today we have the egotistic atheism of communism, capitalism and the brave new world or "the jihads and crusades of one religion against another" (*HS*, 206). The market and the sale values of the New York Stock Exchange are the 'confessions' of shareholders, together with the global war against terrorism, which use and fight the "tremendous force of religion" (*HS*, 205). Huxley's confessed Buddhism proves that he does not want to be identified with any religion acting on behalf of power-hungry worldly interests.

8. Ecology

Huxley was one of the earliest ecologists in literature. *Brave New World* has no problems with the environment because overpopulation is avoided and the natural resources are strictly controlled by the Decemvirate. Even food can be fully synthethized but some old-fashioned labour has to be offered because otherwise troubles and an excessive consumption of *soma* would be invited by too much leisure for the working class. Huxley is more worried about the future of mankind on our planet. *Island*, Huxley's ecological utopia,[17] his essays on "Overpopulation" (*BNWR*, 9–23), "Man and his Planet" (*HS*, 12–27) as well as "The Politics of Ecology: The Question of Survival" (see Rohmann, 185) are important proofs of his engagement in favour of a sustainable use of nature.

In 1959 Huxley lectured:

The 2.8 billion people who are now inhabitants of the planet depend upon a layer of soil rarely more than about ten inches thick—and it takes three hundred to one thousand years to create an inch of it, so one sees the extreme danger of any process causing soil destruction. (*HS*, 20)

The quality of the soil determines all plant life, which determines all animal life, while both determine desert or fertility standards of human life on our planet. The cutting of forests around the Mediterranean was followed by over-grazing with cattle from cows down to sheep and goats, "'the mere skeleton of the land being left'" (*HS*, 21). This description of Attica was translated from Plato's *Critias*, dated ca. 400 B. C.

In general, Huxley argues that "man has lived only too frequently on his planet almost like a parasite living upon the host it infects. And whereas many parasites are sensible enough not to destroy their host, [...] man is *not* one of the sensible parasites" (*HS*, 15). A chief example is man's use of natural resources:

When one considers that the amount of planetary capital consumed by the United States since the end of the First World War is greater than the entire amount of metals, fuels, and minerals consumed by the entire human race before that, one realizes what a fantastic drain upon resources is now going on. (*HS*, 102)

The Industrial Revolution from 1780 to 1914 is nothing compared with the exploitation of non-renewable resources between 1918 and 1959 and the continuing waste of nature by capitalism. Outside the United States and the European Union an ever larger and hungrier population 'mines the soil.' The destructive process of erosion and deforestation will be speeded up and lead to totalitarian surveillance systems:

Where more people are competing [...], each individual will have to work harder and longer for his ration, and the central government will find it necessary to intervene more and more frequently in order to save the [...] economic machine from total breakdown. (*TTT*, 165)

The only hope, our last hope, are birth control and N.G.O.s such as Greenpeace, the World Wide Fund for Nature, or ATTAC. No change can be expected from Big Business and Big Government. Their brave new world is not the pacifist "Global Village" but the transnational globalisation of culture-despising capitalism.

9. Education

As there is no freedom without education, Huxley wants the Magna Carta act of *habeas corpus* (1215/1679) to be extended to *habeas mentem* (see *BNWR*, 153–154). In *Brave New World,* as in most societies of our time, there is no real education 'leading up,' but only mental fast food 'weighing down' people: advertising, superficial values, the tabloid press, discos, movies, computers, fun, games, drugs and, finally, TV, the time killer and enemy of good reading:

> The nature of psychological compulsion is such that those who act under constraint remain under the impression that they are acting on their own initiative. The victim of mind-manipulation [...] believes himself to be free. [...] His servitude is strictly objective. [...] the psychological slave trade [...] makes nonsense of the whole democratic process. (*BNWR*, 154–155)

American election campaigns are Hollywood shows. In Europe many voters abstain because they see no chance to stop political corruption. The competitive Western world cannot be endured without drugs because drugs help to transform disappointments into ecstatic experiences. The old dictators fell because they could not give their subjects enough mild yet dangerous distractions. The modern mind-manipulators have succeeded in making most men and women grow up to love their servitude. Without critical and lifelong eduction for freedom, human beings cannot become fully human.

10. Human Potentialities

If the human needs for food, peace, love, belongingness, recognition, self-respect, knowledge, order, meaning in life and expression are fulfilled, then we have the best environment to realize our latent inborn capacities. "Kulturelle Kompetenz ist [...] das Alpha und Omega erfolgreichen Wirtschaftens [...]."[18] Undrugged by *soma*, educated people achieve high performance creativity under stress and in moments of crisis. While deception leads to foolishness, clear perception is the way to competent problem solving. Neurosis, habit and routine, misplaced intellectualism, daydreaming, prejudice, and hate are obstacles, whereas confidence, love, will, imagination, acceptance and language competence improve the art of seeing which is a learned activity:

> The more discriminating and acute and precise our perceptions are, the better [...] will be our general intelligence. [...] We have to know what surrounds us; we have to know how to react to what surrounds us; we have to know what is happening in our bodies; and we have to have a clear idea of what it is that we are thinking and feeling and wishing and willing. (*HS*, 243)

The essential precondition for the actualization of all human potentialities is old Socrates' 'Know Thyself.' In *Brave New World* only the Great Inquisitor, Mustapha Mond, knows himself. Marx is not a Co-Controller, as a new history of British, Irish and American Literature wants to make us believe,[19] but a poor victim of the transnationally globalized but anti-culturally and therefore inhumanly conditioned World State.

[1] See Nancy Andreasen, *Brave New Brain* (Hamburg, 2002).

[2] See Christoph Bode, *Intellektualismus und Entfremdung: Das Bild des Intellektuellen in den frühen Romanen Aldous Huxleys* (Bonn, 1979). An anticipation of Huxley's quest for new values is *Those Barren Leaves* (1925).

[3] See K. Burmeister, Karlheinz Steinmüller, *Streifzüge ins Übermorgen: Science Fiction und Zukunftsforschung* (Weinheim, Basel, 1992), 54. See also Richard Saage, *Utopieforschung* (Darmstadt, 1997), 167.

[4] According to *Brave New World* (London, 1963), 51, the new era (A.F.) begins with "the introduction of Our Ford's first T-model." Hereafter, *BNW*. [Editors' note.]

[5] Aldous Huxley, "Foreword" (1946), *BNW*, 14.

[6] Arno Schmidt, *Die Gelehrtenrepublik* (Frankfurt/M., 1973 [1957]) owes its genetic engineering to *Brave New World* and the chimeras of mutations to *Ape and Essence*.

[7] Aldous Huxley, *Ape and Essence* (New York, 1948).

[8] See Fred Spier, *Big History* (Darmstadt, 1998), 104-105.

[9] See also Aldous Huxley, *Brave New World Revisited* (London, 1958), 15. Hereafter, *BNWR*.

[10] Aldous Huxley, *The Human Situation: Lectures at Santa Barbara, 1959*, ed. Piero Ferrucci (London, 1978), 52. Herafter, *HS*.

[11] [Editors' translation: 'The rapid growth of the world population, and the effects of the increasingly important ecological regulation system in which man is involved and which he manipulates, affect the whole of the global regulation system.']

[12] See Aldous Huxley, *Tomorrow and Tomorrow and Tomorrow* (New York, 1964), 129. Hereafter, *TTT*.

[13] See Gerd Rohmann, "Unacknowledged Legislators of the World?: Sidney's *Defence of Poesie* and Shelley's *Defence of Poetry*," *Romantic Discourses*, ed. Horst Höhne (Essen, 1994), 157–167.

[14] Claudia Finkbeiner, "Zur affektiven und kognitiven Dimension beim Lesen: Bericht von einer Untersuchung zum Zusammenwirken von Interessen und Lernstrategien," *Zeitschrift für Fremdsprachenforschung*, 8 (1997), 192–212.

[15] Ulrich Thielemann, "*Transzendentale Ökonomik*: Bemerkungen zur Ökonomisierung der Wissenschaften," *Glanzlichter der Wissenschaft*, ed. Deutscher Hochschulverband (Saarbrücken, 2004), 135. [Editors' translation: 'When thinking becomes economised, the theory of truth will be replaced by the theory of competition. It is not the scientific community that establishes the validity of scientific propositions any more, but the market.']

[16] George Orwell, "The Principles of Newspeak," *Nineteen Eighty-Four* (London, 1989 [1949]), 323.

[17] Gerd Rohmann, "*Island*: Huxley's Ecological Utopia," *"Now More than Ever": Proceedings of the Aldous Huxley Symposium Münster 1994*, ed. Bernfried Nugel (Frankfurt/Main, 1995), 175–185. Hereafter, Rohmann.

[18] Peter Bendixen, *Das verengte Weltbild der Ökonomie* (Darmstadt, 2003), 36. [Editors' translation: 'Cultural competence is the Alpha and Omega of successful management.']

[19] See Hans-Peter Wagner, *A History of British, Irish and American Literature* (Trier, 2003), 195.

A. A. Mutalik-Desai

(Dharwad, India)

ALDOUS HUXLEY AS EDUCATOR

Aldous Huxley has much to say on education, on educational institutions imparting instruction all the way from the elementary to the highest levels in universities, on educators and, less frequently, on students as well. Let me begin with some of his unflattering remarks and references in his fictional and non-fictional works. In *Antic Hay* (1923) Theodore Gumbril, Jr., roundly expresses his distaste for his unteachable students, the pedantic teachers, the bullying, domineering headmaster and, above all, the irrational system:

> [The] sickly piety [of the] two ugly, stupid-looking louts, who ought to have been apprenticed years ago to some useful trade. Instead of which they were wasting their own and their teacher's and their more intelligent comrades' time in trying, quite vainly, to acquire an elegant literary education.[1]

A little later he is pouring over tutorial essays on the Italian nineteenth-century Risorgimento written in response to an assignment which reads, "Give a brief account of the character and career of Pope Pius IX, *with dates wherever possible*" (*AH*, 13). Even the names of the schoolboys are chosen for sardonic effect: Falarope Major, Sopwith Minor, Clegg-Weller and the like. They seem to come straight from Charles Dickens's London. Soon Theodore denounces his calling. His father, too, despite the protestations of his friend Mr Porteous, a Latin scholar and teacher, expresses his Shavian reservations about the teacher's calling, "the last refuge of feeble minds" (*AH*, 20), as he puts it.

There are also jibes at professors, as in the note on Udaipur in *Jesting Pilate* (1926).[2] Oxford accent in *Point Counter Point* (1928) comes up for its share at the expense of Sidney Quarles whose "voice was resonant and full of those baa-ings with which the very Oxonian are accustomed to enrich the English language."[3] Cambridge does not escape attention either, as in *After Many a Summer* (1939): Jeremy Pordage, "a product of Trinity College, Cambridge, [had] a small, fluty voice, suggestive of evensong in an English cathedral."[4] And also in the 1946 special preface to *Brave New World* (1932) Huxley is clearly peeved at academics. Critics' response to *The Perennial Philosophy* (1946), it is said, had disappointed him. He reacted with a rare, angry outburst and remonstrance:

> I have been told by an eminent academic critic that I am a sad symptom of the failure of an intellectual class in time of crisis. The implication being, I suppose, that the professor and his colleagues

are hilarious symptoms of success. The benefactors of humanity deserve due honour and commemoration. Let us build a Pantheon for professsors. It should be located among the ruins of one of the gutted cities of Europe or Japan, and over the entrance to the ossuary I would inscribe, in letters six or seven feet high, the simple words: SACRED TO THE MEMORY OF THE WORLD'S EDUCATORS. SI MONUMENTUM REQUIRIS CIRCUMSPICE.[5]

His response may be an overshot: he is uncharacteristically carried away. But then anger hath a privilege.

However, Huxley, despite his occasional ribbing and sardonic comments and even an angry tirade, is on the side of education and educators. It is evident that to him educators, understood in the widest sense, must assume the high moral ground. Their aims must comprise a well-integrated, all-round building of character. They must help students to equip themselves in matters physical, intellectual, moral and spiritual. They are social reformers, keepers of conscience, philosophers, seekers of the ultimate reality of life, visionaries and futurists. In his novels they exhibit redemptive traits. They are his alter egos and they speak for him.

What Sybille Bedford has described as his "genetic lottery" deserves attention.[6] The two clans, the Huxleys and the Arnolds, such important members of the intellectual aristocracy in nineteenth-century England, were educators. His paternal grandfather Thomas Henry Huxley was a teacher, a proponent of science and Charles Darwin's 'bull-dog' in his role as a champion of *The Origin of Species* (1859). His father Leonard was a publisher, an editor, a biographer and a man of letters known for his wide-ranging learning, for the company he kept and for the role he played in his time. His older brother Julian was a scientist, a biologist, a liberal agnostic humanist, a professor at Rice University, Houston, Texas, the first Director General of UNESCO, author of books on science and of autobiographical writings as well as winner of coveted awards and prizes. His maternal great-grandfather Dr Arnold of Rugby, an eminent Victorian, was an educational reformer. His maternal grand-father Thomas Arnold was a cleric and a religious rebel. His maternal great-uncle Matthew Arnold was a poet, a critic, a defender of culture and taste, a classicist, a polemicist against Philistinism, and his mother Julia Arnold Huxley was a teacher, the founder of a girls' school at Prior's Field. They were all educators.

Huxley championed the cause of education. He spoke again and again about the need for it as it leads to sanity, proportion, order and enlightenment. A tireless reformer committed to the betterment of life here on earth, an unabashed liberal, progressive humanist, a product of the English upper-class who nevertheless spoke on behalf of the less fortunate members of humanity everywhere, he frequently returned to the role education must play.

The primary sources, his studies and his detailed observations and comments, may be listed here. Long essays are "Education" in *Proper Studies*

(1927), another, also entitled "Education," in *Ends and Means* (1937), "The Education of an Amphibian" in *Adonis and the Alphabet* (1956) and "Education for Freedom" in *Brave New World Revisited* (1958). There are also minor sources like "Literature and Examinations" in *The Olive Tree* (1936), "Can We Be Well Educated?" in *Esquire* (1956), his preface to *A Vision of Education, Being an Imaginary Verbatim Report of the First Planetary Conference* by J. H. Burns (1929) and passages in the *Memorial Volume* edited by Julian Huxley (1965), with truthful and sometimes uncomfortable revelations about Huxley's short teaching career. In the way of critics' views there are assessments in journals, reviews of his books, discussions on related matters in monographs from differing points of view, unpublished doctoral dissertations as well, such as those by Francis Larsen and Jacob Schmitt. This article will deal with the main sources as repositories of his faith in education, his criticism of the systems of education and the directions in which, according to him, the entire field of education must turn—if there is to be hope. Of hope he never despaired: even at his gloomiest he always pursued an unconquerable hope.[7]

In his first long essay on "Education" Huxley starts off with an axiomatic statement: "To enable every individual to attain and preserve [...] maximum efficiency is the aim of all education."[8] Considering the rational systems of physical education, he states that an individual's willing submission to the rigour and discipline involved lead to the highest state of physical attainment. But while mental education in general must aim at enabling every student to attain similar efficiency, Huxley, disenchanted and enraged, criticizes the "enormous blunders and stupidities which characterize [the] systems of mental education" (*PS*, 89) in the 1920s. Or again, "there are excellent reasons for supposing that they [i. e., those in charge] make it entirely impossible for the minds of their victims to develop to the full" (*PS*, 90). Therefore, one must oppose the mechanical ways of teaching and avoid the horrors of the resulting distortions. Furthermore, the educational hypotheses accepted are inept and have had baneful influence. If in physical education there is an adequate understanding of the body, there is no corresponding comprehension of the human mind as it is being educated. It is psycho-analysis which comes in for the most severe indictment:

> Of recent years the psycho-analysts have added a sort of basement, in whose almost unrelieved darkness the vermin of the conscious crawl and pullulate. "On the threshold," says Dr. Freud, "there stands a personage with the office of doorkeeper, who examines the various mental excitations, censors them, and denies them admittance to the reception room (of consciousness) when he disapproves of them." The result of the combined activities of all these sensations, associating ideas, emotions, conations, censors, and the like is an individual—is you or I. [...] The first mistake of the psychologists was to take their own visual metaphors too

> seriously; they reduced the living mind to a mere receptacle. [...]
> The psychologists have hypostasized, and indeed almost
> personified, their abstractions. (*PS*, 94–95)

Huxley contrasts what can be achieved with the visible body with what has
not been achieved with the invisible mind. The mind does not absorb
everything nor are all minds alike. Therefore, systems of educating them must
vary in a commensurate degree.

What is the way out? It is best "to teach the child to teach himself" (*PS*,
103). Train their senses, give them something to do, such as plain, simple
work they will do with their own hands. Avoid abstractions. Let them act,
make-believe, narrate stories and thus gain confidence. Let them play with
mud, sticks, water. Let them call upon their own imagination, "the herald, as
Goethe called it" (*PS*, 110) to perceive phenomena like islands, lakes,
mountains and rivers. Their own immediate experiences will interest them.
These observations have not lost their relevance today eight decades since:

> Children should learn as the human race learned; they should set out
> from the immediate and the concrete to discover the abstract, the
> general, and the remote. History and geography should begin with
> the family and the native place. The sciences must blossom out of
> the local flowers, must be born with the familiar animals, spring
> from the neighbouring rocks and waters, be deduced from the
> practice of the local crafts and industries. Geometry must arise as it
> arose among the Egyptians—from the measurement for practical
> purposes of definite individual spaces. Arithmetic must solve the
> actual problems of daily life. (*PS*, 104)

When the minds are young and if they fail to digest what is imparted, he
suggests that flogging or bullying them will not do: "...thou shalt teach them
diligently unto thy children" (*Deuteronomy*, VI, vii). Persuade, stimulate and
even amuse them, which strategies can facilitate gaining what is within their
reach. Even if they cannot reach the levels of their gifted or more able peers,
they will have improved. "It pays," he adds, "to treat the minds of idiots as
though they were delicate living organisms requiring careful nurture" (*PS*,
101). He recognizes the merit of the system followed in the Kindergarten and
the Montessori Schools.

Higher education, he complains, "is so remote from ordinary life that it
hardly affects the majority of learners" (*PS*, 104–105). Universities indulge in
subjects "so completely disconnected with life that it never even occurs to the
learners to absorb them into the practical workaday part of their minds" (*PS*,
105). Subjects like philosophy, science and literature are learnt and forgotten.
Mr Babbitt remains untouched, unmodified and, therefore, uneducated, the
Philistine he was before entering the portals of a university. Huxley's
indictment is absolute: "A twentieth-century material civilization cannot be

worked by people whose minds are predominantly mediaeval or even prehistoric" (*PS*, 106).

In addition to these basics, he further elaborates why "the official system"
cannot help: "The child is too often regarded as existing for the System, not
the System for the child" (*PS*, 108). Even the wording is typically Huxleyan.
He advocates an education which fully takes into account the individuality of
the child at any level. He is just as critical of large classes which hamper, not
promote, the inculcation of the essential skills and values in any frontier of
knowledge. They are inherently rigid Procrustean beds and intolerant. They
lead to boredom. What is missing is the process of self-discovery. Sacrifice of
the individual for the system, psychologically unsound methods of teaching
and irrational ways of imposing discipline are, therefore, the culprits.

In contrast, Huxley suggests innovative ways such as the "Dalton Plan,"
the main features of which are "the emancipation of the individual from the
system" (*PS*, 122), the promotion of students effected without the straight-
jacket of a time-bound plan, an emphasis rather on learning than on teaching
and thus no tyranny of the classroom and the teacher. There is no "Gadarene
rush" (*PS*, 126) to leave the classroom as soon as the bell is sounded. The
ironic allusion to *Matthew*, VIII, 32 ("the whole heard of swine ran violently
down a steep place into the sea, and perished in the waters"), echoes what
Gumbril thought of his flock.[9]

What, in 1927, is Huxley's interpretation of liberal education which he
considered the democratic ideal? It comprises "the humanities, literature, pure
science, languages, and mathematics" (*PS*, 126). He explains:

> It is supposed that youths who have been taught the grammar of
> various dead and living languages, who have learned a certain
> amount of mathematics and natural science, who have read extracts
> from the best authors and practised the art of composition, will be
> thereby fitted to solve all the problems and deal with all the
> emergencies of practical life. [...] In other words, ability acquired in
> academic studies is transferred to other activities. (*PS*, 126–127)

Long cherished, advocated and adopted in various ways, has it worked?
His matter-of-fact response is: "to some extent, but not so completely as was
once supposed" (*PS*, 127). When interest is created or fostered, the ideal could
be reached. But most pupils in the classrooms do not possess any interest nor
is it *created* in them at any level. Liberal education suits those who are
intellectually inclined.

Towards the end of this essay, Huxley challenges the system of lectures as
the sole or dominant means of providing instruction. He wishes that lecturers
became a thing of the past. Once when books were expensive and rare,
lecturing was necessary, he concedes. But, at the present time, when printing
is cheap and books are readily available, why should the lecturer carry on as if
it were still the age of Thomas Aquinas? Huxley rightly condemns

universities which take on futile, insignificant, flimsy and almost comical subjects. "The modern scientific literary researchers produce nothing but boring trivialities" (*PS*, 135), it is forthrightly pointed out. As academics in the fields of English and American literature, European and Comparative literature, literatures in translation from every corner of the world, the more recent waves of multi-ethnic and multi-cultural works etc., we can testify that if Huxley's assessment was then accurate, timely, perspicacious and prophetic, its potent urgency in the nascent years of the twenty-first century cannot be denied.

However, is he not too idealistic and impractical on the subject of the institution of lectures? If lecturing too large numbers does not fulfil its primary and academic function of creating enthusiasm for the subject-matter among those who are supposed to be listening, if it cannot produce at least a few converts to embrace the cause of philosophy, physics or poetry, if the everlasting verities of liberal education are not adequately conveyed to awaken a few minds, then indeed lecturing, and, along with it, liberal education have failed—which is a stark reality in too many colleges and universities, especially where I come from, India. Other countries in financial and socio-political constraints are hemmed in the same way. Our classes must become smaller. We need bigger and bigger legions of properly trained, motivated and dedicated teachers. We need the classic Oxford and Cambridge tutorial system. We need libraries with books, periodicals and other ancillary facilities. But are not these too ambitious dreams in most places? As a teacher having taught at the highest levels in the prosperous West as well as in a third-world country, I must state with genuine regret that the droning and braying of the teachers and the drowsiness of the students will continue with all the imperfections which are easily palpable and damaging to the educational process. The fact is that, with exceptions, lawfully and democratically constituted modern nation states and their governments are unwilling to invest in education to the extent necessary so that education may produce what it is expected to. At a second glance it is apparent that Huxley, too, was aware of the odds, as his concluding words in "Education" show:

> The ideal educational system is one which accurately measures the capacities of each individual and fits him, by means of specially adapted training, to perform those functions which he is naturally adapted to perform. A perfect education is one which trains up every human being to fit into the place he or she is to occupy in the social hierarchy, but without, in the process, destroying his or her individuality. [On the other hand], there is every reason to suppose that the world will become even more completely technicized, even more elaborately regimented, than it is at present. (*PS*, 136–137)

To be fair, he does not retreat from his idealism, his oft-repeated noble resolve about the nature and function of education. But these last words quoted betray a growing sense of resignation towards life around. Is there also in them a suggestion of the fears of the dystopian brave new world which was to occupy him only a few years later and of which there was already a hint in his first novel *Crome Yellow* (1921)?

A decade after his first essay on education, which was published when he was still in his early thirties, Huxley, in *Ends and Means*, picked up where he had left off. In this renewed attempt written at a time when the Second World War was at the doorstep of Europe, he calls upon Jesuits as well as Freudians (and revisionists among them), refers to the old patriarchal traditions and the modern systems, turns to Bertrand Russell, revisits Dr Maria Montessori and takes into account St Augustine and Calvin, the ancient Romans and the seventeenth-century Puritans, the Samurai, even Mussolini and Stalin, his own ancestor Dr Arnold of Rugby, F. M. Alexander, John Dewey and H. G. Wells (as in his *The Anatomy of Frustration*, 1936). He now lays more stress on moral and intellectual instruction and even more on what must be avoided. Wells, too, emphasized the vast difference between the nature of education during a child's early years and that which follows as the student matures. "The charm, the alert intelligence, the fearless freedom of the modern child of six or seven," wrote Wells, "[contrasts sharply with] the slouching mental futility of the ordinary youth in his later teens."[10] Endorsing Wells, Huxley's train of thought from the 1920s continues: "We educate young children for freedom, intelligence, responsibility and voluntary co-operation; we educate older children for passive acceptance of tradition and for either dominance or subordination" (*EM*, 178). In the late 1930s, in Western Europe one had to be cognizant of a changed order in public life and the need for altering and adjusting one's philosophic strategy. As a result, the claim to independence (the ideal) and the need for a degree of acquiescence (the reality) clashed, the need for giving children freedom and responsibility (the ideal) ran counter to their need for security and support (the reality).

But, while children need and deserve freedom, is excessive freedom not itself a strain on them? Do they not need some security, "the support of a firm framework of moral laws and even of rules of polite conduct"? (*EM*, 178). Building on his diagnosis presented in *Proper Studies*, Huxley now attends to the child's later education "for freedom, for justice, for peace" (*EM*, 181). He is deeply concerned by the rise of fanatical nationalism and the totalitarian regimes in Europe which ruthlessly imposed stern discipline, blind obedience, subservient behaviour and the most passive methods of acquiring knowledge. The results were a militaristic mentality "at once obedient and domineering, cowardly and brutal" (*EM*, 181), a general servility and an inferiority complex. After the Russian revolution in October 1917, for example, the sweeping changes introduced assured that the free play allowed during a child's impressionable years was snuffed out. Sport, too, as Huxley had feared in 1927, came to be practised for promoting individual and group vanity, greed, intolerance and hatred (attributes which would characterize future militarists) and not as a means of instilling a sense of endurance, courage, fair play and respect for rules. Elsewhere in Europe, too, the exploitation of education for political and ideological indoctrination was alarming. Huxley's humanism and pacifism were deeply irked by how educational institutions which should aim at building a state of freedom, justice, peace, enlightenment and the ultimate ideal of non-attachment, had instead moved towards creating a climate of utter cynicism, idolatry and senseless slaughter. His despair increases:

> Instruments of marvellous ingenuity and power [such as newspapers, news magazines, music and the cinema] on the one hand; and, on the other, ways of using those instruments which are either idiotic, or criminal, or both together. Such are the moral and intellectual fruits of our system of education (*EM*, 191).

A more discerning, enlightened Huxley, now in his forties, is teased by fundamental questions. A sense of identity or selfhood may indeed be derived from the militaristic ethos. But, instead, may one not search for it from the inward-looking Eastern, Hindu point of view implicit in the emphasis on the philosophy of non-attachment, which is the ideal of the 'Sthitahprajna' as propounded in the *Bhagavad Gita*?[11] Such disquiet, such probing, already part of his outlook in *Ends and Means*, was to possess him even more in the post-Second World War years—his last phase as a writer, thinker, and exponent of mysticism.

However, in 1937, mundane matters occupy him. Under the contemporary circumstances, should one let young minds loose "into a hierarchical, competitive and success-worshipping society" (*EM*, 179), even if they are equipped with the most desirable type of education? There are no easy solutions. Still, apart from what has been said already in this essay, a number of specific prescriptions follow:

(1) Humans belong to various types. There is the cerebrotonic (one who is immersed in intellectual pursuits), the viscerotonic (one who is involved in emotions), and the somatotonic (one who is inclined towards muscular activities). With such radically different minds in a classroom, it is not possible to devise a schedule of studies to suit them all. Even the tests administered, such as the IQ test, are far from perfect.

(2) Teaching needs to be reformed. The teachers' scholarly and pedagogical fossilization and petrifaction must be prevented by timely sabbaticals and even the assignment of jobs entirely unconnected with the academic.

(3) The examination system must be reformed by doing away with the one single, decisive examination.

(4) Liberal education should be reformed so that it takes heed of everyday problems. Technical education, on the other hand, should become more

liberal. Both should become integrated, i. e., the student must learn "to establish relations between the different elements of his sum of knowledge" (*EM*, 196). Such integration or building of a network of even seemingly disparate elements is vitally important in Huxley's scheme of education. He argues that only thus "the accomplished intellectual [who] understands the relations subsiding between many sectors of apprehended reality" (*EM*, 196) will gain a genuine continuum of knowledge and a perception of it. The same principle is explained as one "that will co-ordinate the scattered fragments, the island universes of specialized or merely professional knowledge; a principle that will supplement the scientifico-historical frame of reference [...], that will help [...] to transform [intellectuals] from mere spectators of the human scene into intelligent participants" (*EM*, 198–199). In his general indictment, the English Public Schools are not spared either, as their "rules, customs and loyalties which constitute the supporting framework [belong to] a hierarchical, competitive, imperialistic society" (*EM*, 202).

(5) Change the old worn-out systems. Move away from ancient hierarchies.

(6) Combine theory with practice as did Dr A. E. Morgan of Antioch College, Yellow Springs, Ohio.

(7) Get rid of fossilized professors.

(8) Let the fine and performing arts play a more important role.

(9) Encourage feeling and thinking.

(10) Introduce the experience of literature in a "bovaristic" manner, i. e., through reading one should glean examples and models one can adopt and follow. Such are portraits of non-attached beings and of people who not only possess compassion and charity, but who also respect the virtue of an action and perceive the role of the individual within society and the cosmos.

(11) Give creative intelligence its due, which is possible only in free and open societies and not under dictatorships.

(12) Expose the duplicity of advertisers, "modern commercial propagandists" (*EM*, 216).

(13) It is the business of educators to tell their wards (and, by implication, society) the plain, unvarnished truth stripped of "picturesque or empty phrases" (*EM*, 216) which dress up and hide political propaganda and are used to justify wars in the name of national or religious credos. Wars must be eschewed as freedom is their first casualty.

(14) Huxley returns to the ways of organized Christianity, one of his persistent targets. There is a doctrinal inadequacy among its moralists, he argues, not conducive to the emergence of "intelligently virtuous, adultly non-attached" persons (*EM*, 209), as they do not emphasize the right way of living. For example, can one be a true Christian and profit from armament factories or speculate in stocks and shares which might hurt the well-being of fellow-Christians or practise imperialism at the same time (see *EM*, 209)?

(15) In words recalling Juvenal (*"Quis custodiet custodes?"* [*EM*, 210], i.e., 'Who shall guard the guards themselves?'), Huxley asks who is to educate the educators to ensure that they will discharge their obligations, for their message must reach moralists, scientists and technologists and rulers alike. Without rightful education it is but a short leap from uncertain democratic societies to dictatorial regimes where freedom stands banished and education is propaganda, where every means of entertainment, information and communication is under state control, where pharmacology could be summoned to facilitate the brutal imposition of the ruler's will—all these conditions being the ominous shades of the dystopias of *Brave New World* or George Orwell's *Nineteen Eighty-Four* (1949).

(16) Psychology must be wedded to ethics, knowledge to experience.

(17) Education must make it possible for people to rise above the mere acquisition of a marketable skill and to relate one to the task of living a life distinguishing between good and evil, well-being and suffering.

(18) Therefore, Huxley asks his ideal educators to face an historic challenge and be men and women of conviction in order to undertake this mission of civilization.

In the meantime, time's winged chariot is hurrying faster and faster. Turning his critical gaze away from educators, Huxley exhorts us all to stop "purposeless reading, purposeless listening-in, purposeless looking at films," for they are forms of "ad-dictions, psychological equivalents of alcoholism and morphinism" (*EM*, 212). He fears that science might "be able very soon to supply us with micro-pocket-flasks and micro-hypodermic-syringes, micro-alcohol, micro-cigarettes and micro-cocaine" (*EM*, 213). Again, the onus is on education to create awareness in society to prevent such negative visions from becoming reality. This 1937 essay on education concludes with Huxley's reminder, "I have spoken in turn of education as character-training, education as instruction, education as training of the emotions [as well as] education of the body" (*EM*, 219) and adds that the world needs practical, curative morality to be obtained, of course, through education. Thus, without at all abandoning the tenets he always advocated, he has fine-tuned his thinking and the philosophic strategies for education. He has developed with the changing times and the new challenges faced by democratic societies.

When early in the twentieth century universal education was launched as a supreme goal, there were high hopes. But the results were discouraging. Humanitarianism declined. Unquestioning acceptance of those in power increased. Never since the days of Cesare Borgia (1476–1507), Huxley reminds us, had politics touched such low. If politics were bad, public life too had sunk deplorably. Hand in hand with mass education tabloids, pulp fiction, pulp magazines, morally squalid movies, bad music and propaganda proliferated. How, in the midst of this, one should go about fostering education for the non-attached and peace-loving men and women, remained a constant in his *Weltanschauung*. Fearless and uncompromising, he argued that "large numbers of boys and girls [...] are unable to derive much profit [from] academic [or liberal] education" (*EM*, 192), which was a conclusion derived from observed facts, not a reflection of any bias, as it has been alleged. Of all the controversies that beset him, this one had him labelled an elitist—a charge hurled at him by leftist critics like K. S. Shelvankar[12] and others who turned a cheap variety of populism into a religion, a sacred cow which cannot be spurned. The truth of the matter is, as Huxley objectively stated, many are "*congenitally incapable*" (*EM*, 192; my italics) of receiving higher education to which academics can attest.

Building new bridges, networks, being able to relate, to integrate, to live in harmony with all that surrounds you and not in isolation—such thoughts should remind us of another liberal humanist of the twentieth century, a near-contemporary of Huxley, who, too, agonized over incomplete and broken selves and fragmented lives. The reference here is to E. M. Forster and his *Howards End* (1910), in which the second Mrs Wilcox, Margaret, wishes to help her husband Henry

> to the building of the rainbow bridge that should connect the prose in us with the passion. Without it we are meaningless fragments, half monks, half beasts, unconnected arches that have never joined into a man. [...] Only connect! That was the whole of her sermon. Only connect the prose and the passion, and both will be exalted, and human love will be seen at its highest. Live in fragments no longer.[13]

Forster and Huxley may differ in details. Their common humanity, regardless, aims at elevating, enriching life, making it a whole, a complete entity in the classical manner, either through personal relationships and human love or through the right variety of education. But there is humanity's ultimate perversity, as Ovid has it in his *Metamorphoses*, "*Video meliora proboque; Deteriora sequor*," Huxley's repeated reminder, which he translates as: "To see and approve the better is useless, if one then regularly proceeds to pursue the worse" (*EM*, 214). Life, society and many of its institutions and practices are marked by this unshakable cussedness which brings about our miseries, our failures, our fall.

To restate, then, the essence of Huxley's 1937 essay "Education": Lay the foundation of a student's character within the framework of life under democracy. Establish the value of cooperation, which will lead to an individual's sense of responsibility. Inculcate a willing and well-informed sense of discipline. These are the three pillars, the three means that should lead to ideal education. Indeed, there has been some shift in emphasis since 1927, some recognition of the facts of life as they confronted Western intellectuals in the 1930s, as "the low dishonest decade" (in the words of

W. H. Auden) marched on inexorably. But Huxley's faith in education became even more solidified.

In *Adonis and the Alphabet*, "The Education of an Amphibian" covers a wide variety of complex and demanding concepts. Huxley argues that the almost wholly verbal nature of organized education does nothing to train the kinaesthetic sense, to promote Western and Eastern spirituality, or familiarize the student with, for example, the kinesthetic sense, tachystoscopic training, catalepsy, the reversal of peristalsis and so forth.[14] But is it pragmatic to attend to such esoteric areas? Can they be of use in actual and extensive practice? Huxley is noncommittal: "I can give no answer," he writes, a great deal of research is needed to deal with "the disintegrative effects of the kind of the civilization, under which our technology compels us to live."[15] And he concludes: "Time alone will show. Meanwhile, we can only hope for the best" (*AA*, 38).

In *Brave New World Revisited*, written against the background of the ever-increasing threat of a nuclear holocaust and the ecological destruction of the planet, he yet again gives prominence to education. He turns to freedom and its enemies as he deals with the importance of values and refers to philosophers, scholars and specialists in the field (e. g., William James, W. H. Sheldon, B. F. Skinner, J. B. Watson, etc.). The goal, as always, is to channel education properly. But what is Huxley's specific motivation in the central essay, entitled "Education for Freedom"? Even if it deals primarily with the education of mid-twentieth century Western men and women, the enunciation of goals and the adoption of appropriate techniques for their realization assume a higher significance. Advocating the goal of freedom and the need for a spirit of tolerance, the discussion takes on a more distinctly socio-political stance than before although he shies away from the claims put forward by Skinner, Watson or the nineteenth-century ideas of Herbert Spencer. Despite popular theories to the contrary, his faith in the uniqueness of a human being remains firm. If tyranny, in any form and whatever its source, is to be forestalled and defeated, educators must strive to sow the seeds of truth and freedom in children and grown-ups, even though the opposite attributes might appear more 'thrilling.' It is language which has separated humans from animals and made civilization possible. But language can be and is deliberately misused by those who wield power. Systems of education and educators have a part to play in preventing this folly which is assuming alarming proportions—what with all the tools made available by the latest technology. It is in such a context and for such a purpose that he turns to the role of education in 1958. Sadly, in the last half century since his warnings the world has moved more towards a denial of freedom and made the pursuit of truth more arduous.

Casting his net far and wide in these studies and elsewhere Huxley hoped for an education which is holistic and which leads to a life of independence, democratic governance, a sense of responsibility, a spirit of co-operation and character-training, and which is not aimed merely at the pursuit of Mammon. In his lifelong search for means of improving the quality of life here and now on this planet, he trusted immensely in what education can achieve. As the two essays on education discussed in the preceding pages show, he compels our attention by the profundity of his thought, its abiding, universal relevance and his manifest commitment to the cause. It is important to note that, whether as a mystic or a utopian, he developed over the years, even decades. As a champion of education, too, he similarly responded to the changes in Western Europe from the 1920s to the 1960s.

I have tried to underline the continued significance of Huxley's role as an educator even as mankind has stepped into the third millennium. I wish to conclude by expressing my conviction that he looked upon teachers or educators as true friends to man. In doing so, I believe, he echoes words of wisdom from India's ancient past. There is a well-known dictum in Sanskrit which defines who is a true and ideal friend and how he is supposed to play that role. I wish to quote those words, first because, regardless of time and place, regardless of one's national, ethnic, religious, philosophical and cultural affinity, they seem to convey moral awareness and idealism, and secondly because to Huxley India was a kind of spiritual home. He looked to the teachings of the *Bhagavad Gita*, the Vedas and the Upanishads, among other sources, for enlightenment. Written over three thousand years ago, the dictum reads: "Papat parityajyate iti tat mitram." I will paraphrase it somewhat freely: A true and ideal friend is one who, without any consideration for what may be in his own interest (such as preserving his goodwill and even his friendship) and always mindful of his duty, will dissuade others from committing what is sinful, morally wrong, wicked or evil, and insist that they retrace their steps. Aldous Huxley was such a friend to mankind: unfailingly honest, unswerving in what he saw as his duty or call of his conscience, ever ready to pay a price (which he did) for advocating what was so unequivocally his testament of faith.

---

[1] Aldous Huxley, *Antic Hay* (1923), Collected Edition (London, 1949), 9. Hereafter, *AH*.

[2] See Aldous Huxley, *Jesting Pilate* (1926), Collected Edition (London, 1948), 92. See also *Ends and Means* (London, 1937), 204. Hereafter, *EM*.

[3] Aldous Huxley, *Point Counter Point* (1928), Collected Edition (London, 1947), 349.

[4] Aldous Huxley, *After Many a Summer* (1939), Collected Edition (London, 1950), 4.

[5] Aldous Huxley, *Brave New World* (London, 1932), viii. (Translation: 'If you seek a monument, look around you.')

[6] Sybille Bedford, *Aldous Huxley: A Biography* (New York, 1974), 18.

[7] I will limit myself to the main sources, as his own writings form a consi-derable corpus. For a comprehensive look at this subject a full-length monograph will be needed. As a novelist of ideas, too, he is an educator. *After Many a Summer* turns to education, and *Island* (1962) is about education.

[8] Aldous Huxley, *Proper Studies* (London, 1927), 89. Hereafter, *PS*.

[9] See *AH*, ch. I, where Gumbril Junior heavily criticizes the educational system, see above, 79.

[10] Huxley quotes Wells' words; see *EM*, 178.

[11] The ideal way or conduct through life is that of the "Sthitahprajna." So, how is this ideal man, this seeker with his steadfast and unwavering consciousness to be defined? Arjuna, the warrior hero of the *Mahabharata*, greatly anguished over having to fight his own kith and kin, asks Lord Krishna, in response to which follows a discourse on living according to the highest tenets of Hinduism: Free yourself from all earthly desires, remain unshaken by sorrows and pleasures alike, eschew passion and rage, loathing and rejoicing, turn away from a life of the senses. Then you have become a "Sthitahprajna," who is dispassionate, unattached, free from earthly passions, untroubled by pleasures as well as sorrows, rejoicing or loathing, good or evil. (The preceding is a condensed version of S. Radhakrishnan, *The Bhagavadgita* [Bombay, 1985], 122–124.)

[12] Shelvankar, author of *Ends "Are" Means: A Critique of Social Values* (London, 1938), held diplomatic posts in erstwhile North Vietnam and the USSR.

[13] E. M. Forster, *Howards End*, ed. Oliver Stallybrass (Aylesbury, Bucks, 1988), ch. XXII, 187–188.

[14] The kinesthetic sense is the mind's ability to control the limbs; tachystoscopic training refers to that which measures and guides the exposure of objects to the human eye; catalepsy is a state of trance in which the body is insensate, and peristalsis is the involuntary muscular movement of one's intestines.

[15] Aldous Huxley, *Adonis and the Alphabet* (London, 1956), 37–38. Hereafter, *AA*.

Claudia Rosenhan

(University of St Gallen)

'THE KNOWLEDGE ECONOMY': ALDOUS HUXLEY'S CRITIQUES OF UNIVERSAL EDUCATION

T he aim of this essay is to give a coherent analysis of Aldous Huxley's critiques of universal education with the purpose of reconstructing his cultural criticism within its historical context and evaluate its usefulness as a contribution to today's debate on the problems of formal education. In order to achieve this aim, my objectives are first of all to classify Huxley's arguments on education and divide them into five categories for which education has a particular significance, secondly to illuminate the historical, ideological and theoretical background against which Huxley's arguments attain cogency, and finally to present his solutions and assess their relevance with respect to current concerns in Western education. I begin with education and human nature, since a prevailing theory of human nature inevitably determines the prevailing theory of education.

I. Education and Human Nature

Huxley's first critique of universal education attacks the prominence it affords to nurture over nature, and in his own survey of humankind, *Proper Studies*, he sets out to refute what he calls the "entirely false conception of individual human nature,"[1] namely the ideology of the 'blank slate.'[2] It is furthermore his contention that modern institutions such as schools have evolved to fit this erroneous view. Since he claims that "the only social institutions which will work for any length of time are those which are in harmony with individual human nature," he predicts that "institutions which deny the facts of human nature either break down more or less violently, or else decay gradually into ineffectiveness" (*CE*, II, 146). In his view this has happened to education. Huxley's critique is rooted in a partisan understanding of human nature that is mirrored in some important aspects by Steven Pinker's recent study *The Blank Slate: The Modern Denial of Human Nature*.[3] Like Pinker, Huxley felt that the denial of human nature is in itself treacherous because it puts too much trust in the efficacy of social engineering.

The conception of the 'blank slate' furthermore leads to two important misunderstandings about the human mind, the first concerning egalitarianism. Locke declared: "The Difference to be found in the Manners and Abilities of Men, is owing more to their *Education* than to anything else" (Locke, 137–138).[4] Thus education came to be regarded as the central formative influence on people and the only viable explanation for existing inequalities (see "The Idea of Equality" [1927], *CE*, II, 155). The Aristotelian postulate that men are in essence and originally equal and the Cartesian tenet that reason is the same in all men prompted eighteenth- and nineteenth-century political and social reformers to declare that all members of society have an equal capacity to be reasonable and could therefore be educated for a rational life. Yet by refusing to acknowledge the Hobbesian "universe of Behemoth and Leviathan"[5] with its pessimistic view of human nature, reformers like Godwin were, according to Huxley, taken in by a false psychology.[6] He claims instead that people react more readily to appeals to their lower passions and that "no amount of education or good government will make men completely virtuous and reasonable, or abolish their animal instincts" ("The Future of the Past" [September 1927], *CE*, II, 93; see also "On the Charms of History and the Future of the Past" [1931], *CE*, III, 137).

The second misunderstanding is based on the belief that the Lockean mind is uniform in its ability to achieve anything, and Huxley thinks that this behaviourist theory exercises a "baneful influence on current systems of education," first by regarding the mind as a box into which ideas can be introduced with impunity and second by treating all minds as identical ("Education" [1927], *CE*, II, 194, 197–198; see also "The Idea of Equality" [1927], *CE*, II, 155). The—in Bantock's words—"uniformitarian tendencies"[7] of nineteenth-century reform were a logical reaction to the unregulated, haphazard and fairly rudimentary educational system in existence at that time, because only by believing in the homogeneity of human ability could a standardised system succeed.[8] But for the future Huxley hopes that such a reductive science of mental processes is replaced by a new "psychological realism" in education ("The Outlook for American Culture: Some Reflections in a Machine Age" [August 1927], *CE*, III, 193), by which he proposes "simply applied psychology, applied heredity and applied psycho-physiology" ("Education" [21 December 1932], *CE*, III, 350).

First steps to diverge from uniform standards were taken in the 1920s. IQ testing[9] as a regulative measure to override the still existing class bias in education, or IQ-elitism, as Gordon and White call it, was an attempt to realise a meritocracy, a Platonic denial of class-bound intelligence and ability.[10] Another approach was to classify the mind into three categories, abstract, mechanical and concrete, for which a tripartite system of grammar, secondary modern and technical schools was devised.[11] However, the link between meritocracy, IQ testing and social success is not self-evident. It implies that the "technocratic-meritocratic ideology" is inherently egalitarian and that social success is solely based on technical and cognitive skills.[12] Even though access to grammar schools was thereby eased for lower classes, Gordon shows how the provision of scholarships to disadvantaged children and the extension of selection principles did not counteract the demands of the 11+ examination in which social factors still played an important role.[13] Huxley's view of IQ testing and tripartism is similarly negative. He believes first of all that the mind, "hereditary make-up and acquired attainments," is an organic whole whose constituent parts cannot be isolated in this way ("Varieties of Intelligence" [1927], *CE*, II, 181). He also realises that educational provisions were in effect based on status and income, not ability: "Class and money determine not the nature of the individual's intelligence but the way in which it shall be used and the ends which the individual sets himself to attain" (*CE*, II, 192).

Huxley concedes that universal education is by necessity democratic and standardised, but that even standardised education should provide for people the opportunity to benefit individually from it. His favoured educational strategy was the Dalton Plan, by which children with individual talents, abilities and aptitudes control their own learning process in an environment geared towards mutual support and cooperation (see "How Should Men Be Educated?" [December 1926], *CE*, II, 75).[14] The Dalton system addresses all the problems Huxley identified with universal education. It takes individual human nature for granted and does not believe in mechanistic teaching methods that treat the mind as a uniform receptacle. He blames the failure to adopt Daltonised schools as a standard educational provision on the endurance of Lockean and Helvétian doctrines, the "blank page of pure potentiality [...] capable of being molded by education into any desired form" ("Where Do You Live?" [1956], *CE*, V, 175). It remained his lifelong conviction that Helvétius's *De L'ésprit* is a preposterous book and that Watson's and Skinner's work was tainted by their oversimplification of human nature. Huxley fears that in order to solve the conundrum of universal education, governments might go further than just pretend that every child has the same intellectual potential. In the grip of a totalitarian doctrine, social engineering leads to a brave new world instead of a democratic utopia (see *Brave New World Revisited* [1958], *CE*, VI, 279–286).

II. Education and Social Control

The excessive 'uniformitarianism' of the brave new world may be a dystopian vision, but throughout the nineteenth century the 'blank slate' was commandeered to prove the efficiency of education in controlling required outcomes and initiate fundamental social and political changes. Working-class and middle-class educators each attempted to assume control over popular education, yet this class-struggle reinforced the instrumental function of education as a means of social control rather than social change. Andy Green illustrates in *Education and State Formation: The Rise of Education Systems in England, France and the USA* how the monitorial system set the institutionalised parameters of universal education by enforcing industrial and capitalist values like punctuality, obedience and discipline.[15] When the state finally took over the provision of popular education at the end of the century, it put similar emphasis on the non-cognitive values of discipline and authority, thus transforming education into a political acculturation to the values of a dominant class. In "Nationalizing Education" (1916) John Dewey asserts how exploiting it for such ends undermines the democratic claim of education and helps "refeudalizing" the system.[16]

This charge is not new. Universal education as a means for social control had previously been criticised by the philosophical radicals. J. S. Mill commented: "A general State education is a mere contrivance for moulding people to be exactly like one another; and as the mould in which it casts them is that which pleases the predominant power in the government [...] it establishes a despotism over the mind."[17] Mill's estimation feeds into Huxley's investigation into the nature of ideals, *Ends and Means*, in which he identifies what lies at the bottom of the contemporary crisis in education, namely that the "strict authoritarian discipline of state schools" emphasises values which primarily benefit a hierarchical and militaristic social organisation. In Huxley's opinion it is therefore no wonder that the "decline of democracy has coincided exactly with the rise to manhood and political power of the second generation of the compulsorily educated proletariat" ("Education" [1937], *CE*, IV, 269–270). In this light "universal education has proved to be the state's most effective instrument of universal regimentation and militarization, and has exposed millions, hitherto immune, to the influence of organized lying and the allurements of incessant, imbecile, and debasing distractions" ("Politics and Religion" [1941], *CE*, V, 12). Only a ruling oligarchy benefits from the social engineering education provides, be it in the form of an uncritical mass-consumerist population or an army of specialized stooges for political ends (*Science, Liberty and Peace* [1946], *CE*, V, 273–274). Huxley's warning of universal education resulting effectively in the decline of democracy came after it had earlier become reality in Italy and Germany.

However, the dream of positive social engineering was not yet dead at the beginning of the twentieth century. Progressives like Dewey still regarded education as a countermeasure to the authoritarian bias in popular education and still believed in it as "the fundamental method of social progress and reform" ("My Pedagogic Creed" [1897], Dewey, 234), if only the syllabus and the methodology emphasises freedom and responsibility enough. Yet Huxley is sceptical that "any great scheme of human regeneration," be it religious, economical or political, could be achieved through education, simply because history has shown how these intentions were habitually reverted to the opposite. A "religious faith in the efficacy of education" had by the end of the 1920s not succeeded in abolishing the Edwardian stratified society ("The New Salvation" [September 1929], *CE*, III, 212–213), because, in Bernstein's words, "education cannot compensate for society."[18]

The reason that radicals and socialists initially lobbied against state education was not only because they feared its abuse as a means of social and political control by the government, but, as Alan Richardson shows, also because they were suspicious of the knowledges and methodologies that such an education system perpetuates, such as overtly imperialist, capitalist and nationalist doctrines.[19] A. V. Kelly asserts that these knowledges are often treated as positivistic facts, decontextualised and compartmentalised in order to be transmissible by the teacher and passively absorbable by the students.[20] Yet Huxley exposes such "reasonable" world-views we obediently accept as "metaphysical entities" ("Varieties of Intelligence" [1927], CE, II, 191) based upon cultural preferences ("No Disputing About Reasons" [May 1927], CE, III, 143–144). He criticises that "we are taught in terms of rigid formulas, we are made to believe dogmatically that only one thing can be true or right at one time and that contradictions are mutually exclusive" ("Some American Contradictions" [October 1929], CE, III, 213). His criticism thus anticipates the postmodern crisis of epistemology which in Kelly's definition regards "knowledge as a social, even a personal construct," an ideological device for the maintenance and exercise of power (Kelly, 63).

Stripped of any supreme claim to truth, knowledge is thus not only ideologically determined but also hierarchical. The ability to project its own convictions onto others, which then becomes the "natural" way of seeing the world, is what Antonio Gramsci termed the hegemonic power of the dominant social group.[21] The definition of cultural capital transferred via education represents such a moral-intellectual leadership, and it is, as Pierre Bourdieu in "Cultural Reproduction and Social Reproduction" has shown, only valuable to those who, by descent and privilege, already own it.[22] The education system reproduces cultural and social values and exercises hegemonic control over those who do not own cultural capital and is thereby again closely linked to social control and discipline.[23] Post-World-War-II attempts to level out this hierarchy and elevate popular "lowbrow" disciplines to the same status as traditional "highbrow" subjects are in Huxley's eyes equally misguided. Pandering to a culture-free concept of knowledge, the resultant "anarchy of values" merely leads to "conformity to current conventions of personal and collective behaviour" ("Knowledge and Understanding" [1956], CE, V, 213). Yet he concedes that the perennial values of a highbrow curriculum are not always relevant to contemporary life and should therefore be adapted to match the realities of the modern world (see CE, V, 215–216).

Huxley feels that what is generally termed the 'essentialist' approach to education places too much emphasis on remote and externally imposed learning objectives.[24] This entails conserving and transmitting a common conservative culture and does not initiate independent inquiry. Teaching is based on rigour and achievement and passing exams is as important as discipline. In contrast Huxley puts forward a disinterested model of moral education based on the non-attached individual. This model emphasises personal autonomy and can, for instance, be projected via the "bovaristic" quality of literature that offers models for judicious analysis of society (see "Bovarism" [27 May 1933], *CE*, III, 362–364). By building "up in the minds of their charges a habit of resistance to suggestion" teachers instil in children the necessity to rely on their own resources and resist external stimulation ("Education" [1937], *CE*, IV, 288–290), thereby underpinning the democratic freedom to question loyalties.

III. Education for National Efficiency

Yet education is often perceived not as instruction for life but training for a livelihood. Huxley's third critique of universal education condemns its utilitarian emphasis on human capital and the economic value of skills. National efficiency, a highly prized function of education at the beginning of the twentieth century, was impeded by what adherents to the 'two cultures' controversy called the breakdown in communication between the arts and the sciences. It fuelled the 'declinist' view of economic history that a humanistic prejudice in education left Britain without properly trained specialists and workers. By refuting that the measure of man is only his "socially valuable abilities" ("Education" [1927], *CE*, II, 216), Huxley is an outspoken critic of the increasingly specialised "second heroic age of industrialisation" at the beginning of the twentieth century ("Abroad in England" [May 1931], *CE*, III, 271, and "On the Charms of History and the Future of the Past" [1931], *CE*, III, 135). He asserts: "The worship of success and efficiency constitutes [a] menace to our world" ("Spinoza's Worm" [1929], *CE*, II, 330),[25] a premonition of the technocratic nightmare of World War II. Huxley's criticism of students entering "the world, highly expert in their particular job, but knowing very little about anything else and having no integrating principle in terms of which they can arrange and give significance to such knowledge as they may subsequently acquire" ("Education" [1937], *CE*, IV, 276) blamed what was to become the ground for the war-mongering machinery.

    Still, educating a skilled and specialised workforce was the primary aim of nineteenth-century utilitarian education, and a second was projected social mobility for the lower classes.[26] But basic literacy and the diffusion of 'useful knowledge' did not have the desired effect since, well into the twentieth century, only a tiny minority could climb the ladder of opportunity and attend the necessary secondary schools.[27] It was not until the late 1930s that attempts were made to re-fashion the education system on one based on 'parity of esteem,' which afforded technical education the same social kudos as grammar school education. But the quick demise of technical schools as the third column of tripartism in the 1940s soon minimised the choices for the lower and middle classes again. The paucity of technical schools and the low esteem in which scientific and technical education was allegedly held in England, was, according to Wiener, based on the gentrification of the nineteenth-century middle classes, which were in his eyes reluctant to support a more efficient and vocational education system. In fact, the middle-class mandate for more vocational training was fulfilled when, e.g., the home and imperial civil services began to recruit on a meritocratic system of competitive exams and instruction at grammar schools became more academically rigorous after 1870.[28] This progression from patronage to merit actually imposed what Harold Perkin called the "entrepreneurial ideal" on secondary and higher education.[29] At first glance it looks as if Huxley confirms Wiener's prejudice of an inherently anti-modern culture at public schools and universities when he concedes that these institutions were often nothing more than a "delightful social club" ("Education" [1927], *CE*, II, 214). Furthermore he agrees that the liberal ideal is not one that should be elevated to a universal ideal.[30] Yet his critique must be located within the revisionist school against the Wienerian thesis.[31]

In contrast to Wiener, Huxley does not see the liberal ideal winning out against the vocational. On the contrary, he believes that a humanistic education is under attack by technocrats and that more students go to universities because the pragmatics of the job market demands it (see "Literature and Examinations" [1936], *CE*, IV, 62), despite Huxley's contention that a liberal education cannot lead to social success for the many (see "Foreheads Villainous Low" [1931], *CE*, III, 248). In turn, university subjects in the humanities were taught according to scientific standards, even though "the scientific student of literature is one of the most comical figures of our day" ("Education" [1927], *CE*, II, 215). Huxley maintains his position also in post-war times by emphasising that humanities "do not lend themselves to being taught with an eye to future examinations and the accumulation of credits" ("Censorship and Spoken Literature" [October 1955], *CE*, V, 323).[32]

Thus by the 1930s scientific methodology and the emphasis on quantifiable outcomes were winning out against a culture of disinterested, 'useless' knowledge. In Huxley's eyes, technical and vocational education threatened to overwhelm a more eclectic liberal syllabus and narrow the horizons of those it educated to a point of absolute specialisation which, as mentioned above, ultimately led to the technocratic nightmare of World War II. In order to avoid a recurrence of this dangerous one-sided barbarism,[33] he advocated the integration of scientific and emotional truths, for which the study of literature is again a valuable foundation. First, it has practical value. Students learn how to express themselves in writing and speech and evaluate the opinions of others (see "Literature and Examinations" [1936], *CE*, VI, 59–62).[34] In addition, its immediate and moral point of view can mingle with the objective point of view of science in order to address fundamental questions about human nature, truth and social harmony.[35] Huxley's answer to the 'two cultures' debate is thus one that integrates what he calls Snow's "bland scientism" and Leavis' "moralistic literarism" (*Literature and Science* [1963], *CE*, VI, 90–91).[36]

IV. Education and Cultural Degeneration

So it seems as if literature was the ideal subject for an integrated and disinterested education, though Huxley's fourth critique of universal education shows how literacy was a double-edged weapon in the fight for social improvement and acculturation. On the one hand, book reading is traditionally the tool for self-improvement and, as an heir to the Arnoldian tradition, Huxley feels that "culture is not derived from the reading of *books*—but from thorough and intensive reading of *good* books" ("Reading, the New Vice" [August 1930], *CE*, III, 48–50).[37] On the other hand, lower class literacy after the French Revolution was regarded as subversive, so that the dominant social powers strove to control the reading material of the newly literates, a process Harvey J. Graff calls "recreating cultural hegemony".[38] Alan Richardson similarly illuminates how, as soon as it was realised that a substantial number of the populace could spell, political, religious and utilitarian groups vied for the attention of the reading public with useful, spiritual or improving literature in order to contain any seditious thoughts that may result from the "unfettered" literacy of the lower orders (Richardson, 44).[39] This inhibited the development of a confident literary and cultural taste amongst the lower classes and resulted, according to Huxley, in an inverted snobbery.

Now as then, the hierarchy of cultural capital posits a literate culture at the top, controlled, according to Graff's "literacy myth," by the middle classes (Graff, 335). For the lower classes, imperfect reading skills and the lack of opportunity made it difficult for them to cross this cultural divide. Instead, their culture was dictated to them by the dross and trivia of popular mass publications particularly at the beginning of the twentieth century, and they were regarded as particularly hapless in their choice of reading matter.[40] Even though Jonathan Rose has recently denied this thesis,[41] Huxley judges the keenness of barely literate workers to access the nation's cultural capital rather more pessimistically. Commenting in 1934 on the newly literate Mexican Indians, whose situation in many ways mirrors that of nineteenth-century British workers, he underlines that a love for reading cannot make up for a lack of understanding (see *Beyond the Mexique Bay* [1934], *CE*, III, 578, 602).

This combination of untutored literacy with an intrinsic debased taste is held responsible for the perceived cultural degeneration of the early twentieth century. Although virtually all popular reading matter was derided as sensationalist and culturally impoverished, it provided for many the only chance to own their reading skills without feeling inferior.[42] In any case, functional literacy was applied to activities of which book reading accounted for only a small percentage.[43] Most workers, as Mitch similarly illustrates, preferred the Sunday papers and sports journals (see Mitch, 60–1). Despite the fact that leisure seemed to be the main incentive to acquire literacy (see Mitch, 78), reading was for pleasure rather than improvement.[44] In light of this, Huxley punctures the utopian dream of unlimited leisure leading to enlightenment and disinterested scholarly activity, as people would not in general devote themselves willingly to a "rational existence" ("Work and Leisure" [1925], *CE*, I, 416). Simultaneously he understands how literacy does not necessarily present the cultural pinnacle. Prompted by his interest in mysticism, he commended the staple of modern mass entertainment, the radio and the gramophone, as a didactic tool,[45] modelled on the old traditions of an oral and auditory culture.[46] But by then a hegemonic literary culture had largely destroyed the old oral traditions, and the common sensibilities of the people, fed on a "peculiarly shoddy kind of sensational and sentimental trash" ("Paper" [5 February 1932], *Hearst*, 318–19), were twisted into nationalistic and militaristic doctrines.

Thus the philanthropic dream of an enlightened rational existence for the masses is limited by what Huxley terms the "law of diminishing returns" ("Boundaries of Utopia" [1931], *CE*, III, 127; see also "Work and Leisure" [1925], *CE*, I, 415). It puts Mill's dream of a "reign of reason and democracy" based on universal literacy out of reach (*Science, Liberty and Peace* [1946], *CE*, V, 254; see also "Propaganda in a Democratic Society" [1958], *CE*, VI, 242–243). Even though literacy enables us to understand our place in our culture, culture can also be "a negative force, a something which prevents persons, living in certain places and at certain times, from being able to think certain thoughts or adopt certain styles of expression" ("Variations on a Philosopher" [1950], *CE*, V, 97). Huxley also says: "If we want to understand, we must uproot ourselves from our culture, by-pass language" and generally leave behind all emotional links to the world. But knowledge is often rooted in an unhealthy and "almost maniacal over-valuation of words" ("Knowledge and Understanding" [1956], *CE*, V, 219). So as a remedy for the failings in universal education, the overspecialisation of technocrats, the indoctrination of the populace and the degeneration of culture, education must include thorough linguistic training.

V. Language and Critical Thinking

By the beginning of the twentieth century, language itself had become the focus of investigation. The paradigmatic change came with Saussure's structuralist approach that severed the study of language from mainly philological concerns and created a system in which the signifier and the signified interact to create meaning devoid of reference to an objective material reality. Another strand of linguistic theory emerging in the early twentieth century was that of relativism, emphasising the power of language to manipulate, constrain or even render incapable the understanding of a particular reality if language does not provide for it. The binary bind between language and thought is sometimes judged to be so strong by cognitive scientists that, as Mark Turner explains, "speech and writing could be ways for the brain of one person to exert biological influence upon the brain of another person."[47] In other words, language can physically change the way people are able to think. Huxley similarly believes that the self-sufficiency and separateness of the Western alphabet conditions thought processes. Thus he views the invention of the alphabet not only as humanity's highest achievement, but also as its most dangerous weapon (see "Adonis and the Alphabet" [1956], *CE*, V, 235–239). The view that language can only give an inadequate and conventional view of reality and that it is riddled with ambiguity and vagueness, was influential in what has been termed the "linguistic turn" in philosophy.[48] Huxley's musings on the nature and importance of language and thought are thus crypto-linguistic inquiries into the workings of language in an ideological context, emphasising its power to manipulate the understanding of a particular reality. He regards language as a vague system bearing no relationship to an unknowable reality, even though our being is determined by words. He feels that education unfortunately puts too much significance on the importance of words, and the resulting verbalized, abstract knowledge is therefore only a kind of pseudo-knowledge (see "Can We Be Well-Educated?" [December 1956], *CE*, VI, 206 and "The Education of an Amphibian" [1956], *CE*, V, 199). Huxley stresses: "As we believe, so we are. And what we believe depends on what we have been taught".[49] The first step to thorough understanding, he advises, is to become more knowledgeable about the linguistic reality that surrounds us.

Today, Critical Language Study underlines the "significance of language in the production, maintenance, and change of social relations of power".[50] This methodology uses the strategies of discourse analysis to investigate the expression and reproduction of social identities and social power relations. Norman Fairclough quotes Michel Foucault: "'Any system of education is a political way of maintaining or modifying the appropriation of discourses, along with the knowledges and powers which they carry'" (Fairclough, 65). He puts forward a model in which language and discourse are described, interpreted and explained so as to raise awareness of the social operation of linguistic features. His model aims to facilitate emancipation not only in newly literate societies (which is the main focus of Paolo Freire's path-breaking project in Brazil) but also in developed countries like Britain. I propose that Huxley may have had a similar model in mind when he criticised the dangerous distortions of meaning which language underwent in the late 1930s. Huxley claims that "all propaganda directed against an opposing group has but one aim: to substitute diabolical abstractions for concrete persons" ("Words and Behaviour" [1936], *CE*, IV, 57–58). In reference to Hartley,

Huxley feels that the most important part of language teaching is the art of dissociating ideas. But "that the art of dissociation will ever be taught in schools under direct state control is, of course, almost infinitely improbable" ("Education" [1937], *CE*, IV, 292; see also "Education for Freedom" [1958], *CE*, VI, 284–285).

Huxley's concerns were in unison with those of other cultural critics. Orwell famously stated: "Political language [...] is designed to make lies sound truthful and murder respectable, and to give an appearance of solidity to pure wind."[51] The ideological distortion of language has furthermore been examined by Mikhail Bakhtin and his model of the dialogic nature of understanding has been tremendously influential in postmodern theory.[52] He states: "The very same thing that makes the ideological sign vital and mutable is also, however, that which makes it a refracting and distorting medium" (Bakhtin, 55). In "The Dialogic Imagination" he makes clear that "language is not a neutral medium that passes freely and easily into private property of the speaker's intentions; it is populated—overpopulated—with the intentions of others" (Bakhtin, 77). Although it is unlikely that Huxley was familiar with Bakhtin, the Russian usefully augments Huxley's link between language, social interaction and political consciousness, even though the Marxist view of relations between human consciousness and the material world should be opposed by Huxley as an advocate of human nature. Yet this assumed discrepancy could be resolved if we bear in mind that unawareness and lack of self-knowledge was, according to Huxley, one of the major weaknesses of modern civilization. Language can be decoded if people were made able to tap into their innate abilities, something akin to Pinker's "language instinct."

Teaching the "capacity for autonomous thinking and decision-making," which A. V. Kelly defines as the basis of democratic education (Kelly, 112) was for many educationalists epitomised by the classical syllabus of the grammar school.[53] Yet the way the classics were taught, viz as passive absorption of knowledge through rote learning, made it ineffectual in producing real understanding. At grammar schools, for instance, most students would sweat over Latin and Greek translations without really understanding the content, a fact on which Huxley has often remarked (see, e.g., "Doodles in the Dictionary" [1956], *CE*, V, 429). What is more, critical thought and self-knowledge, which Huxley regards as an important educational goal (see "Ethics" [1937], *CE*, IV, 401), cannot be assessed in standardised exams. Huxley himself submitted *The Perennial Philosophy* in 1946 as an educational reader for people who want to attain total awareness, but feels it is important to provide alternative ways of achieving an understanding that "comes when we are totally aware" ("Knowledge and Understanding" [1956], *CE*, VI, 225). For those who cannot derive any benefit from a liberal education Huxley advocates non-verbal education as a way to understanding and self-knowledge.

Huxley was an enthusiastic supporter of the Dalton Plan, because it made the learning experience relevant to the life experience of the child (see "How Should Men Be Educated?" [December 1926], *CE*, II, 75). It presents a shift in emphasis from what is learned to how the learning process is handled (see "Education" [1927], *CE*, II, 212–30). Physical activity is an important aspect of it, and Huxley, like Dewey, is a keen supporter of F. M. Alexander's kinesthetic training (see "How to Improve the World" [December 1936], *CE*, IV, 139–140). Yet for Huxley Dewey's learning-by-doing approach does not go far enough, because the ideal non-verbal education must also cater for the "not-selves," our spiritual and vegetative soul ("The Education of an Amphibian" [1956], *CE*, V, 197–208). He furthermore speculates that mind-enhancing drugs in connection with a superior kind of education will have revolutionary results,[54] because drugs "potentiate the non-verbal education of adolescents and [...] remind adults that the real world is very different from the misshapen universe they have created for themselves by means of their culture-conditioned prejudices" (article in *Playboy* [November 1963], *Moksha*, xix). In "Education on the Nonverbal Level" (1963) Huxley lists a whole range of (unlikely) subjects that should be taught at school to aid awareness, such as yoga, meditation and Tantrik exercises as well as Gestalt therapy. Techniques for elementary pain control (auto-suggestion, hypnosis) and ethical training as well as auto-conditioning also potentially generate self-awareness (see *CE*, VI, 311–316).

VI. The End(s) of Education

As a supporter of the progressive child-centred approach, which, despite several attempts, never seemed to get a foothold in the traditional British education system,[55] Huxley has a jaded view of education as a means of perfection. He insists that education must address the individual differences of human beings in order to be effective—differences that include varied levels of ability and intelligence. In addition, he questions not only the means of education but also its ends. Many educational activists declare that only an educated person can make a valuable contribution to society,[56] but this humanistic objective has resulted in indoctrination for political ends and specialisation for economic gains. So Huxley's critiques of universal education overlap with his cultural criticism, because he is not blind to the fact that formal education can influence the future of human society. His hopes are for a future in which next generations would grow up impervious to political propaganda, advertising and religious indoctrination, fortified by a balanced and integrated education and instruction how to attain self-awareness and understanding. This could not be accomplished by the standardised, authoritarian and specialised system that emerged at the beginning of the twentieth century. Yet Huxley was also aware that social experiments cannot be conducted under laboratory conditions. In 1933 he presciently averred that "whenever new educational methods are introduced, we can only watch and wait how the experiment will unfold" ("Discipline" [8 August 1933], *Hearst*, 370–371), a statement he repeated in 1956 (see "Can We Be Well-Educated?" [December 1956], *CE*, VI, 203). Today we are now in the position to judge tentatively if universal education has proved to be a successful experiment or if Huxley's arguments still have some validity. In any case, the continuing debate about education signifies that concerns about the ends of education have not yet been satisfactorily resolved.

Looking back on Huxley's suggestions, first of all his call for a non-competitive, individual education, we can see that the actual implementation of the Comprehensive System in the early 1970s with the aim of abolishing selection and providing for children of all abilities may have been a step into the direction Huxley favoured. Yet today the current trend is again towards more selection under the cloak of diversity and choice. The inevitable result is segregation on mainly social factors, determined by parents' buying powers in desirable catchment areas. Comprehensive schools were also the first institutions attempting to change instead of reproduce the existing inequalities in society. Today, education has the status of a human right whose provision cannot depend on a return for society in terms of useful skills and manpower, even though A. V. Kelly reiterates how most governments would nevertheless treat it as an investment in the economic and political future of the state and its members (see Kelly, 107, 119, 124). Joel Spring's exploration of Article 26 of the 1948 Universal Declaration of Human Rights also exposes that education is continually and habitually misused for political and religious indoctrination.[57] Thus the hold of the government over those it educates has actually increased. The National Curriculum, introduced in 1988, specifies what children must study and what they are expected to know at certain key stages. This does not leave much room for the cultivation of critical faculties. Even the introduction of 'Citizenship' as a foundation subject in 2002, with a mission statement highlighting 'knowledge and understanding' is imposed by the state and cannot therefore count as a step towards Huxley's call for 'disinterested' education.

The National Curriculum is also based on an extensive system of tests at every key stage to check whether children are meeting the pre-set targets. Test results, league tables and the need to quantify educational outcomes is not in any real sense a way to encourage children to learn at their own pace and in a cooperative environment. Furthermore, parcelling knowledge up into disparate disciplines works against a system of integrated education. Twenty-eight years after Lord Callaghan's Ruskin Speech, the current government continues to uphold that education must profit society in terms of a competitive national economy, for which the term 'knowledge economy' has been coined. The trend for educating for the workplace has infected the humanities to such a degree that they "now seek to justify their value in terms of 'embedded transferable skills' of potential use to employers."[58] The purely functional aspect of education also impinges on the teaching of literacy and numeracy. The former Minister of Education, Kenneth Baker, said in 1986 that literacy is valuable only for the job market.[59] In any case, analytical linguistic skills may be no longer adequate for today's visual culture, so that Huxley's advice to supplement reading with the new skills of looking and listening seems prophetic (see "Audible Books" [11 June 1934], *Hearst*, 278). Finally non-verbal education has been totally neglected in formal education, and physical education is often merely a once a week break from the classroom routine. But why should students not learn how to meditate or how to use their body correctly? Learning in a stimulating environment remains the domain of children with special needs and primary school children.

On the whole, educational underachievement in deprived areas, inequality of opportunity via selection and the application of market principles to educational problems are but some aspects which allow for some disturbing parallels to be drawn between the provision of universal education in Britain in the nineteenth century, when parental consumers of education were sovereign, and today's 'parentocracy.' Marketisation, privatisation and choice have failed to provide answers to what most experts perceive to be a crisis in modern formal education in Britain. In light of these findings, it seems as if Huxley's critiques of universal education still supply some useful reference points for a new approach to schooling, provided parents and the state alike put as high a premium on the emotional well-being of children and their precious curiosity about the world as on league table results.

---

[1] "Measurable and Unmeasurable" (1927), *Aldous Huxley: Complete Essays*, ed. with commentary by Robert S. Baker and James Sexton (6 vols., Chicago, 2000–2002), II, 147. Hereafter, *CE*.

[2] Locke's coinage of the *tabula rasa* is not original but goes back to Aristotle's conception of the mind as a blank receiver, or Pelagius' *non pleni* (cf. "non pleni nascimur, et ut sine virtute, ita et sine vitio procreamur," Pelagius, *Pro lib. arb.* 1. <http://www.sant-agostino.it/latino/grazia_cristo/grazia_cristo_2.htm>), and even appears in John Earle's *Microcosmographia* of 1628, see George Boas, *The Cult of Childhood* (London, 1966), 43. Yet its prominent position at the end of *Some Thoughts Concerning Education* (1693, 1705), where Locke states his intention to consider the child as a "white paper, or wax, to be moulded and fashioned as one pleases" accords it superior status in educational thought. See *The Educational Writings of John Locke*, ed. James L. Axtell (Cambridge, 1968), 325.

[3] (New York, 2002). Pinker refers, e.g., to modern architecture (Le Corbusier) and urban planning (170–171), two of Huxley's pet hates.

[4] Occasionally his bias towards nurture was tempered by an acknowledgment of individual "Makes and Tempers" of human minds (Locke, 206). See also "God has stampt certain Characters upon Men's Minds, which, like their Shapes, may perhaps be a little mended; but can hardly be totally alter'd, and transform'd into

the contrary" (Locke, 159). Axtell in his edition of Locke's writings points out that there are further occasions where Locke gets caught up in the nature-nurture dichotomy; see, e.g., §§ 66, 108, 139, 216.

5 Aldous Huxley, "On Grace" [January 1931], *CE*, III, 119.

6 William Godwin actually had surprisingly similar arguments to Huxley's with regard to the varieties of intelligence and his refutation of Helvétius. In Essay II of *Thoughts on Man* Godwin clearly states that he believes in a common human nature while at the same time acknowledging that "every human creature is endowed with talents, which, if rightly directed, would shew him apt, adroit, intelligent and acute, in the walk for which his organisation especially fitted him" (*The Political and Philosophical Writings of William Godwin*, VI, ed. Mark Philip [London, 1993], 53). Like Huxley, he deplores how "the practices and modes of civilised life prompt us to take the inexhaustible varieties of man, as he is given into our guardianship by the bountiful hand of nature, and train him in one uniform exercise, as the raw recruit is treated when he is brought under the direction of his drill-sergeant" (Godwin, 53).

7 G. H. Bantock, *Studies in the History of Educational Theory*, I: *Artifice and Nature, 1350–1765* (London, 1980), 226.

8 It alone can "induce that equality of outcome which was the logical result of subjecting beings of a similar original nature to an identity of influence" (Bantock, 258).

9 See Cyril Burt, *How the Mind Works* (London, 1933), in which he defined intelligence as an inborn and unspecified ability that can be accurately measured. See also Percy Nunn, *Education: Its Data and First Principles* (London, 1920). Standard IQ testing (such as the later tests devised by H. Eysenck [e.g., *Know Your Own IQ* (1962)] derives from the collaborative work of Alfred Binet and his student Theodore Simon. An early description of the Binet-Simon scale for testing the intelligence of 'subnormals' was published in *L'Année Psychologique*, 12 (1905), 191–244. See also C. Spearman, "'General intelligence,' objectively determined and measured," *American Journal of Psychology*, 15 (1904), 201–293.

10 See Peter Gordon and John White, *Philosophers as Educational Reformers: The Influence of Idealism on British Educational Thought and Practice* (London, 1979), 178, 213.

11 See John Stevenson, *British Society 1914–45* (London, 1984), 263. See Hadow Report (1926), Spens Report (1938) and Norwood Report (1943).

12 See A. H. Halsey, A. F. Heath and J. M. Ridge, *Origins and Destinations: Family, Class, and Education in Modern Britain* (Oxford, 1980), 6–7.

13 Peter Gordon, Richard Aldrich and Dennis Dean, *Education and Policy in England in the Twentieth Century* (London, 1991), 114.

14 For a detailed outline of the Dalton Plan at A. J. Lynch's West Green Elementary School, Tottenham, see "Education" (1927) *CE*, II, 209–11. Also Lesley Fox Lee, "The Dalton Plan and the loyal, capable intelligent citizen," *History of Education*, 29 (March 2000), 129–138. A. J. Lynch was a member of the Labour Party's Advisory Committee for Education.

[15] Andy Green, *Education and State Formation: The Rise of Education Systems in England, France and the USA* (New York, 1990), 251.

[16] *The Essential Dewey*, I: *Pragmatism, Education, Democracy*, ed. Larry A. Hickman and Thomas M. Alexander (Bloomington, 1998), 268.

[17] John Stuart Mill, *On Liberty* [1859], ed. with an introduction by Gertrude Himmelfarb (London, 1988), 177.

[18] See Basil Bernstein, "Education Cannot Compensate for Society," *New Society*, 387 (26 February 1970), 344–347.

[19] See Alan Richardson, *Literature, Education, and Romanticism* (Cambridge, 1994), 89. However, Ross McKibbin points out that the Board of Education recommended an anti-imperial bias for teaching history after World War I (see *Classes and Cultures, England 1918–1951* [Oxford, 1998], 218).

[20] A. V. Kelly, *Education and Democracy: Principles and Practices* (London, 1995), 101.

[21] See, e.g., Antonio Gramsci, "The Intellectuals," *Selections from the Prison Notebooks*<http:/www.marxists.org/archive/gramsci/editions/spn/problems/intelle ctuals.htm> (International Publishers, 1971). Hegemony presupposes that account be taken of the interests and tendencies of the groups over which hegemony is to be exercised, and that a certain compromise equilibrium should be formed, based on compromise and consent.

[22] See *Power and Ideology in Education*, ed. J. Karabel and A. H. Halsey (New York, 1977), 493.

[23] See Amanda Coffey, *Education and Social Change* (Buckingham, 2001), 68–83.

[24] See Dewey in "Democracy and Education" (1916), where he argues that educational aims are often seen as being dependent on the needs of society in preparation for a remote future and disconnected from the experience of the child and can impact negatively on the intellectual freedom of the student (Dewey, 255).

[25] Huxley refers to 'Taylorism,' the principles of scientific management. Ross McKibbin claims that Britain was the only European economy where 'Taylorism' had been adopted on any significant scale. See *The Ideologies of Class: Social Relations in Britain 1880–1950* (Oxford, 1990), 158.

[26] In some areas elementary instruction in literacy and numeracy was an essential means of social mobility. Miners, John Hurt reports, were keen for their children to acquire literacy skills because that would enable them to work on the surface. Furthermore, railway companies only employed workers who could read and write. See *Elementary Schooling and the Working Classes, 1860–1918* (London, 1979), 32–33.

[27] Also, in Julia Wrigley's eyes, the diffusion of "useful knowledge" at mechanics' institutes brought little practical advantages to the workmen who attended lectures on science and technology. See "Technical Education and Industry in the Nineteenth Century," *The Decline of the British Economy*, ed. Bernard Elbaum and William Lazonick (Oxford, 1986), 164–165, 168.

[28] See Green, 288. Martin Wiener is arguably the most influential commentator who prescribes to the view of 'entrepreneurial failure,' and his thesis firmly puts education at the centre of his critique. See *English Culture and the Decline of the Industrial Spirit, 1850–1980* (Cambridge, 1981).

[29] *The Origins of Modern English Society, 1780–1880* (London, 1969), 258.

[30] The tradition of liberal education does not preclude certain vocational aspects, such as statesmanship or, on a smaller scale, the enlightened governance of the estate. See Christopher Winch, *Education, Work and Social Capital: Towards a New Conception of Vocational Education* (London, 2000), 35–36. Locke's educational theories are similarly based on the education of the gentleman as manager of his estate.

[31] See *The Cambridge Economic History of Modern Britain*, II: *Economic Maturity, 1860–1939*, ed. R. Floud and Paul Johnson (Cambridge, 2004). For an overview of revisionist literature against Wiener's thesis see David Edgerton's annotated bibliography *Science, Technology and the British Industrial 'Decline,' 1870–1970* (Cambridge, 1996).

[32] This in opposition to some critics who fear that the fashionable academicisation of scientific subjects today makes them useless in the workplace.

[33] Specialists and technocrats are dangerous barbarians whose education is based on passive acceptance of positivist knowledge, not on independent enquiry (*Science, Liberty, and Peace* [1946], *CE*, V, 256).

[34] Huxley's belief that literature can indeed be a valuable educational tool springs from his affinity with his ancestor Matthew Arnold. Arnold regarded poetry as a criticism of life and therefore a vital contribution to our understanding of reality (see "The Study of Poetry" [1880], *Democratic Education*, ed. R. H. Super [Ann Arbor, 1962], 171).

[35] See "Integrate Education" [1959], *The Human Situation: Lectures at Santa Barbara, 1959*, ed. Piero Ferrucci (London, 1978), 3–10.

[36] Nadezhda Krupskaya, Lenin's wife, was one of the founders of the Soviet system of public education. See also Lev Semenovich Vygotsky (1896–1934), Russia's eminent psychologist and pedagogue. Huxley comments on the fact that in Russia attempts were made to redress this over-specialisation by balancing intellectual and manual skills and to unite specialised and general knowledge (see "Thinking with One's Hands" [11 February 1933], *Aldous Huxley's Hearst Essays*, ed. James Sexton (New York, 1994), 339–340. Hereafter, *Hearst*. See also "Cultured People" [3 May 1934], *Hearst*, 266. But he fears that this old 'Hebrew' ideal of education is no longer adequate (see "Education" [1937], *CE*, IV, 282–284).

[37] The repository of perennial wisdom and knowledge has, by the 1930s, become a "literary torrent" of knowledge: "Culture is in danger of being buried under the avalanche of books" and the mind is in danger of being paralysed ("Too Many Books" [22 April 1932], *Hearst*, 88–89).

[38] Harvey J. Graff, *The Legacies of Literacy: Continuities and Contradictions in Western Culture and Society* (Bloomington, 1987), 264.

[39] See Hannah More's *Cheap Repository Tracts* [1795] or Maria Edgeworth's *Popular Tales* [1804]. Socialists preferred technical reading material which appealed to the autodidactic culture of the artisan elite; see Owen's *New Views of Society* [1813–1816] (see also Richardson, 214, 226).

[40] Cramped housing and inadequate lighting was not conducive to the disinterested study of literature or newspapers in the evenings. See David Vincent, *Literacy and Popular Culture: England 1750–1914* (Cambridge, 1989), 212–213. In the path of self-improvement also lay the unavailability of cheap books and the lack of leisure time to read them (see Richardson, 263).

[41] Jonathan Rose's examination of working-class culture claims, in the tradition of Hoggart, that workers were not merely passive consumers of popular literature. Their eclectic reading based on the random availability of books was in fact marked by a distinctive literary sophistication. See *The Intellectual Life of the British Working Classes* (New Haven, 2001), 375.

[42] See David F. Mitch, *The Rise of Popular Literacy in Victorian England: The Influence of Private Choice and Public Policy* (Philadelphia, 1992), 54, and Vincent, 217–223. Broadsheets catered for illiterate audiences as well as varying standards of literacy by including pictures and ballads as well as written reports. But broadsheets also featured reprints of canonical literature, heralding the cheap editions of classical libraries in later decades (see Vincent, 203–204, 208).

[43] Harvey J. Graff, "Literacy, Jobs, and Industrialization in the Nineteenth Century," *Literacy and Social Development in the West: A Reader*, ed. H. J. Graff (Cambridge, 1981), 332–333, 337, 245).

[44] Before 1914 not many workers had the money, time or energy to pursue recreational activities. A decrease in working hours, the introduction of half-day Saturdays and the provision of cheap railway travel facilitated a new leisure culture (see Gordon [1991], 142). After 1920 the average working week came down from 54 to 48 hours. See Andrew Davies, "Cinema and Broadcasting," *Twentieth-Century Britain: Economic, Social and Cultural Change*, ed. Paul Johnson (London and New York, 1994), 264.

[45] Documentaries and newsreels tapped into the didactic potential of film (see Gordon [1991], 148). In 1924 an Education Department was set up by the BBC under J. C. Stobart to examine the educational possibilities of broadcasting. In 1924 10% of British households held a licence, 48 % by 1933 and 71% by 1939 (see Davies, 267).

[46] In "The Outlook for American Culture: Some Reflections in a Machine Age" [ref.] Huxley describes how the educational contributions of machinery could lead to a rich universal culture. Huxley thinks that the spoken word of a sound recording has historically a greater impact than the written word and also reaches those who have no pleasure in reading or who cannot read (see "Censorship and Spoken Literature" [October 1955], *CE*, V, 323–324). His support for an oral culture grew out of his interest in mysticism, which was steeped in the oral tradition (see "Can We Be Well-Educated?" [December 1956], *CE*, VI, 205). In *Beyond the Mexique Bay* (1934) Huxley accounts for the crisis in popular culture by the migration of rural people to the cities, which meant that new paradigms of culture replaced oral and localised patterns and political propaganda and commercial advertising replaced traditional myths (see *CE*, III, 502, 578).

[47] Mark Turner, *The Literary Mind* (New York, 1996), 159.

[48] *Language and Reality: An Introduction to the Philosophy of Language*, ed. M. Devitt and Kim Sterelny (Cambridge, MA, 1999), 236.

[49] *Vedanta for Modern Man*, ed. Christopher Isherwood (London, 1952), 43.

[50] Norman Fairclough, *Language and Power* (3rd ed., London, 1991), 1.

[51] "Politics and the English Language" [1946], <http://www.george-orwell.org/Politics_and_the_English_Language/0.html>. See also George Steiner, "The Hollow Miracle," *Language and Silence: Essays 1958–1966* (2nd ed., London, 1985, repr. 1990), 117–132.

[52] See Mikhail Bakhtin, "Marxism and the Philosophy of Language" [1929], *The Bakhtin Reader: Selected Writings of Bakhtin, Medvedev, Voloshinov*, ed. Pam Morris (London, 1994), 35.

[53] See, e.g., T. S. Eliot, "Modern Education and the Classics [1932]," *Selected Essays* (London, 1999), 507–516.

[54] See "Drugs That Shape Men's Minds" [1958], *Moksha: Writings on Psychedelics and the Visionary Experience 1931–1963*, ed. Michael Horowitz and Cynthia Palmer (London, 1980), 152–153. Hereafter, *Moksha*.

[55] Child-centred approaches and the progressive writings on infant education by Maria Montessori, John Dewey and Friedrich Froebel were very influential at the beginning of the twentieth century, but the enthusiasm for it was not shared by the president of the Board of Education, Lord Eustace Percy, who was a strict opponent of Dewey and his followers (see Gordon, [1991], 59, 160). After World War II, disapproval of the progressive approach by the Black Paper critics (see Gordon, [1991], 85) and the preferred emphasis on vocational training meant that education, especially at secondary level, would rarely pick up on progressive theories of education, even though subsequent reports, like the Plowden Report in 1967, continued to pay lip service to a curriculum centred on activity and experience at primary level (see Gordon, [1991], 59).

[56] See Kevin Manton, *Socialism and Education in Britain, 1883–1902* (London, 2001), 146.

[57] He quotes the eminent educationalist I. L. Kandel, who established how western educational systems were historically indoctrinating, propagandising, nationalistic and discriminatory. See *The Universal Right to Education: Justification, Definition, and Guidelines* (Mahwah, NJ, and London, 2000), 17.

[58] Michael Sanderson, *Education and Economic Decline in Britain, 1870 to the 1990s* (Cambridge, 1999), 105. He is clearly not alone in his opinion that "we need to see the education of the people less as a kind of humane charity and social service and recognise it more as 'fundamental and essential for the promotion of economic growth'" (Sanderson, 107, quoting Szeter).

[59] Quoted in Fairclough, 236.

Rolf Lindemann

(University of Münster)

OVERPOPULATION AND SUSTAINABILITY—A CULTURAL GEOGRAPHER'S REAPPRAISAL OF HUXLEY'S PERTINENT CRITICAL ESSAYS[1]

Any author about to write an utopian novel would have to take regard to several restrictions likely to limit his or her artistic freedom. One would be that the action of the novel would have to take place in the future as the times when sailors could hope to discover utopian states on some remote island somewhere in the Atlantic are definitely gone in our age of spy satellites. Since geography can no longer be exploited for new utopias, authors have to resort to time. Novels must be set in 1984 when its author is writing in 1948 or somewhere seven centuries after Ford.

Another restraint which the early utopians as well as contemporary authors have had to struggle with and which is more to the point of this critique is the problem that the author has to devise an utopian society or an utopian state that has come to the end of its development, indeed a society where any development whatsoever is or has been made impossible. This state must be perfect and must have attained the utmost in either goodness or, preferably, badness. And it must be of global extension in these times when, as stated, all remote islands have been discovered. The only exception to this rule could be that there are three states, practically identical and interchangeable as devised by Orwell.

But constructing an absolutely stable society is not as easy as it might seem. For neither nature herself nor human nature are stable. Nature is characterised by climatic and geological catastrophes and revolutions. And one of the gravest threats to a stable society and a stable state is an inordinate development of its population. Mankind being what it is, humans tend to produce more children than are needed to maintain a stable population. The early utopians solved this predicament by shipping the superfluous population to some other island. But there are no virgin islands any longer. Therefore, any utopian state and its population must reach sustainability. Neither natural catastrophes even on the scale of global warming can be allowed to shake the robustness of its fundaments, nor disturbances from within, first and foremost uncontrolled population growth. Aldous Huxley found a—I think, ingenious—device to come out of this second predicament: he separated sex and child propagation. Only so many embryos were put into bottles and decanted as were needed to maintain a stable population.

Huxley was quite aware of the role a stable population played for the maintenance of his brave new world. He explicitly says so in *Brave New World Revisited* published twenty-six years after the novel itself.[2] But it is not only in the context of justifying his design of his *Brave New World* that he takes up the question of how population development and what he calls overpopulation will affect mankind and its future constitution and prospects. He repeatedly gives his opinion on these matters, often combined with the related subjects of landscape degradation and what we today call sustainability. Huxley leaves the world of fiction and enters that of Cultural Geography and Population Studies. Thus it is not so much Huxley the artist this article is focussed on but Huxley the thinker and critic.

Welcoming Huxley within the realms of Cultural Geography, one is *ex officio* obliged to analyse and evaluate three key categories of his thinking: population development, overpopulation, and the consequences of overpopulation.

1. Population Development

> At the rate of increase prevailing between the birth of Christ and the death of Queen Elizabeth I, it took sixteen centuries for the population of the earth to double. At the present rate it will double in less than half a century. And this fantastically rapid doubling of our numbers will be taking place on a planet whose most desirable and productive areas are already densely populated, whose soils are being eroded by the frantic efforts of bad farmers to raise more food, and whose easily available mineral capital is being squandered with the reckless extravagance of a drunken sailor getting rid of his accumulated pay. (*BNWR*, 17)

Huxley here and elsewhere joins the ranks of a multitude of more or less popular authors painting a very black picture of our common future indeed. Expressions and book titles like "the population bomb,"[3] "the population explosion"[4] and other more or less martial similes immediately come to mind. Typical for this type of quasi-scientific literature is a German book with the best-selling title of—literally translated into English—'Standing Room for Billions?'[5]

Some of these prophets of impending absolute doom[6] earned quite a lot of money with their 'prophecies.' Huxley—I contend—ought to have known better. Of course the diminishing phases between the doubling of the world's population are true. Of course world population is—or was in Huxley's time—growing at an accelerating pace. But to all serious demographers it was quite obvious that this extreme growth was part of what was called 'demographic transition' and that the growth rates would go down again as indeed they have. Human growth rates have fallen from 2.1 % in the 1960s to 1.3 % (1995–2000). Somewhere around 2050 these rates will come to a standstill—world population will then be around 9.3 billion—and then slowly become negative. Today demographers and population geographers are no longer so much interested in world population growth, it is the aging of world population that is on the agenda now. While this is already a growing problem in the industrialized countries today it will be an unbearable burden to the developing countries in the future, which will hardly have any money to spare for old-age institutions.

The concept of 'demographic transition' has been used as an elementary model in every text-book on population geography over the last sixty years. The model relates birth rates and mortality rates of a country to each other and views their progress through history. Diagram 1 (see following page) shows the population transitions for England/Wales and Sweden together with an idealized version of the model. These two countries are usually taken to document the transition because both have excellent historical statistics and both have not had their boundaries changed since the eighteenth century. Germany would have been an absolutely inappropriate example here. Besides, both countries had practically no immigration. This criterion rules out the United States, for instance.

Both nations show very high birth and death rates during the first phase, England/Wales until about 1740, Sweden until about 1820. It is characteristic for this first period that both rates fluctuate very much. The extreme peak of the mortality rate in Sweden in 1812 is the outcome of the Napoleonic wars; not of the war itself, of course, but of the accompanying famine and epidemics. Then the death rate drops abruptly leaving the nativity rate high in the air. We are in phase 2 now, characterized by growing population numbers. At about 1870 the birth rate begins to descend as well in both countries, initializing phase 3, which is still a phase of rapidly growing populations as both rates are parallel but far apart. Then in phase 4 the death rate levels out so that the still falling birth rate can come nearer. At about 1940 both rates are parallel again with only a small distance between them (phase 5). This fifth phase is comparable to the long period before demographic transition, resulting in only very limited population growth, being blown up, however, by the baby boom after World War II and by immigration.

Some researchers would add a sixth phase with the nativity rate falling below the mortality rate, resulting in declining population figures. Most of the European nations are in this phase now, the developing countries will follow.

It took England about two centuries and Sweden about 140 years to proceed through the demographic transition. If we take the well-documented case of Mauritius, a small island southeast of Madagascar in the Indian Ocean, which is usually grouped with the so-called developing nations, we find that this country entered into phase 2 very late, at around 1950, but passed through the whole transition in about one generation. What took seven generations in England and four in Sweden Mauritius achieved in one.

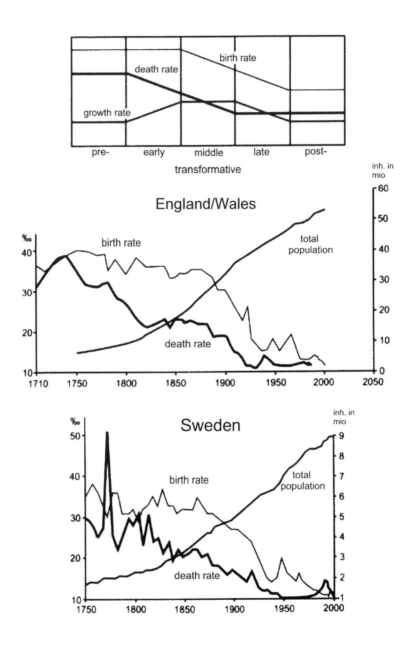

Diagram 1: The concept of demographic transition: idealized model (above) and historical processes in England/Wales and Sweden. (Source: Jürgen Bähr, *Bevölkerungsgeographie* [Stuttgart, 2004], 220; modified.)

There are two rules which can be set up after having followed the demographic transition in the majority of nations in the world:

1. All nations follow this pattern.[7]
2. The later a nation begins the transition the more rapidly it will pass through it.

A word of caution must be added regarding the character of the model. Since it was included into the textbooks of population geography, there has been a heated debate on the question whether it is a true and scientific model or not. Without going into details, it has to be admitted that it is 'only' descriptive and not prescriptive as a true model should be and that it provides no reasons at all, neither for the onset of the different phases nor for the transition itself.

Be that as it may, the 'model' gives an explanation for the extraordinary growth rates noticed by Huxley and others. It was the time when the big nations like China, India, Indonesia, Brazil and others entered phase 2. Today there are only a few countries that show a growth rate of more than 3 % but regarding their momentum they are of rather low significance (Mauretania, Angola, Tchad). But could Huxley have known that these growth rates were transient as indeed they have proved to be? In my opinion—but I am just a cultural geographer and no professional Huxleyite—he is very likely to have known.

The concept of the model was developed back in the 1930s, textbooks being a bit controversial and undecided about who really used the term and the model first. But it was propagated by Frank W. Notestein, who was an eminent and influential American demographer at the end of World War II and immediately afterwards and as such had enormous influence within the arising United Nations, which very early took up global population questions as part of their investigation and publication agenda. Some of the campaigns of the UN during their first decades can be regarded as attempts to accelerate the passage of a country through the demographic transition by applying measures to bring down both death and birth rates. As Huxley was very interested in both the United Nations and in population problems, I think it highly unlikely that the fundamental model of transition should have escaped his notice. As early as 1934 he wrote:

> In most countries the rate of increase has recently declined; so much
> so, that it looks as though population would soon become stable, or
> would even diminish.[8]

The time lag in population increase between Europe and the developing countries is mentioned in his essay "The Double Crisis" (1950),[9] and Huxley notes the "startling suddenness" of the decrease of the death rate in 1958 (*BNWR*, 16) and again in 1959 (*HS*, 45). In "The Double Crisis" he also states that the "over-all birth-rate has sharply declined" in Western Europe and North America ("DC," 231) and even observes:

> World population is bound to rise to at least three billions before it
> starts to decline. ("DC," 247)

A possible reason why Huxley did not mention the demographic transition
and its consequences is that it would have endangered his argumentation
about overpopulation inevitably leading to dictatorship and to a brave new
world.

2. Overpopulation

> For overpopulation is not compatible with freedom. ("DC," 235)

> Overpopulation leads to economic insecurity and social unrest.
> Unrest and insecurity lead to more control by central governments
> and an increase of their power. [...] the probability of over-
> population leading through unrest to dictatorship becomes a virtual
> certainty. It is a pretty safe bet that, twenty years from now, all the
> world's overpopulated and underdeveloped countries will be under
> some form of totalitarian rule—probably by the Communist party.
> (*BNWR*, 21-22)

There seldom was a prophecy that was so completely wrong. It is not only
unfair, however, but it is utterly futile to sneer about Huxley's blunder in
prophesying the political future. There were quite a few others that were
wrong here. And it is much more rewarding to analyse Huxley's assumed
close connection between population pressure and political order.

Huxley never exactly defines what he means by "overpopulation." The
nearest approach to a definition is "an unfavourable relationship between
numbers and resources" ("DC," 235). This is of course a rather elastic
definition which in a way goes back to Thomas Malthus, who in 1798
postulated that human numbers grow in a geometrical way while resources
increase only arithmetically. Sooner or later these divergent developments
would lead to catastrophies ("negative checks," according to Malthus).[10] In
his conviction that, given the uncontrolled propagation of mankind,
population pressure is inevitable, and that this population pressure will
unavoidably lead into dictatorship and a brave new world Aldous Huxley
must be classified as a Neo-Malthusian.

What do demography and population geography think about Malthus
today? The most obvious argument is, of course, that if Malthus had been
right then most of us would not be here. The race between the stork and the
plough was not as hopeless as it seemed to be to Malthus himself and to his
many followers. Of course we have hunger and malnutrition in the world of
today but it is at least contestable whether we have more hunger and worse
malnutrition today if we see them in relation to 1798. What Malthus and his
disciples did not take into account is the huge progress mankind has made by
inventions and improvements in technology, plant and animal genetics,

fertilisation and other devices, unimaginable in those times. While Malthus saw the outer limits of agricultural land use (oecumene) which have not been extended so much since his life-time, he overlooked the enormous potential which lay and still lies in increasing the intensity of agriculture.

This of course touches the concept of the carrying capacity of the earth. Trying to figure out how many people could live on earth was a favourite subject—and playground—of many geographers in the 1930s. The numbers which they so assiduously calculated have all by far been surpassed by the world population of today. Theirs was the same mistake that Malthus made: they underestimated the potentials which lie in intensifying food production.

To return to Huxley: he feared that overpopulated regions and states would attack their neighbours, forcing them to militarise their own state, to abandon freedom and democracy and to turn into dictatorships. Thus, Huxley argues, demographic crises underlie most political crises. That is what he calls the double crisis. To quote him:

> So long as the relationship between population and natural resources remains as hopelessly unfavourable as it now is [...] in the greater part of Europe, above all in a defeated Germany, it will be for all practical purposes impossible for democratic institutions to take root and develop. ("DC," 236)

Huxley was wrong here again. True, there was bitter hunger in Germany after the war but democracy grew nevertheless. This shows, and examples could be multiplied, that there is no such intimate connection between overpopulation and the growth of totalitarianism.

Huxley's main mistake appears to be that he uses deterministic argumentations, which may have some legitimacy in natural sciences, also in the sphere of human society, where they simply are not applicable. This equally applies to the last point I will analyse: Huxley's thoughts about the consequences of overpopulation.

3. The Consequences of Overpopulation

While Aldous Huxley's arguments regarding overpopulation are rather threadbare, he walks on very thin ice indeed when he considers the consequences of overpopulation.

Among the several of consequences that Huxley foresees, there is the following:

> Within any nation whose birth-rate is declining, there is a tendency for the decline to be most rapid among the most accomplished and gifted members of the population, least rapid among those whose hereditary and educational endowment is the lowest. [...] The future population of Western Europe and North America will be constituted, in the main, by the descendants of the least intelligent persons now living in those areas. [...] Differential birth-rates

within any national community lead [...] to a qualitative deteriorate-
ion of the population as a whole. ("DC," 232–233)

He also quotes "an eminent English authority, Sir Cyril Burt" ("DC," 232),
who maintains that the average intelligence of the British population will
decline by five IQ points until the end of the twentieth century. Are Britons on
their way to become Epsilons? This is how Huxley had already seen it in the
1930s:

> *If conditions remain what they are now, and if the present tendency*
> *continues unchecked, we may look forward in a century or two to a*
> *time when a quarter of the population of these islands will consist of*
> *half-wits. What a curiously squalid and humiliating conclusion to*
> *English history!* ("WHP," 150; Huxley's italics)

Of course nobody will deny the possibility of a deterioration of the average
intelligence within a population. But Huxley is unique in ascribing this—if it
really occurs—to differing rates of birth-rate decline between the social strata
of a population. If one thinks along these lines there would be the inevitable
conclusion that those nations which started early with their demographic
transition would today show an average IQ far below those countries which
are still in the earlier phases. I think it is sufficient to point out that today the
overwhelming majority of Nobel Prize Awards goes to the countries of the
Western World.

To return to the British on their way down the ranking scale of
intelligence, I fear that, in quoting Sir Cyril Burt, Aldous Huxley fell victim to
a very dubious witness:

> After Burt's death [in 1971], striking anomalies in some of his test
> data led some scientists to reexamine his statistical methods. They
> concluded that Burt manipulated and probably falsified those IQ-test
> results that most convincingly supported his theories on transmitted
> intelligence and social class [...], many accepted that he fabricated
> some data.[11]

Equally astounding is Huxley's further contention:

> In countries where the birth-rate is sharply declining, there has been,
> during the last forty years, a marked increase in the incidence of
> neurosis and even of insanity. ("DC," 248)

There is no evidence to support this argument neither does Aldous Huxley
give any.

To sum up: Huxley tends to apply quasi-natural laws, mostly derived from
biology, to society and its development.[12] This deterministic way of thinking
together with its derivation from biology was rampant within geopolitics, a
'science' within geographical thinking during the 1930s. It was most
pronounced in Germany, where it had evil consequences, but existed in other
countries as well. It is still not quite dead as books like Huntington's *The*

Clash of Civilizations show. Modern Geography, especially Political Geography, strives to expose and deconstruct these arguments.

Aldous Huxley was a child of his time. He obviously adopted some of the short-sighted arguments and short-cuts from the thinking of the twenties and thirties and used them in his essays in order to make his *Brave New World* more real, more imminent, and more dangerous. But *Brave New World* is not the real world. For his construction of a fictional world I certainly admire Aldous Huxley, but I have my doubts as to his abilities to explain the real world.

---

[1] Revised version of a lecture at the Third International Aldous Huxley Symposium, Riga, 25–28 July 2004. I would like to thank the Deutsche Forschungsgemeinschaft for a grant towards the costs of my journey to Riga.

[2] See Aldous Huxley, "Overpopulation," *Brave New World Revisited* (London, 1958), 9–23. Hereafter, *BNWR*.

[3] Best known is Paul R. Ehrlich, *The Population Bomb* (London, 1971).

[4] One of several examples: Richard M. Fagley, *The Population Explosion and Christian Responsibility* (New York, 1960).

[5] Heinrich von Loesch, *Stehplatz für Milliarden?* (Stuttgart, 1974).

[6] It is interesting to note that Huxley himself used "The Population Explosion" as title of one of his Santa Barbara lectures in 1959. See Aldous Huxley, *The Human Situation*, ed. Piero Ferrucci (London, 1978), 42–58. Hereafter, *HS*.

[7] See George J. Stolnitz, "The Demographic Transition: from High to Low Birth Rates and Death Rates" [1964], in: *Population Geography: A Reader*, ed. George J. Demko et al. (New York, 1970), 71: "Demographic transitions rank among the most sweeping and best-documented historical trends of modern times."

[8] Aldous Huxley, "What is Happening to Our Population?" [hereafter, "WHP"], *Nash's Pall Mall Magazine*, xciii (April 1934), reprinted in: *The Hidden Huxley: Contempt and Compassion for the Masses 1920–36*, ed. David Bradshaw (London and Boston, 1994), 155.

[9] See Aldous Huxley, "The Double Crisis," *Themes and Variations* (London, 1950), 231–232. Hereafter, "DC."

[10] See Thomas R. Malthus, *An Essay on the Principle of Population, as it Affects the Future Improvement of Society, with Remarks on the Speculations of Mr. Godwin, M. Condorcet, and Other Writers* (London, 1798).

[11] *The New Encyclopædia Britannica*, II (2003), 667.

[12] In 1959 Huxley deplored that political leaders "just don't think in biological terms" (*HS*, 53) and painted the picture of an American president versed in practical biology. Evidently, the same short-cut between biology and population problems that I have analysed in this essay can be found in Huxley's political thinking (see also *HS*, 48).

Irina Golovacheva

(State University of St Petersburg)

THEORIES OF THE MIND AND PSYCHOTHERAPY
IN THE WORKS OF ALDOUS HUXLEY

> There is intelligence in relation to the not-self and there is
> intelligence in relation to the self. The completely intelligent person
> is intelligent both in regard to himself and to the outer world. [...] If
> one is to deal intelligently with oneself one must be aware of one's
> real motives, of the secret sources of one's thoughts, feelings, and
> actions, of the nature of one's sentiments, impulses and sensations
> [...] No self can go beyond the limits of selfhood, either morally [...]
> or mystically [...], unless it is fully aware of what it is, and why it is
> what it is. Self-transcendence is through self-consciousness.[1]

This argument presented in Huxley's *Ends and Means* (1937) places the
question of the role of psychological studies in Huxley's art and thinking
among the most important ones. It invites Huxley scholars to analyse his
definitions and interpretations of concepts such as personality, mind,
consciousness, and the self because they are fundamental to all further
theorizing. It also opens a discussion of his views of psychology as a science
and its medical, moral, religious, political, educational and personal
implications.

Most Huxley critics assume that his views of the mind, psyche, and
consciousness were predominantly shaped by Eastern psychology. Indeed, it
was evident in the mid-1950s—not without the influence of Eastern thought—
that the salvation of the human race might be achieved through the salvation
of personalities. Eastern psychology earned more and more respect in
Huxley's lifetime, due not only to his own writings and those of his friends—
Gerald Heard and Christopher Isherwood among them—but also to the
writings of psychologists like C. G. Jung, Timothy Leary, Gordon Allport,
and Alan Watts. To some extent an acquaintance with the East was for most
of them the symbolic expression of the connection that they were trying to
establish with the strange elements in the Western mind. There is no doubt,
however, that besides his profound knowledge of Eastern wisdom Huxley was
also an expert in Western psychology.

Eastern psychology stresses that the central problem of most mental
disorders and of general unhappiness lies in a state of anxiety caused by
excessive agitation and worry. Huxley's approach to the treatment of anxiety
is twofold. The first instrumental feature of the healing process is a
fundamental insight that can be hoped for as an instantaneous revelation but
is, in most cases, achieved through the cultivation of a clear picture of human

nature and its potentialities, and/or through special training. The second remedy for anxiety is the state of no-mind in Zen and Taoism.[2]

Understanding the difficulties of the Eastern way for an average person of the Western mind, Huxley claimed that before seeking self-transcendence or collective happiness one should take the trouble to become a *person*, a physically and mentally healthy, fully conscious and purposeful human being. In this frame of thinking cure and prevention became central metaphors in his numerous books, essays and prefaces exploring what he called the "sixty-four-billion-dollar question"[3] of mental health. This question reveals the writer's concern about the general psychological regression he noticed, i.e., the vast increase in neuroses accompanying technological progress. Huxley hoped that psychology, the science exploring the connection between psyche, *soma* and brain dynamics, would be of great practical value to medicine, education and sociology. The most important field of research was, in his view, psychosomatic studies. He found it immensely more useful than mere abstract speculation about tensions and stresses.

How did Huxley's keen interest in psychological and medical issues develop in the 1950s? What led him to take part in numerous professional conferences as well as in sometimes dangerous experiments involving hypnosis, healing currents and psycho-pharmacological substances? Let us put together a chronology with a special focus on our present topic.

As a matter of fact, as early as in the 1930s Huxley had spoken of the necessity of a World Psychological Conference, considering it the only realistic means to the end of solving the problems of nationalism and war.[4] By the early 1950s he had become an active participant in a variety of projects and events related to psychology and medicine. In 1952 he and Alan Watts discussed and actually started writing a project aimed at research into the deeper layers of the mind (that is, deeper than personal). Huxley even suggested his own reading list—a fact revealing the scope of his knowledge of the field. The undertaking was to be part of a bigger educational project—incorporating, among other things, the study of psychotherapeutic techniques—with which they were to approach the Ford Foundation. Huxley commented on the project in two letters to Watts, specifying their mutual interest in the "'molar' phenomena of the human organism as a whole,"[5] in hypnosis, progressive relaxation, mescaline therapy, as well as in contemporary studies in psychosomatic medicine with their insistence on the personal ego's capacity for interfering with the beneficent action of the automatic not-self (see *Letters*, 656–658).

In late 1953 he accepted an invitation to Mills College and lectured on the training of the psycho-physical instrument as the basis of education. Referring to numerous books, he explained methods of gaining control of the secondary nervous system, and pointed out exercises that help coordinate "the conscious self and the various non-selves, personal subconscious, entelechy, collective subconscious, superconscious and Atman-Brahman" (*Letters*, 695).

1953 turned out to be a very special year for Huxley. It was then that he first met Dr Humphry Osmond and took part in pharmacological experiments tackling medical, religious and artistic issues. Osmond even sent him his paper "Inspiration and Method in Schizophrenic Research" for editing (see *Letters*, 687), which was an unmistakable sign of his recognition of Huxley's proficiency in the field.

In September 1954 Huxley discussed the idea of a psychiatric text book with Osmond, emphasizing that it had always been his dream to do something like that for students or a professional audience (see *Letters*, 711). In April he had attended a parapsychological conference at St Paul de Vence (see *Letters*, 17, 704); thirteen months later, in May 1955, Huxley participated in the meeting of the American Psychiatrists' Association at Atlantic City, where he communicated on professional issues with Karl Menninger, the leader of American psychiatry, and Abram Hoffer, one of the originators of the psychopharmacological project (see *Letters*, 742–743). The following month he went to a conference on "Unorthodox Healing" and attended discussions of various untraditional healing methods:

> The discussion of the hypothetical force involved in healing by laying on of hands, as opposed to 'faith healing', suggestive healing, healing at a distance, healing by prayer etc., was most interesting. Some recent evidence tending to confirm von Reichenbach's hypotheses (revived in our days by Dr Wilhelm Reich) was mentioned. (*Letters*, 749–750)[6]

In the above letter Huxley advocates hypnosis produced by psychological means as well as Eeman's "relaxing circuit," both of which he successfully practised himself. In September 1955 he wrote a letter to Mrs Barry Stevens, discussing what he called physiological intelligence or *entelechy*, the deeper self and the possibilities of ridding it of the harmful obstructions which the conscious, superficial ego puts in its way. He mentions two methods, that of recalling buried material (abreaction) and the induction of physical disturbances like sobbing, shaking, twitching that would finally loosen the visceral and muscular knots resulting from psychological knots (see *Letters*, 765–766).

In October 1956 Huxley attended a conference on "Meprobamate and Other Agents Used in Mental Disturbances" at the New York Academy of Sciences, where he met Dr Berger, the inventor of Miltown, and Dr James Miller of Ann Arbor, the director of an interdisciplinary project concerning human behaviour (see *Letters*, 810). In November he travelled to St Louis for a discussion—and TV interview—about "The Actualization of Human Potentialities" (see *Letters*, 812).

In 1956 Huxley also corresponded with Dr Osmond about the urgent necessity to apply the brand-new psycho-pharmaco-spiritual approach to both sick and healthy people. It was his strong belief at the time that the approach suggested by Osmond and Hoffer was transcendental, that it was operationally verified and pragmatically confirmed as it worked both in the field of therapy and in that of normal behaviour (see *Letters*, 813–814). Moreover, he hoped that the method would not only normalize at least 50 per cent of neurotics but that it would also serve as a contrast to ineffective psychoanalysis.

At the end of that year Huxley submitted the text of his article on psychoanalysis, "The Oddest Science," to *Esquire*. It appeared in March 1957. He had had to do extensive reading for the essay (see *Letters*, 814). In 1957 he contributed to a discussion of the management, structure and architecture of mental asylums. He was terrified by the hair-raising, harmful atmosphere of those hospitals induced by big wards and endless corridors that looked like the nightmarish tunnels described in Poe's "The Fall of the House of Usher" (see *Letters*, 846). Huxley remained interested in the subject until his last days.

In the same year he wrote to his brother Julian that he had been asked to write a series of articles on methods of altering thoughts and behaviour by by-passing the conscious and rational self and working on human weaknesses and the psycho-physical machine from which the individual personality develops and by which it is conditioned. The methods included the use of drugs, sleep-teaching, hypnosis, subliminal projection, etc. The series was published as a supplement to the paper *Newsday* and then as his book *Brave New World Revisited (*see *Letters,* 837).

In August 1958 Huxley was interviewed on thought control by Mike Wallace (ABC channel). The text appeared in *The Listener* in September.[7] Five months later he participated in a conference on the pharmacological approach to the study of the mind in San Francisco. On 26 January 1959 he gave his talk "The Final Revolution" at the conference dinner meeting.[8] In the fall of 1959 his second lecture course at the University of California at Santa Barbara took place. This time he concentrated more intensely on psycho-logical issues. His lectures "The Problem of Human Nature," "The Ego," "The Unconscious," and "Latent Human Potentialities" reveal his profound and advanced knowledge of psychological theories.[9]

In March 1960 Huxley began his six-week tenure at the "Holy of Holies of Psycho-Analysis" (*Letters*, 888), the Menninger Foundation in Topeka, Kansas. In the fall of that year he took part in the Topeka conference that tackled the problems of anxiety. It was the sixth conference of that type. This time there was a gathering of psychiatrists and clergymen. The objective was to explore the twofold nature of anxiety, which was regarded as a curse and a blessing at the same time.[10]

In June 1960 he participated in the Tecate Symposium on Human Potentialities (see *Letters*, 892), where he gave a talk emphasizing the necessity to shift our attention from the insoluble problems caused by national power to the difficult but soluble problem of individual development. In September he went to Dartmouth College to join the "Convocation on the Great Issues of Conscience in Modern Medicine" (see *Letters*, 893, 895). It was the first conference on bioethics in history. Among others, it hosted geneticists and medical doctors. The hottest topics were genetics and eugenics. Some scientists declared that the advances in medicine had created the most difficult problems of medical ethics, like that of prolonging life. Geneticists worried that the gene pool was becoming polluted because the early deaths of people with serious abnormalities were now preventable. Huxley was disappointed by the fact that the discussion centered upon the problems of physical health and the prolongation of life instead of turning to the topics of mental health and brainwashing.

In a letter to Julian written in December of that year, Huxley mentioned his plans to attend another conference on the control of the mind in San Francisco. The conference was to be preceded by a brief trip to New York, where the NBC wanted him to prepare the way for broadcasting the event. From San Francisco he was to go to Oregon to meet Maxwell Jones, pioneer of the Open Ward system in English mental hospitals, who was introducing his methods at the State Hospital at Salem at that time (see *Letters*, 901).

In August 1961 Huxley attended the Copenhagen Congress on Applied Psychology, where he read an address on visionary experience; on 22 August he went to Zurich to meet Albert Hofmann, the discoverer of LSD (see *Letters*, 919). In September he spent a night at Colgate University having a long talk with George Estabrooks, professor of psychology at Colgate University and an expert on hypnotism.[11] After their discussion he decided to take part in the Symposium on Hypnotism at Colgate University in April 1962 (see *Letters*, 919-920).

If one looks at his list of the books he needed most after his house, including the library, had burned down in May 1961, one will find there Alexander's *The History of Psychiatry*, Bromberg's *The Mind of Man*, and Jacobi's *Psychological Reflections*, which is actually an anthology of all the writings of C. G. Jung.[12]

Huxley's last letter to Humphry Osmond (at least the last in Grover Smith's edition) had as its subject their common project which was to be a collection of papers on human resources. In this letter he suggested that Osmond should devote a "chapter [...] to the best emotional contexts in which the learning of new ways to use the mind should be placed" (*Letters*, 963).

And finally, Huxley's last book, *Literature and Science* (1963), discusses psychology among other subjects. So the questions remain: Why did he indulge so much in scientific and scholarly activity? How precise or how subjective was his assessment of psychological concepts and schools? How original were his views of the psyche? To find answers one should look into his primary and secondary sources.

As for the first of these questions, quite obviously there were personal, biographical reasons for Huxley's curiosity in this field. Laura Huxley believes that psychotherapy and therapy in general interested him because of his family history.[13] He was seriously dissociated from a great deal of the real world. His partial—at times total—blindness, the loss of his mother when he was still very young, his brother's suicide—all isolated him. Indeed, this devastating experience demonstrated the extent to which life may depend on the kind and the quality of treatment one can get.

Other explanations of his psychological and medical interests can be found in numerous memoirs of his friends and relatives. To give a few examples, Peggy Kiskadden, in her discussion of the reasons for Huxley being a scientist manqué and specifically for his interest in medicine and psychology, said that it was his desire to better the human condition. As for the infatuation with psycho-pharmacology, in her view, "it was always the subconscious thing that he wanted and that's what would come out under the drugs."[14] Juliette Huxley also thought that "he was always interested—tremendously interested—in what could *improve* human appreciation, health, or almost anything" (HM 56882, 8).

Ellen Hovde said that "he was a little disconnected with his body. [...] I think it was a sort of anguish for him. If you have to take a serious drug in order to cry, you're in trouble in terms of your body. I think that a lot of time he was" (HM 56897, 36). Claire White also thought that "Aldous felt imprisoned by his brain" (HM 56897, 39). Christopher Isherwood remembered Aldous as an "exceptionally sensitive human instrument":

> His health was correspondingly variable. One week he would look fresh and healthy and even robust; the next, wan, shattered, almost spectral. He suffered from all kinds of ailments; but they seemed to interest him quite as much as they distressed him. He would talk about them at length, objectively and without complaining. ... Both he and Maria were great connoisseurs of doctors; it sometimes seemed to their friends that they were prepared to consult absolutely anyone, at least once, in a spirit of disinterested experimentation.[15]

Laura, who became a successful practising psychotherapist in the mid-1950s, was the strongest personal influence that fortified Huxley's preoccupation with psychology. She administered a few LSD sessions to her husband, combining them with techniques of dianetics to bring out his childhood memories.

The story of her becoming a psychotherapist is very unusual. At the time when her close friend Virginia Pfeiffer was very seriously ill (Laura was still single then), Virginia went to see her sister, Pauline Hemingway, in Florida. In order to entertain Laura, Virginia sent her L. Ron Hubbard's *Dianetics: The*

Modern Science of Mental Health (1950). Laura liked the book and decided to employ the ideas. Then Hubbard came to lecture in Los Angeles. She became still more enthusiastic and soon began to write her "Recipes for Living and Loving." She published the book ten years later under the title *You Are Not the Target*. It immediately became a bestseller. Aldous had written a foreword to the book, confessing that following those recipes he was forced to practise what, as "a theorist of human nature," he always preached—to attack the many-faceted life-problems of man as a multiple amphibian simultaneously by different techniques. Moreover, he emphasized his literary debt, pointing out that he borrowed some of Laura's ideas for *Island*:

> Some of her recipes (for example, those for the Transformation of Energy) have found their way, almost unmodified into my phantasy. Others have been changed and developed to suit the needs of my imaginary society and to fit into its culture.[16]

Laura never got any special training. Yet she was bold and inventive in adopting and adapting theories and practices. The thing that was missing, as she felt, in dianetics, was body work. She added special body-mind practice in order to work out what she called "precious negative energy" (L.H., interview) through activities of the body such as weeping, screaming, dancing, exercising, etc. Aldous also believed that such physical disturbances could be very beneficial to the process of liberation because they loosened many knots, which are the obstacles that the conscious superficial ego puts in the way of the deeper self. As he stressed in one of his letters, Laura obtained "remarkable results" (*Letters,* 881) in psychotherapy mostly due to her intuitive knowledge of what to do at any given moment, what technique to use in each successive phase of the patient's mood and feeling. Aldous would often supply Laura with ideas for her therapy sessions and books.

Apart from personal reasons for this interest in psychology, there certainly was the general curiosity of a scientist manqué in Huxley that made his mind play over the vast and controversial ground of psychological and physiological concepts. The picture of the human mind that he offered was the synthesis of contemporaneous psychological theories and philosophical observations of such non-psychologists as Gerald Heard, Bertrand Russell, Julian Huxley and Joseph Krutch. Some of his ideas echoed almost literally somebody else's argumentation. In some cases Huxley exhibited much greater freedom, mixing points of view in the melting pot of his imagination.

His radical views of Freudism have been analysed by Peter Firchow, Jerome Meckier, Robert Baker, and James Hull.[17] Still I believe the discussion of this issue can and should be continued.

Huxley's early—and in some ways fallacious—criticism of Freud resembled that of quite a few men of letters. His overwhelming fear of control caused his contempt for psychoanalytic (as well as behaviourist) therapies since, in his view, all such manipulations were potentially dehumanizing.

Even in a therapeutic sense Freudian technique employed reductive
procedures inhibiting the healing process because it concentrated on the roots
of the problem, that is, on the past instead of the present or the future. Huxley,
though accepting Freudian theory regarding the motion of psychic energy and
the division of the psyche into what is conscious and what is not, was
dissatisfied by the partiality and the inevitable incompleteness inherent in all
psychoanalytical theories:

> "The only unconscious they ever pay attention to is the negative
> unconscious, the garbage that people have tried to get rid of by
> burying it in the basement. Not a single word about the positive
> unconscious. [...] And then look at their idea of what's normal! [...]
> A normal human being is one who can have an orgasm and is
> adjusted to his society. [...] And then what about the society you are
> supposed to be adjusted to? Is it a mad society or a sane one? And
> even if it's pretty sane, is it right that anybody should be *completely*
> adjusted to it?"[18]

However, Huxley—among many others—tended to forget (or probably did
not know) that Freud's intention was to develop an affirmative conception of
the psyche by adding something to his own notion of the predominantly
negative destructive and self-destructive unconscious that has to be controlled
by repressive civilization. In *The Future of an Illusion* (1927) and particularly
in *Civilization and Its Discontents* (1930) Freud envisions culture as a system
of institutions that protect man against nature and organize social order. Yet,
Civilization and Its Discontents also contains warnings against the violation of
freedom and of the individual for the sake of social order. The final goal of
human activity, according to Freud, is to reach an expedient balance between
individual desires and the demands of the masses. He offers the ambivalent
scheme of the "pleasure-principle" versus the "reality-principle" and advances
a project for attaining the feeling of wholeness, "the oceanic feeling," which
he considers to be initial and fundamental for the psyche.[19]

Certainly Freud was by no means a naive poet of utopia. On the contrary,
he kept reminding the reader that many systems of civilization had become
neurotic under the pressure of the civilizing trends. The severity of the
individual super-ego as well as of the communal super-ego, inflicting the
sense of guilt, is to be weakened in order to moderate their demands. He
thought that the price of progress in civilization—the forfeiture of happiness
—was perhaps too high. Freud presented a list of methods to help avert
suffering, in ways other than becoming a neurotic. It is quite a bizarre mixture
of tips, including voluntary isolation, intoxication, practising yoga,
displacements of libido through art, research, social work, etc. What is most
important—Freud himself thought that the solution can be found in a new "art
of living," in a libidinal approach to life, rather than in the above-listed
displacements of libido. But this, he states, can be practised only individu-

ally—through "talking cure," i.e., by applying theoretical and practical discoveries of psychoanalysis and thus establishing libidinal (not only sexual) relations in society.

By the early 1950s Huxley attained a more moderate view of psychoanalysis by incorporating more advanced conceptions into it. On the whole, no matter how strongly he was dissatisfied by Freudian psychologists who paid more attention "Original Sin" than to "'Original Virtue,'" (*Letters*, 635), he never rejected the basic concept of the unconscious:

> The hypothesis of unconscious mental activity is valid and of great practical importance. Without it, we should be compelled to fall back on primitive notions of supernatural intervention. With it, we can offer partial explanations of some kinds of normal behavior and can help some of the victims of the milder forms of mental illness to get rid of their symptoms.[20]

His attitude to traditional psychoanalysis remained ambiguous. On the one hand, his dislike is explicit in his letters and non-fiction. On the other hand, in his prose—for example in *The Genius and the Goddess*—he consistently used psychoanalytic ideas. It cannot be incidental that Freudian concepts such as the Oedipus complex, the theory of instincts, infantile sexuality, and the like were fictionalized in quite a few of Huxley's texts, *Island* among them. The major change that he made in the original model of the unconscious was expressed in Sheldonian terms:

> On the deepest level our unconscious equals our constitution: we are determined by what we physically and temperamentally are. [...] It is quite pointless to talk about the unconscious unless we see it rooted in the constitutional differences which make us the individuals we are. (*HS*, 151)

Huxley's criticism of the deficiencies of Freudism revealed his approval of certain schools of psychotherapy that modified Freud's theories. Neo-Freudians, such as Alfred Adler and Otto Rank, offered a substantial revision of the original. Their ideas were motivated by a desire to respond to the defeat of rationalism, by their general quest for a solution to the problem of the human situation, and by the psychological need to reestablish the link between the individual and the creative source of life. Huxley's theory of self-transcendence is based not only on his religious beliefs but, among other things, on Adler's and Rank's standpoints. In *Understanding Human Nature* (1927) Adler wrote:

> The soul, indeed, seems to consist chiefly of a force moving towards a goal, and Individual Psychology considers all the manifestations of the human spirit as though they were directed to such a goal.[21]

In *Beyond Psychology* (1939, English translation 1941) Rank criticized Freud's psychoanalysis for being a science of causal motives which left out spiritual values without which the self goes to pieces. Rank spoke about the urge to immortality as man's forceful drive to be impersonal, as the wish to surpass individuality. (Of course, any belief in immortality was, for Rank, hardly more than a psychological fact.)

C. G. Jung also warned that psychology was exhausting itself by causal means and maintained that the mind lives by aims as well. In *Modern Man in Search of a Soul* (1933) he argued:

> Analytical Psychology is no longer bound to the consulting room. [...] It transcends itself, and now advances to fill that void which hitherto has marked the psychic inefficiency of Western Culture as compared with that of the East.[22]

Like Jung, Huxley insisted that psychology should consider the psyche as a whole and include physiology, philosophy, theology and many other disciplines. The fulfilment of psychological work, he argued, lay in the realm beyond psychology. He believed that psychology was to complete its task in history by finding means of transcending itself as a science and leading to "a soul without psychology."[23]

As for another Neo-Freudian, Wilhelm Reich, Aldous knew quite a lot about his Orgon theories and Orgon machine.[24] Laura remembers that some of their friends even had the machine. They were among the first to learn about Reich's prosecution and arrest, and considered the whole story in the overall political context of McCarthyism. Huxley got frustrated when he learned about Reich's death in jail.

Huxley's contempt for determinism in psychology, especially his dislike of behaviourism, is well-known. Yet I believe that some of the ideas inherent in B. F. Skinner's later therapy appealed to Huxley's practical part, to that of the educator and the engineer of utopias. We know that Huxley read Skinner's major works and from time to time discussed the pros and cons of operant conditioning with a special emphasis on the role of the environment and that of positive reinforcement. Skinner's utopia *Walden Two* (1948) may actually have provided some ideas for *Island*.

Another school, phenomenological psychology, was much admired by Huxley since its basic assumptions corresponded with his own views and represented a reaction against both the behaviourist tradition, with its emphasis on measuring responses to external stimuli, and the psychoanalytic view of human beings as motivated by unconscious impulses. From the 1940s onwards his favourite psychological concepts became those of growth, spontaneity, self-awareness, self-actualization and affection. His theorizing was concerned with problems identical to those faced by humanistic psychologists who dealt with existential problems in their practice, for example with the questions of meaninglessness, boredom, self-estrangement, valuelessness and future shock. According to Erich Fromm, "in the nineteenth century the problem was that *God is dead*; in the twentieth century the problem is that *man is dead*."[25]

Phenomenologists were the first to reconsider the concept of normality. The view of normality closest to that of Huxley belonged to Fromm and Alan Watts. Both felt that it was unavoidable for the psychotherapist to be forced into social criticism since it was evident that the so-called normal state of consciousness was the context and the breeding ground of mental disease. Huxley refused to treat normality as the adjustment to others or to social norms and institutions. Psychotherapy, he claimed, should represent a life philosophy independent of society. It should relate to the natural order instead of any superimposed artificial order. In his "Foreword" to Hubert Benoit's *The Supreme Doctrine* (1955) he drew a parallel to Fromm's *The Sane Society*, published the same year. Huxley maintained that by 'normality' he understood the normality of perfect psycho-physical functioning, of actualized potentialities, of nature in its fullest power:

> This normality has nothing to do with the observed behaviour of the greatest number. [...] A psychotherapist, the Oriental philosopher tries to help statistically normal individuals to become normal in the other, more fundamental sense of the word. He begins by pointing out to those who think themselves sane that, in fact, they are mad, but they do not have to remain so if they don't want to.[26]

The phenomenologists Carl Rogers and Abraham Maslow, with whom the Huxleys were personally acquainted, had, perhaps, a major impact on the Huxley's outlook. These psychologists advocated the idea of actualization, meaning the growth and fulfilment of basic potentialities. According to them psychotherapy must be seen as a quest for a purposive life and society—a quest with a psychologically satisfying end. Huxley believed that, so far, the science of psychology had been much more successful on the negative than on the positive side. It had revealed too much about the abnormality of the human condition. Like major psychologists of the existential and humanistic schools he was certain that psychology had not stood up to its full height and that it should free itself from the effects of very limited and pessimistic views of human nature. First of all, to be cured man had to learn from the doctor or the scientist how to understand human nature and how to appreciate the errors he had made in his life, his wrong evaluation of his inferiority or superiority.

For Huxley, the special charm of Maslow's views was the psychologist's dream of a totally self-actualized society consisting of spontaneous, unfrustrated human beings who felt no need for repression or hostility: "The key concepts in the new dynamic psychology are spontaneity, release, naturalness, self-acceptance, impulse-awareness, gratification."[27]

Maslow saw psychotherapy as an ideal human relationship. Unlike Freudians, he studied the generally healthy personality. His utopian imagination envisioned psychotherapy as a tremendously extended form of treatment, dealing with millions upon millions of people. Maslow's wishful thinking pictures the psychology of values as a practical guide for ordinary people as well as a theoretical frame of reference for philosophers.

Laura often saw Maslow after Aldous's death. When she had psychological problems he was the one to treat her—apart from Milton Erickson, whom she paid for hypnotherapy. However, it was Carl Rogers whom the Huxleys preferred to the other people of his trade. They used to call him "the best" (L.H., interview). Often they would meet him at conferences, and sometimes he visited them at their place. Huxley found the idea of non-directive therapy very promising, possibly because his previous reading (on entelechy) and his personal experience had prepared him to accept the new counseling methods developed by Rogers:

> Therapeutic procedures should not be directive, but should be suggested by the deeper self, which can generally be relied on to come up with something of use to the organism, if it is politely asked to do so—e.g. some memory which requires to be talked out several times until there is no further emotional reaction to it, or else some symbolic image which may not be significant at the moment [...]. There is a part of the sub-conscious not-self which is much less stupid than the self and the personal subconscious, and can be relied upon to provide help if asked. (*Letters*, 648)[28]

Rogers's explanation of the nature of neurosis must also have appealed to Huxley. Indeed, instead of seeing neurosis either as maladaptive behaviour—as did B. F. Skinner—or as the repressed, now unconscious past, Rogers treated neurosis as an interruption in the process of self-actualization and suggested that it should be approached as a "here and now" problem.

It is noteworthy that Huxley, like Rogers, saw conscience as a total organismic experience in which the self is a discriminated part, perceived by the individual as the awareness of being. He also emphasized the conscious capacities of the individual, believing that the patient is responsible for the rediscovery of his/her own experience. Like Rogers, Huxley tended to find the roots of mental illness and evil in the distortions of reality that prevent the actualization of human potentialities. According to him the perspective chosen by the individual psyche is mostly dependent on the person's subjective awareness of himself and of the world around him. Our reactions are based on the way we view reality. Hence, objective reality itself is not the most important determinant. Only when it is conceptualized does it become a real force that can be potentially dangerous:

> A man can be an excellent practical psychologist and yet be completely ignorant of the current psychological theories. What is even more remarkable is that a man can be well versed in psychological theories which are demonstrably inadequate, and yet remain, thanks to his native insight, an excellent practical psychologist. On the other hand, a wrong theory of human nature

> [...] may evoke the worst passions and justify the most fiendish of cruelties. Theory is simultaneously not very important and very important indeed.[29]

Huxley saw human nature as basically positive. Evil springs mainly from socially constructed models. This is one of the reasons for his dislike of behaviourism and neo-behaviourism based on social conditioning. Differential reinforcement can no doubt shape desirable responses. However, in many cases it is social conditioning rather than instinctive drives that leads to violence. Man should be accepted for what he is. In this case the good in him will enhance both himself and society. It was this assumption that got Huxley to explore the paths leading to the discovery of the true reality of the psyche. The intermediate purpose of such experimenting was the openness of the individual, his responsiveness to experience.

Huxley's last novel, *Island*, reveals his infatuation with phenomenological psychology as well as with one of the schools of so-called humanistic psychotherapy, namely Gestalt therapy. Together with Zen Buddhism, Gestalt therapy provided guidelines for his understanding of man and the world, and for his blueprint of a perfect society on the island of Pala. Gestalt therapy is discussed in several of Huxley's letters, and one can be certain that he read at least one of the books about it—*Gestalt Therapy: Excitement and Growth in the Human Personality* (New York, 1951) by F. S. Perls, R. F. Hefferline, and P. Goodman (see *Letters*, 829–30, 902). This book was among the first which Aldous gave to Laura when they started dating. She was already a practising consultant then. They were not acquainted with either Hefferline or Goodman,[30] but they knew Fritz Perls personally. In fact, he came to visit them in their house.

Island is filled with Gestalt therapy recommendations. Huxley felt sure that the method was "extremely therapeutic" (*Letters*, 902) since it trained perceptual receptivity and could provide, as he hoped, the basis for a genuinely realistic treatment of the mentally ill by attacking their problems on all fronts. The book differs from other works of literature (from other utopian novels, too) since it deals with personal psychology, interpretations of the functions of the self, and the treatment of the latter's disorders rather than with interpersonal relations or social problems. It focuses on the protagonist's obsessive neurosis, his mental history and therapy. The author provides the reader and the critic with a completely new type of genre—the psycho-therapeutic Bildungsroman. The islanders' prosperity is based on highly developed self-understanding and advanced psycho-therapeutic techniques rather than on social equality or a balanced economy. It is remarkable that Huxley employed some Skinnerian recipes in the novel too. Perhaps it was because he had to finally admit that Rogers's approach undervalued the negative side of human nature—"the Freudian rats and black-beetles [...] in the Freudian basement" (*Letters*, 647)—or maybe because behavioural psychotherapy offered a shorter cut to cooperative harmony.

Huxley must have realized that he supplied the reader with a new and attractive utopia which held out the hope of achieving genuine harmony by means of authentic self-understanding and individual as well as group psychotherapy. It was probably for the first time that psychology—or, more precisely, its concepts—found itself in the very center of the literary scene. Laura Huxley also thinks that *Island* is a novel about psychotherapy. Moreover, she is going to write a book entitled "Recipes for Living, Loving, and Dying from *Island*" (L.H., interview), extracting the psychotherapeutic recommendations from the novel.

Comparing Huxley's ideas to those of professional psychologists I did not mean to deprive his theorizing of its uniqueness. The point was rather to emphasize its syncretic character. Indeed, each school of psychology and psychotherapy had something precious to add to the writer's understanding of human nature. Each was stimulating for his personal life, scientific outlook, his art and beliefs. He thought it absolutely legitimate to apply whatever he found available and workable in his quest for knowledge, awareness and perfection. Finally he arrived at a more or less comprehensive and integrative concept, drawing on, and transforming, the most advanced theories of consciousness of his time.

Huxley's main concern was not primarily medical. His position may be called a kind of moral philosophy which aims at healing the total personality by replacing the crashed values with psychologically effective spiritual qualities—not only for their own sake but also for the purpose of restoring a meaningful social life. Naturally, this approach connected psychology with Huxley's pedagogical explorations and his religious studies. Like C. G. Jung and Gordon Allport, who maintained that psychology and religion had similar views regarding the origin and nature of—as well as the cure for—mental distress, Huxley regarded the relationship between religion and psychology as one of desirable supplementation:

> A sensible and realistic religion should be one which is based upon a set of psycho-physiological operations, designed to help individuals to realize their potentialities to the greatest possible extent [...], to heighten their awareness, so that they become conscious of the Unconscious [...] and at the same time fully conscious of other human beings. (*Letters*, 827)

---

[1] Aldous Huxley, "Ends and Means," *Complete Essays of Aldous Huxley*, ed. Robert S. Baker and James Sexton (hereafter, *CE*), IV: *1936–1938* (Chicago, 2001), 400, 402.

[2] Examples of the Eastern approach can be found in D. T. Suzuki, *The Zen Doctrine of No-Mind* (London, 1949), and Alan Watts, *Behold the Spirit: A Study in the Necessity of Mystical Religion* (New York, 1947), books which Huxley evidently read. As for Watts's work, it was definitely influenced by Huxley's philosophy.

[3] "Madness, Badness, Sadness," *CE*, VI: *1956–1963* (Chicago, 2002), 188.

[4] See Aldous Huxley, "Do We Require Orgies?" *Yale Review* (March 1934), 466–483, and "Wars and Emotions," *Life and Letters* (April 1934), 7-26.

[5] See *Letters of Aldous Huxley*, ed. Grover Smith (New York—Evanston, 1969), 659 (hereafter, *Letters*). Huxley is employing Kurt Koffka's terminology insisting that we distinguish between molar and molecular behaviour. The latter takes place only within the organism and is initiated by various stimuli, whereas the former takes place in an environment, i.e. in an external setting. See the chapter "Behaviour and Its Field: The Task of Psychology," in: Kurt Koffka, *Principles of Gestalt Psychology* (London, 1935), 24–68.

[6] The letter reveals Huxley's infatuation with vitalist theories like that of Dr Karl Baron von Reichenbach (*Researches on Magnetism, Electricity, Heat, Light, Crystallization and Chemical Attraction in Their Relations to the Vital Force*, 1845), who had studied various manifestations of the vital force which he named Odic force. Von Reichenbach also thought that this force explained the phenomenon of mesmerism. Huxley believed that the nominally different 'vital forces' described by Wilhelm Reich, von Reichenbach, Eeman, Fahnestock and some others did, in fact, refer to one and the same life force. The books concerning radiological theories and therapies (including those employing various methods of hypnosis and relaxation) that Huxley read and commented on are: W.B. Fahnestock, *Statuvalism, or Artificial Somnambulism* (1871); Hans Driesch, *The History and Theory of Vitalism* (1914)—the term *entelechy* appears there; Dr Edmund Jacobson, *Progressive Relaxation* (1924); David Harold Fink, *Release from Nervous Tension* (1943); Leon Ernest Eeman, *Cooperative Healing: The Curative Properties of Human Radiation* (1947); A. L. Kitselman, *E-Therapy* (1953).

[7] Mike Wallace, "Aldous Huxley on Thought Control," *The Listener*, 59 (September 1958), 373–374.

[8] See Aldous Huxley, "The Final Revolution," *A Pharmacological Approach to the Study of the Mind*, ed. Robert M. Featherstone and Alexander Simon (Springfield, 1959), 216–228. The essay also appeared in *Contact: The San Francisco Journal of New Writing, Art, and Ideas*, 2 (1959), 5–18.

[9] See Aldous Huxley, *The Human Situation: Lectures at Santa Barbara, 1959,* ed. Piero Ferrucci (New York, Hagerstown, San Francisco, 1977). Hereafter, *HS*.

[10] For the diverse approaches to the issue of anxiety see the conference papers, *Constructive Aspects of Anxiety,* ed. Seward Hiltner and Karl Menninger (New York, 1963).

[11] Huxley most certainly read *The Future of the Human Mind* by George Estabrooks and Nancy E. Gross (New York, 1961). He was impressed by their discussion of the body-mind paradigm in its relation to the voluntary and the

involuntary nervous systems. The authors maintain that hypnosis belongs to the former, whereas the basic body functions are expressions of the latter.

[12] See *Letters*, 922-923. Huxley seems to have forgotten the title of another book by Franz Alexander (1891–1964), the eminent psychiatrist and leading expert in psychosomatic disorders. My guess is that he also knew *The Scope of Psychoanalysis, 1921–1961: Selected Papers of Franz Alexander* (New York, 1961). As for the other two books, the exact references are: Walter Bromberg, *The Mind of Man: A History of Psychotherapy and Psychoanalysis* (New York, 1959) and C.G. Jung, Psychological *Reflections: A New Anthology of His Writings 1905–1961,* ed. Jolande Jacobi (Princeton, NJ, 1953).

[13] Mrs Laura Huxley agreed to talk to me at her home in Hollywood in June 2004. I am very grateful to Professor Bernfried Nugel for this arrangement. Our talk concerned Huxley's connections with the field of psychology and his acquaintance with contemporaneous methods of psychotherapy. Hereafter, L.H., interview.

[14] David Dunaway, "Aldous Huxley Oral History Papers," Huntington Library, HM 56885, 5. Hereafter, HM.

[15] *Aldous Huxley 1894–1963: A Memorial Volume*, ed. Julian Huxley (New York, 1965), 157.

[16] Aldous Huxley, "Foreword," in: Laura Archera Huxley, *You Are Not the Target* (New York, 1963), XIII.

[17] Robert Baker, *"Brave New World": History, Science and Dystopia* (Boston, 1990); Peter Firchow, "Science and Conscience in Huxley's *Brave New World,*" *Contemporary Literature*, 16 (Summer 1975), 301–316; Peter Firchow, *The End of Utopia* (Lewisburg, London and Toronto, 1984); Jerome Meckier, "Our Ford, Our Freud and the Behaviorist Conspiracy in Huxley's *Brave New World,*" *Thalia*, 1 (1977–1978), 35–59; James Hull, *Aldous Huxley: The Growth of Personality* (Zurich, 1955).

[18] Aldous Huxley, *Island* (London, 1979), 79–80.

[19] Sigmund Freud, *The Standard Edition of the Complete Psychological Works of Sigmund Freud,* trans. and ed. J.Strachey (London, 1995), XXI, 80–144.

[20] Aldous Huxley, *Literature and Science* (Woodbridge, CT, 1991), 96.

[21] Alfred Adler, *Understanding Human Nature*, transl. W.B. Wolfe (Garden City, 1927), 29.

[22] C.G. Jung, *Modern Man in Search of a Soul* (New York, 1957), 53.

[23] Otto Rank, *Psychology and the Soul* (New York, 1950), 31. (The book was published in German in 1930).

[24] See, e.g., Wilhelm Reich, *Biographic Material: History of the Discovery of the Life Energy—European and American Period, 1920–1952* (Rangeley, ME, 1953).

[25] Erich Fromm, *The Sane Society* (New York, 1955), 360.

[26] Aldous Huxley, "Foreword," in: Hubert Benoit, *The Supreme Doctrine: Psychological Studies in Zen Thought* (London, 1955), VIII.

[27] Abraham Maslow, *Motivation and Personality* (New York, 1954), 352.

[28] Huxley may have read—or at least known about—Carl R. Rogers, *Counseling and Psychotherapy: Newer Concepts in Practice* (Boston, 1942).

[29] Aldous Huxley, *The Devils of Loudun* (New York, 1996), 158–159.

[30] Aldous, however, was a regular reader of Hefferline's reviews published in *Main Currents in Modern Thought*, a monthly journal he had subscribed to since 1943.

III.

Aldous Huxley, the Artist

Valery Rabinovitch

(Urals State University)

Aldous Huxley's Quest for Ways of Saving Mankind

As a matter of fact, the history of culture is, first of all, the history of the human world-view, of the human interpretations of the so called 'eternal' philosophical, ontological and existential mysteries which have ultimately remained unresolved to this day. What is the universe based on? What is the meaning of a single human life, its justification with regard to a higher order? What is good and, for that matter, what is evil, for a single person as well as for mankind as a whole?

It was the twentieth century that became a turning-point for Western civilization, because the harmonious system of explanations and related values prevailing till then was not only shaken to its very core, but virtually collapsed. Before that, a rather strict system of ideas (partly of religious origin, partly going back to the rationalistic conceptions of the Enlightenment) had existed, but from the beginning of the twentieth century "God was dead" (as Nietzsche said). On the one hand, this radical position meant a good deal of liberation, but on the other it exposed the helplessness of the human mind in dealing with the incomprehensible. The twentieth-century world, depicted in many great works of literature, appeared empty of God, fragmented into micro-elements, decentralized, and deeply deprived of sense (this was displayed most clearly in the literature of the 'absurd,' which included leading writers such as Eugene Ionesco or Samuel Beckett).

At the same time, however, and as a kind of counter-reaction, the quest for novel values and first principles (and sometimes even for a new God, resulting, for example, in the deification of the charismatic political leader) became one of the dominant features of twentieth-century culture in a world which had lost its former certainties. It was just within the course of such a quest for new values that the intellectual and artistic development of Aldous Huxley took place—a writer who is considered one of the greatest figures not only in twentieth-century literature but in the century's culture as a whole.

The early Huxley—up to the beginning of the 1930s—was a convinced skeptic, even an agnostic, and a 'polyphonist.' This was the time when outstanding and disturbing novels such as *Antic Hay* (1923), *Point Counter Point* (1928), or the dystopia *Brave New World* (1932), very popular in Russia, were published. These works just absorbed the modern world-view, showing a world fragmented into single components, a world where there was no single, absolute truth, but, on the contrary, a multitude of positions which were all equally valid. To some extent, Huxley, at this time, was fascinated by this world, which constituted a polylogue of truths, none of which being a truth in the absolute sense of the word, but each pretending to be prophetic. In this regard, one may refer to a memorable and, indeed, novel-shaping metaphor from *Point Counter Point* : the whole world appears as an orchestra in which every musical instrument independently pursues its own part, and all are equally 'right' and equally 'wrong,' while the players disregard any instrument but their own. The result is a general cacophony.

In each of Huxley's earlier novels one can find the so-called 'auto-biographical hero,' onto whom Huxley projects himself and who voices some of his own artistic principles. As a result of Huxley's general outlook, this 'autobiographical hero' tries to view the world from all possible angles—with the eyes of a believer, of a scientist, of an economist, of a simple man in the street. This is what Philip Quarles, Huxley's *alter ego* in *Point Counter Point*, explicitly states. In Huxley's earlier novels there are, indeed, convinced believers as well as positivistically minded biologists, but also simple people absorbed in conventional family life—philistines, so to speak. And none of them really listens to what the others have to say.

A concentrated expression of the early Huxley's world-view can be found in his little-known play "Happy Families," published in *Limbo* (1920). In fact, one can argue that this play anticipates the theatre of the absurd. Long before the ideological and theoretical foundations laid by Ionesco, long before the appearance of the cult plays written by Ionesco and Beckett, Aldous Huxley wrote a short play which fully incorporates the standard ingredients of absurdism. The majority of cause-and-effect relationships seem destroyed, there is no real communication between the characters, and their utterances do not indicate any deeper mutual relations. Even the boundaries between individual characters are on the verge of being obliterated. It sometimes seems that there are no separate characters any more, just an undifferentiated human mass. And through this whole chaotic conglomeration, just in the way of absurdism, some lowest common denominators that cannot be denied surface now and then.

For the time being, such a state of the universe seemed inevitable to Huxley. The only viable alternative would have been an artificial consolidation of the human community under the banner of some relative idea—all ideas had become relative by then—which pretended to be absolute. As a matter of fact, such a system would inevitably have required the manipulation of the majority's conscious and sub-conscious minds, and would therefore have presupposed a division of humanity into a manipulating élite, on the one hand, and the 'herd,' i.e., those who are manipulated, on the other. In the end there would have been a total lack of personal freedom for the masses, and the weeding out those of a different opinion would have been common and required practice. In this vein Huxley, as early as in his first novel *Crome Yellow* (1921), has Mr Scogan, an advocate of a purely rational and functional utopian state (for Huxley that was undoubtedly a dystopian state), assume that the human community could be organized solely by a division into separate categories such as the "Directing Intelligences," the "Men of Faith," and "the herd."[1] Furthermore, there would have to be a strong uniting ideology and a strategy to impress it on the general public. The development of this strategy would be the business of "the Men of Faith." These would be fit for temporary use only, depending on the validity of the ideology promoted by them. And for those morally too scrupulous to belong to the ruling intellectuals or too skeptical to be among the "Men of Faith," or, for that matter, not foolish and obedient enough to humbly pasture together with "the herd," there would be a "lethal Chamber" (*CY*, 247). This, one should keep in mind, was the year 1921. The real gas chambers were to follow in the not too distant future.

In 1932, Huxley's famous dystopia *Brave New World* appeared. Later, it became a cult book in post-communist Russia, along with George Orwell's novel *Nineteen Eighty-Four* and Evgeny Zamjatin's novel *We*. The reasons for this popularity are obvious—Russia itself had just gone through terrible decades of building an 'ideal society' but had, finally, been able to throw off the communist yoke. *Brave New World* was read as a warning never to put the idea of individual, personal freedom at stake again.

Huxley's dystopian world is absolutely cold and rational. Mustapha Mond, the World Controller, explains:

> 'The world's stable now. People are happy; they get what they want, and they never want what they can't get. They're well off; they're safe; they're never ill; they're not afraid of death; they're blissfully ignorant of passion and old age; they're plagued with no mothers or fathers; they've got no wives, or children, or lovers to feel strongly about; they're so conditioned that they practically can't help behaving as they ought to behave.'[2]

All this is achieved by a complex system of absolute 'programming' of the population before and, this goes without saying, after birth. Babies are produced artificially in laboratories just as the World State, the only remaining country, needs them. Every individual's fate is determined long before his birth when he is assigned to a special social caste—there are five of them: 'Alphas,' 'Betas,' 'Gammas,' 'Deltas' and 'Epsilons'—and submitted to corresponding chemical treatment. 'Alphas' are destined to be rulers and hence allowed to fully develop their intellectual abilities, while 'Epsilons' are meant to lead a completely submissive life and are, therefore, deprived of almost all their intellectual power.

After birth, every child—and this includes 'Alphas,' too—is put through a comprehensive programme of conditioning—for example, in the form of sleep-teaching, or Pavlovian conditioning—to ensure everybody's un-questioning and life-long loyalty to the World State's principles as well as deep contentment with the social caste one belongs to. And should anybody still have temporary feelings of unhappiness or dissatisfaction, there is always the possibility of consuming the State's official drug, *soma*, which is distributed freely and regularly to everybody.

As for the few 'Alphas' who are nevertheless able to lead an intellectual life which is too independent of, and thus dangerous to, the World State, they are simply deported to distant islands where they cannot do any harm. The World Controller adds: "It's lucky [...] that there are such a lot of islands in the world. I don't know what we should do without them. Put you all in the lethal chamber, I suppose" (*BNW*, 269–270). Remarkably, the image of the 'lethal chamber' comes up again, eleven years after it appeared in Huxley's imagination in *Crome Yellow*, and only a few years before it turned into horrible reality.

Brave New World was much discussed in Soviet Russia. Some detractors, following the party line, tried to prove that Huxley had, indeed, the Soviet Union in mind when he wrote the novel, and consequently condemned the book. Others, just to rehabilitate Huxley in the eyes of the Soviet authorities, argued that his target was not in the least the Soviet Union but, on the contrary, the Western consumer society. The truth probably lies somewhere between these extremes because one remarkable fact must not be forgotten: in Huxley's dystopian vision direct or indirect reference is made to some important (near-)contemporaries from both the 'communist' and the 'capitalist' spheres. There are Marx and Lenin with their communism, there is Ford with his new system of mass production, there is Pavlov with his work on conditioned reflexes, and there is Freud with his psycho-analysis, to name but a few. In Huxley's view they have one decisive feature in common—all of them, and this is his fundamental charge, have created methods and systems of manipulating individuals or the masses, thus making it possible to transform a great many single 'egos' into a compact impersonal herd.[3] Up to that point of time, the idea of an 'impersonal' and 'unified' existence could, according to Huxley, only lead to a dystopian vision. He, *a priori*, accepted the chaos of life, in which there was still a place for individuality, for personality, for the soul—and for Shakespeare, too—as the fundamental reality, as something to be valued and defended.

From the beginning of the 1930s the international political scene began to change rapidly. The Nazis triumphed in Germany, and it is important to note that Huxley, as a convinced anti-fascist, left England when he realized that the British government did not take the necessary measures to stop Hitler. Another world war seemed to be increasingly imminent, and even nuclear weapons which threatened the very existence of mankind as a whole were no longer inconceivable. It suddenly appeared that humanity could be destroyed instantly.

As a result Huxley, from the middle of the 1930s, was concerned with developing a metaphysical outlook, one that would not, primarily, focus on the idea of an 'ideal society'—which was out of the question at that time—but that, more basically, would open up ways of saving mankind from self-destruction. His progress from absolute skepticism to a more positive view is clearly portrayed in the spiritual development of Anthony Beavis, his 'autobiographical hero' in his novel *Eyeless in Gaza* (1936). At times the younger Beavis even seems to toy with the gruesome vision of *Brave New World*: Let there be unfreedom! Let there be manipulation! Let there be higher and lower castes! If only the ruling intellectuals, like psychiatrists in a mental hospital, will stop insane mankind from tumbling down the abyss.[4] However, by the time he wrote *Eyeless in Gaza*, Huxley, just like the older Beavis, had lost faith in the idea of improving life through social changes, whatever their direction. The only promising alternative, he thought, consisted in the internal improvement of the individual. In this context we may refer to the important Russian writers Dostoevsky and Tolstoy with their ideal of 'self-improvement.' Both writers were very much appreciated by Huxley.

Huxley had, by that time, arrived at the conviction that the reason for all social quarrels and cataclysms is the fact that every single person, by his inherited nature, sees the world almost exclusively through the tinted glasses of his own ego and selfish interests. Men strive to defend their own territory and—if it seems to their advantage—even conquer another's. Most communities, be they large or small, are guided by this egoistical principle, which, in fact, permeates all areas of life. From it all nationalisms have been derived—Nazism, of course, being the most radical case—and wars must be attributed to it, too. It is exactly man's self-centredness which prevents mankind from solving the big, world-wide problems jointly.[5]

However, in Huxley's view, a means of rescue is now available—"'Liberation from personality.'"[6] This is the idea put forward by Mr Propter, the saintly character in *After Many a Summer* (1939), Huxley's first novel after his move to America. According to this concept, the way out of the dilemma is to acquire—or, better, to restore—the ability to see the world as objectively as possible by coming to regard one's self in a completely new light—as but a small fraction of an all-encompassing, interrelated whole. This does not at all mean that the self is suppressed or forcibly dissolved in a crowd. On the contrary, the process can be described as a voluntary and deliberate outgrowing and surmounting of the self, achieved only under the highest possible personal freedom and security. As long as one must defend one's own poor individuality from being encroached upon, anything like 'liberation from personality' retreats into the background. Mr Propter underlines: "'Slavery and fanaticism intensify the obsession with time and evil and the self. Hence the value of democratic institutions and a sceptical attitude of mind. The more you respect a personality, the better its chance of discovering that all personality is a prison'" (*AMS*, 109).

Significantly, Propter proposes his theories in wealthy and posh Los Angeles—against the background of a pompous castle inhabited by the Californian multimillionaire Joe Stoyte. The setting symbolizes modern civilization with its ideal of consumption, its expansion of the personal 'ego' into eternity and infinity, its longing for unlimited physical abilities and even for physical immortality. Indeed, Stoyte wants to become immortal. For this reason he pays his personal doctor, Sigismund Obispo (there is certainly an allusion to Sigmund Freud here) millions to find an 'immortality recipe.' Obispo, however, pursues his own interests and brings the rich man more and more under his control. He manipulates Stoyte, who is but an interesting test subject for him.

Finally, the proud multimillionaire's dream appears to have come true—not without far-reaching concessions, however. For the sake of physical immortality Stoyte is ready to descend the ladder of evolution and degenerate into a monkey. The motif of 'devolution' is, in fact, quite productive in Huxley's oeuvre. This is especially remarkable since he was the grandson of T. H. Huxley, Darwin's associate. The two evolutionists had drawn a long line of development from ape to modern *homo sapiens*, while Aldous Huxley, disgusted at the direction in which humanity was heading, simply reversed the process. According to him modern man, mindlessly driven to consumption, was returning to an apelike state. Freudian psychologists, who stressed man's animal components, substantiated his view.

In 1948, sixteen years after *Brave New World*, an even gloomier dystopia appeared: *Ape and Essence*. In this book,[7] which shows the deep impact of the traumatic experience of the Second World War, Huxley depicts the ultimate downfall of human civilization. The monkey within man, the ape which embodies his savage nature, fully takes over. The most detestable manifestations of modern life, such as ruthless self-assertion, excessive physicality, suppression of others, lack of culture, and dull consumption, dominate while the mind has been reduced to an instrument in the hands of a monkey, assisting it in achieving its primitive aims.

Thus, in the "Script" section of *Ape and Essence*, the reader is introduced to wretched and downtrodden replicas of Faraday and Einstein who are actually kept on leashes by monkeys in military boots. The monkeys are in charge of the intellectuals, who are solely needed for military purposes. The monkey rules, and the human intellect has been completely submitted to it. A nuclear war follows, leading to the loss even of these last personifications of the intellect—the human faculty which had, at first, enabled man to be gratified by the illusion of his own power, but which, later on, did not stop him from gradually being taken over, even in appearance, by the ape, which more and more dictated its will to him in the times of seeming progress.

The aim was chosen by the ape, while the means of its achievement were contributed by man—this is how Huxley defines the essence of modern civilization in the 1940s. Moreover, he clearly assumes that the development of mankind has been a steady movement towards a catastrophe, which was evidently imposed on people by evil, devilish forces. That is why in the 'post-nuclear,' largely depopulated world of *Ape and Essence* the traditional belief in God has been replaced by devil worship. The Devil has become the only real sovereign: instead of wearing crosses, the clergymen of the new religion bear horns, and the main moral postulate (according to the Devil's will) is not to let others do unto you what you yourself would like to do unto them. Formerly sacred notions such as love or maternity have been damned and abolished, and the whole world is ruled by a single hope, i.e., that the Devil, under the name of Belial, will postpone, if only for some time, the final annihilation of mankind. That is the natural end of a civilization dominated by the ape.

The last years of Huxley's life were a new period of his spiritual quest. Huxley qualified his former ideal of the 'liberation of the individual' because it had been too absolute and categorical in character. Thus, he gradually formulated a new ideal—that of a synthesis of different truths and different values, liberal and fundamental, eastern and western, and other opposite features. While, previously, the views held by a religious believer, a scientist, an economist, or a philistine had, in Huxley's opinion, been equally valuable but unrelated statements about the incomprehensible world, he now fostered the idea of a possible unity of all these incompatible truths. The basic requirement, he thought, was that the different disciplines paid attention to one another and appreciated one another's findings so that, as a result, a new valuable unity, a common foundation underlying the contradictory truths, might be found.

It is on these ideas that he based his unique lecture series entitled "The Human Situation" in 1959. Here he regards a thinker as a *pontifex*, whose mission is to build 'bridges'—between different world views, different values, and different truths. Huxley considers historically formed dichotomies and other opposite poles from different sides, and in each case the essential truth seems to lie not merely in the middle, but in a unity. Thus Huxley erects his famous 'bridges' between scientific knowledge and spontaneous perception, between the predetermination of a human fate through inheritance of characteristics and its dependence on the individual's free will, his environment and education, between a person's private life and his being 'part of history,' and many more. And throughout there is no talk of absolutes, but there is always a certain 'measure' or 'degree' of absoluteness.

From the same point of view Huxley also regards the question of progress in "The Human Situation." In fact, he confronts the idea of continuous forward movement, i.e., of persistent progress, with the concept of motion in time as an eternal rotation, where a 'rise' is inevitably followed by a 'fall,' and it appears to him that both assumptions are quite possible. On the one hand, he points out the factors precipitating the end of civilization, such as the exhaustion of natural resources, the threat of a nuclear war, and others, but at the same time he thinks it possible that there will be further progressive development—on condition, however, that the many conflicting human communities are transformed into one big world community, a vast unity ruled by one world government. As might be expected, his attitude to the realization of such a world-wide project is rather skeptical at that moment: "Undoubtedly, the best thing for world government under law would be an invasion from Mars. Unfortunately, this is rather unlikely to take place" (*HS*, 101).

Huxley's final work was *Island* (1962)—this time a utopian novel, written exactly thirty years after the dystopian *Brave New World*. At the very end of his life, on the brink of death from cancer of the tongue, Huxley worked out a fictional model of a perfect society. It is founded on the same ideal of unity— unity at all levels. In the ideal society of Pala, an island somewhere in the Indian Ocean, the most important philosophical achievements of the West and the East have been perfectly fused (significantly, this society was created both by an educated rajah and a no less educated doctor from Scotland) so that Western rationalism and Eastern mysticism go hand in hand (it is not by chance that the people on Pala are bilingual—they speak the ancient language of Pala as well as English). This means that the Western liberal ideal, which focusses on the individual and the expression of the personal self, and the Eastern concept of the 'liberation from personality' are both valued according to their respective benefits.

Furthermore, even some of the ideas used in *Brave New World* reappear, albeit in drastically changed shape and context. Although the institution 'family' is still alive, it is by no means undisputed because the 'Mutual Adoption Club' enables children who do not get along with their parents to be adopted by a different family. There is the possibility of voluntary artificial insemination to guarantee genetically healthy offspring. Those about to die are prepared for death psychologically.[8] On the island people are also divided into groups of types, but there is no artificial predetermination by scientists, like in *Brave New World*. There is merely some registration of striking inherited characteristics. For example, those who are "sheep-people" by nature "love ritual and public ceremonies and revivalistic emotion; their temperamental preferences can be directed into the Way of Devotion."[9] "Cat- people," on the other hand, "like to be alone, and their private broodings can become the Way of Self-Knowledge" (*Island*, 206). And then there are "marten-people," who always "want to *do* things" (*Island*, 206). They must somehow be led onto the "Way of Disinterested Action" (*Island*, 206), while aggressive "Muscle People" as well as neurotic "Peters Pans" (*Island*, 151) are to be 'reprogrammed' psychologically from their very childhood so that they cannot grow into dangerous Stalins or Hitlers. Like in *Brave New World*, there is even an official drug on Pala, but in contrast to *soma* the *moksha-medicine* is taken to open the doors of perception and get in touch with the eternal One.

The principal aim pursued in the Palanese society is to overcome the traditionally sanctioned system of values which is based on egoistic interests as a stimulating motive (producing various forms of violence) as well as on a volitional, forced negation of egoism (leading to a cultivation of suffering). Through appropriate social measures and the practice of 'reprogramming' people everything is arranged in such a way that love for one's neighbour is the primary power of the human soul. People feel happy when they do good to each other, while doing harm, even by accident, naturally makes them suffer.

This is achieved by uniting various values and ideals, and, consequently, the Palanese world is, in some respects, culturally poorer than ours. However, there are no absolute, final losses like in *Brave New World*. In the latter, Shakespeare's works, for instance, have not only become obscure but they have, in fact, been banned completely. It would be of no use, it would even be detrimental to the unsuspecting Brave New Worlders to read them. On Pala there is no such ban—literature and art are still to be found, but they are not appreciated as highly as in our world, and not all the works regarded as 'high' art in our civilization would be understood there. How should the happy inhabitants of a utopian world fully comprehend, say, a tragedy dealing with phenomena dictated by destructive passions when they do not feel them?

To illustrate this, a performance of *King Oedipus* is staged on Pala, a play epitomizing our civilization with its passions and sufferings. However, here the play has a happy ending—Oedipus is dissuaded from putting out his eyes, and Jocasta is prevented from committing suicide: It is all so simple! You see, Oedipus did not know that it was his father he killed and that it was his mother he was sleeping with. Then where is his guilt? Only in this way can the happy residents of Pala interpret the play. *Oedipus* could not be staged in any other way on the island (see *Island*, 243–248).

The type of the 'rioter' found in *Brave New World* also underwent a fundamental change in *Island* : while in the former he is a 'noble savage' who challenges the artificial harmony of the World State in the name of personality, soul and Shakespeare, and finally dies for his principles, in the latter he appears in the form of hypocritical and treacherous egoists who ruthlessly destroy the natural, blissful harmony characterizing life on Pala—and with it the very essence of the utopia.

In conclusion, one must regard Huxley not only as a fine and extraordinarily talented writer, but as a bright thinker, reflecting on the fortunes of humanity. Sometimes his deductions may seem extravagant, even naive nowadays. But nevertheless, particularly in our time of a new 'clash of civilizations,' when the West is threatened by Eastern fundamentalists, when it seems rather doubtful if it will be able to maintain its foundations (liberty, human rights, freedom of speech, to name but a few), in the face of a terroristic war, Aldous Huxley can perhaps show mankind a possible way out. A synthesis of the best that has been thought and said in the West and the East may, in fact, be the only alternative to their mutual destruction. It would certainly be worth giving it a try.

---

[1] Aldous Huxley, *Crome Yellow* (London, 1921), 243. Hereafter, *CY*.

[2] Aldous Huxley, *Brave New World* (London, 1932), 259–260. Hereafter, *BNW*.

[3] This, among other reasons, explains Huxley's life-long aversion to Freud's ideas. He believed that, by his discoveries, Freud, too, was playing into the hands of the ruling élites, offering them a powerful instrument for the manipulation of people.

[4] In a belated preface to *Brave New World*, published in 1946, Huxley stressed the same idea: "Procrustes in modern dress, the nuclear scientist will prepare the bed on which mankind must lie; and if mankind doesn't fit—well, that will be just too bad for mankind" (New York, 1946), xv.

[5] Later in his career, Huxley did, in fact, develop the idea of a "world government" (Aldous Huxley, *The Human Situation*, ed. Piero Ferrucci [London, 1978], 101; hereafter, *HS*).

[6] Aldous Huxley, *After Many a Summer* (London, 1939), 109. Hereafter, *AMS*.

[7] The larger part is written in the form of a film script.

[8] Here, of course, death is understood to be the transition to a happier state. When his fist wife, Maria, terminally ill with cancer, was suffering before his eyes in the mid-1950s, Huxley came to realize that it is not death itself which is the most horrible thing, but the very process of dying, when a human being, barely alive, seems to turn into something less than human. See *Letters of Aldous Huxley*, ed. Grover Smith (London, 1969), 734–737 (note).

[9] Aldous Huxley, *Island* (London, 1962), 206. Hereafter, *Island*.

Michael Szczekalla

(University of Greifswald)

THE SCOTTISH ENLIGHTENMENT AND BUDDHISM— HUXLEY'S VISION OF HYBRIDITY IN *ISLAND*

It is not to be expected that postmodern advocates of hybridity feel drawn to the society of Pala. In *Island* (1962),[1] Huxley attempted a complete fusion of two civilisations. The result is an entirely homogeneous culture with very little potential for conflict. Tolerant Mahayana Buddhism has been provided with an injection of science or scientism—administered by a belated representative of the Scottish Enlightenment, Andrew MacPhail, who also happens to resemble the author's famous grandfather. In spite of the Scotsman's "ominous surname,"[2] Pala's ultimate failure results from the machinations of the unreconstructed world outside—or so the reader is made to believe.

Criticism of Huxley's last novel should therefore focus on the internal fissures of this utopian legacy, which constitutes the culmination point of Huxley's career as a writer and cultural critic who had long since moved away from his benign cynicism of the 1920s and early 1930s. Though, to use a formula suggested by himself, the post-war Huxley may still have been an agnostic, he was incessantly striving to become a gnostic.[3] To the critic who wants to get a grip on this peculiar variety of 'sceptical gnosticism,' as I want to call it, the improbable synthesis of Buddhism and the Scottish Enlightenment offers a good starting point. However, I have to state clearly that I am not going to engage in a detailed examination of either Huxley's Buddhism as it manifests itself in his writings or of his attitude towards eighteenth-century Edinburgh as a European "capital of the mind" (to use the title of a recent publication on the Scottish Enlightenment[4]). Rather, these two concepts provide me with a kind of shorthand which makes it easier to address two issues of paramount importance in *Island*: education and the "science of the human mind" (*Island*, 144). Huxley was an educationalist who tried to achieve no less than a radical transformation of Enlightenment thought. In his later writings, the very concept has acquired religious overtones—if it has not become completely void of any secular meaning.

Though *Island* is infused with a spirit of modesty (in its professed limitation to the feasible it is Aristotelian rather than Platonic[5]), it forms a solid basis for a critique of utopian thinking. Its pessimism, which hardly seems unwarranted, may even be seen to invite such a critique. Thus, in the novel's final chapter, Pala is conquered by a third-world strongman, the head of a neighbouring state where he has initiated a Western-style modernisation programme. But what about the cracks and crevices of the edifice itself, the internal fissures I have referred to?

To begin with, Pala, erected by an early nineteenth-century Raja, who was assisted by the Scottish itinerant physician Andrew MacPhail, is not much of a state, that is to say, Huxley did not concern himself with devising a political structure that merits sustained critical attention. This may either be seen as a shortcoming or explained away by using a genre-based argument. Serious utopian fiction divides into two types. In their attempts to criticise contemporary societies, the authors of the one lay great store by political, those of the other by scientific innovations.

It could be argued that Huxley follows Bacon's *New Atlantis* were it not for the fact that his concept of science is thoroughly anti-Baconian. Neither may we assume Huxley to have liked the paternalistic, not to say hieratic trappings of Bacon's imaginary island of Bensalem. The virtuosi or scientists of Solomon's House, the richly endowed academy this island boasts of, partake of the roles of father and priest.[6] However, in spite of the novel's emphasis on "democracy and plenty" (*Island*, 163), a toned-down version of paternalism appears to be a recognisable feature of *Island*. Huxley may have felt ill at ease with it, but the elaborate educational schemes successfully implemented by Pala's tiny elite require it as a premise. And though Huxley probably considers the sacerdotal function obsolete,[7] he is bound to revere the mystagogic one as he pleads for a "sacramental vision of reality" (*DP*, 19). There have to be teachers of mysticism.

The novel's emphasis on education, especially the dim view it takes of the benefits which may be derived from studying great literature, reminds one of Plato's *Republic*. In both works, art is rejected on moral as well as metaphysical grounds. Thus Huxley's daringly dismissive attitude is not merely consistent with the conceptual framework of his utopia. It is in fact required by it. To have understood this appears to be the one and only reason why Huxley, not unlike Plato, deserves praise for embracing a view justly considered untenable by humanists.

The members of Pala's governing class are thoroughly committed to practical wisdom (perhaps a version of Aristotle's 'phronesis'[8]), especially in the field of education. For all their scepticism, they also acknowledge a foundational discipline called the "science of the human mind," which belongs to the intellectual heritage Andrew MacPhail bequeathed to Pala. But there is a problem here. The term occurs only once in the entire novel (*Island*, 144), and the discipline itself has been transformed almost beyond recognition. It is my contention that this new "science of the human mind" functions as the novel's substitute for politics.

No wonder then that Huxley cared so little for an exposition of Pala's political system. Pala is a constitutional monarchy, as William Farnaby, the novel's Hythloday figure is informed early on by Murugan, an adolescent who is soon to become the new Raja, the island's ruler, and whom Huxley is at pains to describe as a spoilt brat. There is a cabinet, a house of representatives, and a privy council, which represents the Raja during his minority. Murugan's official role is not confined to representative functions. He is going to rule and not just reign (see *Island*, 42–43). Though the reader has to accept much of this on the authority of Murugan himself, there is nowhere the slightest hint that he cannot be trusted when he expounds the constitution.

Woe to the state whose future ruler is the product of an education which has been a complete disaster! It takes some time to fully realise the strangeness of such an exclamation if it is meant to refer to a mid-twentieth-century utopian novel. Little effort is required to understand that critics who think highly of *Island* tend to be squeamish about the awkward truth it expresses. Admittedly, the novel allows for the view that Murugan's deficiencies have merely accelerated the demise of the Palanese experiment, which would have been inevitable any way. Less immature, it is true, Murugan would not have so easily become a victim of Colonel Dipa's sexual advances. At least, this latter-day Hadrian on the payroll of an international oil company would have found it more difficult to exploit both Pala's beautiful Antinous and its rich oil wells. Yet, in the end, it is the advent of a global economy which puts paid to Pala's splendid isolation.

So much for the novel's view of world politics. I reserve judgment on its soundness for now. To make up one's mind about Huxley's hybrid civilisation, it is better to begin by locating the novel in the context of utopian literature and by focussing on the kind of problem solving meant to be undertaken in this genre. References to other literary utopias, which I try to keep as short as possible, serve the purpose of clarification on the options and constraints that define this kind of writing.

1. A Hybrid Civilisation

Whereas Huxley's emphasis on science reminds one of Bacon's *New Atlantis* and his zeal for education of Plato's *Republic*, his preference for biology may be called Aristotelian. As in *Brave New World* or even in *Ape and Essence*,[9] the life sciences are of paradigmatic importance. It is in the context of a discussion of Pala's reformed system of family life with its peculiar institution of Mutual Adoption Clubs, which allow youngsters a temporary escape from their biological parents, that the most important concept of this novel of ideas occurs for the first and only time. If people from different families intermingle, a lot of strain is taken from the smallest units of society and the lives of individual members are enriched by a multiplicity of potentially rewarding contacts. This process is explicitly referred to as the "hybridization of micro-cultures" (*Island*, 99). Huxley celebrated hybridity long before it became an academic fashion.

Pala has been enriched by a foreign civilisation through a complicated process of assimilation and reform. It may be said to be based on a mutual adoption programme writ large. On the highest level of abstraction, its "best-of-two-worlds"[10] approach to social engineering attempts to infuse Western science with the distrust of conceptual knowledge that characterises Eastern philosophy and religion. It realizes, in the realm of the literary imagination, Huxley's dream of a science that does not terminate in a complete 'desiccation' of our 'spiritual faculties.' This has a distinctly nineteenth-century flavour. It reminds one of Comte and Mill, the great positivists who were worried about the effects of the 'dry light,' the Baconian metaphor for scientific or instrumental reason. If we think of Mill's cautious admiration for the author of *Sartor Resartus*, we may wonder whether Huxley wished to become his grandfather's Carlyle. Mill, however, never compromised the fundamental principles of his *System of Logic* whereas Palanese science poses a problem precisely because it is used to buttress claims made on behalf of mysticism. In a cogently argued paper, Christoph Bode has pointed out the epistemological inconsistencies Huxley's later works are fraught with in this respect.[11]

If we disregard such criticism, valid though it is, and concentrate on science proper as we encounter it in *Island*, we may begin by mentioning the strong emphasis on agriculture, the importance attached to Rothamstead-in-the-Tropics, as the leading research centre is called (see *Island*, 146). Here the Palanese have profited from the advances made by British agronomists and agriculturalists. Incidentally, farming is done by small-scale producers and co-operatives, though—apart from a reference to the German social reformer Raiffeisen[12]—we do not learn much about this. With *Science, Liberty and Peace* (1947), Huxley became an advocate of such structures. They are a Western legacy, though hardly mainstream economics. Idealistically as well as apolitically, Huxley invokes the principle of Emersonian self-reliance (see *SLP*, 42).

The Palanese also believe in eugenics (see *Island*, 213–14). They have got sperm banks and practise artificial insemination. Medical studies are pursued with an emphasis on prevention. But good antibiotics are also readily available. And that's all about it. No physics, very little engineering, let alone large smoke-stack industries, no consumer culture. To anyone familiar with the history of utopian thought such austerity should not come as surprise. The Palanese have reached such a high level of contentment that sumptuary laws seem to be quite unnecessary. Huxley does not encourage us to suspect that the government might, at least occasionally, use coercion. The Palanese simply do not want to change anything. Murugan, their future Raja, whose favourite reading material are mail-order catalogues, heartily despises them for their conservatism.

In *Science, Liberty and Peace*, Huxley distinguishes between the basic needs of humankind—food, mental health, and the opportunity to develop one's latent potentialities—and our spiritual needs. Having recourse to a theological language whose bold syncretism is likely to cause some uneasiness, he speaks of a "Final End," which he conceives of as "the unitive knowledge of ultimate Reality." It amounts to the realization that "Atman and Brahman are one," that "the body is a temple of the Holy Ghost," that "Tao or the Logos is at once transcendent and immanent" (*SLP*, 22). Whatever our reservations about it might be, such a rhetoric of inclusiveness does not only accord well with the fundamental axiom of Huxley's *The Perennial Philosophy*, his belief in the essential unity of Western and Eastern mystical thought, it also prepares us for the semi-religious assumptions underlying the utopian experiment of Pala.

At the beginning of *Island*, Farnaby is given a kind of primer, the so-called Old Raja's *Notes on What's What*, which are said to contain the underlying principles of the Palanese experiment (see *Island*, 36). The short treatise does not merely deal out spiritual advice. Surprisingly polemical in spirit, it denounces the eloquence of Western philosophers and theologians. Above all, it finds fault with their 'dualism,' which Huxley seems to regard as the *peccatum originale* of Western thought. The Old Raja's own position is to be found in an elaboration of a Sanskrit formula: "*Tat tvam asi*, 'thou art That'" (*Island*, 81, see also *PP*, 8)—our innermost nature is ultimate reality. The formula has far-reaching implications. It amounts to no less than the rejection of all forms of 'dualism.' God, we learn in *The Perennial Philosophy*, is not a "what," he is a "That" (*PP*, 44). Nothing can be predicated of him. There is no discursive knowledge of the 'Divine Ground.' If we want to experience 'Pure Being,' we have to escape from the world of symbols.

Many readers who admire *Island* may not feel drawn to the spiritual teachings of *The Perennial Philosophy*, although the novel is based on them. The doomed utopia of Pala boasts of a *philosophia perennis*. The Leibnizian or Thomistic associations of the term, however, could hardly be more misleading. Huxley's book is an anthology of mystical literature interspersed with the compiler's own reflections. A fairly competent expounder of ancient texts, he arranges his material in such a way that he can demonstrate the essential unity of mystical thought.

The anthology has a distinctly anti-Aristotelian, perhaps we should say, anti-philosophical bias. Aristotle was content to know about the unmoving mover, "from the outside and theoretically," whereas the "perennial philosophers" are "primarily concerned with liberation and enlightenment" (*PP*, 78). Having thus identified a common concern which allows him to establish connections between the writers of the Upanishads and the

Cambridge Platonists, Huxley can drive home the message that "it is a fact, confirmed and re-confirmed during two or three thousand years of religious history, that the ultimate Reality is not clearly and immediately apprehended, except by those who have made themselves loving, pure in heart, and poor in spirit" (*PP*, 5).

The speculative Hindu prose treatises, known as the Upanishads, which assert the unity of Brahman and Atman, may contain humankind's most venerable mystical lore. Hence I cannot see any need to raise objections when Huxley claims that St Bernard, Master Eckhart, and William Law (the non-juror who attacked Bishop Hoadly and later became a mystic) in some way shared the belief that Atman, the individual self or the principle of life, is known after 'enlightenment' to be identical with Brahman, the primal source and ultimate goal of all beings. Suffice it to say that Eckhart's insistence that the knower and the known are one means the end of all discursive knowledge (*PP*, 19).

The mystic or sage who has attained a state of genuine 'enlightenment' has purged himself of "selfness" (*PP*, 58). This attainment, which is a divestment, seems to have the greatest appeal to Huxley. Yet mysticism is not for everyone. The inhabitants of Pala practise meditation—according to their individual needs, not as a compulsory exercise though it is also on the school curriculum. As an occasional treat, they are offered *moksha*. Hallucinogenic mushrooms open the doors of perception and help them to attain momentary states of "'luminous bliss'" and "knowledgeless understanding" (*Island*, 302, 303), as the journalist Farnaby learns upon his initiation. Murugan rejects the mushrooms. His open disdain for the dope, the novel wants to make us believe, offers a true measure of his shortcomings, which are the effects of his bungled education.

Huxley shows himself fully aware that most of his readers are likely to be sceptical about the cognitive claims made on behalf of mystical experiences, be they drug-induced or not. To buttress such claims he does not shrink from appealing to science. Like Huxley's description of the effects of mescaline in *The Doors of Perception*,[13] the Old Raja's definition of faith in *Island* is couched in the language of empiricism: "For Faith is the empirically justified confidence in our capacity to know who in fact we are" (*Island*, 38). To many Westerners the absence of dogma constitutes the greatest appeal of Eastern religion. Yet what we end up with here may be nothing but "cunning pseudo-affirmations," to borrow a phrase John Updike has put into the mouth of one of the many ministers that people his fiction, in this case, to dismiss Emersonian transcendentalism.[14] Huxley, the 'sceptical gnostic,' may have believed that Mahayana Buddhism, the later, more supernaturalist and syncretist form of Buddhism, possesses "a hard core of sense" beneath layers of "silliness and superstition" (*Island*, 81). At least, these are the very words used by a likeable young Palanese, the boyfriend of the nurse who attends on the injured Farnaby.

Comparing *The Perennial Philosophy* with *Island*, we should be aware of the differences of genre. It could easily be proved in a comparative analysis, ranging from Johnson's *Rasselas* to the twentieth-century novel, that, owing to the subtleties of narrative technique, works of fiction almost always lend themselves to the expression of sceptical views. They tend to erode the dogmatism we come across in our treatise literature. This observation holds true even for religious writers. In *Island*, however, Huxley's dogmatism reveals itself in the denial of a disjunction between Western science and Eastern religion. Thus the hybrid civilisation of his literary imagination is a far cry from postmodern concepts of hybridity, which tend to vacillate between integration and deconstruction.

2. Utopian Education

It took Huxley some time to become an advocate of integration. For Philip Quarles, in *Point Counter Point*, the "art of integral living" (*PCP*, 326) is still a mere formula. Once the transformation had been achieved it had momentous consequences for Huxley's attitude towards education. In his second novel there is the figure of a cranky architect who dismisses the whole teaching profession by referring to their calling as "the last refuge of feeble minds with classical educations" (*AH*, 20). The architect's son and principal character of the novel has only recently escaped from the boredom of a teaching position, which included duties like correcting sixty-three holiday task papers on the subject of the *Risorgimento* (see *AH*, 12), a satirical thrust at the defenders of a liberal education. Like his friends and acquaintances, Theodore Gumbril belongs to a generation that is suffering from a post-war depression amounting to a veritable crisis of values. By dancing the 'antic hay,' these denizens of a modern metropolis transform themselves into 'Marlovian goats.' No wonder they do not want to be educators.

In *Island*, however, Huxley confronts us with a utopian community whose success depends on nothing so much as offering the right education to all of its members. He seems to have what many readers would take to be a teacher's attitude towards the elimination of social evils. The earlier cynicism is just the reverse side of the coin which now shows us a state-maintained system of education that produces nothing but virtuous citizens whose happiness is too conspicuous to be ignored. We should, however, emphasise their happiness rather than their virtue. Huxley's eudemonism, unlike Aristotle's,[15] can do without the latter as long as there are science and mysticism.

The almost complete lack of coercion, which seems to characterize the system, is all the more surprising as the most prominent misfit of Pala's closely-knit society is the future ruler himself. And it is certainly no compliment to the framers of Pala's constitution that the elite has to squabble about educating the successor to the throne. Thus Murugan's guardians tried to undertake his *éducation sentimentale* by providing him with a girlfriend (see *Island*, 56). Their exertions were to no avail. The Rani, Murugan's overbearing mother, had managed to take her son abroad for a couple of formative years. It is difficult to imagine a greater disservice to the future of a utopian state which happens to be a monarchy. Huxley describes the Rani as a woman who dabbles in false spirituality. A theosophist bent upon a religious campaign she calls the "Crusade of the Spirit" (*Island*, 45), she behaves like "a female tycoon who [has] cornered the market, not in soya beans or copper, but in Pure Spirituality and the Ascended Masters, and [is] now happily running her hands over the exploit" (*Island*, 53). Incidentally, she may be seen as a literary ancestor of the heroine of John Updike's 1988 epistolary novel *S.*, a woman who also has a genius for combining business acumen with a penchant for an American-style do-it-yourself religion with Eastern trappings.[16]

When all is said and done, we are left with the observation that Pala's constitutional monarchy lacks any safeguards against both educational disasters and genealogical accidents. Giving Farnaby a crash course on the history of the island, Dr MacPhail briefly mentions a former Raja who was "an ass" but "happily made up for it by being short-lived" (*Island*, 36). This might tempt us into observing that a serious problem is treated with inexplicable nonchalance did we not know that Huxley was an educationalist rather than a political philosopher.

The reconciliation of analysis with vision, science with mysticism is the most ambitious goal of Pala's system of education. This means educating children "on the conceptual level without killing their capacity for intense non-verbal experience," or, in the idiom of a great Romantic, preventing "the glory and the freshness from fading into the light of common day" (*Island*, 231). There is a demonstration lesson attended by Farnaby dedicated to this educational objective (see *Island*, 244–248). It starts with observations on the dichotomy of public symbols and private feelings to prove the necessity for every child to move beyond discursive knowledge in order to become a little 'knower of suchness.' The suggestive questions of the instructor and the eagerness of the pupils who are led into 'discoveries' they believe to be their own betray an innocence that can hardly be shared by any informed reader. Yet when, in *The Perennial Philosophy*, Huxley refers to Wordsworth's 'Intimations Ode' to comment on the poverty of analytical thought (*PP*, 27), I take him to be fully aware of the irony that he uses one of the most egotistical of all modern poets to make his point.[17]

Having recourse to literature in works of fiction poses a problem. It is true that the Savage in *Brave New World* and Dr Poole in *Ape and Essence* do the same. The former's dissident views are couched in Shakespearean phrases (see, e.g., *BNW*, 105, 118, 126), and Shelley's "Epipsychidion" gives expression to the latter's newly-found bliss (see *AE*, 163). Though the bilingually educated inhabitants of Pala are said to have produced an Anglo-Palanese literature (see *Island*, 147), great works of art are incompatible with their happiness for two reasons.

As Plato did not want children to learn about the foul things which, according to Hesiod, Kronos did to his father Uranos as well as to his own children,[18] Pala's elite thinks it wise to improve upon Aesop's anthropo-morphic fictions. Betraying exactly the same zeal for political correctness, they have devised little "ecological fables with built-in, cosmic morals" (*Island*, 242). Ecology is after all the coping stone that tops their system of scientific education—like dialectics in Plato's utopia (see *The Republic*, 534e). We may wonder whether Huxley felt happy with this kind of pedagogically motivated censorship. The second reason is to be found in the *Notes* of the Old Raja. In a remarkably honest statement, he declares good life to be incompatible with good literature because the latter is premised on 'dualism' (see *Island*, 199). According to Plato, the poets from Homer downwards had no grasp of truth but merely produced a superficial likeness (see *The Republic*, 600e) If 'dualism' is epistemologically discredited, as Huxley clearly holds it to be, the same must be said about a tragic world view. Besides, tragedy requires social instability, as the World Controller explains to the dissident Bernard Helmholtz (see *BNW*, 200).

Nothing could better explain the decline of art. In the capital of Pala, *Oedipus* is transformed into a puppet show for children, in which a clever girl reasons the incestuous parricide out of his desire to maim himself (see *Island*, 279–284). It becomes the equivalent to *Three Weeks in a Helicopter* in *Brave New World* though the latter does not serve a didactic purpose (see *BNW*, 155). The Greek hero's tragic entanglement and blindness, the view that humans may become the sport of the gods (not the position of Sophocles but of later versions of the same myth) have become incomprehensible. As the happy children of Pala are also completely ignorant of the hierarchy of relationships within traditional families, of a stern authority operating through harsh constraints, they could not even make sense of Freud's interpretation of the myth should they hear about it. Such is the price that has to be paid for happiness.

There can be no mistake about what constituted the novel's appeal in the sixties. Apart from its unashamed recommendation of hallucinogenic mushrooms, it portrays the Palanese as a happy people because they practise *maithuna*. Sex is upgraded, if that is the word, through the equation of sacred with profane love (see *Island*, 82). Colonel Dipa's Ganymede, the future ruler Murugan, is full of contempt for the love lives of the inhabitants of Pala. But he is not completely blinded by his strong feelings. Perspicaciously he comments on their total aversion to change. The true reason for their conservatism is to be found in nothing else but in their 'lineaments of gratified desire.' Of course that is not the way Murugan chooses to express it. "'They like everything,'" he complains to Farnaby, "'to go on as it is, in the same old disgusting way, for ever and ever'" (*Island*, 47, see 152). From his point of view, Pala can only be vanquished by an outside aggressor. There is no inevitable decline. In modern parlance, *maithuna* functions as a safeguard against entropy.

The way the novel describes Murugan, as a beautiful adolescent with an exquisitely Grecian nose who is restlessly fidgeting and yawning during the *moksha* ceremony because he does not like the dope (see *Island*, 185, 189, 192), should be seen against the backdrop of the counter-culture of the sixties and Huxley's partial anticipation of it. In order to realise that he can hardly have been its true prophet, we have to become aware of the clash between the content and the form of his literary imagination.

Huxley assumes the pose of an old-fashioned, but essentially well-meaning pedagogue who leads a strayed child back to the path of virtue—with a firm but gentle hand. Yet it is not virtue this teacher recommends but *moksha* and *maithuna*. Murugan is a poor boy whose mind has been stuffed with the wrong notions and who has consequently committed himself to the wrong allegiances: "Only Mother and masturbation and the Ascended Masters. Only jazz records and sports cars and Hitlerian ideas about being a Great Leader" (*Island*, 80). Jazz music appears to be the oddest item on this list. German readers are reminded of Adorno who could also write about jazz and Fascism on the same page.[19] In the latter's case, the prejudices of the old German *Bildungsbürgertum* may be offered as an explanation, but what excuse does Huxley have after his sweeping condemnation of high art?[20]

3. A 'Science of the Mind'

When Dr Andrew MacPhail, the co-founder of the new Pala, started his project of social engineering, he began by carefully assessing the intellectual heritage he had brought from his native Scotland to this tropical island. In order to succeed with his best-of-two-worlds project, the Calvinist turned atheist had to learn a lot. Thus we are being told that he knew nothing about the "science of the human mind" (*Island*, 144). This is the only time this term occurs in the entire novel and it is not easy to make sense of it in the context established by Huxley. There is, however, a significant parallel to the novel's use of the term 'enlightenment.' The 'science of the mind' known to this physician was Scottish moral philosophy. As a young medical student who had to spend his days in the dissecting room he had studied Hume on miracles as well as other writers hostile to Calvinism or revealed religion. Hence we may assume him to be familiar with a way of accounting for the phenomena of the human mind that, though far from atheistic in its consequences, hardly lends itself to Huxley's theorizing about immanence and transcendence. Its incompatibility with the Buddhist notion of 'Mind at Large' (see *Island*, 156, *DP*, 59) hardly needs to be pointed out.

When Dr Andrew's descendant Dr Robert MacPhail tries to convince Farnaby of the kind of 'enlightenment' that may be had via mystical experiences, he has to counter the latter's sceptical objection that the "'whole caboodle is inside your skull'" (*Island*, 155). The doctor begins by making a subtle distinction. Whereas Farnaby seems to think that the brain produces consciousness, he prefers the view that it functions as a transmitter of consciousness—that is to say, of what Huxley was happy to call 'Mind at Large'. But, as the author (or his fictional mouthpiece) cannot even quite convince himself, Dr McPhail ends by saying that it would not make any practical difference if he could be proved to be wrong, which of course he cannot (*Island*, 156). The physiological effects of *moksha* do not depend on one's theory of consciousness. The Palanese are officially encouraged to seek transcendental experiences and, at the same time, to be sceptical about them (see *Island*, 166, see also 88). And who is going to worry about giving or withholding assent in such matters if knowledge about ultimate reality can never be propositional?

The appearance of so much tolerance, however, may be deceiving. Utopians have to believe that their ideas cannot be improved upon. They usually brook no interference with their blueprints. Huxley's late utopia relies on his 'anti-dualist' science as a substitute for politics, and on a system of education which implements its most important findings. And it is precisely here that a strain of authoritarianism becomes all too visible: "In religion," the Old Raja writes, "all words are dirty words. Anybody who gets eloquent about Buddha, or God, or Christ, ought to have his mouth washed out with carbolic soap" (*Island*, 37). We can hardly be surprised that, in this novel, intolerance should come in the guise of such rather old-fashioned, not to say school-marmish educational fantasies about inculcating the virtue of cleanliness.

Consequently, it is not the liberal education he ridiculed in *Crome Yellow* and *Antic Hay*[21] that the older Huxley returns to. Such a move would have been incompatible with his dismissal of tragic art, which is still held in high esteem in *Eyeless in Gaza*, whose hero, while musing on Hamlet, convincingly defines tragedy as a surfeit of knowledge. The prince of Denmark would have been happy had he been as ignorant as Polonius (*EG*, 92). If Huxley falls back behind such insights in *Island*, we have to blame his 'science of the mind'.

In his book *The Closing of the American Mind*, which may have been the most eloquent plea for a liberal education in late twentieth-century America, Allan Bloom, a political philosopher and a classicist, explains what Socrates stands for—the firm conviction "that the unexamined life is not worth living."[22] Taken seriously, this can only mean that a liberal education "puts everything at risk and requires students who are able to risk everything"

(Bloom, 370). A readiness to do so includes the willingness to face the "lack of cosmic support for what we care about" (Bloom, 277). Huxley's intermittent scepticism notwithstanding, this is a far cry from the position of an author who is looking for an escape from the world of symbols and who wants us to recover, at least momentarily, the "perceptual innocence of childhood" (*DP*, 21).

Moreover, in his late utopia, Huxley has not merely got rid of a liberal education, but of liberalism as well. This may either be explained by referring, once again, to the genre. Thus the critique of utopian thinking implicit in this interpretation of *Island* is bound to yield the result that there simply cannot be a liberal utopia. Aristotle's obsession with virtue, Huxley's emphasis on science and mysticism effectively preclude such an option. Or, alternatively, we may point to Huxley's disaffection with the nineteenth century. The hero of his last novel is called William Asquith Farnaby because the old Farnaby was an "ardent Liberal. Even when he was drunk. Especially when he was drunk" (*Island*, 15). This is how the journalist introduces himself upon his arrival on the island. In *The Road to Serfdom*, which was first published in 1944, the economist and social philosopher Friedrich August Hayek sums up his argument by saying that his contemporaries made "a mess of things" because, feeling superior to their forebears, they thought it wise to abandon nineteenth-century liberalism.[23] Bashing the Victorians was very much *en vogue* in the 1920s and beyond. It seems that *Island* still owes much to the intellectual climate of the inter-war years. Huxley could only have become first a *dystopian* and then a *eutopian* writer because he had long ago ceased to believe in liberalism. Readers of *Island* may see Pala as a close approximation to paradise. But they should be ready to acknowledge that true freedom is to be found in the unreconstructed world outside. And so are wickedness and misery. Christian 'dualist' writers like John Updike have always known this. Without such knowledge there is little hope for a sound understanding of politics.

---

[1] Aldous Huxley, *Island*, with an introduction by David Bradshaw (London, 1994). Hereafter, *Island*. I have used the following editions of Huxley's other works: *Antic Hay* (London, 1977; hereafter, *AH*), *Ape and Essence* (Chicago, 1992; herafter, *AE*), *Brave New World* (London, 1994; hereafter, *BNW*), *Crome Yellow*, with an introduction by Malcolm Bradbury (London, 2004; herafter, *CY*), *Eyeless in Gaza,* with an introduction by David Bradshaw (London, 1994; hereafter, *EG*), *"The Doors of Perception" and "Heaven and Hell"* (London, 1977; hereafter, *DP*), *The Perennial Philosophy* (London, 1950; hereafter, *PP*), *Point Counter Point* (New York, 1984; hereafter, *PCP*), *Science, Liberty and Peace* (London, 1947; hereafter, *SLP*).

[2] Peter E. Firchow, "Brave at Last: Huxley's Western and Eastern Utopias," in: *"Now More Than Ever": Proceedings of the Aldous Huxley Centenary Symposium Münster 1994*, ed. Bernfried Nugel (Frankfurt a. M., 1995; hereafter, *"NMTE"*), 226.

[3] See Dana Sawyer, *Aldous Huxley: A Biography* (New York, 2002), 188.

[4] James Buchan, *Capital of the Mind: How Edinburgh Changed the World* (London, 2003).

[5] See the motto from Aristotle's *Politics*: "In framing an ideal we may assume what we wish, but should avoid impossibilities" (*Island*, [xiv]).

[6] See Francis Bacon, *New Atlantis*, in: *The Advancement of Learning and New Atlantis*, ed. A. Johnston (Oxford, 1974), 215–247.

[7] There is, however, an old priest who conducts the *moksha* ceremony. The enraptured congregation listens to his "splendid rumble of Sanskrit" (*Island*, 185).

[8] 'Practical wisdom' ('phronesis') enables the citizens to find out which laws are best and which of them suit a particular constitution (*Politics* 1289a). Unlike Aristotle, Huxley is not enough of a political philosopher to think about the process of legislation. His major concern is education.

[9] It is surely no coincidence that Dr Poole, one the principal characters in *Ape and Essence*, is a biologist.

[10] *Island*, 253. This ambitious-sounding attribute occurs already in *Eyeless in Gaza*, whose principal hero shows a penchant for mysticism (*EG*, 77). The dystopian vision of *Ape and Essence* constitutes the very opposite of such an ideal, a 'demonocracy' erected after a nuclear Armageddon combining the worst in both civilisations. To prove this point, the Arch-Vicar of Belial encourages the captive Dr Poole to make a counterfactual assumption by imagining that the best synthesis had been achieved instead—a blend of Western science and Eastern mysticism (*AE*, 184). *Brave New World* does not fit into this scheme because its dystopian world state has got a utilitarian basis.

[11] See Christoph Bode, "Epistemological Inconsistencies in Aldous Huxley's Later Works," in: *"NMTE"*, 319–333.

[12] There are no commercial banks but credit unions inspired by Raiffeisen (*Island*, 164).

[13] It is certainly part of the book's uniqueness in the field of drug literature that it avails itself of a Lockean terminology (see *DP*, 23, 43).

[14] See John Updike, *In the Beauty of the Lilies* (London, 1996), 16.

[15] See Plato, *Politics*, 1323b.

[16] See John Updike, *S.* (Harmondsworth, 1988).

[17] True 'enlightenment' remains unattainable as long as one does not get purged of one's "selfness" (*PP*, 58).

[18] See Plato, *The Republic*, 377e.

[19] See Theodor W. Adorno and Max Horkheimer, *Dialektik der Aufklärung: Philosophische Fragmente* (Frankfurt/Main, 1984 [¹1944]), 133.

[20] In *Point Counter Point*, Philip Quarles may not know what a "complete human being" is. Therefore his nearest approach towards a definition is by negatives: "Not a newspaper reader, not a jazzer, not a radio fan" (*PCP*, 308).

[21] Whereas Theodore Gumbril has become thoroughly disillusioned with teaching, the young poet Denis Stone offers abject apologies for being overeducated (see *CY*, 17).

[22] Allan Bloom, *The Closing of the American Mind* (New York, London, Toronto, 1988).

[23] Friedrich August Hayek, *The Road to Serfdom* (London, 1997 [[1]1944]), 178.

Grzegorz Moroz

(University of Bialystok)

FROM CENTRIFUGAL BUMBLE-PUPPY TO FREE CLIMBING—
REPRESENTATIONS OF SPORT IN *BRAVE NEW WORLD*,
EYELESS IN GAZA AND *ISLAND*

Aldous Huxley's life-long quest for "the Godhead," "the Ground," made him concentrate much more on the spiritual than the corporeal. But, as he wrote himself in *Eyeless in Gaza*, "mind-body is indivisible except in thought,"[1] and in his fiction as well as non-fiction we get numerous representations of the human body in action. We get them in 'realistic' novels set in Britain in between the wars or just before the Second World War, for example in *Crome Yellow* or *Eyeless in Gaza*, but sport is also an integral part of the 'non-realistic' dystopian society presented in *Brave New World* as well as in the utopian Palanese society depicted in *Island*.

As one of Huxley's biographers, Dana Sawyer, observed, the marriage of Aldous Huxley's parents Leonard and Julia "was more than a marriage of two people; it was the marriage of two great Victorian families, the Huxleys and the Arnolds; [...] who, though not of 'noble blood,' nonetheless constituted the intellectual aristocracy of the British Empire."[2] Being born at that time and that place meant that he entered the system of British public schools with its emphasis on the role of sports and particularly team games in the education of the new generations of the British Empire's élite. Aldous Huxley went first to Hillside School and then to Eton; this was the heyday of public school games, whose role in élite education had been growing steadily since the 1850s. By Edwardian times they were absolutely pivotal in the system, as Richard Holt observed in *Sport and the British*:

> Although in principle sport was not supposed to be compulsory, in practice it was. Refusing to play took even more courage than participating. Games were the core of a kind of inclusive culture that sociologists nowadays identify with 'total institutions' like army barracks or prisons from which there is no escape and where an individual eats and sleeps, works and plays in collective isolation.[3]

Huxley was not much of a sportsman and probably most people familiar, or vaguely familiar, with his biography, would put it down to his eye disease which led to his near-blindness in the summer of 1911 and whose consequences continued to trouble him for the rest of his life. However, these problems apparently did not begin till the winter of 1911, when Aldous was 17 and long past his Hillside days. To try to explain Huxley's lack of success in sport one should turn to the theory of personality and its correlation with corporeal constitution which was proposed by Dr William Sheldon and which

Aldous Huxley took extremely seriously and wrote about copiously, mostly in his non-fiction, to explain such diverse phenomena as people's inability to communicate with one another due to extreme somatotonia,[4] or different religious dispositions.[5] Sheldon's theory seemed to be able to explain also why most of us have no chance at all of success on a competitive level in most sports. In an article published in *Harper's Magazine* in 1944 Huxley wrote: "For example, less than ten out of every hundred are sufficiently meso-morphic to engage with even moderate success in the more strenuous forms of athletics. Hence the almost criminal folly of encouraging all boys, whatever their hereditary make-up, to develop athletic ambitions."[6] Sports physiologists today use terms like slow or fast twitch muscle predominance and/or kinesthetic intelligence to explain why most of us have no chance to become top athletes no matter how much we dream of it, try or are pushed to do so.

Let me start with *Brave New World* (1932). There sport is not such an important part of an educational process of forming character and team spirit as it was, has been and still is deemed by most nineteenth- and twentieth-century British, American or Australian educators; it is reduced to the role of entertainment, it is a distraction from reality. In *Brave New World Revisited* (1958) Huxley states:

> A society, most of whose members spend a great part of their time not on the spot, not here and now and in the calculable future, but somewhere else, in the irrelevant other worlds of sport and soap opera, of mythology and metaphysical phantasy, will find it hard to resist the encroachments of those who would manipulate and control it.[7]

And a little earlier in the same paragraph, a popular game in the World State, Centrifugal Bumble-puppy is recalled together with others of Huxley's own coinages for popular entertainment:

> In *Brave New World* non-stop distractions of the most fascinating nature (the feelies, orgy-porgy, centrifugal Bumble-puppy) are deliberately used as instruments of policy, for the purpose of preventing people from paying too much attention to the realities of the social and political situation. (*BNWR*, 280)

Sport is a distraction and a form of entertainment, but also a part of the World State's capitalist economy. When the Director of the Central London Hatchery and Conditioning Centre takes his students to the Infant Nurseries, the Neo-Pavlovian Conditioning Rooms, and shows them babies treated with electric shocks while being shown pictures of books and flowers, he concludes: "'We condition the masses to hate the country. [...] But simultaneously we condition them to love all country sports. At the same time, we see to it that all country sports shall entail the use of elaborate apparatus. So that they consume manufactured articles as well as transport.

Hence those electric shocks."[8] Later on, while watching a game of Centrifugal Bumble-puppy, the Director says:

> "Strange to think that even in Our Ford's day most games were played without more apparatus than a ball or two and a few sticks and perhaps a bit of netting. Imagine the folly of allowing people to play elaborate games which do nothing whatever to increase consumption. It's madness. Nowadays the Controllers won't approve of any new game unless it can be shown that it requires at least as much apparatus as the most complicated of existing games."
> (*BNW,* 35)

That is the view of the capitalist theory of economics, but it seems that Huxley's creativity in presenting 'the consumer sports' in practice was restricted mostly to linguistic coinages: thus, golf becomes "Obstacle Golf" and "Electro-magnetic Golf"; tennis is "Riemann-surface tennis," squash becomes "Escalator Squash," cricket becomes simplified to "Centrifugal Bumble-puppy." We are not given the exact rules nor do we see any of the major characters actually participating in any of these sports. The idea of sport as a stimulus for the development of the transport industry as well as the manufacturing industry is envisaged just once and only fragmentarily when Lenina Crowne is flying with Henry for a round of Obstacle Golf:

> Lenina looked down through the window in the floor between her feet. They were flying over the six kilometre zone of parkland that separated Central London from its first ring of satellite suburbs. The green was maggoty with fore-shortened life. Forests of Centrifugal Bumble-puppy towers gleamed between the trees. Near Shepherd's Bush two thousand Beta-Minus mixed doubles were playing Riemann-surface tennis. A double row of Escalator Fives Courts lined the main road from Notting Hill to Willesden. In the Ealing stadium a Delta gymnastic display and community sing was in progress. (*BNW*, 58)

Looking at this problem from the perspective of the beginning of the twenty-first century, it should be acknowledged that tennis, golf or squash are still popular and in some cases even more popular in Western societies and keep sports gear manufacturers busy. But in the meantime other sports have appeared that are much closer to the World Inspector's ideals of consumption, namely sports like windsurfing, mountain biking and, more than anything else, alpine skiing—a sport that is popular with people from all layers of society, be they members of Royal families, celebrities, executives and top politicians or simple working class people. They buy or rent expensive gear which is outdated technologically after two or three seasons, although it is often still in mint condition. Apart from skiing equipment special clothes and accessories are required as well as lifts, pistes, pensions, hotels, restaurants, discos, airplanes or motorways and petrol. In 2002 Austria alone made around ten billion euros on the skiing industry.

As far as Britain is concerned, Andrew Adonis and Stephen Pollard tell us in *A Class Act* :

> Every sport has its class labels. Ascot is for toffs, the Grand National for 'the people'; Cowes is for debs, rugby league for miners. [...] Next are sports such as cricket and golf which attract 'all sorts.' Although the 'sorts' are segregated between municipal golf courses and Wentworth Golf Club, for instance—when they do mix there can be trouble.[9]

They do not mix in the brave new world either: "Beneath them lay the buildings of the Golf Club—the huge lower-caste barracks and, on the other side of a dividing wall, the smaller houses reserved for Alpha and Beta members" (*BNW,* 65). This way they can enjoy their social, so to speak, 19th hole separately. However, it seems that there is no class distinction regarding the two types of golf, Obstacle and Electro-magnetic: "'What were you playing this afternoon? Obstacle or Electro-magnetic?'" (*BNW*, 70), Bernard Marx is asked by Morgana Rothschild, and "blushingly he had to admit that he had been playing neither" (*BNW*, 70). Golf in the brave new world is played by men and women together.

So is tennis, as we have seen in the passage quoted above, "two thousand Beta-Minus mixed doubles were playing Riemann-surface tennis." The impression created by "two thousand Beta-Minus mixed doubles" certainly is that of the common lower middle class. In Britain, for a long time mixed doubles were the only game in which men and women participated together; and tennis as such was a game that the upper and middle classes played together. Going down the social ladder, we have in the same passage "a Delta gymnastic display" in "the Ealing stadium"; this is the only activity or sport for the bottom classes of the brave new world, and it seems to reflect the socially low position of gymnastics in Britain at the beginning of the twentieth century, which was probably best summarized in the slogan of that time: "games for the classes; gym for the masses" (Holt, 118).

But it seems that in the brave new world they have one game for the masses, or at least for the masses of children:

> The Director and his students stood for a short time watching a game of Centrifugal Bumble-puppy. Twenty children were grouped in a circle round a chrome steel tower. A ball thrown up so as to land on the platform at the top of the tower rolled down into the interior, fell on a rapidly revolving disk, was hurled through one or other of the numerous apertures pierced in the cylindrical casing, and had to be caught. (*BNW*, 35)

Huxley takes the simple, traditional game of bumble-puppy and converts it into Centrifugal Bumble-puppy which becomes a sort of simplified and mechanised cricket, with the socially more prestigious aspects of cricket, that is, bowling and batting, being taken over by the Centrifugal Bumble-puppy towers and catching being left for the entertainment of children. We do not learn if the children playing Centrifugal Bumble-puppy are Alphas or Deltas or Epsilons and there is no other moment in the novel when this game is played. So its low social status is not directly stated but only implied, as it is the case in the passage quoted above from *Brave New World Revisited*, where Huxley puts Centrifugal-Bumble-puppy alongside other entertainment for the masses, such as orgy-porgy and the feelies.

If we jump to the other end of the social spectrum, we find that the sport with the highest social status is Elevator Squash. Again, as in the case of Centrifugal Bumble-puppy, this status is presented in a rather implicit way. Thus, when Bernard and Lenina, on their way to the reservation, stay overnight in a hotel in Santa Fé, Lenina considers this hotel so posh and excellent that she is unwilling to go on and says: "'I almost wish we could stay here. Sixty Elevator-Squash Courts...'" But Bernard interrupts her, remarking: "'There won't be any in the Reservation'" (*BNW*, 85).

Bernard Marx and Helmholtz Watson are both Alpha-Plus intellectuals. They get together because they feel alienated from their own class; Bernard because he, by some fault in his Hatchery production, has "too little bone and brawn" and is eight centimetres shorter than the standard height for his caste, Watson for very different reasons: "This Escalator-Squash champion, this indefatigable lover (it was said the he had had six hundred and forty different girls in under four years), this admirable committee man and best mixer had realized quite suddenly that sport, women, communal activities were only, as far as he was concerned, second bests" (*BNW*, 62). This opinion about "second bests" may be a truly individual intellectual fad of Watson's, but the narrator's list of his honours is clearly supposed to reflect the hierarchy of the Alpha-Plus values. It is not his intellectual skills as a committee man nor even his top lover status (and we are in an ultra-promiscuous society), but his being the Escalator-Squash champion that comes first on the list. And somehow, his status of great lover and committee man may be seen as a result of his squash mastery, the game requiring more "bone and brawn" than most ball games; the game—to use Sheldon's terminology—for extreme mesomorphic somatotonics to win and for Alphas (and maybe Betas) to play.

There are two distinct, if short, representations of spectator sports in *Brave New World*. The first occurs, while the Savage visits his dying mother Linda in the hospital:

> Linda was lying in the last of the long row of beds, next to the wall. She was watching the Semi-finals of the South American Riemann-Surface Tennis Championship, which were being played in silent and diminished reproduction on the screen of the television box at the foot of the bed. Hither and thither across their square of illumined glass the little figures noiselessly darted, like fish in an aquarium—the silent but agitated inhabitants of another world. (*BNW*, 157)

Nowadays, when the All England Cricket and Lawn Tennis Club has just announced that it is going to spend millions of pounds on building sliding roofs over some of the Wimbledon courts in order to please TV broadcasters unhappy with frequent coverage distractions due to rain, Huxley's predictive, almost prophetic skills should be stressed. But it can be argued if the second passage representing sports is even more prophetic or if his sardonic jibe at masculine hegemony in the English upper middle class backfired and has become true now with women competing in world championships in sports like boxing, kick-boxing, weight-lifting and wrestling. After all, there is quite a long discussion between Lenina Crowne and Bernard Marx on where to go on their first date: "In the end she persuaded him, much against his will, to fly over to Amsterdam to see the Semi-Demi-Finals of the Women's Heavyweight Wrestling Championship" (BNW, 77). This episode can perhaps be linked to an experience Huxley had in Paris, which Nicholas Murray reports in his biography: "The Huxleys were starting to enjoy Paris, however, and sampling some of its pleasures, which included a Lesbian bar featuring 'a wrestling match between two gigantic wrestlers.'"[10]

Sport in the brave new world may look trivial and childish (for example, Centrifugal Bumble-puppy) and yet because it distracts people from living here and now and sends a considerable part of the economy spinning, it is compulsory and may thus lead to very ominous consequences. Bernard Marx considers Electro-magnetic Golf a waste of time (his partner Lenina Crowne even finds it difficult to conceive what is meant by this: "'Then what's time for?' asked Lenina in some astonishment" [BNW, 77]), and he prefers walking in the Lake District, which is one of the reasons why the Director of the Central London Hatchery and Conditioning Centre exclaims: "'By his heretical views on sport and soma, by the scandalous unorthodoxy of his sex-life [...] he has proved himself an enemy of Society, a subverter, ladies and gentlemen, of all Order and Stability, a conspirator against Civilization itself. For this reason I propose to dismiss him, to dismiss him with ignominy from the post he has held in this Centre; I propose forthwith to apply for his transference to a Sub-Centre of the lowest order'" (BNW, 121).

Extreme mesomorphs became captains of their English public schools' first elevens, as did Mark Staithes in Huxley's Eyeless in Gaza, or champions in Elevator Squash, as does Helmholtz Watson in Brave New World, which elevated their positions within their own class considerably. On the other hand, weak ectomorphs and endomorphs, preferring walks in the Lake District, as did Brian Foxe in Eyeless in Gaza or Bernard Marx in Brave New World, found it extremely difficult to make their way in their respective societies.

In Eyeless in Gaza there are no direct representations of sports, but many passages show how the central role of sport in the British public school system affects key characters like Anthony Beavis, Mark Staithes or Hugh

Ledwidge. Anthony Beavis, who is usually assumed to be, to a large extent, a *porte-parole* of Huxley himself, reports to his father in a letter from Bulstrode, dated June 26th, 1903: "'We had two matches yesterday, first eleven v. Sunny Bank, second v. Mumbridge, we won both which was rather ripping. I was playing in the second eleven and made six not out'" (*EG,* 134). This passage corresponds quite well with the account of Aldous's cousin, Gervas Huxley, from Hillside: "By 1905 or 6 he was quite as strong as I was. He was never an athlete but enjoyed games—he was scorer for our cricket eleven and in our last year he and I helped to make up a highly unprofessional halfback line in the soccer team—and he was a tremendous walker and climber and very keen on it."[11] But making six not out for the second team is still a long way from Mark Staithes, a mesomorphic captain of the first eleven whose thoughts about Anthony Beavis are reported by the narrator in this way:

> Looking round the table, Mark Staithes saw that that wretched, baby-faced Benger Beavis wasn't laughing with the rest, and for a second was filled with a passionate resentment against this person who had dared not to be amused by his joke. What made the insult more intolerable was the fact that Benger was so utterly insignificant. Bad at football, not much use at cricket. The only thing that he was good at was work. Work! (*EG,* 40)

Many years later, long after their school days, Mark and Anthony have become friends. When their common lady friend, Miss Pendle, learns that they were at school together she asks Anthony what sort of boy Mark was then. Anthony answers: "'He bullied me a good deal'"(*EG,* 219) and then adds: "'Being so good at football he had a right to bully me'"(*EG,* 220). Now, Anthony can afford to be clearly ironic about this sport/bullying syndrome, but in *Eyeless in Gaza* one can also see real trauma caused by it. Even long after his schooldays Hugh Ledwidge, who was much worse at sports than Anthony, cannot bear to face "their reminiscences of how he had funked at football; of how he had cried when it was his turn, at fire-drill, to slide down the rope; of how he had sneaked to Jimbug and had then been made to run the gauntlet between two lines of them, armed with wet towels rolled up into truncheons"(*EG,* 121).

However, sport in *Eyeless in Gaza* is shown to have some positive potential as well. Football may be a curse for non-mesomorphic students at public schools at home, but at the same time it is seen by Dr Miller as the best British export. Games, he claims, "'are the greatest English contribution to civilization [...] much more important than parliamentary government, or steam engines, or Newton's Principia. More important even than English poetry. Poetry can never be a substitute for war and murder. Whereas games can be. A complete and genuine substitute'" (*EG,* 389–390). And although Mark Staithes derides the idea of substitutes as such, Dr Miller insists on teaching football to the Indians and organizing matches between villages as a substitute for vendettas (see *EG,* 380).

Yet, it is not through games or competitive sports that Huxley's characters are allowed to attain bliss. In Helen Amberley's case it is achieved through dancing:

> Dancing she lost her life in order to save it; lost her identity and became something greater than herself, lost her perplexities and self-hatreds in a bright harmonious certitude; lost her bad character and was made perfect; lost the regretted past, the apprehended future and gained a timeless present of consummate happiness. She who could not paint, could not write, could not even sing in tune, became while she danced an artist; more than an artist; became a god, the creator of a new heaven and a new earth, a creator rejoicing in his creation and finding it good. (*EG,* 166–167)

Similarly, Anthony Beavis, who takes Helen on a boatride, displays grace and mastery: "He lifted his trailing punt pole and swung it forward with a movement of easy grace, of unhurried and accomplished power; the punt shot forward, the end of the pole lifted from the river-bed, trailed for a moment, then gracefully, once more, easily, masterfully was swung forward" (*EG,* 153). Much later, in his diary, Anthony stresses awareness and control causing the mind-body dichotomy to collapse: "Skill acquired in getting to know the muscular aspect of mind-body can be carried over into the exploration of other aspects. There is increasing ability to detect one's motives for any given piece of behaviour [...]. Re-educate. Give back correct physical use" (*EG,* 223). Huxley was by then clearly walking briskly on the path leading to *The Perennial Philosophy* and *Island.*

In *Island* there are no team games; sport, or to be more precise, physical activities that are supposed to keep us sane, fit and healthy are gardening and mountain climbing; incidentally, both stereotypically perceived as exquisitely British. Mountain climbing was the favourite outdoor activity of Victorian and post-Victorian intellectuals and gentlemen. There was a wide range of forms, from walks in the Lake District, via the climbing of Snowdon and the Matterhorn to George Leigh Mallory's three Mount Everest expeditions in tweeds and home-knits and his death there near its summit in 1924. In a 1961 London interview, Huxley admitted that after his eye trouble started, "many things that I liked doing, like mountain climbing and so on, became difficult or impossible to me" (Bedford, 54). In *Those Barren Leaves* Francis Chelifer describes an Easter Sunday climb of Snowdon with his agnostic father, who "considered a walk among the mountains as the equivalent of church-going,"[12] peaking (pun intended) with the latter's recitation of a passage from Wordsworth's *Prelude.* In *Island,* "climbing is an integral part of the school curriculum."[13] One of its goals is to channel the excessive energy of extreme mesomorphs, but the main one, the one that makes it a crucial part of Pala's initiation rite, is beautifully described in this way:

> Danger deliberately and yet lightly accepted. Danger shared with a friend, a group of friends. Shared consciously, shared to the limits of awareness so that the sharing and the danger become a yoga. Two friends roped together on a rock face. Sometimes three friends or four. Each totally aware of his own straining muscles, his own skill, his own fear, and his own spirit transcending the fear. And each, of course, aware at the same time of all others, concerned for them, doing the right things to make sure that they'll be safe. Life at its highest pitch of bodily and mental tension, life more abundant, more inestimably precious, because of the ever-present threat of death. But after the yoga of danger there's the yoga of the summit, the yoga of rest and letting go, the yoga of complete and total receptiveness, the yoga that consists in consciously accepting what is given as it is given, without censorship by your busy moralistic mind, without any additions from your stock of second-hand ideas, your even larger stock of wishful phantasies. You just sit there with muscles relaxed and a mind open to the sunlight and the clouds, open to distance and the horizon, open in the end to that formless, wordless Not-Thought which the stillness of the summit permits you to divine, profound and enduring, within the twittering flux of your everyday thinking. And now it's time for the descent, for a second bout of the yoga of danger, time for a renewal of tension and the awareness of life in its glowing plenitude as you hang precariously on the brink of destruction. Then at the foot of the precipice you unrope, you go striding down the rocky path towards the first trees. And suddenly you're in the forest, and another kind of yoga is called for—the yoga of the jungle. (*Island*, 202–203)

And Huxley ends this memorable paragraph with the words:

> And not merely a reconciliation. A fusion, an identity. Beauty made one with horror in the yoga of the jungle. Life reconciled with the perpetual imminence of death in the yoga of danger. Emptiness identified with self-hood in the Sabbath yoga of the summit. (*Island*, 203)

Island is often perceived as Huxley's utopian vision merging the philosophies of the East and West; nowhere is this fusion more apparent than in the passage quoted above.

From the yoga of mountain climbing one may profitably turn to another extremely important, if not equally epiphanous, yoga, the yoga of gardening. The Palanese concept of the advantages of gardening are explained to Will jointly by Vijaya and Dr Robert McPhail in Chapter 9. When Will comments that they "'dig and delve'" (significantly, the Chaucerian phrase is used here by Huxley) in the form of a "'Tolstoy act,'" Vijaya replies: "'Certainly not. I do muscular work, because I have muscles; and if I don't use my muscles I shall become a bad-tempered sitting-addict'" (*Island*, 173), to which Dr Robert adds: "'With nothing between the cortex and buttocks [...]. Or rather with everything—but in a condition of complete unconsciousness and toxic stagnation. Western intellectuals are all sitting-addicts. That's why most of you are so repulsively unwholesome. In the past even a duke had to do a lot of walking, even a moneylender, even a metaphysician'" (*Island*, 173). And when asked by Will if the Palanese treat gardening as a form of therapy, Dr Robert answers: "'As prevention—to make therapy unnecessary. In Pala even a professor, even a government official generally puts in two hours of digging and delving each day'"(*Island*, 174).

Seen from today's perspective of keeping fit, the Palanese recipe for physical wellness leading to holistic wellness more than fulfils the 1970s sport physiologists' famous formula 3x30x130, which tells us that in order to keep our cardio-vascular system in shape one should do physical exercise three times a week for 30 minutes raising the heart rate to approximately 130 beats per minute. I checked my heart beat with my heart monitor while digging my mother's garden; hard digging certainly does the trick, but I see two problems here: one is that in the temperate zone digging and delving are very seasonal activities which cannot be performed over long spells of time; the other is described in a letter written by Maria Huxley from France on 4 May, 1935: "But what is more comic still is that Aldous has decided to take violent exercise for the sake of his health and that that exercise is the most concisely found in the form of gardening. So he digs every spare inch of the ground and causes havoc all round him to the despair of the gardener" (Bedford, 298).

---

[1] Aldous Huxley, *Eyeless in Gaza* (New York, 1964), 255. Hereafter, *EG*.

[2] Dana Sawyer, *Aldous Huxley: A Biography* (New York, 2002), 22.

[3] Richard Holt, *Sport and the British: The Modern History* (Oxford, 1997), 97.

[4] See Aldous Huxley, *The Doors of Perception* (New York, 1990), 14.

[5] See Aldous Huxley, *The Perennial Philosophy* (New York, 1945), 150–151.

[6] Aldous Huxley, "Who Are You?" *Harper's Magazine, 189* (1944), 515.

[7] Aldous Huxley, *Brave New World Revisited* (London, 1987), 280. Hereafter, *BNWR*.

[8] Aldous Huxley, *Brave New World* (Harmondsworth, 1972), 30. Hereafter, *BNW*.

[9] Andrew Adams and Stephen Pollard, *A Class Act: The Myth of British Classless Society* (Harmondsworth, 1998), 229.

[10] Nicholas Murray, *Aldous Huxley: An English Intellectual* (London, 2003), 218.

[11] Sybille Bedford, *Aldous Huxley: A Biography* (New York, 1975), 15.

[12] Aldous Huxley, *Those Barren Leaves* (New York, 1925), 130.

[13] Aldous Huxley, *Island* (New York, 2002), 91. Hereafter, *Island*.

Rodica Dimitriu

(University of Iasi, Romania)

ALDOUS HUXLEY REWRITTEN BY MIRCEA ELIADE

Mircea Eliade, internationally acclaimed writer, literary critic and historian of religions, was one of the key figures in mediating the dialogue between Aldous Huxley and his Romanian readers in the inter-war (pre-Communist) years. Moreover, his works have contributed to establishing the British author's continuing popularity in Romania in later periods of reception. Eliade's response to Huxley was a complex one, comprising both literary criticism and literary pieces—one novel in particular—written along the lines of Huxley's novels of ideas. In what follows, I shall consider all these texts as 'rewritings' of some of the English writer's works for the Romanian readership.[1] The term as such draws attention to the fact that the—inevitably subjective—image of Huxley thus projected for the reader is filtered through a series of culturally as well as personally determined grids, which may coincide with, but also considerably differ from, other interpretations of Huxley's works in Romania, Britain and worldwide.

Aldous Huxley and the Romanian 'Existentialist Group'

In the 1930s Eliade provided his rewritings of Huxley as one of the leaders of a cultural group of brilliant young intellectuals alternately called 'The New Generation,' 'The New Spirituality,' 'The Experimentalists' (P. Comarnescu), or, more frequently in recent times, 'The Existentialists' (I. Negoiţescu). Although this circle comprised strikingly different personalities and despite the fact that there were divergences between its members' political beliefs, they felt the need for some unifying texts to acknowledge the principles that they shared. Since theirs was the first young generation to enjoy, for almost two decades, a period of peace, prosperity and democracy, they could afford to concentrate on more sophisticated issues such as their own spiritual development, theoretically claiming a break with the past in every respect. Their iconoclastic attitude was, in fact, similar in many ways to Huxley's and to that of the young British generation of the 1920s. Their discourse was mainly informed by the irrational and mystical trends in philosophy (particularly Spengler's, Keyserling's and Berdiaev's theories) that had come into full blossom in Europe after World War I. Emil Cioran, who, later on, wrote his philosophical works in France, was also a member, whereas Eugène Ionesco, who was not part of the group as such and who had written about Huxley in less enthusiastic terms,[2] was nevertheless one of Eliade's avowed disciples at the time.[3]

As a group, 'The New Generation' were primarily concerned with cultural issues or, more precisely, with spiritual ones. In spite of claims for an irrationalist bias, Mircea Eliade was, in fact, trying to fuse mysticism with self-awareness, contending that the two concepts did not exclude each other. In 1928 he was already sketching out the ideology of the group:

> What does this polyvalence [of the spirit] mean? The possibility of [...] tasting and appreciating all the planes of reality: the aesthetic, the ethical, the rational, the human, the physiological ones. There is no continuity, no bridges over these separate levels. Instead, there is a transcendent religious reality. Religious experience is absolute.[4]

These words anticipate, in some respects, Huxley's own views from the mid-1930s onwards. But whereas Eliade was gradually turning into an outstanding scholar of religions who ironically rejected 'fake' prophets such as Krishnamurti and the Theosophical Movement that was becoming fashionable in Romania, too,[5] Huxley was getting increasingly convinced by them. However, there were other philosophical and aesthetic reasons why Huxley was held in high esteem among the members of this group and ranked beside writers and philosophers such as Nietzsche, Dostoevsky, Gide, Unamuno, Valéry, and Papini. In Petru Comarnescu's programmatic "Observații provizorii asupra mentalității tinerei generații" ['Some Provisional Remarks on the Young Generation's Mentality'], published in 1932 in the newly issued review *Azi* ['Today'], the author insists on the importance that 'The Existentialists' attached to the authenticity of experience as such.[6] In his opinion, the foreign models cited above had in common an unconventional outlook on life as well as a constant yearning to reach the deep sources of personal experience.

'The Existentialists' were keeping pace with the ongoing cultural events in Europe, taking part in conferences, seminars, and reunions. Comarnescu had met and listened to Huxley, Gide, Malraux and E. M. Forster (less familiar to Romanian readers at the time) at the International Congress for the Defence of Culture (1935).[7] Discussing Huxley's speech, Comarnescu reports on the distinction the British author made between the literature of the imagination and that of propaganda. Huxley claimed that the former was much more influential than the latter. The term 'propaganda' referred to Communist literature and, according to Comarnescu, the remark was all the more objective as it came from a writer with antifascist views. Here is Huxley's own account of the event:

> I had hoped for serious, technical discussions [...]but it made one angry when one thought of what might have been done and wasn't, when one saw the cynical indifference of the Communist organizers to the *wretched little delegates from the Balkans, etc.* [my italics] who had been hoping for some serious effort on the part of other writers to understand their problems, and who found [...] only

endless Communist demagogy in front of an audience of 2000 people.[8]

The review of the main issues of the Congress—Huxley's opinions included—was actually undertaken by Comarnescu in order to alert the public opinion to the necessity of defending Romanian culture against all those political regimes that destroyed 'authentic' expression on extra-cultural grounds.

'The Modern Aldous Huxley'

Of all the members of 'The Existentialist Group,' Mircea Eliade was the one who offered the most exhaustive rewritings of Huxley's works. One way of doing this was by publishing two interesting critical articles on the British writer in 1932. It is significant to note that Eliade's reading was perfectly synchronized with the publication of Huxley's books in Great Britain. The critic was among the very few Romanians to read these texts in the original at a time when almost everybody was using French translations.[9] In March 1932, when Eliade's first critical article came out, its author had already read Huxley's latest collection of essays, *Music at Night* (1931), and was prepared to make value judgements based on an overall evaluation of Huxley's books up to that date. Eliade's very early acquaintance with Huxley's writings is actually hinted at by a series of essays published in various periodicals of the 1920s. These essays, which comprise literary criticism as well as travel notes and deal with religious issues, but also matters of more general interest, echo, both in terms of topics and style, the miscellaneous journalism Huxley wrote for *The Athenaeum*.[10]

The title of the first article, "Modernul Aldous Huxley" ['The Modern Aldous Huxley'][11] suggests from the start that the British author had been adopted by Eliade and his generation as one of their emblematic writers. The Romanian critic goes beyond the 'sparkling' surface of Huxley's books, finding deeper, more fundamental truths about him that were not obvious at that early date even to British readers.[12] One of those rarely discussed aspects which Eliade promptly notices is that in his already impressive work Huxley introduces 'a new kind of humanism with its roots in physiology and its fruit in the secret joy of contemplation' ('The Modern Huxley,' 85). The fact that the English writer managed to build up a worldwide reputation is due, according to the Romanian critic, not only to his brilliant talent, but also to 'his fervent search for the seeds of a new humanism beyond the great modern heresy' ('The Modern Huxley,' 85). In other words, Eliade was one of the few professional readers of Huxley's work to detect the ultimate seriousness of the English author's message, and his general interpretation of Huxley's books is fully compatible with the writer's intentions. Eliade also mentions the importance of D. H. Lawrence's writings for Huxley's literary creations in the period under discussion, a fact that was equally overlooked or ignored by most critics at the time.

In keeping with the tenets of the existentialist circle, Eliade stresses Huxley's 'increasing interest in moments of *irrationality*, of *moral irresponsibility* [my italics], without giving up the idea of structure and harmony' ('The Modern Huxley,' 85). Another matter of discussion is Huxley's marked antipathy—which he shared with Lawrence—towards any absolute system of thought, for the simple reason that 'reality is, by definition, *incomprehensible* [my italics]' ('The Modern Huxley,' 85).

The italicized words occur again and again in the critical and philosophical discourse of Eliade's group and, when related to Huxley's writings, for which they hold true to a certain extent, one is never sure of how much they are actually triggered by the texts and how much by the ideological framework that the critic wishes to apply. A brief review of Huxley's novels and short stories is a good opportunity for Eliade to draw attention to 'some of the best pages of the English contemporary novel': *Those Barren Leaves*—part IV, *Antic Hay*—chapter XIV, *Point Counter Point* (see 'The Modern Huxley,' 86). As far as the first two of these novels are concerned, they were, more often than not, left out by British and American critics in the period between the two world wars. Moreover, Eliade is able to anticipate—before *Eyeless in Gaza* was written—that the collection of essays *Do What You Will* (1929) already marked a turning point in the writer's literary career. Huxley's critic—and disciple—sharply notices that the British author is gradually leaving modernist positions, turning to the classics in his aspiration for 'a more humane harmony and a more direct contemplation of a few mysteries and miracles' ('The Modern Huxley,' 86), while some facile effects characterizing his early works have been left out. In the same allusive style Eliade also speaks of an 'invitation to deeper meditation and to a longer journey' ('The Modern Huxley,' 86) that the author makes to his readers. Like many other critics afterwards, Eliade is right in stating that 'there is no sense of humour in this development' ('The Modern Huxley,' 86). If one now reconsiders the title of the article, one may even detect a touch of mild irony in it.

Yet, the prophetic note of the previous lines is somewhat annihilated by the conclusion of the article, which claims that 'the most important and most complex English novelist is squaring his last accounts with himself and with his contemporaries' ('The Modern Huxley,' 86). From the diachronic perspective that we can provide today, we know that Huxley's 'long journey' was just about to start and was going to last much longer.

Aldous Huxley: Fundamental Unity in Diversity

Eliade published his second, more detailed article on Huxley a few months later in August 1932.[13] This time, the arguments of his critical essay are triggered by his challenging statement that 'Huxley is not only a complex writer whose work is full of variety, he is also monotonous' ('The Road,' 286). By 'monotonous' Eliade means that, in spite of an impressive literary production—besides novels and short stories Huxley wrote poems, essays and articles, which Romanian and French readers were less familiar with at the time—'the writer's entire work could be read as one book'('The Road,' 286). In other words, the critic emphasizes the fundamental unity of Huxley's oeuvre, a remark that has maintained its relevance to this day, in spite of subsequent developments of the author of *Point Counter Point*. How does Eliade account for Huxley's 'monotony' or, rather, what are the unifying elements in the English writer's work?

Before answering this question, he wittily compares Huxley's writings to the world of his travel notes (*Jesting Pilate, Along the Road*), so full of contrasts and still 'agreeably the same' ('The Road,' 286). Another unifying aspect refers to the characters, who are 'static' and 'classic' ('The Road,' 288). Eliade distinguishes three types of characters that are reiterated in all the novels: the inefficient intellectual who is not able to really communicate with others, the *raisonneur*, and the neurotic woman. A third aspect concerns the plots of the novels, which are similar in many ways: 'All the novels could be reduced to a short story in *Brief Candles*, all his writings—to a page of criticism in *Proper Studies*' ('The Road,' 288). This does not at all deprive Huxley of his originality, which is 'amazing' and 'authentic' ('The Road,' 288).

In the course of the study Eliade undertakes an analysis of Huxley's typical characters, as they develop from one novel to another. Thus, for instance, Denis, the ridiculous romantic intellectual from Huxley's first novel, *Crome Yellow*, turns into Gumbril Junior in *Antic Hay*, the young man who needs a beard to counterbalance his social helplessness, and then into the emotionally sterile Philip Quarles in *Point Counter Point*. However, the type that, according to Eliade, best reflects Huxley's philosophy is that of the *raisonneur*: Scogan (*Crome Yellow*), Cardan (*Those Barren Leaves*) or Rampion (*Point Counter Point*). One should state at this point that, whereas it is true that these characters often revert to some of their author's witty speculations in his essays, they only provide one perspective, one point of view in the novels among many others that are meant to be equally 'valid.' The fact that Mark Rampion, the *raisonneur* in *Point Counter Point*, actually expresses D. H. Lawrence's ideas rather than Huxley's, a fact that perhaps made Eliade dismiss him as 'too sterile an imitation of Lawrence' ('The Road,' 290) is a case in point. That is why one may assume that if Eliade—and not Huxley—chooses to give intellectual precedence to this type, it is because it best suits the Romanian critic's (and his group's) own ideology: 'All these *raisonneurs* have come to the conclusion that existence is incomprehensible, irrational, that there is no causal, logical, continuous link between its episodes, no rational motivation' ('The Road,' 290).

In fact, as Eliade himself would confess many years later, the novel *Huliganii* ['The Hooligans'] that he wrote in 1935 was full of such *raisonneurs*, who were sharing with Huxley the same outlook on life. At the plot level, the irrationality of existence is suggested by 'some stupid, unexpected, useless, unmotivated events' ('The Road,' 290). According to the critic, *Antic Hay* is the novel that accumulates the highest number of sequences of this kind. One of the most interesting parts of Eliade's study is, in my opinion, his analysis of the third 'type' of character in his classification, i.e., that of the neurotic woman. In revealing the total novelty of this type for the modern novel in general, Eliade once again opens up new directions in Huxley criticism, for few critics have concentrated in a systematic way on this striking aspect of the novels. The topic would, in fact, provide excellent material for feminist approaches both to Huxley and to Eliade himself. Characters like Myra Viveash (*Antic Hay*), Mrs Wimbush (*Crome Yellow*), Mrs Aldwinkle (*Those Barren Leaves*), says Eliade, are true-to-life embodiments of the twentieth-century English woman, quite ridiculous in her snobbery, artificiality and, especially, her 'contagious and depressing fatigue' ('The Road,' 291). With very few exceptions, the only impression that these characters leave is one of emptiness, of a spiritual void, particularly when they get older. No other novelist before Huxley, Eliade says, has captured their mimetic structure so brilliantly, the fact that they live by 'social tropisms, fashions, undigested ideas, superficial feelings' ('The Road,' 293). Eliade even ventures a comparison between the sexes that seems to him to work for Huxley's characters in general: 'Whereas men can learn something from life—even if they do not understand it—women learn nothing, they live by tropisms' ('The Road,' 293). *Two or Three Graces* provides the most obvious instance of this kind of mimesis, the neurotic 'type' being, of course, Grace Peddley, the woman who changes according to her lovers' personality. This metaphysical contempt for women was very much part of Eliade's own ideology. Besides creating a male-dominated society in his own novels, he would, as a journalist, write articles on the necessity of 'building up a manly country and a manly culture.'[14]

All in all, Huxley's array of characters appears to the critic as one of the most vivid and original in English literature, and their author as a truly gifted novelist. In spite of echoes from Joyce, Lawrence and Proust, Huxley develops his own novelistic techniques, the only 'influence' being the one that comes from his own essays. Analysed in a distinct section, the essays are regarded as real masterpieces, even if there is a prestigious, almost intimidating tradition in this field in English literature. What Eliade mainly admires about them is 'the author's secularization of the absolute,' 'their superb independence from contemporaries and predecessors' ('The Road,'

293). Reverting to the problem of the author's neo-humanism, emphasis is laid this time on the fact that Huxley's humanism does not draw on theology, classicism, history, mediaeval psychology but on sociology, psychoanalysis, pedagogy and eugenics (see 'The Road,' 297).

The image of Huxley that Eliade wants to convey to the Romanian audience through his critical studies is that of a lucid, skeptical mind who 'suspects the absolute and still cannot go beyond the uncertainty that the existential farce may hide some kind of tragedy' ('The Road,' 297). Hence the depth and humanity of Huxley's works, which are sometimes triggered by 'a musical piece heard at night, an Italian landscape or a painting by Goya' ('The Road,' 298). Once again Eliade's views run against the interpretive clichés of the time, which overemphasized the writer's intellectual dryness and his lack of emotions, suggesting a basically non-affective involvement of his readers. In the Romanian critic's opinion, such lyrical moments do occur in Huxley's books and some of his descriptions of nature or of works of art are instances in which the author's feelings are displayed, eliciting his readers' emotional participation.

Eliade's 'The Hooligans,' a Romanian Rewriting of Huxley's "Point Counter Point"

That Mircea Eliade's *Huliganii* ['The Hooligans'] is probably the only Romanian novel whose intertextual dimension includes Huxley in a substantial way is not a matter of mere speculation and assumption. By 1935, when the book was published, Eliade had already become acquainted with all the essays and novels Huxley had produced up to that date.[15] Although literary critic George Călinescu had placed Eliade's novels under the Gidean sign in most categorical terms,[16] the Romanian novelist denied any particular influence the French author might have had on his own writings. In his memoirs Eliade considers his personal life experiences and ideas to be more solid ground for the evaluation of his inter-war accomplishments.[17] Years later, when he referred to this book of his youth again, he avowed to Claude Henri Rocquet that its characters are 'a group of intellectuals and pseudo-intellectuals who had a lot in common with the characters in Huxley's *Point Counter Point*.'[18]

The previous statement can be regarded as an openly admitted instance of a particular kind of response to Huxley's novel.[19] Intertextuality and rewriting as key notions for this type of investigation account for the way in which the Huxleyan text (and spirit) pervades Eliade's novel, the final result being what P. Constantinescu, using his generation's terminology, called 'one of the most authentic works belonging to the young generation of novelists.'[20] Apart from Eliade's own declaration and the admiration for Huxley that he expressed in his articles, neither the characters nor the implied author make any specific reference to the British writer or to *Point Counter Point* in the novel. The only allusion to English (Huxley's?) *raisonneurs* occurs when the latter are compared to one of the characters in the book. Intertextuality as 'direct quotation' is not present here and should, therefore, be sought on other levels.[21]

What has traditionally been called 'spiritual affinities' might explain well enough Eliade's decision to effectively incorporate Huxleyan patterns of thought and some of the British author's formal solutions into his novels. Both writers were dedicated intellectuals who had shown scientific and literary preoccupations ever since their school years, trying to balance them in different ways throughout their lives. Their sensuous natures were strongly counteracted by their intellectual force. They also shared an interest in religion and an Indian experience. Huxley's trip to India preceded Eliade's stay there by two years and lasted only a couple of months (October 1925–February 1926). Eliade, on the other hand, spent three years (November 1928–December 1931) mainly in Calcutta and in the Himalayas and made in-depth studies of theosophy, Yoga and Sanskrit. It was in India that Eliade actually read most of Huxley's books published up to that date.

A common historical background dominated by World War I had given rise, both in Romania and in Britain, to a generation that was trying to hide its uncertainty and confusion behind excessive individualism and a hedonistic way of life. In *Point Counter Point* a female character declares: "Nowadays people are bored and world weary before they come of age. A pleasure too often repeated produces numbness."[22] In *Huliganii* a young man discerns 'an unavowed weariness, a hidden discontentment'[23] in jazz music, in the consumption of alcohol and in the erotic atmosphere of a party. It is not surprising then that Eliade who, like Huxley, was emblematic of his time, could easily incorporate and make use of comparable types of characters.

In these two novels written by, for and about intellectuals, the authors recruit their protagonists from limited social categories: most of them belong to the upper and middle classes of the late twenties (Huxley) and mid-thirties (Eliade), and the occasional presence of the lower classes stands in sharp contrast to the rest. The intellectual charge of the texts is put into discussions on the relation of art to life, mind to body, man to society or, in other words, reflections on the human condition, on the relationship between the sexes, on socio-political, literary and artistic issues. However, in *Point Counter Point* Huxley emphasizes the body-soul dilemma and the way it could be solved in Lawrencian terms, as well as the meaninglessness of the human condition. In *Huliganii* the characters' problems are more deeply rooted in the ongoing ideological debates of the time in Romania. In his memoirs Eliade writes:

> I wanted to assign a certain existential and axiological prestige to some Romanian ways of behaviour that had either been interpreted as purely sociological facts or condemned and 'moralised' in literature. [...] My 'hooligans' existed on a different level: what they

> were mainly interested in was a life-style that would have allowed
> them to create and triumph in History. [...] I believed in the
> possibility of a Romanian Renaissance and that is why I could
> afford to create such heroes. ('Memoirs,' 332)

Therefore, in spite of their fundamental moral flaws, the 'hooligans' reveal a good deal of determination and energy in accomplishing 'their own destiny' through artistic creations or obscure political involvement that most of Huxley's characters find pointless or seem to lack.

Like Huxley, Eliade needed a suitable framework to express his ideas. It is on the structural level that the similarities between the two novels become even more manifest, as the Romanian author adopts and adapts the formal innovations in *Point Counter Point* in a less ambitious and intricate way. The advantages of the contrapuntal technique introduced into the modernist novel by Huxley are obvious: narrative sequences, moods and themes run parallel or clash so as to facilitate situational ironies. In this way, the illusion of simultaneity can be created and the perspectives on reality are multiplied. Consistent flashbacks make the reader feel as if he could freely travel through space and time. Both authors handle a fairly large number of characters that discuss matters of general interest in restaurants or at parties, whereas private talks usually occur among couples, at somebody's house or in pubs. As in *Point Counter Point*, the main social event in *Huliganii* is a *soirée*, this time given by a rich family in Bucharest. Although it takes place in the second part of the story, it is a focus of interest from which many other simultaneous sub-plots are derived. In this way, in the Romanian novel, too, the characters' selfish and vain attempts to be happy are brought into relief from an ironic perspective.

The 'sensational' side of the plot is not left aside either. In *Point Counter Point* it culminates in a child's pointless death, a pointless murder and a suicide. In *Huliganii* it comprises a theft, a rape and a suicide. Through shocking events, the reader is made to realize that the borderlines between tragic, grotesque or merely ironic facts are very shaky indeed.

The structure of the books also allows for the inclusion of other documents. In *Point Counter Point* there are Lucy Tantamount's letters from Paris, an expression of her essential boredom and weariness in her futile quest for physical pleasure. In *Huliganii* the correspondence between Alexandru and Petru seems to be more successful than their actual encounters, since through letters they can more freely reveal their opinions and 'experiences' without running the risk of being interrupted or contradicted by the other. Still, in *Point Counter Point* Huxley's more ambitious formal project includes the *mise-en-abîme* device, which consists in the insertion of a novelist's notebook with theories on how a novel should be written. This gives the Huxleyan text a metafictional, explicitly aesthetic dimension that *Huliganii* lacks. It is quite clear that Huxley strives to apply in his novel what Philip

Quarles writes down in his diary. For Eliade, this technical artifice seems to be irrelevant and is only ironically sketched out. In *Huliganii* the presence of a writer at work has no motivation in terms of plot construction. The Romanian novelist-in-the-novel, Anton Dumitraşcu, is a failure, being totally deprived of Quarles' intellectual complexity.

In spite of Eliade's consistent use of the contrapuntal technique no association is made in his book with the musical device from which it derives. However, music as such is frequently mentioned and also produced and listened to, just like in Huxley's novel. In *Point Counter Point* the presence of Bach's suite at the Proustian gathering at the beginning of the novel as well as of Beethoven's A minor quartet at its end demonstrates that "an ideal order does exist, at least in the mind, with which man has contacts by means of art and in which the disorders of real life are reconciled."[24] To Spandrell's exalted mind it is the ultimate proof of the existence of God. In *Huliganii* ideal musical harmony at the piano lessons (as a hint, for instance, at a possible harmonious relationship between Petru and Anişoara) is never achieved. For Petru, a composer himself, music is a supreme ideal, but he sees its fulfilment as related to an undeniable assertion of the self through creation (a form of exacerbated selfishness). In both novels, however, jazz music stands for the fundamental disorder and dissipation in the characters' lives, an idea previously used by Huxley as early as in *Antic Hay*.

Counterpoint as a formal device also has the function of "weaving all the themes together through a variety of characters giving the novel a solid structural and thematic unity."[25] Eliade's characters, following Huxley's, are meant to illustrate ideas and, although most of them have adopted their generation's mannerisms and life-style, their theories account for the numerous modulations on the main themes. They fall, roughly, into similar categories and types: successful and unsuccessful artists, rich, childish, inefficient scientists, professional politicians, etc. There are also common human types that make intertextuality even more obvious at the character level: sentimental fools rejected by the 'object' of their passion, neurotic women, *raisonneurs*, etc. Generally, the couples within the novels, whether married or not, are not joined together by mutual love or affection because of some 'flaw' in one partner (for example, Philip Quarles' over-intellectualism or the monstrous selfishness characterizing John Bidlake, Sidney Quarles, Alexandru Pleşa, Petru Anicet, Lucy Tantamount). However, the more numerous young male characters involved in couples in *Huliganii* stand out through their cynical attitudes to women. There is an unmistakably male universe in Eliade's book from which women are severely banished.

When discussing *Point Counter Point* in his second critical article on Aldous Huxley, Eliade mentions that almost all the people in the novel 'have reached the conclusion that existence itself is incomprehensible and irrational, that between its episodes there are no causal, logical or continuous links'

('The Road,' 290), concluding that the British writer must have drawn upon Bertrand Russell's philosophy of events. Eliade does exactly the same in his own novel, probably appreciating the existential outlook as such as well as the technical devices used for its expression. Still, neither of the novels is decentralized.

Both books have a 'nucleus' character, a spokesman providing a main 'melody,' an intellectual who enjoys a certain prestige among the others, since they all approach the centre he represents. In *Point Counter Point* it is Mark Rampion, the Lawrencian character, who opposes his more balanced views on the body-soul dilemma to all the others' eccentricities that he pertinently diagnoses: "All perverts. Perverted towards goodness or badness, towards spirit or flesh, but always away from the central norm, always away from the humanity" (*PCP*, 408). David Dragu, the 'centre' of Eliade's novel, also balances and nuances the other characters' excessive views on 'hooliganism' or on political issues. His definition of 'hooliganism' is more complex and has more to do with one's creative powers than with the immoral, cynical connotations that the term might imply. Yet, Dragu's function of a 'preacher' is less obvious than Mark Rampion's, his opinions are more controversial and, in a way, he is more 'true to life' than his English counterpart.

By putting Philip Quarles' outlook into the novel Huxley tries to rise above his own way of seeing things. Indeed, his satirical indictment of Quarles is probably the sharpest of all those directed against his many fictional self-portraits. Dragu is also a *porte-parole* character, as many of the theories and ideas he stands for can also be found in the essays and articles Eliade used to publish in *Cuvântul* and in *Vremea* between 1932 and 1935. However, no satirical intention can be traced in the writer's treatment of his character.

The narrative perspective that suits both novels is the omniscient one. In this way, characters are ironically kept at a distance. The elegance and the precision of style betray the essayist in both authors. Verbal irony is part of it, too. Many passages like the following prove that Eliade was also rewriting Huxley in a stricter sense of the word:

> Burlap walked home. He was feeling pleased with himself and the world at large. "I accept the Universe," was how, only an hour before, he had concluded his next week's leader. "I accept the Universe." He had every reason for accepting it. Mrs. Batterton had given him an excellent lunch and much flattery. (*PCP*, 434)

> [Mitică] had an excellent opinion of himself that evening. It seemed to him that he could always find the right answer, that his intelligence was lucid and still communicative. He was only sorry that none of his former schoolmates had been there to listen to what he had to say. (*H*, 101)

Huxley's more consistently ironic voice and his more elaborate use of irony on a structural level convey strong satirical accents to *Point Counter Point* which are absent in *The Hooligans*. Eliade reveals an ultimate seriousness about his generation that reminds us that he himself was only twenty-eight when the book was published. Where Huxley is mercilessly destructive (while keeping Rampion for 'what was to be done' and with a clear moral purpose in mind), Eliade, whose attitude is more ambivalent, is trying to build a different world, using his paradoxical generation of 'new men.'

Both novels fulfil a documentary function regarding their respective source culture, dwelling upon issues that, in many cases, are still of interest to present-day readers. At the same time, Aldous Huxley's *Point Counter Point* acted as a catalyst for the creation of *Huliganii* both on a structural and ideological level. It is no exaggeration to say that in the same way in which Huxley introduced the novel of ideas—encapsulated in a specific form—into British modernist literature Eliade, drawing on the English writer, rewrote this genre for an unmistakably Romanian readership.

Consequences

Eliade continued his exhaustive readings of Huxley after the publication of *Huliganii* (1935).[26] However, he never wrote other articles fully devoted to Huxley. This silence could be interpreted as a result of his surprise at Huxley's mystical turn, which no longer corresponded to the image of the independent-minded, irreverent prestidigitator of ideas that had so much attracted the Romanian young generation, and the author of *Huliganii* in particular. Hence the reserve of the scientist, of the expert in Buddhism (and the matter is not deprived of irony) to the newly converted Buddhist from *Eyeless in Gaza* and from subsequent books. An entry in Eliade's 1959 diary is most significant in this respect:

> I met Sir Julian Huxley at John Nef. I talked to him about Aldous, of course. I wanted to know since when and after what 'intellectual' meeting had Aldous become a mystic. 'He has always been one,' Sir Julian answered. 'Remember what he says about music and poetry.'[27]

As for Huxley's response to Eliade's writings, in two of his letters—one of them written in 1961, the other in 1962—he advises his addressees, Anthony Brooke and Timothy Leary, to use Eliade's books as scientific support for their study of non-violent behaviour (see Eliade's *The Sacred and the Profane*) and the practice of Tantra Yoga, respectively.[28]

Eliade's rewritings of Huxley's early works are one of the warmest tributes paid by the Romanians to the British author. The republication of his studies in recent years still paves the way for the English writer's reception in this country. As for his rewriting of *Point Counter Point* via *Huliganii*, it not only introduced the novel of ideas into Romanian culture, but it also contributed, as Nicolae Manolescu shows, 'to the creation of a new, ambitious, experimental and intellectual Romanian novel, keeping pace with everything that was going on in European literature.'[29]

[1] In my view, 'rewriting' is actually more comprehensive a term than is suggested, for instance, in André Lefevere's definition, which does not include novels in this category. In his opinion, translations, literary histories, critical studies, anthologies and reviews "are all responsible for the image of a writer, a work and even a literature that is presented to [...] the reading public" (*Translating Literature: Practice and Theory in a Comparative Literature Context* [New York, 1992], 2). From the broader perspective that I adopt here, a text that was written, in a detectable manner, as a form of thorough and consistent response to another text (or to more than one text) may be regarded as a rewriting. Hence the significant difference from intertextuality, which may only consist of isolated (implicit or explicit) references to a source in parts of a text. In this light, rewritings may incorporate intertextual instances.

[2] In *România literară* ['Literary Romania'], 25 (1932), 6, Eugène Ionesco interpreted Huxley's *Point Counter Point* in the light of the reading conventions introduced to the French—and the world's—readership by Balzac's and Proust's novels.

[3] See, for instance, Marie-France Ionesco, *Eugène Ionesco* (Bucureşti, 2003), 26.

[4] Mircea Eliade, "Spiritualitate şi ortodoxie" ['Spirituality and Orthodoxy'], *Viaţa literară* ['Literary Life'], 93 (1928), 2. All translations in this paper are mine, unless stated otherwise.

[5] See, for instance, Eliade's article "Spiritualitate şi mister feminin" ['Spirituality and Feminine Mystery'] in *Azi* ['Today'], 2 (1932).

[6] See *Azi*, 2 (1932), 183.

[7] See Petru Comarnescu, "Congresul internaţional pentru apărarea culturii" ['The International Congress for the Defence of Culture'], *Vremea* ['The Time'], 398 (1935), 5.

[8] Letter to Victoria Ocampo, cited in Sybille Bedford, *Aldous Huxley: A Biography* (2 vols., London, 1973–1974), I, 304.

[9] The first Romanian translation of a Huxley text was that of the short story "The Rest Cure" (*Brief Candles*, 1930), published in 1934; his essays only started being translated in the Communist period (1968).

[10] Some of Eliade's essays written in 1927 were subsequently gathered by Mircea Handoca in the volume *Mircea Eliade: Itinerariu spiritual* ['Mircea Eliade's Spiritual Development'] (Bucureşti, 2003).

[11] Mircea Eliade, "Modernul Aldous Huxley" ['The Modern Aldous Huxley'], *Azi*, 1 (1932), 85–86. Hereafter, 'The Modern Huxley.'

[12] For early reviews and criticism of Huxley's books see *Aldous Huxley: The Critical Heritage*, ed. Donald Watt (London, 1975).

[13] Mircea Eliade, "Aldous Huxley," *Cuvântul* ['The Word'], August–September 1932. The study was republished in 1943 and 1991; see *Insula lui Euthanasius*

['Euthanasius's Island'] (Bucureşti, 1943), 232–251, and *Drumul spre centru* ['The Road to the Centre'] (Bucureşti, 1991), 285–298. Hereafter, 'The Road.'

[14] See, for instance, Mircea Eliade, "Criza românismului" ['The Romanian Crisis'], *Vremea* (10 February 1935), 5.

[15] Besides my previous evidence in this respect, in *Şantier* ['The Building-Site'], a full-length novel by Eliade that was published in 1935, too, the protagonist, like Huxley's Philip Quarles, keeps a diary in which he writes down: 'I was just finishing *The Tillotson Banquet* by Aldous Huxley and was extremely amused by it, when I heard footsteps on the stairs and knocks at the hall door. The story was too exciting for me to interrupt my reading" (*Şantier* [Bucureşti, 1991], 131).

[16] In his seminal history of Romanian literature (1941) George Călinescu writes: 'Mircea Eliade [...] is the most faithful embodiment of the Gidean spirit in Romanian literature' (*Istoria literaturii române de la origini până în present* ['History of the Romanian Literature from Its Origins up to the Present Time'] [Bucureşti, 1982], 956).

[17] See Mircea Eliade, *Memorii, jurnale* ['Memoirs and Journals'], I (Bucureşti, 1991). Hereafter, 'Memoirs.'

[18] Quoted by Mircea Handoca in *Scriitori români comentaţi* (*Comments on Romanian Writers*) (Bucureşti, 1993), 37.

[19] *Huliganii* is a novel of discussion, located in Bucharest, in the 1930s. Most of the characters are young people (artists, writers, actors and actresses, teachers, clerks, prostitutes, etc.), rich or poor, who try to find out, through their discussions, a number of 'essential truths' about their (and Eliade's) own generation. They strive to break away from the past and replace bourgeois values by radical (moral, artistic, sexual, political) behaviour for the purpose of achieving self-fulfilment on a strictly individual level. Several plots are interwoven, one of them involving, for instance, the formerly rich Anicet family (Petru and his mother) that react in different ways to their social and financial disaster: Petru is one of the 'hooligans' who wants to become a great composer and restore his family fortune. For this, he seduces the youngest daughter of the Lecca family, whom he teaches the piano, and then asks her to steal her family's jewels. His mother commits suicide ashamed, humiliated and shocked at her son's behaviour. Another plot focuses on Alexandru Pleşa, Petru's friend, whose ideal is, for a while, a military career that exalts bravery and physical force. On the sentimental plane he is directly responsible for his former girlfriend's suicide and repents by getting married to a woman whom he occasionally meets at a party and whom he eventually abandons. Mitică Gheorghiu, a rich young man working in a bank, falls madly in love with an actress who rejects him, rapes her on the train to Vienna and ultimately discovers he no longer wants to marry her. Besides the witty conversations between the characters, the novel successfully recaptures the mood of the Romanian young generation of the 1930s as well as the atmosphere of the old aristocratic families in Bucharest.

[20] Pompiliu Constantinescu, review of *Huliganii*, *Vremea* (12 January 1936), 9.

[21] We fully agree with David Lodge that "there are many ways by which one text may refer to another: parody, pastiche, echo, allusion, direct quotation, structural parallelism" (*The Art of Fiction* [London, 1992], 92).

[22] Aldous Huxley, *Point Counter Point* [1928] (London, 1975), 53. Hereafter, *PCP*.

[23] Mircea Eliade, *Huliganii* (Bucureşti, 1991), 269. Hereafter, *H*.

[24] George Woodcock, *Dawn and the Darkest Hour* (London, 1972), 105.

[25] Peter Firchow, *Aldous Huxley: Satirist and Novelist* (Minneapolis, 1972), 99.

[26] For instance, in a diary entry written in 1936, when he was in London, Eliade states: "I bought Aldous Huxley's latest novel, *Eyeless in Gaza*, and I read it holding my breath" ('Memoirs,' 345). Even his comments to Sir Julian Huxley in the 1950s show that he was fully aware of Huxley's subsequent development.

[27] Mircea Eliade, *Jurnal*, I (Bucureşti, 1993), 140.

[28] See *Letters of Aldous Huxley*, ed. Grover Smith (London, 1969), 923, note; 929.

[29] Nicolae Manolescu, "Romanul românesc modern: creaţie şi analiză" ['The Modern Romanian Novel: Creation and Analysis'], in: *Istoria literaturii române-studii* ['Studies in the History of Romanian Literature'], ed. Zoe Dumitrescu-Buşulenga (Bucureşti, 1979), 242.

IV.

Panels
for Young Huxley Scholars

Janko Andrijašević

(University of Montenegro)

ARS MORIENDI: HUXLEY'S FINAL EXAM

Whenever we are confronted with existential problems, many questions, which rack our brains in everyday life, seem to lose their significance. One of such questions concerns the relationship between an author's biographical data and the inner life of his books. Is there specific evidence that connects these two worlds or not? Whatever the answer, it remains rather shallow and irrelevant in the light of such powerful themes as, for example, the experience of death in Huxley's works. What matters is the fact that the spectre of the grim reaper haunts both Huxley's life and his books from beginning to end. From an eschatological point of view, his existence on Earth as well as his literary heritage can be seen as a series of lessons in the art of dying. On the other hand, whose life isn't a lesson in this most difficult of all arts? But the decisive question is whether we are ready and courageous enough to learn these painful lessons, as Huxley was, or if we rather choose to close our eyes and ignore whatever hurts us.

In an ancient Egyptian poem quoted by Huxley in *Texts and Pretexts* it says that "death is before me to-day, / like the recovery of a sick man, / like going forth into a garden after sickness."[1] The Lebanese poet Kahlil Gibran once said that to die is "to stand naked in the wind and to melt into the sun."[2] The fragrant blossoms of death intoxicate only those who "knew how to live," as Huxley has Rivers say in *The Genius and the Goddess*.[3] The enigma of death seems to lie within the enigma of life, "for life and death are one, even as the river and the sea are one" (Gibran, 101). But how is such a solemn, peaceful and meaningful experience of death to be reconciled with what we fussily take as the darkest moment of each individual life? This skill is certainly so difficult to learn that, while learning it, our most vulnerable inner being is pierced by sharp and rusty pointed wires of pain. Still, it seems that this great uncomfortable effort pays in the end. For learning how to look death in the eye means reaching profound wisdom and spiritual stability. Huxley seems to have touched upon these deep inner layers of his eternal existence, although he asked for a shot of LSD on his deathbed, and although the uncried tears of a lifelong struggle with spirits choked him to the very end. The day President Kennedy was assassinated was also the day Huxley passed his final and irrevocable exam of a lifetime. The price for such a divine accomplishment was a long, fierce and gloomy preparation, but also a rewarding one.

The dark gate of death opened before Huxley in his childhood, when his mother, terminally ill with cancer, was forced to leave her emaciated body and her bereaved family behind. Aldous took it, as his doctor Max Cutler said, with "dignity and courage."[4] He didn't cry, he rarely ever talked about it. However, his fiction echoes hidden chants of pain, because, according to Juliette Huxley, he "was never to outlive [...] an annihilating sorrow" (*MV*, 42) caused by his mother's death. The suicide of his brother Trev a few years later only reinforced his "awful fear of death."[5]

In his early works Huxley almost masochistically worshipped death as a sinister divinity: "[...] of all the Gods / Death only cannot die."[6] He called it "the thickening darkness,"[7] he said "there is no glittering eye of water to be seen at the bottom,"[8] he asked himself why we are "allowed to become gradually less than human"[9] and why "only death remains faithful."[10]

In the mid-1930s, while going through a "dark night of the soul,"[11] i.e., a long crisis before the appearance of the first shimmers of deeper lights within his being, the cocoon of death's black horror started to crack. The dark butterfly within was terrifying, but beautiful. Then already Huxley felt what he expressed later in *The Genius and the Goddess*, viz that it was time he "ought to be learning" (*GG*, 10) the art of dying, that he ought to start looking at it with different eyes.

In his novel *Go Tell It on the Mountain* James Baldwin writes: "The way to death was broad, and many could be found thereon; but narrow was the way that led to life eternal."[12] At that stage Aldous took a turn towards light, even though it was oppressed with so much darkness.

After *Eyeless in Gaza*, Huxley's inner sight broadened. It cast some light even on the horrors of his earlier years. Grappling with the inevitability of physical demise now became more promising. The greatest test before his own departure from the known earthly room was his wife Maria's long, fatal, but dignified and awe-inspiring fight with cancer. She said she was just going from the common room to an unknown one, just that. And she let herself be carried away by the loving whispers of her husband who told her to "let go of this poor old body"[13] and join the spouting flood of light. When eventually she did join the red glow of love on the other side, Huxley felt like an "amputated organism."[14] His emotions were caged in a dark cellar of sadness, but he still felt elated because he knew that "the living can do a great deal to make the passage easier for the dying."[15]

Not too many years passed before the shadow of cancer, which devastated so much of Huxley's emotional empire, cast a shadow on his own lank and awkward bodily frame. The illness set out from the tongue, and in a couple of years it spread throughout his body. The menace was gloomily on its way to take a victory over his "*vis medicatrix naturae*."[16] Utter pessimism could rightfully have been justified in such a patient. However, Huxley did not surrender himself to it. Of course, he never said he was happy to be dying from cancer, but he admitted that even in such a dead-end street of life light can be found: "There had been sadness, of course [...] but there had also been the spectacle" of Huxley's "joyful serenity, and even, at one remove, a kind of participation in the knowledge of which that joy was the natural and inevitable expression" (*TMHS*, 280–281).

His second wife Laura was by his deathbed helping him to build bridges to the "country from whose bourn no traveller returns."[17] Huxley was learning from what was happening to him and trying to be fully aware all the time. Full awareness, after all, is "the whole art of dying" (*Island*, 274).

Joe Stoyte of *After Many a Summer* had consoled himself that "perhaps there really and truly wouldn't be any death."[18] The inhabitants of the brave new world tried to ignore it completely. All had been wrong, because "life always ends in death."[19] However, life is also "renewed through death" (*HS*, 200), but this rejuvenation of life does not occur by closing one's eyes before the look of the grim reaper. On the contrary, it happens only when we summon up enough courage to kiss his bony face. Only then do we learn that the dance of our days is "impartially of death and of life" (*Island*, 190), like Shiva's play or the whirling of dervishes, and only then do we know with Penelope Fitzgerald that "the resurrection, for those who understand how to change their lives, takes place on this earth"[20] and that death only passes us on. Nothing we hold on to in this life "is forever, nothing is to infinity. Except, maybe, the Buddha Nature" (*Island*, 320).

Reading the lessons in *ars moriendi* in Huxley's work, we ignore the "cold dispute of what is fit, and not"[21] in modern approaches to literature, and we stand back, amazed, enchanted and terrified, before the testament of a man who told us so much about himself and who unselfishly told us even more about our own selves. It is up to everybody to digest Huxley's words in their own way. I cannot but be deeply impressed by Huxley's 'heart of the matter' which, as it seems to me, lies nowhere else but in the heart of the soul and in the heart of the universe, which are one. This heart floats between body and spirit, mind and emotions, light and darkness, and it is the root of all creation. It cannot easily be expressed in a definition or even in volumes of books. And whenever we think we have managed to encompass the wisdom of life and the nature of art, whenever we feel like coming close to an end of a journey, there is a universal voice shattering our illusions: "Finished? [...] But it's only just begun" (*TMHS*, 284).

---

[1] Aldous Huxley, *Texts and Pretexts* (London, 1932), 298.

[2] Khalil Gibran, *The Prophet* (Harmondsworth, 1992), 102.

[3] Aldous Huxley, *The Genius and the Goddess* (London, 1955), 10. Hereafter, *GG*.

[4] *Aldous Huxley: A Memorial Volume*, ed. Julian Huxley (London, 1965), 123. Hereafter, *MV*.

[5] Aldous Huxley, *Time Must Have a Stop* (London, 1945), 133. Hereafter, *TMHS*.

[6] Aldous Huxley, "Orion," *Verses and a Comedy* (London, 1946), 121.

[7] Aldous Huxley, *Those Barren Leaves* (Harmondsworth, s.a.), 186. Hereafter, *TBL*.

[8] Aldous Huxley, *Antic Hay* (London, 1994), 206.

[9] Aldous Huxley, *Brave New World* (New York, 1950), 304.

[10] Aldous Huxley, Eyeless in Gaza (Harmondsworth, 1962), 267.

[11] A. Sally Paulsell, "Color and Light: Huxley's Path to Spiritual Reality," *Twentieth-Century Literature*, 41 (1995), 85.

[12] James Baldwin, *Go Tell It on the Mountain* (New York, 1983), 34.

[13] Aldous Huxley, *Island* (London, 1994), 299. Hereafter, *Island*.

[14] Sybille Bedford, *Aldous Huxley* (London, 1993), 646.

[15] *Letters of Aldous Huxley*, ed. Grover Smith (New York, 1969), 900.

[16] Aldous Huxley, *The Art of Seeing* (London, 1943), 1.

[17] William Shakespeare, *Hamlet*, in: *The Collected Works of William Shakespeare* (New Lanark, 2001), 389.

[18] Aldous Huxley, *After Many a Summer* (New York, 1939), 45.

[19] Aldous Huxley, *The Human Situation* (London, 1978), 200. Hereafter, *HS*.

[20] Penelope Fitzerald, *The Beginning of Spring* (London, 1989), 177.

[21] George Herbert, "The Collar," *The Norton Anthology of English Literature*, ed. M.H. Abrams (NewYork, 1986), 1349.

Andrei Vasilenko

(University of Latvia)

THE DYSTOPIAN VISION OF THE WORLD IN ALDOUS HUXLEY'S *BRAVE NEW WORLD* AND VLADIMIR SOROKIN'S *BLUE FAT*

This essay will begin with a brief examination of the dystopian cosmology of Huxley's fictional world and will then focus on the recent ironic postmodern dystopia by the Russian writer Vladimir Sorokin (Владимир Сорокин) in order to find out in which ways the two novels may be related.

In *Brave New World* we see the successful results of introducing absolute order and stability into society. These goals are noble enough to call a society that has reached them a *utopia* ; however, the price we would have to pay for such an extraordinary achievement prevents us from doing so. Considered to be the primary cause of instability and unhappiness, traditional human values have been abolished in the era of Ford, the new lord of the technocratic, standardised society, and this may be the basic reason for calling the novel a *dystopia*, which, according to *The Penguin Dictionary of Philosophy*, may be defined as "a fictional account of bad political and social conditions."[1] The institution of the family has been stamped out, and the words *father* and *mother* have become obscene. The right to choose, this cornerstone of democracy, has been liquidated as another factor threatening stability. Human beings are now produced in test tubes, and from the early stages of their life they are conditioned to become a member of one of the five castes as well as to pursue a certain activity assigned to them. In order to maintain a state of complete happiness the inhabitants of the brave new world receive the pacifying drug *soma*. However, the most flagrant practice in Huxley's vision of the future is the abolition of high art and literature in particular, because they give glimpses of an unhappy, disordered, disarrayed world of uncontrolled emotions and unpredictable behaviour. The present paper will focus on this particular dystopian aspect of *Brave New World*, namely on the fact that it is a world without literature.

In a grotesque scene of postnatal conditioning, a group of babies crawling towards books with beautifully illuminated pages are subjected to electrical shock as well as exposed to loud noise. Thus they learn to hate literature. Antithetically, the protagonist of the novel, John, the modern version of a noble savage, has been under the influence of Shakespeare's works from his early childhood. In the scientific parlance of the brave new world, he has been 'conditioned' to like literature, although we would say that he has adopted traditional human values that have no place in the brave new world. John the Savage has become a receptacle of Shakespearean passions: he talks of dignity and chastity, he believes in winning true love by accomplishing noble deeds, he is ready to confront dangers and overcome them. From the viewpoint of the new world, he has become addicted to instability. This fact is thoroughly examined in chapters 16 and 17, in which John talks to Mustapha Mond, one of the ten World Controllers. The disillusioned John, who has been longing to see the world outside the reservation and, quoting Miranda from *The Tempest*, has dubbed it 'brave new world,' has an opportunity to argue in favour of his cause. Unfortunately, all his arguments are defeated by the iron logic of Mond. For example, the impossibility of reintroducing such a masterpiece as *Othello* into the brave new world is explained in the following way: "Our world is not the same as Othello's world. You can't make flivvers without steel—and you can't make tragedies without social instability. The world's stable now."[2] And later Mond stresses: "You've got to choose between happiness and what people used to call high art. We've sacrificed the high art. We have the feelies and the scent organ instead" (*BNW*, 220). Mustapha Mond rightly observes that literature, especially good literature, is inseparable from anguish and misery, which are usually part of its subject matter. Therefore, to enjoy this source of instability is the prerogative of the World Controllers, who, like many totalitarian rulers, prohibit the vices which they themselves enjoy. His final verdict is: "Our civilization has chosen machinery and medicine and happiness. That's why I have to keep these books locked up in the safe. They're smut" (*BNW*, 234).

Although it is hard to approve of the monotonous, sterile world that has been created by the World Controllers, one has to concede that there is a point in Mond's argument: Shakespeare's work, it is true, contains not only beautiful, but also extremely violent passages. John makes a reference to *King Lear*, in which there are graphic scenes of murder and torture, things that actually took place in a world where literature still existed and that have become obsolete in the brave new world, where there is none. This leads us to the issues tackled in Vladimir Sorokin's novel *Blue Fat* (*Голубое Сало*), which one can read as an ironic response to the dystopian vision of Aldous Huxley. In this work Sorokin replies, as it were, to John's defiant yearning for the return of high art into human life by creating a world where there is nothing but literature, where the literary text has acquired global significance and unprecedented sway. The result is a nightmarish world of unspeakable cruelty and violence.

Like *Brave New World*, Sorokin's novel is set in the distant future. The place is Siberia, which has become a vast chaotic territory where an intimate fusion of the Russian and Chinese cultures has taken place. The characters speak a barely comprehensible mixture of Russian and Chinese, sprinkled with obscure neologisms. The main goal of a research group at a secret laboratory is to obtain blue fat. This precious substance, analogous in its significance to Huxley's *soma*, has zero entropy and is earmarked for strategic use in a lunar atomic reactor. In order to produce blue fat, it is first of all necessary to make clones. The references to cloning and breeding humans out of incubators echo the respective episodes set in the Central London Hatchery and Conditioning Centre in *Brave New World*. But while in Huxley's novel all humans are conditioned to hate literature, in *Blue Fat* cloning is directly connected with it, for it is great Russian writers who are cloned. The precious blue fat accumulates on the cloned writers' bodies after the so-called script process, which used to be called writing in the past. All in all, there are seven clones: Tolstoy 4,[3] Chekhov 3, Nabokov 7, Pasternak 1, Dostoevsky 2, Akhmatova 2 and Platonov 3. The texts they produce correspond in some measure to the deceased classics' original works and thus reflect the degree of Sorokin's faithfulness to the models imitated in his pastiches. Although the texts are written in the style of Nabokov, Tolstoy, Platonov etc., they also contain, owing to the new technologies used in producing them, all the destructive elements of the subconscious involved in this artistic process, which would have been concealed behind innocent phrases under ordinary circumstances, but are in this context open to being deciphered by a literary psychoanalyst. In fact, these texts reflect all the anguish and suffering that has been invested in their production, something that has been denounced by the adherent to stability and happiness Mustapha Mond. Here it seems apposite to mention the Belorussian scholar Irina Skoropanova (Ирина Скоропанова), who has highlighted Sorokin's tendency to expose the destructive potential of libido in his writing, calling it a kind of schizoanalysis, which is a notion borrowed from the French philosophers Gilles Deleuze and Félix Guattari.[4]

Doubtless the texts are preposterous. For instance, the narrative imitating Dostoevsky's style recounts a high society party at a certain Count Reshetovsky's which is regularly disrupted by the intrusion of incoherent phrases reminiscent of surrealist automatic writing and ends with three characters sewing themselves together with the help of some mysterious gizmo. The exquisite Nabokovian style is used to narrate a spine-chilling sacrifice performed by a married couple of bloodthirsty perverts. The text produced by Platonov's clone is much gloomier than those of the original Platonov, which is hard to imagine but certainly true. It tells the story of a steam engine driven by two proletarians who stoke the furnace with pieces of flesh of members of the bourgeoisie. The world outside those texts is even more violent. Wanton atrocities committed by the members of various groups in order to get hold of blue fat are so numerous and so shocking that one starts wondering at the chaos reigning in a society that has found the means of exploiting the unadulterated essence of literature manifested in blue fat.

The brave new world that is unaware of Shakespeare is dull, monotonous and predictable. It is a vapid dystopia which has been deprived of genuine human emotions and feelings. John the Savage, who has grown up reading Shakespeare, is terrified by this world of uniformity and standardisation, and so are we, the contemporary readers of Huxley. But what would the world be like if it was solely inhabited by Johns, by those who carry not only the positive values of literature but also its hidden destructive potential? There is no doubt that John is the most violent character in Huxley's novel: he whips up Lenina, who is completely innocent, simply being a product of her time, he starts a brawl in the hospital, and finally commits suicide. Moreover, John's self-flagellations hint at some inherent masochistic traits. My answer is that a world of pure literature created for the likes of John would resemble the nightmarish universe of *Blue Fat*. After changing numerous hands, the blue substance is delivered to the world of an alternative history in which Stalin and Hitler have won the Second World War against the allied forces and finally plot to become the incontestable masters of the world by using the blue fat extract. The result is the apocalyptic destruction of the earth precipitated by the injection of this blue liquid into the Soviet dictator's brain:

> Мозг разорвал его череп, раздулся бело-розовым шаром, коснулся стены и стола. [...] К трем часам правое полушарие столкнуло в Атлантику обезумевший Лиссабон и рухнуло следом, подняв километровую волну. Левое полушарие, раздавив Москву и Санкт-Петербург, уперлось в Уральские горы и поволокло их по тундре Западной Сибири, счищая землю с вечной мерзлоты. Мозжечок, расправившись со Скандинавией, ухнул в Ледовитый океан, тревожа тысячелетние льды. К вечеру Последнего Дня Земли мозг Сталина накрыл полмира. Другая половина скрылась под водой. Еще через сутки Земля, перегруженная мозгом Сталина, сошла со своей орбиты и притянула к себе Луну.

> [The brain burst open his skull; it swelled into a pinkish white ball that reached the walls and the table. [...] By three o'clock the right hemisphere shoved the panic-stricken Lisbon into the Atlantic Ocean and plummeted immediately after it, raising a wave a kilometre high. The left hemisphere, having squashed Moscow and St Petersburg, ran against the Ural Mountains and pushed them along the tundra of Eastern Siberia, scraping the permafrost clean of the soil. After making short work of Scandinavia, the cerebellum crashed into the Arctic Ocean disturbing the peace of the millennial ice. By the evening of the Last Day of the Earth Stalin's brain covered half of the world. The other half disappeared under the water. A day later, the overloaded Earth left its orbit and attracted the Moon].[5]

As it turned out, the Stalin of this alternative world underestimated the destructive force lurking behind literature, something that did not escape Mustapha Mond. There is no great literature without great tragedy, and, although it is bitter to recognise this, we can enjoy the best literary products also because people suffer and inflict pain both to other people and themselves. We might suppose that Sorokin kept this in mind when creating his improbable *grand guignol*.

In conclusion, bearing in mind the definition of dystopia quoted above, I have to add that my reading Aldous Huxley against the backdrop of Vladimir Sorokin has led me to re-define this concept as a fictional account of a future society brought to extremes. The peaceful and stable life induced by the pacifying drug *soma* is as abhorrent as an existence in the cannibalistic world of unrepressed desires obsessed with the production of blue fat. The renowned Riga-born critic Pyotr Vail (Петр Вайль) said some wonderfully apt words in one of his interviews. He pointed out that the most disquieting sight would be that of underground trains full of people reading Joyce, arguing that a country in which everybody read Joyce would be dangerous and unpredictable, and that any sane individual should flee it at once.[6] Accordingly, my vision of a utopia is a society whose members have a choice to read nothing except Joyce, or, for that matter, Huxley, but are reasonable enough not to limit themselves so drastically.

---

[1] *The Penguin Dictionary of Philosophy*, ed. Thomas Mautner (London, 2000), 157.

[2] Aldous Huxley, *Brave New World* (New York, 1998), 220. Hereafter, *BNW*.

[3] Each figure refers to the ordinal number of each clone, e.g., there have been 3 clones of Tolstoy: Tolstoy 1, Tolstoy 2, Tolstoy 3, but they died, so the scientists used the fourth clone, i.e., Tolstoy 4, who proved to be suitable for the process of accumulating blue fat.

[4] See *Русская постмодернистская литература* (Москва, 1999), 38-39, 260-261, 278).

[5] Владимир Сорокин, *Голубое Сало* (Москва, 1999), 337–338 (my translation).

[6] See Радиостанция «Эхо Москвы»: Интервью, 30.11.2002, accessed 08.06.2004 via http://echo.msk.ru/interview/20467/index.phtml.

Katja Reinecke

(University of Münster)

THE ORDER OF FOLLY OR THE FOLLY OF ORDER: ALDOUS HUXLEY'S CRITIQUE OF IDEALS BASED ON GOYA'S "EL SUEÑO"

"The dream of Order begets tyranny, and the dream of Beauty, monsters and violence."[1] This quotation taken from *Ape and Essence* is not only reminiscent of Francisco de Goya y Lucientes' etching "El sueño de la razón produce monstruos" but also epitomizes Huxley's criticism of ideals and his scepticism about utopian ideas. Huxley himself regarded this etching from Goya's cycle *Caprichos* as the essence and moral of Goya's later work, "with the horror and mindlessness and animality and spiritual darkness" of all those creatures that haunt Goya's works.[2] His interpretation, however, did not start from the common translation, 'the sleep of reason produces monsters' but from his own, "the dream of reason produces monsters." According to Huxley, the title of the picture lends itself to more than one possible interpretation. If one follows the traditional English translation of 'sueño' as 'sleep,' the interpretation Huxley suggests must be: "When Reason sleeps, the absurd and loathsome creatures of superstition wake and are active, goading their victim to an ignoble frenzy" (*TV*, 215). But, Huxley argues, reason can also dream without sleeping. Thus, the dream of reason produces the same terrifying visions as the sleep of reason. This latter interpretation seems to be more important for Huxley because it includes both his critique of ideals and that of the means of achieving them:

> Reason may also dream without sleeping; may intoxicate itself, as it did during the French Revolution, with the day-dreams of inevitable progress, of liberty, equality and fraternity imposed by violence, of human self-sufficiency and the ending of sorrow, not by the all too arduous method which alone offers any prospect of success, but by political re-arrangements and a better technology.[3]

As early as in his essay "Spinoza's Worm" in *Do What You Will* (1929), Huxley, attacking George Bernard Shaw's *Back to Methuselah*, had emphasized that the state of reason and perfection was by no means an ideal one but, on the contrary, produced horror and distress. Thus, Huxley did not consider Shaw's play a utopia but a dystopia. He regarded the inhabitants of George Bernard Shaw's "spectacle of a future Earth" as "sexless old monsters of mental and physical deformity."[4] Accordingly, he concluded programmatically with regard to ideal and utopian notions:

> As usual, the highest turns out in a strange way to be the lowest. We aspire in circles, and when we imagine that we are most superhuman we suddenly find ourselves below the beasts. Mr. Shaw's earthly

> paradise turns out to be a charnel-house. Under the galvanic stimulation of his wit the mummies frisk about like so many putrefied lambs; it is all very amusing, no doubt, but oh, how gruesome, how unspeakably horrible! (*DWYW*, 71)

Huxley had developed his attitude towards ideals and, more specifically, towards utopian notions, in the introduction to *Proper Studies*. He called those social theorists and reformers whose notions showed an insufficient empirical understanding "the Utopians."[5]

In the face of the political and social chaos during the depression of the thirties Huxley depicted the excess of total efficiency by presenting the nightmarish society in *Brave New World*: "Ours was a nightmare of too little order; theirs, in the seventh century A.F., of too much."[6] The perfect efficiency in *Brave New World* does not leave any room for liberty or personal initiative. In *Brave New World Revisited* Huxley considered his dystopian vision not only as a literary experiment but as a real possibility in totalitarian regimes and democracies.[7]

Against the background of this situation Huxley pleaded for a less perfect society. In *Ape and Essence* and in *Eyeless in Gaza,* the belief in order and perfection and its realisation in the political field is judged as "sub-human [...] and diabolic" (*AE*, 6). Analogously, the sociologist Anthony Beavis in *Eyeless in Gaza* describes the greed for fame and perfection as the "last infirmity of [the] noble mind, the primary, perhaps only, source of sin."[8] The attempt to put a theoretically perfect order into practice without taking into account the concrete human needs is characterized by various ideal notions.[9]

The question of how the realisation of ideals on a social plane can come true is part of the content of Anthony Beavis' projected treatise on sociology in *Eyeless in Gaza*.[10] Beavis inserts a digression about different notions of human ideals. The crucial point of his digression is the question of how thoroughly the realization of human ideals could modify highly developed western societies. Beavis identifies European societies as heterogeneous communities which do not allow for one standard human personality. He regards the attempts of fascist and communist ideologies to introduce and establish a kind of sacrosanct model of personality as inadequate and doomed to failure. Beavis reaches this conclusion because the establishment of an artificial homogeneous society implies the erasure of human differences. However, the structure of highly developed western societies is based on differences.[11] Against the visions of total organisation, human perfection, and perfect beauty, Huxley tried to put forward his own notion of ideals. He demanded what he called realistic idealism.[12]

Significantly, Huxley's last novel *Island* is orientated towards such a realistic idealism. As a motto he introduces the Aristotelian quotation: "In framing an ideal we may assume what we wish, but should avoid impossibilities." [13] In the course of his journey through Central America in

1933 this aspect had already become more topical when he wrote: "We shall have to ask ourselves very seriously which is better worth having—pyramids and a perfectly efficient, perfectly stable community; or personal liberty with instability, but the possibility, at least, of a progress, measurable in terms of spiritual values."[14] Hence, Pala's society is neither orientated towards a utopian dream in the sense of absolute perfection nor is it based on an absolute ideal, which Huxley defines in *Proper Studies* as impossible and unrealizable.[15] Following this interpretation of ideals, Susila explains to the journalist Will Farnaby that Pala's is an open society which is to be considered as a "working model of society at large" (*Island*, 92) From Huxley's point of view it is characteristic of this society that it does not give in to what he calls the social drive towards conformity but allows difference while avoiding inequality.

For Huxley, the question of the nature of ideals touches on another aspect, which is the question of the functional role of ideals and its relevance in conjunction with social behaviour—in other words the question concerning the ends-means relation in human behaviour.[16]

In *Ends and Means* Huxley claims that the choice of an ideal is to be determined by the means to achieve this ideal and that the means are not to be justified by the ideal itself.[17] Since the vision of a better human being and that of a better society are a common characteristic of most ideals, there seems to be a general consensus as to the content of the aims of such visions. What they have in common is the dream of liberty, peace, justice, brotherly love. However, there is a lack of agreement on how to achieve the goal, i.e., on the means.[18]

In *Ape and Essence* Huxley exemplifies the different methods or alternatives of implementing ideals. The Arch-Vicar explains the consequences of the ideals and values of modern western civilization to Dr Poole. In his view, the ideals of progress and of nationalism inevitably led to the Third World War, of which both Dr Poole and he are survivors. The Third World War has almost extinguished western civilization, which he describes as follows:

> "Bigger and better, richer and more powerful—and then, almost suddenly, hungrier and hungrier. [...] Back to hunger. The New Hunger, the Higher Hunger, the hunger of enormous industrialized proletariats, the hunger of city dwellers with money, with all the modern conveniences, with cars and radios and every imaginable gadget, the hunger that is the cause of total wars and the total wars that are the cause of yet more hunger." (*AE*, 92)

In the course of industrialization and of man's ever increasing control of nature, technique and progress are declared the highest values for their own sake. Man not only experiences himself as a conquerer of nature, but he also regards himself as a kind of creator and gradually destroys the basis of his own existence, failing to recognize that the will to control and domineer nature must in the end ruin the natural balance. As the Arch-Vicar argues, the ecological catastrophe was man's own fault, who for the sake of progress ignored this fact although the outcome of this process was irreversible. It was this cause, among others, that led to the catastrophe of the Third World War. The particular ecological problem of exhausted resources led to battles for the remaining ones. Thus the ideals which determined western civilization before the Third World War, viz progress and nationalism,[19] inexorably led to the overall catastrophe.

The Arch-Vicar describes political and moral progress as a myth. This myth is motivating insofar as it leads to violence and destruction in the name of nationalism and progress. He regards these ideals as mere alibis or pretexts. In this context Huxley recurs to an idea he introduced in *Proper Studies*, viz that striving for an ideal interpreted as a myth spurs people on to action. The Arch-Vicar considers the destructive consequences of the ideals of a former civilization and comments on them cynically from his perspective, which is a postcivilized and historical one. It is this position in time which allows him to describe the inevitability of the consequences of those ideals.

A similar perspective is maintained by Pierre Abdul Bahu in *Island*. Bahu, in his Cassandra-like function, considers Pala's ideals doomed to failure in the face of the circumstances and ideals that prevail in the rest of the world. He is introduced not only as the ambassador of Rendang but also as Colonel Dipa's counsellor. In fact, Bahu is obviously Dipa's servant. However, his interests and his power reach far beyond this function, as can be derived from a comment Ranga makes: "'He's the unofficial ambassador of all the oil companies'" (*Island*, 72).

Bahu acts out of his own aspiration to power and in favour of his own interests. In his function as political counsellor Bahu consolidates his position, and from this perspective he also interprets the role and function of ideals and religions. For him, ideals are an instrument of manipulation which is used to control the masses and to strengthen the power of a small elite:

> "He goes about giving lectures about the need for a religious revival. He's even published a book about it. Complete with preface by someone at the Harvard Divinity School. It's all part of the campaign against Palanese independence. God is Dipa's alibi. Why can't criminals be frank about what they're up to? All this disgusting idealistic hogwash—it makes one vomit." (*Island*, 72)

Against this background Bahu defines his position in Pala as that of an outsider and a representative of a foreign power. This is the perspective from which he judges not only Pala's ideals but also the development of its society.[20] Thus Bahu interprets Pala's failure as inevitable because of the external circumstances but by no means because of Pala's internal ones. Pala's ideals and society appear not to be able to survive because of the increasing terror in the rest of the world and because of the global industrial networks. Bahu denies Pala its right to be different and supports the historical interpretation that the global development and Pala's destiny are inevitable.

Against the backdrop of economic interests, the political situation and the balance of power, Pala's oil resources attract violent attacks from other countries on behalf of the oil monopolists which Pala can neither evade nor ignore. In this overall context the Rani as well as Pala's future ruler Murugan declare it a goal to reintroduce a monotheistic religion of redemption. They readily agree with Bahu's views on religion. The kind of religion they propagate serves as an official excuse for the oil industry on the one hand and as a justification for Rendang's hegemonic claims on the other.

The necessity of such a religion, which is emphasized by Bahu, corresponds to the social and psychological needs of a society which is characterized by fear and lack of freedom, and for which a religion of redemption serves as a means of compensation.

Will Farnaby's ironic comment on this plan is as follows: "'So now,' said Will, 'you're proposing to make them miserable in the hope that this will restore their faith in God. Well, that's one way of producing conversion. Maybe, it'll work. And maybe the end will justify the means'" (*Island*, 59)

Bahu's analysis of Pala's ideals fits in this context. The realized ideals of Pala like freedom and happiness and the means of achieving them are judged by Bahu as follows:

> "Perfectly wrong because all too perfectly right. [...] Perfectly right [...] because so perfectly designed to make every man, woman, and child on this enchanting island as perfectly free and happy as it's possible to be. [...] And there can be no doubt that the policies inaugurated by the original Reformers and developed over the years have been admirably well adapted to achieving these two goals. [...] But unfortunately they're out of context, they've become completely irrelevant to the present situation of the world in general and Pala in particular." (*Island*, 58)

Thus it can be concluded that any motivation or ideal in Bahu's world is no longer based on a friendly optimistic *appetitus socialis* (as Ernst Bloch formulated it) but on boundless selfishness: *homo homini lupus, ergo bellum omnium contra omnes.*

---

[1] Alous Huxley, *Ape and Essence* (London 1949), 7. Hereafter, *AE*.

[2] Aldous Huxley, "Variations on Goya," *Themes and Variations* (London, 1950), 215. Hereafter, *TV*. Originally this essay was published as the foreword to *The Complete Etchings of Goya* (NewYork, 1943).

[3] (*TV*, 215–216). In his essay "Variations on *The Prisons*" Huxley comments in a similar way on German concentration camps: "In the Nazi concentration camps hell on earth was not of the old Hogarthian kind, but neat, tidy, thoroughly

scientific. Seen from the air, Belsen is said to have looked like an atomic research laboratory or a well-designed motion picture studio" (*TV*, 196).

[4] Aldous Huxley, *Do What You Will* (London, 1929), 71. Hereafter, *DWYW*.

[5] Aldous Huxley, *Proper Studies* (London, 1927), x. Like the Italian sociologist Vilfredo Pareto, to whose *Trattato di sociologia generale* he explicitly refers in *Proper Studies*, he rejects utopian thinking. He demands a realistic view of social and human prerequisites for the development of ideals and social planning. In this light the quotation from Nicolas Berdiaeff at the beginning of *Brave New World* is to be regarded as a warning. The realization of a utopian vision understood as the wish for a perfect order not only implies the origin of a real dystopia—as Huxley explains in *Brave New World Revisited*—but it also presents the literary basis of his experiment in *Brave New World*.

[6] Aldous Huxley, *Brave New World Revisited* (London, 1958), 11. Hereafter, *BNWR*.

[7] See *BNWR*, 11–12: "I feel a good deal less optimistic than I did when I was writing *Brave New World*. The prophecies made in 1931 are coming true much sooner than I thought they would. The blessed interval between too little order and the nightmare of too much has not begun and shows no sign of beginning. In the West, it is true, individual men and women still enjoy a large measure of freedom. But even in those countries that have a tradition of democratic government, this freedom and even the desire for this freedom seems to be on the wane."

[8] Aldous Huxley, *Eyeless in Gaza* (London, 1936), 150.

[9] In *Ape and Essence* Huxley describes aesthetic, moral, political, social and human ideal notions as follows: "But from the Parthenon and the *Timaeus* a specious logic leads to tyranny which, in the *Republic*, is held up as the ideal form of government. In the field of politics the equivalent of a theorem is a perfectly disciplined army; of a sonnet or picture, a police state under a dictatorship. The Marxist calls himself scientific, and to this claim the Fascist adds another: he is the poet—the scientific poet—of a new mythology. Both are justified in their pretensions; for each applies to human situations the procedures which have proved effective in the laboratory and the ivory tower. They simplify, they abstract, they eliminate all that, for their purposes, is irrelevant and ignore whatever they choose to regard as inessential; they impose a style, they compel the facts to verify a favourite hypothesis, they consign to the waste-paper basket all that, to their mind, falls short of perfection. And because they thus act like good artists, sound thinkers and tried experimenters, the prisons are full" (*AE*, 5).

[10] See Chapter XI.

[11] In *Eyeless in Gaza* Huxley fictionalized a critique which he had already begun in *Beyond the Mexique Bay* and which he developed and reconsidered in *The Olive Tree*. Huxley regarded it as a fact that European societies are heterogeneous and that only small isolated societies can be homogeneous.

[12] With regard to methodological requirements concerning the understanding of human society, Huxley associated his notion of realistic idealism with a standard he had already put forward in *Proper Studies*, which he later on developed in *Ends and Means* and eventually summarized in his essay "More Nature in Art"

(1959): "We need a philosophy, some form of what I would call realistic idealism, which will harmonize man with nature and which will take account of all the facts" (*The Human Situation*, ed. Piero Ferrucci [London, 1978], 40; see also 58).

[13] Aldous Huxley, *Island* (London, 1962), [6]. Hereafter, *Island*.

[14] Aldous Huxley, *Beyond the Mexique Bay* (London, 1994), 177.

[15] See "A Note on Ideals," *PS*, 263–264.

[16] In comparison, the relation between ends and means is a crucial one also in Pareto's *Trattato*, which, according to Placido Buccolo, can be interpreted as follows: "For Pareto, it was not really that the end justifies the means so much that the means are ends in themselves. From this springs Pareto's modernity and influence which he has had on many of the sociologists and economists of our time" ("Reading Pareto," *The Other Pareto*, ed. Placido Buccolo [London, 1980], 301). Buccolo continues: "Pareto had never supplied any antidotes. At the most he confined himself to indicating where one road or another would lead the men who took it. He did not advise, because he never chose for others. At most he invited others to choose. His science is not exhortatory precisely because it is no other than analysis made coherent only as an instrumental context which he himself has created for the most part, and which in its majesty gives an idea which leaves no doubt about the *relative* position of the author. All he does is to furnish different technical instruments which different people can employ with different wills for different ends. [...] Another thing which he emphasises is that you cannot support a civilisation of mass consumption and at the same time oppose birth-control."

[17] See Aldous Huxley, *Ends and Means* (London, 1937; hereafter, *EM*), 9: "The end cannot justify the means, for the simple and obvious reason that the means employed determine the nature of the ends produced."

[18] See *EM*, 11: "Every one has his own patent medicine, guaranteed to cure all the ills of humanity; and so passionate, in many cases, is belief in the efficacy of the panacea that men are prepared, on its behalf, to kill and to be killed."

[19] See *AE*, 93–94: "'Progress—the theory that you can get something for nothing; the theory that you can gain in one field without paying for your gain in another; the theory that you alone understand the meaning of history; the theory that you know what's going to happen fifty years from now; the theory that, in the teeth of all experience, you can foresee all the consequences of your present actions; the theory that Utopia lies just ahead and that, since ideal ends justify the most abominable means, it is your privilege and duty to rob, swindle, torture, enslave and murder all those who, in your opinion (which is, by definition infallible), obstruct the onward march to the earthly paradise. Remember that phrase of Karl Marx's: 'Force is the midwife of Progress?' [...] And then there was Nationalism—the theory that the state you happen to be subject to is the only true god, and that all other states are false gods; and that all these gods, true as well as false, have the mentality of juvenile delinquents; and that every conflict over prestige, power or money is a crusade for the Good, the True and the Beautiful."

[20] See *Island*, 58: "In those days, Pala was still completely off the map. The idea of turning it into an oasis of freedom and happiness made sense. So long as it remains out of touch with the rest of the world, an ideal society can be a viable

society. Pala was completely viable, I'd say, until about 1905. Then, in less than a single generation, the world completely changed. Movies, cars, aeroplanes, radio. Mass production, mass slaughter, mass communication and, above all, plain mass—more and more people in bigger and bigger slums or suburbs. By 1930 any clear-sighted observer could have seen that, for three-quarters of the human race, freedom and happiness were almost out of the question. Today, thirty years later, they're completely out of the question. And meanwhile the outside world has been closing on this little island of freedom and happiness. Closing in steadily and inexorably, coming nearer and nearer. What was once a viable ideal is now no longer viable."

Eva Oppermann

(University of Kassel)

THE CROWS OF PEARBLOSSOM:
ALDOUS HUXLEY'S FORGOTTEN PICTURE BOOK FOR CHILDREN

Aldous Huxley's works are well known, especially *Brave New World*, but also *Point Counter Point* and *Island* are widely read, and a considerable amount of research has been invested into his critical, essayistic work. However, Huxley was not only the "Man of Letters: Thinker, Critic and Artist" as whom most of us know him today. Among his essays and novels, there is one extraordinary work, nearly forgotten now and written merely for entertainment, a picture book for children entitled *The Crows of Pearblossom.*[1]

Generally, children's books are regarded as minor literary works, although their reputation has increased considerably in recent years. Still, their stigma of being simplistic and childish has not been overcome completely. Especially picture books, whose story is closely interwoven with corresponding illustrations, are in danger of a Mickey Mouse reputation. Together with the fact that the original manuscript of *The Crows of Pearblossom* was destroyed by fire at Huxley's house in 1961,[2] this is the main reason why Huxley's only children's book is known to very few scholars today.

With this paper I would like to rescue *The Crows of Pearblossom* from oblivion. Since I am a scholar of children's literature rather than a Huxley scholar, this book is of special interest to me. Among the serious research done on Huxley's essays and especially his novels, this essay may appear exceptionally light and easy, but nevertheless I consider *The Crows of Pearblossom* worthy of scholarly regard, since it reveals both Huxley's ability to adapt perfectly to the literary needs of children and his knowledge of children's literature along with its typical motifs and strategies. Apart from this, "it is good to have a scherzo in the symphony."[3]

The Crows of Pearblossom was originally written in 1944, when the Huxleys lived at Llano, California, near the Mojave Desert. In his Huxley biography, Theo Schumacher[4] portrays this period in Huxley's life as one of religious study, particularly of the religious beliefs of the Far East. Schumacher describes the ranch at Llano not only as a place of prayer and study but also as a dwelling in which Huxley and some friends tried to establish a kind of independent community apart from the rest of the world. Despite these interests, Huxley was not the sort of hermit one might expect. *The Crows of Pearblossom* clearly testifies to his openness to the world and his interest even in small everyday matters.

It is quite likely that, similar to Carroll's *Alice* Books and Grahame's *The Wind in the Willows*, there was an oral version on which the written text was based. It is recorded that Huxley told many stories to his niece and nephew. However, one should be careful not to create a myth in the way of Carroll's "Golden Afternoon"[5] or that of Kenneth Grahame as Master Bed-Time Storyteller to Alastair, his son.[6] Still, since *The Crows of Pearblossom* is much shorter than a novel, the possibility of an oral origin and the transformation from orality to literality is probable, especially since there are some passages in the text which hint at orality. Reading passages like the following makes it easy to imagine Huxley talking to Olivia and Siggy and imitating Rattlesnake:

> "Two eggs today!" he said; "nyum—nyum." And he smacked his lips, for his mother neglected his education and he had very bad manners. (*CP*, [24])

> All at once he began to have the most frightful stomach ache. "Ow," he said. "Ooh, aie, eeh." But the stomach ache only got worse and worse. "Ow, ooh, aie." Mr. Snake began to writhe and wriggle and twist and turn. (*CP*, [28])

With this connection to orality, and also by mentioning the children for whom the story was invented, Huxley joins a well-developed tradition in children's literature, to which, apart from Carroll's and Grahame's works, also Alan Alexander Milne's *Winnie-the-Pooh* and Beatrix Potter's stories belong. Lucy Carr, to whom Potter's "The Story of Mrs Tiggy-Winkle" is dedicated,[7] appears in the tale, and in "The Tale of Jemima Puddle-Duck" both Jemima and Kep the collie are modelled on Potter's own animals (see Potter, 160).

"The Tale of Jemima Puddle-Duck" and *The Crows of Pearblossom* have more in common than only their adherence to an established tradition and the fact that they both are picture stories. The major motifs are identical as well. Both Jemima and Mrs Crow want to hatch their own eggs, and both are robbed of them. In both cases, too, there is an enemy who destroys the dreams of the birds. In *The Crows of Pearblossom*, it is Rattlesnake, in "Jemima Puddle-Duck" it is "the hospitable gentleman with sandy whiskers" (Potter, 167), a fox.[8]

To me, Jemima and Mrs Crow appear similar in temperament. Both are a little over-emotional, as they both seem not to have the best of nerves. Jemima asserts that only four of her eggs hatched "because of her nerves" (Potter, 172), although, as the narrator notes, "she had always been a bad sitter" (Potter, 172). There are no such authorial comments about Mrs Crow, but the way she talks and behaves clearly reveals aspects of her character:

> "How can you be so coarse and unfeeling? [...] Here am I, working myself to the bone for you; when I'm not working, laying a fresh egg every single day—except Sundays, of course, and public

holidays—two hundred and ninety-seven eggs a year, and not a single chick hatched out. And all you can do is ask if I've been overeating." (*CP*, [12–13])

Both heroines are terribly affected by the attacks on their eggs. However, in the end, Mrs Crow is the one who successfully manages a large household; it is probably her happiness about her many children that helps her to relax.

Beatrix Potter's "Tales" are not the only animal stories which reveal a clear connection to *The Crows of Pearblossom*. In my view, Rattlesnake and Grahame's Toad apppear to be related as well. Both enjoy their lives as much as they can, and both are rather proud of themselves, especially after having done a considerable amount of mischief. Toad sings the last stanza of "The world has held great Heroes"[9]after having caused his last accident:

"The motor-car went Poop-poop-poop,
As it raced along the road.
Who was it steered it into a pond?
Ingenious Mr. Toad!" (Grahame, 199)

Rattlesnake sings a very similar song after having had his most opulent breakfast of Mrs Crow's darling eggs:

"I cannot fly—I have no wings;
I cannot run—I have no legs;
But I can creep where the black bird sings
And eat her speckled eggs, ha, ha,
And eat her speckled eggs." (*CP*, 27])

In both cases, the singers are cured of their boastfulness rather quickly; Toad finds himself hunted by policemen, Rattlesnake begins to have his stomach ache. Then both become impressive images of misery.

Another similarity between both works, and Potter's as well, is the particular degree of anthropomorphization used. The animals wear human clothes (at least sometimes), they have human jobs, and they act in a typically human manner. Old Man Owl, for instance, "shav[ing] and comb[ing] his feathers" (*CP*, [16]) is reminiscent of Toad, "dipp[ing] his hairbrush in the water-jug, part[ing] his hair in the middle, and plaster[ing] it down very straight and sleek on each side of his face" (Grahame, 244).

This method of giving animals certain human qualities appears to be a convention in texts for children. It is perfectly suited to the children's magico-numinous view of the world[10] and turns the animals into persons. The magico-numinous world-view can be described as changing the qualities of a person by the use of outer appearance. For example, a shaman wearing a tiger mask is taken for a tiger, a crow with a hat and a newspaper under his wing becomes an "Assistant Manager in the drug store" (*CP*, [10]), and an owl wearing bedroom slippers and pyjamas is a person that has just got out of bed.

Illustration 1 (*CP*, [17])

Originally, this concept seems to have developed in animal fairy tales. A good example is "The Wolf and the Seven Young Goats" from the collection by the Grimm Brothers,[11] a fairy tale with intertextual connections that are also important in this context. The goats, as well as the wolf (it can be assumed), live like humans; the description of the house is given in detail during the wolf's attack. That the animals wear clothes can be concluded from the fact that the old goat uses needle, thread and scissors, typical tailor's tools, to sow up the wolf's belly after cramming it up with heavy stones.

The motif shared by *The Crows of Pearblossom* and "The Wolf and the Seven Young Goats" is that of the stones causing the enemy's death. Of course, the eggs Rattlesnake swallows are only baked clay, but still, they are as hard as stones—and as hard to digest. The only difference between the stories is that Rattlesnake swallows the eggs himself while the wolf has the stones put into his belly. Both, however, feel the consequences of what they have in their stomachs. The wolf says:

"Was rumpelt und pumpelt
in meinem Bauch herum?
Ich meinte, es wären sechs Geißlein,
so sind's lauter Wackerstein."
['What is rumbling
in my belly?
I thought it was six little goats,
but it is only big stones.'] (Grimm, I, 54)

Similarly, the effect the eggs have on Rattlesnake is "the most excruciating stomach ache" *CP*, [31]).

Originally, there were many different versions of the story, but the one recorded by the Grimm Brothers is known best today. In some of these versions, the wolf turned to stone, in others, the stones were only consumed (see Grimm, III, 15). So, the motif has a long tradition itself.

As regards the many literary models Huxley seems to have taken into consideration, it is surprising that he did not draw on the most important literary genre involving animals, the fable. Neither did Huxley include a moral into his story, nor do his characters show the typical qualities normally ascribed to animals in fables.

The only 'moral' aspects of *The Crows* are the authorial comments on Rattlesnake's bad behaviour and the fact that he is punished for having stolen Mrs Crow's eggs. These comments cannot be regarded as constituting a genuine moral, since Rattlesnake is not punished for his bad manners. The punishment of the proud thief corresponds more with the fairy tale[12] than with the fable. Therefore, the most important element of the fable cannot be detected in *The Crows of Pearblossom*.

Although Huxley's animals are rather flat characters who do not develop in the book, they are certainly created in a much more individual manner than the stereotypical animals in fables. Even Old Man Owl, who, as a "thinker" (*CP*, [15]), fits the image of 'the wise owl', is not just shown as wise, but also as active in the process of making the clay eggs. Apart from that, he appears as the sort of sophisticated bachelor who has managed to develop some taste and whose position in life enables him to use much of his time at his pleasure, despite the fact that he "works on a night shift" (*CP*, [16]) Moreover, he appears to be interested in culture, as his listening to the evening concert on the radio shows. He has a choleric temperament, which reveals itself in his quick and effective actions when he is confronted with a dilemma.[13]

I have already described Amelia Crow as being a little over-emotional; she also appears to be rather forceful, especially when she wants her husband to "go down the hole and kill the snake" (*CP*, [22]). She definitely is the dominant part in the marriage, as the pertinent illustration by Barbara Cooney clearly reveals:

Illustration 2 (*CP*, [12])

Abraham Crow, in contrast, is a little reluctant, and, although he accuses his wife of not being too clever, he himself is not a great thinker either. Nor is he particularly brave or enterprising, otherwise he would not seek rescue under Owl's wings. Abraham seems to be a follower rather than a leader; Owl can order him to be quiet without explaining anything:

> "Abraham, you talk too much [...]. Keep your beak shut and do exactly what I do." (*CP*, [18])

It must be a genuine pleasure for Abraham Crow (and it certainly is for many readers!) that later he is able to rebuke his wife with almost exactly the same words:

> "Amelia, [...] you talk too much. Keep your beak shut and get out of your nest." (*CP*, [23])

Rattlesnake is presented as a rather simple character who is mainly interested in the pleasures of life, in his case, food and sleep. Although he is the destroyer of Mrs Crow's hopes and dreams and indirectly the killer of many young crows, he is far from appearing like the biblical archenemy, even if Cooney's title-page illustration (see below) hints at paradise paintings. His simple-mindedness also makes him different from the wolf in the fairy tale who captures the goats by means of malicious tricks. The only bad quality he has is his greed.

Illustration 3 (*CP*, title page)

The difference of Huxley's characters from the symbolically one-dimensional animals in fables becomes obvious. In fables, owls are nothing but wise, crows nothing but vain, and so on.[14] Huxley's animals do not have a comparable symbolic meaning. He uses the symbolic connection when it fits the context, but no more.

The Crows of Pearblossom is related to many important traditions in children's literature. It can be assumed that Huxley knew the texts which I have taken into consideration here. He was probably even familiar with German fairy tales from the popular *Kinder- und Hausmärchen*, or from his visits to Germany. The *Alice* books, *The Wind in the Willows* and Beatrix Potter's *Tales* are as much classics today as they were fashionable when they were published; it is very likely that Huxley read them to his son Matthew in the 1920s.

In my opinion, *The Crows of Pearblossom* has the quality to achieve an ambivalent status.[15] It appeals both to children and to adults. To children, its oral elements, anthropomorphic characters and humorous attitude are the most appealing factors, both in the text itself and in Cooney's illustrations. For adults, the many allusions and the relationship between the two crows have an attractive potential. Therefore, I hope that *The Crows* will be rediscovered as a valuable piece of literature, not only by children, but also by scholars in general, and Huxley scholars in particular.

---

[1] Aldous Huxley, *The Crows of Pearblossom* (New York, 1967). Hereafter, *CP*. Since this edition has no pagination, page numbers (beginning with the first recto page after the title page) are provided in brackets).

[2] See the editor's postscript, *CP*, [36].

[3] William W. Robson, "On *The Wind in the Willows*," *Hebrew University Studies in Literature and the Arts*, 9 (1981), 98.

[4] Theo Schumacher, *Aldous Huxley* (Reinbek, [2]1992), 77–104, especially 88–90.

[5] Lewis Carroll, "Alice's Adventures in Wonderland," *The Annotated Alice,* ed. Martin Gardner (London, [2]1970), 21.

[6] See Peter Green, *Kenneth Grahame* (London, 1959), 323–333.

[7] See Beatrix Potter, "About this book," *The Complete Tales* (London, [2]1997), 86.

[8] Although the fox does not eat the eggs himself, he intends to, and he also causes the dogs to attack and, in the process, eat the eggs.

[9] Kenneth Grahame, *The Wind in the Willows* (Leicester, 1987), 193.

[10] See Peter Biehl, *Symbole geben zu lernen* (Neukirchen, 1989), 15–160. A detailed study of this phenomenon can be found in: Eva Oppermann, *Englischsprachige Kinderbücher: "Kinderkram" oder auch anspruchsvolle Literatur für Erwachsene?* (Kassel, 2004).

[11] See Jakob und Wilhelm Grimm, *Kinder- und Hausmärchen* (Stuttgart, [2]2001), I, 51–54. All quotations from this text are translated by Eva Oppermann.

[12] See Bruno Bettelheim, *The Uses of Enchantment* (New York, 1989), 147.

[13] See Ole Hallesby, *Dein Typ ist gefragt* (Wuppertal, [9]1996), 59.

[14] An impressive list of animals that appear in fables and of the qualities ascribed to them can be found in Gotthold Ephraim Lessing, "Der Rangstreit der Thiere," *Sämtliche Schriften*, ed. Karl Lachmann (Stuttgart, 1886), I, 221–222.

[15] See Zohar Shavit, *The Poetics of Children's Literature* (London, 1986), 66.

Gisela Hansen

(University of Münster)

A QUEER FISH—
RADCLYFFE HALL, ECCENTRIC CONTEMPORARY OF ALDOUS HUXLEY

While listening to the lecture that Gerhard Wagner gave at the Second Aldous Huxley Symposium in Singapore, one quotation from Huxley's introduction to his anthology of poetry, *Texts and Pretexts*, kept ringing in my ears: "There are more fish in the sea of literature than ever came out of it."[1] At that time, I had already spent a few years in the effort of 'undigging' a forgotten author. Instead of being a literary grave-digger, an image that I came very close to in the course of my research and that I will return to later, I could now look upon myself as a literary fisherwoman, which was an image that I preferred.

When I was thinking about a possible subject for my doctoral thesis, somehow a sense of adventure got hold of me, the excitement of exploring unknown realms, treading off the beaten path and finding hidden treasures. Or, if we again refer to Huxley's original image of the literary sea, I did not wish to re-examine one of the bigger fish that were swimming so close to the surface already, that had been caught, weighed, measured, described, and vivisected so many times before. No, I wanted to dig, or better, I wanted to fish deeper. What I pulled out of the tides of literature was a very strange fish, a weird creature, I could not even tell if it was male or female. It was a queer fish indeed. Its name sounded more like an English country manor or a boy's school: 'Radclyffe Hall,' who on earth was that?

I went to the library and looked through several literary reference books. There was hardly any reference. Only the *Who's Who* stated that "Miss" Radclyffe Hall, daughter of a certain Radclyffe Radclyfe-Hall, had for many years taken a great interest in spiritism, dog-breeding and collecting antique oak.[2]

It does not seem surprising that the *Who's Who* of 1928 was so concerned with her eccentricity and her private life because her novel *The Well of Loneliness* had just created a huge scandal that had involved an obscenity trial and finally resulted in the banning of the book. The reason of this scandal was outrageous at the time, since she had dared to describe the life of a woman who loved other women. The man who had brought the novel to the public's attention was well-known in the literary world. It was none other than James Douglas, the editor of the *Sunday Express*, who had already made a name for himself as hypochondriac and self-appointed guardian of the country's moral well-being. Among his other victims were many modern writers, and Aldous Huxley was favoured on his list. The most infamous sentence of Douglas' article that is still being quoted today is this: "I would rather give a healthy boy or a healthy girl a phial of prussic acid than this novel."[3]

With my sense for adventure, I set out at once to buy and read this highly precarious book. I did not have to go to the adult's section of the book store to acquire it; on the contrary and to my great surprise and astonishment, I found that it was and still is the easiest of all her novels to obtain. Ready for some excitement, I started to read. In vain I looked out for ambiguous descriptions and pornographic depiction. The only sentence I could find was this: "And that night they were not divided."[4]

In spite of its innocence and thanks to James Douglas, the book was suppressed, quite clearly not for its indecency but because of its subject. Radclyffe Hall's fellow writers stepped in to help, stood up against the censorship, and protested for the freedom of speech and literature. They wrote letters and articles. In her famous essay *A Room of One's Own*, Virginia Woolf alluded to the obscenity trial, and together with E. M. Forster she published a letter, ironically asking the government for future instructions how to handle delicate subjects in literature.[5] A very strong reaction came from Aldous Huxley, who took Douglas for his word. In a note with the title "Document," he writes:

> In an article written at the time I offered to provide Mr. Douglas with a child, a bottle of prussic acid, a copy of *The Well of Loneliness*, and (if he kept his word and chose to administer the acid) a handsome memorial in marble to be erected wherever he might appoint, after his execution. The offer, I regret to say, was not accepted.[6]

We do not know what Huxley really thought about the book, or if he had read it at all, but we have enough evidence to believe that its author was not exactly a favourite with her literary companions. Forster, in private, thought the book "ill-written and pretentious,"[7] and Shaw called it "pathetic, serious, unpornographic, [...] so bad as literature."[8] Virginia Woolf, whose well-known cynicism is at its worst when it comes to other women writers, called it a "meritorious dull book"[9] and describes the following scene:

> In the midst of this, Morgan [E. M. Forster] goes to see Radclyffe [...] and Radclyffe scolds him like a fishwife, and says that she won't have any letter written about her book unless it mentions the fact that it is a work of artistic merit—even genius. And no one has read her book; or can read it [...]. So our ardour in the cause of freedom of speech gradually cools, and instead of offering to reprint the masterpiece, we are already beginning to wish it unwritten.[10]

With this, Radclyffe Hall was not only falling from grace with the Bloomsbury Circle, but, what was more, she was also falling through the net of literary history.

The more my research on Radclyffe Hall progressed, the more ambiguous she appeared. Never have I found so many contradictions in one author. Her name, her person, and her infamous novel entered mythology even in her life-time, but her literary achievements were forgotten. If we consider *The Well of Loneliness* as a milestone in her life and work, what happened before and after it? It comes as a surprise that only two years earlier, in 1926, she published the novel *Adam's Breed*, which achieved enormous international success. The book describes the quest of a national outsider, an Italian waiter, who realises the meaninglessness and materialism of London's society in the 1920s and is looking for spiritual nourishment instead of handling real food. The novel won as many literary prizes as Forster's *A Passage to India* and was translated into several languages. Furthermore, Thomas Mann wrote a letter of congratulation and included the German version in the series of English novels he co-edited at the time. Radclyffe Hall's early collections of poems were so popular that several had been set to music by contemporary composers. Her two comical novels *The Forge* and *A Saturday Life* were a great success, too, since they offered a humorous depiction of the disorientation of English society after the Great War.

The Well of Loneliness changed everything for her. She was ridiculed, made fun of, which caused her to withdraw from public life, a bitter and frustrated woman. She even gave up her proud memberships of the PEN Club and the Women Writers' Society. Her last two novels and the volume of short stories that she published in the 1930s hardly gained any attention from the reading public or literary critics. The scandal of her notorious book was still clinging to her. Stigmatised by its theme, she could not and would not let go of it.

Marguerite Radclyffe-Hall, born in 1880 as an only child to a rich Victorian family, died in 1943. Yet the person, the scandal, the myth remain. An astonishing number of five biographies are in existence, plus a biography of her life-time partner Lady Una Troubridge. A volume of her love letters has appeared, but as far as literary research is concerned, there is next to nothing. Only one scholar has undertaken the effort to write a study of her work.[11] The rest has sunken deeply into the darkness of the literary sea.

How is it possible that literary history has not found such a person, an eccentric in her time, worthy of inclusion in its records?

Firstly, there is the subject of her book and its outspokenness. *The Well of Loneliness* being her only novel still remembered, she was likely to be categorised, labelled and thus banned. Therefore, it was not considered worth while paying closer attention to the rest of her work. Other homosexual authors of her time managed to escape public disapproval by either having their delicate texts published posthumously (like Forster's *Maurice* and certain of his short stories) or disguising them with a heterosexual or fantastic cover (like Virginia Woolf's *Mrs Dalloway* and *Orlando*). Thus, they also escaped a very one-sided reception by the reading public as well as by literary scholarship.

Secondly, Radclyffe Hall was not an experimental modernist. She disliked the styles of Woolf and Joyce and preferred more traditional narrative techniques for herself. In this respect, literary history may have to re-consider its established categories and paradigms. In her study *Rebel Women: Feminism, Modernism and the Edwardian Novel*, Jane Eldridge Miller tries to distinguish between what she defines as "modernism of content" and "modernism of form."[12] The new formal achievements of experimental writers sometimes seem to overshadow an objective perception of what can be labelled 'modernist' in literature. In a study called *Outside Modernism*, several scholars undertake the effort to widen the meaning of the term and consider the years between 1900 and 1930 a time of coexistence of more than one narrative style. Moreover, they also state that many authors of this period fall through the net because, as far as their style is concerned, they cannot be regarded as modernists, with the consequence that they do not appear in literary histories at all.[13]

Thirdly, she was not an intellectual. With her financial background but only little higher education, her work cannot be compared to anything as sophisticated and educated as Huxley's or Forster's. As David Bradshaw points out in his introduction to the Flamingo edition of *Point Counter Point*, Huxley privileged content over form, an "anathema to the likes of Virginia Woolf."[14] In my view, the one can never be fully separated from the other, and Woolf's formal experiments helped her to convey a meaning that she would not have been able to express with a more traditional style of narration. Radclyffe Hall, like Huxley, was more concerned with content than with form. Although she was not able to produce novels as witty or as brilliant as her intellectual contemporaries, she was well able to depict the atmosphere of her time, social issues and problems, the consequences of the Great War, and the individual in relation to society. Like Huxley, she was preoccupied in the 1930s with the meaning of existence and wrote about the spiritual quest of the individual.

Finally, she was not a member of, or otherwise connected with, the Bloomsbury Group. Even today, the power of judgement of this circle of intellectuals, writers, artists, and friends has remained strong and highly influential. Their dominance and presence have shaped the annals of literary history as well as contemporary criticism. As a consequence, minor authors like Vita Sackville-West, who were privately connected with this group, experienced a far more favourable reception than Radclyffe Hall. Her fall from grace and Bloomsbury's devastating comments are both reasons for her lasting absence from the literary canons of schools and universities.

Even if Radclyffe Hall may be considered a smaller fish in the sea of literature, she is important not only because she enriches and enlightens the darker depths of literary history, but also because she assumes a contrasting function in relation to the established authors of her time and sheds new light on their artistic merits and achievements. Since writers can never be isolated and separated from their historical and cultural background, it does not seem appropriate to label Radclyffe Hall as scandalous because of a certain book she published. On the contrary, although her style cannot be regarded as experimental and the literary category 'modernist,' as it is used today, may not apply to her, her themes in many ways parallel those of the better known writers of her time. These important common issues within a particular period and a comparison of the handling of similar material in different sources can be a very interesting and useful field for literary study. In addition, taking into account lesser authors can, but need not necessarily, result in a reconsideration of the merits of established writers. On the other hand, it can also help to reinforce their dominant position in the history of literature.

To conclude, although it is generally true that the bigger fish eats the smaller one, both big and small help to complement each other; each has its function and value, and both are in this sense important for the other.

My advice then, especially to younger students and scholars of literature, is this: if you ever set out for a literary adventure, if you want to find hidden treasures and 'dig out' forgotten authors, you never know where it may lead. I for my part can say that I almost met my forgotten author in person. In the summer of 1995, when I was doing volunteer work for the Radclyffe Hall Memorial Fund, I helped clean her vault in London's Highgate Cemetery. One of my jobs was to polish the brass plate on her coffin. I am not suggesting that you need to go as far as this, but I assure you that it is well worth it. Anything is possible, anything can happen. It will bring excitement, but it will also demand a lot of pioneer work. It will bring things to the surface that you might never have dreamed about. But if you are ready, the journey will begin.[15]

---

[1] Aldous Huxley, *Texts and Pretexts* (London, 1932), 10. Gerhard Wagner's paper entitled "Aldous Huxley as Anthologist: *Texts and Pretexts* and *The Perennial Philosophy*" was read on 30 December 2000 and later published in *AHA*, 1 (2001), 145–155.

[2] See *Who's Who* (London, 1928), 1280.

[3] "A Book That Must Be Suppressed," *Sunday Express* (19 August 1928), no pagination.

[4] Radclyffe Hall, *The Well of Loneliness* (London, 1982), 316.

[5] The letter was published in the *Nation and Athenaeum* in September 1928.

[6] Aldous Huxley, "Document," *Music at Night* (London, 1931), 184–185.

[7] Quoted in P. N. Furbank, *E. M. Forster: A Life* (London, 1978), II, 154.

[8] Quoted in *The Journals of Denton Welch*, ed. Michael De-la-Noy (New York, 1986), 73.

[9] Virginia Woolf, *The Diary of Virginia Woolf*, ed. Anne Olivier Bell (5 vols., London, 1977–1984), III, 193.

[10] Virginia Woolf, *The Letters of Virginia Woolf*, ed. Nigel Nicolson and Joanne Trautmann (6 vols., London, 1975–1980), III, 520.

[11] See Claudia Stillman Franks, *Beyond "The Well of Loneliness": The Fiction of Radclyffe Hall* (Amersham, 1982).

[12] Jane Eldridge Miller, *Rebel Women: Feminism, Modernism and the Edwardian Novel* (London, 1994).

[13] *Outside Modernism: In Pursuit of the English Novel, 1900–1930*, ed. Lynne Hapgood and Nancy L. Paxton (Basingstoke, 2000).

[14] David Bradshaw, "Introduction," in: Aldous Huxley, *Point Counter Point* (London, 1994), no pagination.

[15] Meanwhile I have finished and published my doctoral thesis: see Gisela Hansen, *"The Thorns That Pierce" oder Leiden am Anderssein: Das Bild des Märtyrers im Werk Radclyffe Halls*, Münsteraner Monographien zur englischen Literatur / Münster Monographs on English Literature, 31 (Frankfurt a.M., 2007).

Uwe Rasch

(University of Münster)

"NOTHING SHORT OF EVERYTHING": TOWARD A FULL-TEXT HUXLEY DATABASE

1. Why?

A digital edition of any corpus of important texts is always desirable. As much as the printed page may be more sensually pleasing to the book lover, the advantages of computer-based systematical text studies are self-evident to the scholar. There is hardly a more useful tool if one wants to peruse texts for recurrent themes and phrases, for quotations, motifs or simply single words; if one wants to compile indexes or collate variant editions of texts.

For Huxley's writings this is doubly true. On the one hand, there is the prolific literary artist, on the other, there is the thinker. Huxley has repeatedly been called one of the most erudite persons of the twentieth century; his wide-ranging intellect, his ample education, his unresting curiosity and concern have often been praised, sometimes with frank and pleased admiration, sometimes with suspicious bafflement. As writer and artist, as thinker and intellectual, Huxley poses distinctly different tasks to the scholar (less so to the interested reader). Huxley is a mine of erudition, and a major source of twentieth-century thought. His thinking is informed by the great impetus of eighteenth-century Enlightenment and rooted in the skeptical attitudes of Modernity. Huxley was probably the first to recover from the debunking of almost everything that had held Western thought and belief together. Accepting the absurdity of human existence as well as the human need to make sense, he consequently used his skepticism as an instrument in order to try and make better sense.

One of the most common by-words of recent times is that of a pluralistic society: inasmuch as we accept that notion as a fact, regretting the putative loss of grand narratives and foreseeing the end of everything—art, history, mankind, humanity, gender, literature, philosophy—over and over again (it's like the 7th last concert tour by The Who), Huxley was the vanguard of accepting it, knowing at the same time that rejecting the simplistic nature of grand narratives did not mean the end to all intellectual human effort—it just meant that more intelligent answers had to be found, allowing for more complexity and more discernment: "Nothing short of everything will really do."[1] Moreover, Huxley was one of the few intellectuals who kept control over the relativity of the whole pluralistic mess, who realized that all the seemingly hermetic compartments were in reality communing in complex ways.

Huxley's intellectual development, it is true, has been the focus of a number of scholarly essays, and particularly the research of the last twenty years has begun to dissolve the hackneyed cliché that there was a paradigmatic change Huxley's career: the conversion from satirist to saint, from detached aesthete to (a somewhat woolly-headed, mild-mannered, and detached[2]) mystic. A sober look at Huxley's life and work, however, will reveal that the satirical gun in his hand was always warm, and that toward the end of his life he was all but a mystic, and for lack of disciples or a school, he certainly was no guru. All this is very important, I believe, to understand Huxley's comprehensive anthropological approach, in which satire, i.e., the critical attack on outrages, and constructive propositions have from the outset been of equal importance in Huxley's intellectual and social commitment. A lot of Huxley's complex, and necessarily unsystematically expounded, world-view remains uncharted. For somebody who wanted "to bring it all in"[3] he has made it difficult for his listeners and readers to 'bring it all together' and not commit what for Huxley were the original sins of the intellect: "over-abstraction, over-generalization and over-simplification."[4]

There is another point which makes it important to investigate Huxley's thinking and his intellectual stance in greater depth. Aldous Huxley was not only a bridge-builder in the sense of trying to bring together all human answers to existence—religious, cultural, scientific, social, intellectual and intuitive—but he also appears to have been a *pontifex* (*minimus* or *maximus* remains to be established)[5] between the Age of Reason and 'postmodernism.' Endowed with the gifts and curiosity of a Renaissance *uomo universale,* he was a son of the Age of Reason, believing in the controlling function of the intellect to the point of clearly recognizing its limits. The bridges he started to build seem to be leading beyond the haze of the so-called 'post-modern' world-view, and the intellectual forays of his unabashedly undogmatic and sprightly rigorous thinking seem to be fit to inform many of the debates over the challenges of the beginning twenty-first century.

For obvious reasons, at present more digital editions of classical texts are available than of modern texts. There is a greater demand for Chaucer, Shakespeare, Goethe and Cervantes, or the Greek classics, than, say, for George Bernard Shaw or Beckett. Moreover, there are no copyright issues. However, there is a full-text digital edition of one of Huxley's close contemporaries, Virginia Woolf.[6]

2. What?

Present digital editions, such as, for instance, the critical edition of Kafka's Works (S. Fischer), the Weimar edition of Goethe's Works, Shakespeare's Works [all Chadwyck & Healey], Virginia Woolf, Walt Whitman or The Brontës [all Primary Source Media] vary according to editorship, but basically comprise the following materials: reliable editions of the primary texts, basic secondary material, such as monographs, chronologies, bibliographies, images, facsimiles of manuscripts or annotated proofs, and audio material.

All this is very well and should be aimed at in creating a full-text database for Huxley's writings. However, I would suggest aiming further than compiling just a rough-and-ready collection and would keep a gradually extendable database in view. This is why I would suggest a modular approach to the task.

The following features should be included in a comprehensive and user-friendly database:

1. Completeness: a) genres (novels, stories, poems, essays, travel, prefaces, criticism/journalism, letters) b) variants (writings published in different versions, e.g., in American or British editions)
2. Critical apparatus: critical edition of texts, commentary, criticism
3. Search engine (cross-references, links)
4. Collation (comparing variants of writings, see 1.b)
5. Dictionary/encyclopedia/thesaurus: cross-referencing
6. Index of names/sources
7. Index of themes/terms (scientific, aesthetic, philosophical, religious, psychological, sociological etc.)
8. Weblinks: Gerald Heard, F. M. Alexander, D. H. Lawrence, LSD, ESP, hypnosis, to mention a few.
9. Additional resources: didactic materials
10. Extendable features (texts, tools): see, e.g., Wikipedia

Thus the database could be a platform tool (to be extended and used in several domains and directions):

1. scholarly research; interdisciplinary resource
2. general public [literature; ideas; (social, cultural) history]
3. didactic uses (teaching in different contexts)

Modular approach:
1. a) Huxley texts: novels, essays and *belles lettres*, poetry, drama, travel books, criticism etc.
b) Secondary materials where possible: commentary; seminal essays
c) Biography (monographs, testimonies [e.g., *Aldous Huxley: A Memorial Volume*, ed. Julian Huxley; *Aldous Huxley: The Critcal Heritage*, ed. Donald Watt]), chronology, bibliography
e) Images
f) Audio sources: interviews, lectures

2. a) Huxley texts (additions, emendations)
   b) Secondary texts: seminal books and essays on Huxley; further commentary; specialized indexes [s.o.]
   c) Didactic materials: e.g., starting with *BNW*; sources, background: life and times, images

The first module could be completed comparatively quickly, particularly if one concentrates on the compilation and editing of the primary texts. Depending on the amount of funding and the scale of the project, the second module may be completed at a slower pace and after the first edition of the database on CD-ROM or possibly on the Web.

The above attempt at a definition of the goals and scope of a full-text Aldous Huxley database is, of course, only the first step in what creators of electronic texts call "document analysis."[7] Before embarking on the digitization of the originals an encoding methodology needs to be established. In this context, considerations which are standard for any digitization project concern types of encoding, text markup standards, archiving standards for materials such as imagery, structure, classification of document types and their structural differences in order to establish the encoding requirements for their different features, and a clear definition of the targeted user base (academic, secondary schools, general public), its needs, and its hardware and software capabilities. Moreover, a preliminary consideration of the transmission and publication histories of individual documents is prerequisite for encoding decisions and the inclusion of metadata (providing textual history). A thorough document analysis along these lines will also allow to anticipate specific problems that fragile or hardly legible documents may cause in the OCR process.

3. How?

The compilation of a reliable digital edition of Huxley texts and database poses several difficulties. First of all, there is, of course, the collection and critical edition of all available texts, including his published and unpublished letters and other miscellaneous writings. Where necessary, the permission of all owners of rights needs to be obtained.

Wherever possible, extant digital versions of the texts should be acquired, preferably the largely reliable versions used by HarperCollins or Ivan Dee, in order to avoid the time-consuming scanning and re-keying of texts. There are basically two standard procedures to digitize printed texts, which are both time- and money-consuming. In recent years, the most popular procedure for copying large corpora of texts in a reliable fashion has been to use professional keyboarding companies.[8] By employing typists who very often do not know the language that is being captured, the problem of keyboarders subconsciously modifying the text is avoided. A lot of projects have therefore out-sourced the text capturing to Chinese companies or companies employing highly trained Asian keyboarders. Cross-referencing the two typed versions promises an almost 100% accuracy.[9]

The second method, which so far has primarily been employed by individuals for single-document editions, is the scanning of documents or the image capture by high-resolution digital cameras (optical character recognition, or OCR). The world-leading company in this field, Nuance, and their software OmniPage promise a much higher accuracy today than in previous years. In the past, the scanning of texts still was fairly inaccurate and only yielded acceptable results for well-printed, clean, modern texts. OmniPage 16 offers a new "despeckle" feature that promises "to reduce background noise allowing colored, shaded and previously unrecognizable documents to be converted with less human intervention."[10] The problems would, however, largely remain unchanged for manuscripts, typescripts and poor photocopies.

Illustration 1: screenshot from *Major Authors on CD-ROM: Virginia Woolf*, ed. Mark Hussey (see note 5), showing a sample view of the table of contents

Illustration 2: screenshot from *Major Authors on CD-ROM: Virginia Woolf*, ed. Mark Hussey (see note 5), showing a sample view of the index

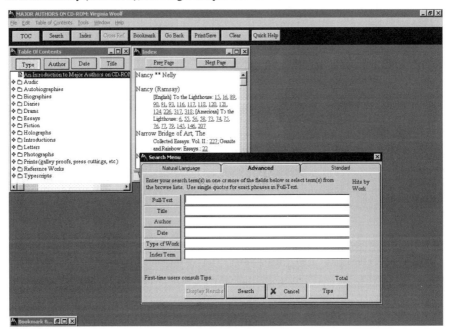

Illustration 3: screenshot of the search engine (and open TOC and index windows) form *Major Authors on CD-ROM: Virginia Woolf*, ed. Mark Hussey

Moreover, the scanning of documents is a comparatively slow process—even if one ignores the problem of getting pages of books to lie absolutely flat on the scanning bed without breaking their spines or having to go through the "despeckling" process:

> The general rule of thumb, and this varies from study to study, is that a best-case scenario would be three pages scanned per minute —this doesn't take into consideration the process of putting the document on the scanner, flipping pages, or the subsequent proofreading. (Morrison et al.)

Even using a stand-alone digital camera would not speed up the process significantly.

In view of the problems that re-keying, which would surely be a costly item, and OCR capture pose, trying to get hold of extant digitized captures of Huxley texts would certainly be the most practical, time- and cost-saving solution. Resources spent on document capture could certainly be put to much better use for the document analysis and project design.

As desirable as this project, especially to Huxleyans, may seem, the major obstacle to its realization, of course, remains the funding. Co-operation with a specialised publisher, such as *Chadwyck & Healey* in Cambridge, UK, or *Directmedia Publishing* in Berlin, should be aimed at, but this would probably only affect the final stage of the production of a CD-ROM. The compilation and editing of the texts and the development of the modular structure for the whole database would have to be financed from different sources. At least two editors would be needed to research, compile, and edit the texts and develop an intelligent and attractive user interface (maybe within the boundaries of a co-operation with a publisher and their standard interface). Software and hardware would need to be provided. Depending on the nature of the employments that could be assigned to the task—full-time, part-time, part of another employment—the time schedule for the project would have to be accommodated accordingly.

The International Aldous Huxley Society and the Centre for Aldous Huxley Studies in Münster would be grateful for assistance, advice, hints or references as to the practical and technical implications, procedures and the funding (organisations, foundations, individuals, grants etc.) of such a project. If you feel you can provide information or advice please contact: Centre for Aldous Huxley Studies, Prof. Dr. Bernfried Nugel, Englisches Seminar / Westfälische Wilhelms-Universität Münster, Johannisstr. 12–20, D-48143 Münster, Germany (<www.anglistik.uni-muenster.de/Huxley>; <nugel@uni-muenster.de>; <raschu@uni-muenster.de>).

---

[1] Aldous Huxley, *Island* (London, 1962), 132.

[2] I would like to take this opportunity to draw attention to the fact that there is a categorical difference between detachment and non-attachment; the indiscriminate use of either term in Huxley studies has sometimes confused the issue. In *Ends and Means* (and *Eyeless in Gaza* at about the same time) Huxley declares the "non-attached man" to be his ideal (*Ends and Means* [London, 1937], 3), which is clearly based on mystic, daoist and Zen-buddhist ideals. As opposed to the 'detached philosopher,' a part that many of Huxley's characters, most notably Philip Quarles, Anthony Beavis and Will Farnaby, grapple with, the non-attached person is involved and engaged selflessly in all human affairs. The detached man, in other words an uninvolved, unengaged egocentric onlooker, is the exact opposite of a Krishnamurtian, daoist, Zen-buddhist observer.

[3] Laura Huxley, *This Timeless Moment* (New York, 1968), 207, 212.

[4] Aldous Huxley, *Adonis and the Alphabet* (London, 1956), 42.

[5] In his Santa Barbara lectures Huxley modestly referred to himself as a *pontifex minimus*, see Aldous Huxley, *The Human Situation*, ed. Piero Ferruci (London, 1978), 4.

[6] *Major Authors on CD-ROM: Virginia Woolf*, ed. Mark Hussey (Reading, UK: Primary Source Media, 1997) includes: complete works of Virginia Woolf in a flexible and accessible format; variant editions, reading notebooks and typescript drafts; Mark Hussey's, *Virginia Woolf A-Z*; offers access to more than 12,000 images—including holographs of manuscripts, diaries and correspondence—from The Henry W. and Albert A. Berg Collection at the New York Public Library and The Monks House Papers at the University of Sussex; the only extant recording of Woolf's voice, an eight-minute talk recorded April 29, 1937 for the BBC radio series "Words Fail Me." Price: US $249.00. See also illustrations 1–3 in this article.

[7] For a full consideration of this stage in the production of a text database see Alan Morrison, Michael Popham, and Karen Wikander, *Creating and Documenting Electronic Texts: A Guide to Good Practice*, Chapter 2: "Document Analysis" (<http://ota.ahds.ac.uk/documents/creating/chap2.html>) at The Oxford Text Archive.

[8] For an overview of all of the problems and procedures mentioned in this passage see Morrison et al., Chapter 3: "Digitization—Scanning, OCR, and Re-keying" (<http://ota.ahds.ac.uk/documents/creating/ chap3.html>).

[9] "One such company, Apex Data Services, Inc. (used by the University of Virginia Electronic Text Center), promises a conversion accuracy of 99.995%, along with 100% structural accuracy, and reliable delivery schedules" (Morrison et al., <http://ota.ahds.ac.uk/documents/creating/chap3.html>).

[10] See <http://www.nuance.com/omnipage/professional/features.asp>. Nuance have brought out two versions of OmniPage 16: a professional version "for business and government organizations of all sizes" and an "entry-level" version for "students, home office and small business users alike" (<http://www.nuance.com/omnipage/>). It seems, however, that the extra-features of the professional version a primarily geared toward business uses and that the features of the "entry-level" version would suffice for the purposes of academic text digitization.

V.

Workshops

Anthony Attenborough

(London)

Anthony Attenborough

(London)

HUXLEY WORKSHOPS ON BATES AND ERICKSON[1]

WORKSHOP 1:
Philosophical Aspects of the Bates Method

I am greatly honoured to have been invited to give this presentation, and although I would like to make it as practical as I can, in order that you can have the chance to experience the energy of what would otherwise be mere exercises, I also want in this workshop to give some idea of what could be called the philosophical background to the practice of what Aldous Huxley called 'the art of seeing.' He is the only person to have given this title to this method and one reason for this is because of his own wide-ranging philosophical and artistic interests.

First I would like to bring to awareness the interconnection of all the senses. The senses enter through the whole of the body, continuously, and, in relation to the dominant activity, a selection is made and then for the most part the process runs on automatic pilot. Meanwhile, in order that when I am speaking you can have some experience of practice, I am going to make a suggestion that we try to bring an awareness of our feet on the floor and at the same time to bring awareness of the whole space of the room whilst I am speaking.

So I am asking you to do two things, and this is an aspect of the Bates Method. I am asking you to focus your attention on the speaking and at the same time to be aware of the whole field. And why am I saying this? The reason is reflected in the structure of the eye itself. The retina of the eye has two parts. The middle part is a very small indented point called the fovea. Because this is a scientific word it is therefore in Latin and not English and that means, from our point of view, it has no meaning so we can paraphrase and say this means 'point of sight' which occupies something like 0.001% of the whole area of the retina. This point is occupied with what could be called focus; the clear point of seeing. The rest of the 99.999% of the retina is field. It does not focus. It brings in the background. It appears that focussing is not possible unless there is a field. There is an interdependence between these two as in active and passive; rather like the focus being an electrical circuit connected in series and the field being an electrical circuit connected in parallel. Everything in the parallel circuit happens altogether, all at once. In the point of the focus it happens one point at a time. It is quite extraordinary that the focus should function one point at a time because the experience that everybody has is that seeing is always in continuous focus. And yet the fact remains that this point of focus is tiny, it functions intermittently, and yet the movement is so fast that even though the picture is continually being formed and reformed in the brain, nevertheless the perception of seeing is that the sight is stable and continuous.

In listening, which in this case would correspond to focussing, there is only the need to focus your attention on my voice as the words unfold. At the same time, the overall awareness, which is general, can be there as a support. If one really tries to maintain this awareness, one may gain the benefit that more will be remembered of what has been spoken. Maybe it will even be provocative so that questions will be produced either in yourself or towards myself. This is something that we do not have to wait to start, and it straight away brings not only a practical element, that is, that we are engaged in a workshop, but it also does something else because, by this act of awareness, we can all be aware of each other together. I am not separate from other people, and that shared energy can be a factor in receiving what I am talking about as though each person's understanding can in some way, which one cannot explain, help another's understanding.

The first quotation I am going to read is from a book by a Frenchman, Jacques Lusseyran. This man was blind. He was blinded at the age of eight, and yet he has more to say about seeing than almost anybody else I have come across. I shall read:

"Barely ten days after the accident that blinded me, I made a basic discovery. I am still entranced by it. The only way I can describe that experience is in clear and direct words. I had completely lost the sight of my eyes. I could not see the light of the world any more. Yet the light was still there. This in myself however. Where was that? In my head? In my heart? In my imagination? Don't you feel that such questions are purely intellectual and worthy only of those adults who have already forgotten the utter simplicity and unquestionable power of true experience. For me I was in my eighth year and lived instead of thinking. The light was there. Its source was not obliterated. I felt it gushing forth every moment and brimming over. I felt how it wanted to spread out over the world. I had only to receive it. It was unavoidably there. It was all there and I found again its movements and shade; that is, its colours which I had loved so passionately a few weeks before. This was something entirely new, you understand. All the more so since it contradicted everything that those who have eyes believe. The source of light is not in the outer world. We believe that it is only because of a common delusion. The light dwells where life also dwells, within ourselves. Yet I had to make the effort to find my way between doors, walls, human beings and trees. As happens to all blind persons, I hurt myself often. But I quickly learned that I knocked against things only when I forgot the light. When I paid constant attention to the light I ran a much smaller risk."

"The second great discovery came almost immediately afterwards. There was only one way to see the inner light and that was to love. When I was overcome with sorrow, when I let anger take hold of me, when I envied those who saw, the light immediately decreased. Sometimes it even went out completely. Then I became blind. But this blindness was a state of not loving any more, of sadness. It was not the loss of one's eyes."

"Because of my blindness, I had developed a new faculty. Strictly speaking all men have it, but almost all forget to use it. That faculty is attention. In order to live without eyes it is necessary to be very attentive, to remain hour after hour in a state of wakefulness, of receptiveness and activity. Indeed attention is not simply a virtue of intelligence, or the result of education, and something one can easily do without. It is a state of being. It is a state without which we shall never be able to perfect ourselves. In its true sense, it is the listening post of the universe. I was very attentive. I was more attentive than any of my comrades. All blind persons are or can be. Thus they attain the power of being completely present. Sometimes even the power of changing life around them, a power the civilization of the twentieth century with its many diversions no longer possesses. Being attentive unlocks a sphere of reality that no-one suspects. If for instance I walked along a path without being attentive, completely immersed in myself, I did not even know whether trees grew along the way, nor how tall they were or whether they had leaves. When I awakened my attention however, every tree immediately came to me. This must be taken quite literally. Every single tree projected its form, its weight, its movement, even if it was almost motionless, in my direction. I would indicate its trunk and the place where its first branches started, even when several feet away. By and by something else became clear to me and this can never be found in books. The world exerts pressure on us from the distance."

Now apart from what Aldous Huxley has written, you may not otherwise know of Dr William Bates, so I will tell you something about him. He was a New York opthalmologist who was born in 1860 and died in 1931, and he worked in various hospitals in New York, in the course of which, making observations on, as he put it, 'thousands of pairs of eyes,' he noticed anomalies in the behaviour of people's sight which did not correspond to the text books. He made the enquiries for himself and as a result, developed, discovered, put together, what now is known as the Bates Method. There is also something that isn't written about, and this is true of all originators of anything of any kind. The originator has often more capacity, more effectiveness, more ability than his followers. That seems to come from the fact that any persons who discover and originate something have had to discover it for themselves. They cannot rely on others, and that seems to generate an energy which can be called a magnetic energy. Thus, when they work with others a transference of some kind seems to take place which may correspond to the induction of a trance, whereby the more hidden unconscious part is awakened and participates. It is very difficult to account for some of the descriptions which Bates gives of the results he had when he worked with people. So let's just give you some of Bates's own words:

"The eye possesses perfect vision only when it is absolutely at rest. Any movement, either in the organ or the object of vision, produces an error of refraction. The act of seeing is passive. Things are seen just as they are felt or heard or tasted, without effort or volition on the part of the subject. When the sight is perfect, the letters on the test card are waiting perfectly black and perfectly distinct to be recognized. The muscles of the body are supposed never to be at rest, the blood vessels with their muscular coats are never at rest, even in sleep thought does not cease, but the normal condition of the nerves of sense, of hearing, sight, taste, smell and touch, is one of rest. They can be acted upon. They cannot act."

"The optic nerve, the retina and the visual centres of the brain are as passive as the fingernail. They have nothing whatever in their structure that makes it possible for them to do anything, and when they are subject to effort from outside sources their efficiency is always impaired. The mind is the source of all such effort from outside sources brought to bear upon the eye. Every thought of effort in the mind of whatever sort transmits a motor impulse to the eye, and every such impulse causes a deviation from normal in the shape of the eyeball, and lessens the sensitivity of the centre of sight. If one wants to avoid errors of refraction therefore, one must have no thought of effort in the mind."

I had better say that again: "One must have no thought of effort in the mind." And let's just look at that. He has put an imperative, 'must.' Already that's a stress. When there is no thought of effort in the mind, *then* there will be relaxation. "Mental strain of any kind always produces a conscious or unconscious eye strain and, if the strain takes the form of an effort to see, an error of refraction is always produced."

He says later on: "The first patient that I cured of presbyopia" (that means long sight) "was myself. The retinoscope showed that when I tried to see anything at the near point without glasses my eyes were focused for the distance, and when I tried to see anything at the distance they were focussed for the near point."

"One day, while looking at a picture of the rock of Gibraltar which hung on the wall, I noted some black spots on its face. I imagined that these spots were the openings of caves, and that there were people in these caves moving about. When I did this, my eyes were focussed for reading distance. Still imagining that the spots were caves with people in them, the retinoscope showed that I had accommodated, and I was able to read the lettering beside the picture. I had in fact been temporarily helped by the use of my imagination."

Now this is interesting, very interesting, because he is bringing up something unexpected. He has caught himself by surprise. His thinking mind has become absent for a moment, and the fact that his imagination started playing with the picture has brought other parts into play, and on that basis I will now make a presumption: the thinking mind, which is the main means by which we in the western world live our lives, is not directly connected to the body, but emotions are. By allowing an emotional feeling to well up, a connection can be made from that route with the sight, but as soon as the thinking again takes precedence, contact with the body is severed. This is another reason why I asked us to be aware of our feet, just in order to permit this connection to be made.

Now I want to return to what I was saying about the point of seeing: that it functions in the moment, intermittently but continuously.

The eye can also be compared to a camera. The sensitive film in the back of the camera corresponds to the retina. Neurologically speaking, the retina is part of the brain. The body of the eye is part of the body. We can make an experiment. If I cover and uncover my eyes with my hands, and open and close my eyes in the same rhythm, then this will be similar to the way the shutter of a camera opens and closes. It is better to do it towards the light so that, when you cover your eyes, you may discover there is an after image left behind. In other words, there is a snapshot left within the eye which will persist for one or two seconds. People who are not accustomed to it may not notice this after-image at first, but with practice it will always be there.

This shows that an image appears regardless of any effort. It also shows that no effort was made to receive that picture, it appears as a result of a natural neurological process, and following this I can experience a brief moment of rest as the eyes close. The eyes open, then close, and the picture is naturally there. Then I can notice whether or not my eyes feel strained or tense in any way.

I can then let the eyes stay closed for two or three seconds so that there is an alternation between the point of focus and the image that is left behind; and then allow the eyes, and even the body, to rest. When this activity is practised intentionally, it becomes one of the most useful and practical of exercises because it is an experience that is given. It is not a trying. It is not a striving. It is not straining. The resulting relaxation that appears may at one moment or another help the eye to see in a different way. The difficulty that many people find with the Bates Method is that, as soon as anybody says, 'I want to improve my eyesight,' straight away a freeze block appears, and that freeze block will act as an interference. Therefore in order to help the eyes see better it is necessary, in some way or another, to bypass judgements, criticisms, evaluations and words in order that the sight can relax and that a moment of better seeing can perhaps appear, which it often does.

Another aspect which Bates talked about a great deal in relation to relaxation was the importance of black—I was going say the colour black, but of course black is not a colour. Black is greatly misunderstood by people who want to understand about the Bates Method. It is not a colour but the absence of light. There is nothing there. Therefore it can be called the ground of seeing. We all of us today live in such a state of tension that if the eyes are covered, which we can try again, and if you let them be covered, almost invariably it will not be blackness that is left behind once the light has faded. It will be some sort of pattern, greyness, mixed up colours, even chaos. (The practice of covering the closed eyes with the hands is called palming).

Palming is accompanied by a difficulty because, when it is said it is a good idea to see black whilst palming then, straight away, an attempt is made to try to see the black. In fact it is better to try something else more accessible. If you imagine that on the one hand you have, let us say, a large paint brush filled with black paint and in front of you a white board, and that when you cover the eyes, you picture just putting a splash of black paint on this board and then with the other hand immediately taking the board away, and then again doing the same thing—you put this moment of blackness on this screen and then take it away—then it becomes possible to bypass the strain of trying.

This principle which I brought in here is an addition to the Bates Method. This question of visualizing something and erasing it was a principle brought by a French therapist, who lived about the same time as Bates, called Roger Vittoz. He based his practice of the treatment of neurasthenia on the visualization of an image and erasing it and the frequent repetition of that. This enabled the people he worked with gradually to gather the power of attention so they could then direct their mind purposefully once more. This way of looking has been brought into the Bates Method at a later date and is a valuable help in showing how to work continually and intermittently, just as the focus of the eye does when relaxed.

Now the question of blackness does not end there because, as I said, it is the ground of seeing, the absence of light, and the association can be made with the Hindu and Buddhist idea of shunyata, nothingness, emptiness. I was saying earlier that the seeing is very wide, the field of vision is very wide. By looking straight ahead, the door on the left and the window on my right are present in my field of awareness. If I allow that seeing to expand, I can ask myself, 'What is beyond that visible field?' There must be something that is beyond, and then I feel in myself a stop. I cannot answer what is beyond with my usual means. There is nothing visible. My ordinary awareness tells me that I see my body sitting here. I see my body sitting here in this room. But, just wait a minute, what I am seeing is contained in my eyes, it is a picture in my brain. My habitual logic comes in and tells me there is nothing beyond what I can see. If, on the other hand, I listen to my body, I can be aware of my body beyond my sight. This leads to a very strange contradiction. I am going to assert that my head is above the ceiling, my chin is below the floor, my ears are beyond the walls. That is ridiculous. How can that be? It is clearly not true. If, on the other hand, I go into my sensing and allow the contradiction to be present, I can allow my sight to stretch out and then I can explore the possibility that what I see is a small picture contained in the back of my head. That means then, by extrapolation, that I can be aware of my head above the ceiling, once I start changing my frame of reference. I can be aware of my chin below the floor, and my ears beyond the walls.

Then something very strange starts taking place, because my ordinary assumptions, my ordinary knowledge will start to react and say, 'This is not true.' Contrarywise my sense of enquiry says, 'There must be something like this taking place, because it is neurologically exact to say the field of seeing is within the back of my head,' so I am caught in a trap. It is like being in a double bind. On the one hand my body must contain what I see. On the other hand all my ordinary conception of the world is calling out saying, 'This cannot be so, this is not true'.

Now if I can stay with that, it produces a sort of friction. It is very interesting, because we are now no longer in the field of trying to improve the eyesight directly. We are now making enquiry into the nature of reality. I am trying to understand, now, what the sight is really about, because it is quite clear the sight is not everything: there are the other senses. A bat, for example, cannot perceive the world as a vulture does, although they both are manifest in it. Now what is beginning to happen is that, whilst I keep this search, this enquiry as to what is possible to experience beyond my frame of seeing, another strange idea comes in. The whole world lives inside myself. For example I can stand on the top of a hill when the sun is setting. There is the sun setting—and also at some time of the month the moon is also rising, I am aware of both—there is the whole vast horizon, the planet earth on which I am standing, I myself, all of it inside me, or indeed anybody who tries such a thing.

I often try this when I walk on hills where there is a wide view. I then walk in an unusual way, and this is an exercise we can try together now. I will demonstrate. I am walking very, very slowly, like this. I am letting myself swing around and take everything in. Now I am interrupting the normal pattern of walking, bringing my balance into question, therefore all the ordinary associations stop—well not quite—but they are interrupted, and there is an awareness of movement, because if there isn't I will fall over, because at one moment I am balanced on one foot and at the same time I am open to seeing. It takes about 20 minutes for the ordinary activity of the mind to quieten and for a different type of feeling to appear. In that feeling, or state, my own reactions start to appear as things to be seen within the field of seeing. It is a strange situation, because, on the one hand I am trying to be open to a different kind of reality, on the other my reactions are still taking place—thoughts, emotions and so on—and in trying to maintain this separation it is as though a friction takes place between the ordinary seeing, the day-to-day seeing, (obviously I do not want to fall over when I am walking), and this enlargement of perception, and that friction sometimes results in the appearance of a very delicate feeling.

Ideally for such an experience to be really effective, there is a need for a wide horizon. It is difficult in a room, even this big, simply because everything in here is man-made and it produces too many associations, and also there is the fact that the practice works better with the infinite width of a wide sky. Practising in this way needs patience. One has to be able to give the necessary time, and not be in a hurry.

The experience of working at something, searching for something, is a necessary precursor to a natural change in the state of the sight. Although what I am talking about is practical from one point of view, it is more connected with the life enquiry which I feel Aldous Huxley would have been interested in, in the sense that it is the meaning and experience behind which validates the process; it is not the striving for results, but the living experience which he himself knew well from, for example, his practice of the Alexander Technique.

I want to read another short quotation from a book on seeing that is almost entirely unknown. It is by an American woman called Flora Courtois. When she went through the experience she described, she was a student at an American university, and without realising it, she was plumbing the depth of understanding which I have been speaking about:

"Then one day, in a class in psychology, the instructor made a casual remark, to the effect that the world as we saw it was simply a projection of neural activity in the visual sectors of the brain. I walked out of the class and along the street, thunderstruck, saying over and over to myself: 'All I know, the whole world, even the universe, is myself. The answer somehow lies in myself.' I was filled with an extraordinary sense of exhilaration with this realisation."

"Shortly after this another incident occurred which made a deep impression on me. Standing at the kitchen window one day, and looking out where a path wound under some maple trees, I suddenly saw the scene with a freshness and clarity that I had never seen before. Simultaneously, as though for the first time, I fully realised I was not only *on* the earth, but *of* it; an intimate part and product of it. It was as if a door had briefly opened. I stood there transfixed. I remember thinking: 'Distant places on the map, such as Tibet and North Africa are extensions of right here, all interrelated.' It was as if for a long time I had been reading books on how to swim, and now for a moment I had plunged into real water."

"After these two incidents, I ceased to search for an answer in reading. I became intensely interested in exploring everyday experience. The very nature of sensation itself absorbed my attention. I became increasingly aware of sounds, sights, touch and smell impressions. Feelings all for their own sakes, and the more observant I became, the more endless the vistas which seemed to open. 'What is more immediate than sensation?' I asked myself. 'Surely reality must somehow permeate immediate sensation. Yet if each sense is so limited, so partial and incomplete, how does one sense a Reality whole, all at once? Is that impossible?'"

And later on: "The small pale green desk, at which I had been so thoughtlessly gazing, had totally and radically changed. It appeared now with clarity, a depth of three-dimensionality, a freshness I had never imagined possible. At the same time, in a way that is utterly indescribable, all my questions and doubts were gone as effortlessly as chaff in the wind. I knew everything and all at once, yet not in a sense that I had ever known anything before."

"All things were the same in my little bedroom, yet totally changed. Still sitting in wonder, on the edge of my narrow bed, one of the first things I realised was that the focus of my sight seemed to have changed; it had sharpened to an infinitely small point, which moved ceaselessly in paths, totally free of the old accustomed ones, as if flowing from a new source."

"What on earth had happened? So released from all tension, so ecstatically light did I feel, I seemed to float down the hall to the bathroom to look at my face in the mottled mirror over the sink. The pupils of my eyes were dark, dilated and brimming with mirth. With a wondrous relief I began to laugh, as I'd never laughed before, from the soles of my feet upward."

"This new kind of knowing was so pure and unadorned, so delicate that nothing in the language of my past could express it."

"It was as if, before all this occurred, 'I' had been a fixed point inside my head, looking out at a world out there, a separate and comparatively flat world. The periphery of awareness had now come to light, yet neither fixed periphery nor centre existed as such. A paradoxical quality seemed to permeate all existence. Feeling myself centred as never before, at the same time I knew the whole universe to be centred at every point. Having plunged to the centre of emptiness; having lost all purposefulness in the old sense, I had never felt so one-pointed, so clear and decisive. Freed from separateness, feeling one with the universe, everything including myself, had become at once unique and equal."

Well, such a possibility may be open even to us. Now in order to get some relief from this constant listening to the monotonous voice speaking, let's now approach, to some extent, the question of relaxation.

First of all, the eyes can be closed. Often when I engage in relaxation, I go through a process I call 'The Guided Tour,' which means a tour around the sensation of my body. However, since there is not much time, it will be enough to give a taste of this practice by reconnecting to the sensation of my feet. It may be also necessary to remember that, although somebody like myself can give a suggestion, and, that no matter how hard I try to act on it, forgetting will take place because my ordinary habits will resist anything new that is offered. So reconnecting to my feet, and becoming aware of the stability of my back, of my arms loosely hanging and my hands resting lightly on my legs, with my eyes closed, I am going to let my head turn very easily and slowly, from side to side, left to right. There is nothing to do. I am not trying to get anywhere. It does not matter what position my head is in, because my eyes are closed and there is nothing to see. I become aware of my head in movement, the sensation of movement of my neck, and because I move my head slowly and evenly, then I can offer up to my head the possibility that it's floating like a hollow ball on water. There's no friction. Many people, indeed, do experience friction on turning the head and neck, but within my possibility I can experience the minimum friction and the maximum of the sensation of movement. And that itself produces a sensation of relaxation.

Bates himself said: "Relaxation is a sensation." Now as I am turning my head, I can open and close my eyes so that snapshots of images enter. Because I am opening and closing the eyes, there's no sense of tension in looking. I can extend my attention rather like extending a very long finger. I can extend my attention so that it touches the floor. I can feel that I extend my attention to touch the wall, or even on a dark clear night I can extend my attention to touch the moon. There may not be any limit to what I can touch with my attention. That means that, if I now turn my head easily from left to right, I now can have an invisible finger which runs over the wall, or indeed any other feature, and pick up its form and its texture. And this is very practical means for helping the sight to be at rest while looking at ordinary things. For example, if you're talking with somebody, you can actually sense their face whilst talking. This possibility is there, because the attention of the different senses can coincide, as indeed in the condition of synaesthesia they do. And synaesthesia is interesting, because it's been found that, when two or more senses meet, in whatever place in the brain they meet, ordinary thinking comes to a stop. All that can be practised is the awareness of the senses. Synaesthesia, and the accompanying freedom from the interference of thinking, may indeed be beneficial to clear seeing.

In a very ordinary way, looking for something is extremely relaxing. It is impossible to know precisely what the history of the human race is, but at some stage or another there is no doubt that people lived by hunting, and many people still do. When people hunt they are looking for, they are searching for, for example, a prey animal, or if not that, perhaps a particular plant for a particular purpose. That 'looking for' is good for seeing. The first thing to encourage anybody to look for is a colour, because a colour is defined by its quality not by its outline. So if I were to say: 'Let's look for the colour red,' immediately everything is brought into movement. We are bringing everything into movement looking for the colour red, so everything else is being discarded.

Now this touches on another important aspect. As Bates said, the process of seeing is passive. That is, the eye, when it sees, is at rest. But there is a contradiction, because it is known that, if the eye is focussed on something fixedly, it will go blind, and yet Bates has said that the eye is only focussed when it is at rest. This can only mean that, although it is not perceptible, the focus focuses on a point, and then immediately rejects it and moves on to the next point. Because the point of focus is so fine, the movement that the eye makes is imperceptible. It is more like a vibration. So the process of seeing is a process of falling away from a point of focus and then catching up with another. It is a strange situation in that there is nothing continuous or fixed in seeing. The eyes get very tired if they are asked to do one thing only for too long. However, the heart itself never stops beating, and yet there is always a brief rest between each beat. Thus the heart, if it is maintained in a healthy body, will beat in a healthy way for the whole of one's life. It could be said that the point of focus is like a miniature heart, the heart of the sight, a slight rhythmic beat, so tiny it cannot be perceived.

As we have been sitting down for rather a long time, we need to stimulate a flow of energy. Can everybody stand up? Let us give the centre of our focus a rest. I am going to cover the front of my eyes with my hands. Now I cannot see anything except hands, but I am going to walk around and interact with everybody. You can all do the same, and you will see that the peripheral sight of your eyes will enable you to avoid bumping into people.

Now I am going to cover my eyes, and I am going to leave a slight gap between the little finger and the ring finger. I am restricting my sight to a small point of focus. We can all do the same, and continue to walk around, and you will have another new experience, that you can certainly see where you are going, but it is alarming because you cannot see what is happening around you.

Again we change the movement. I am looking ahead now, it does not matter where, and I am moving my hands out to the sides, and in again, keeping my hands always in sight. In effect what I am doing with my hands is asking my eyes to stretch their awareness out all the way out to the side. At the same time, this posture is one of both giving and acceptance so there is a symbolic value in it. I am looking straight ahead, or indeed I can look at anything I wish, but because of this movement I cannot but help be aware of what is further out to the sides, and I can see how far back I can stretch the hands and still have visual awareness of them. Then I bring the hands in again, and after a time a sensation appears that feels like a sort of tugging to help the eyes stretch out. It is an unfamiliar sensation. Perhaps we should stop now. It is necessary to be careful not to bore people by doing any activity for too long, because boredom accompanied by daydreaming and staring are three chief enemies of good seeing.

Another exercise to try: I am standing with my feet a shoulder's width apart. Letting my eyes be closed, I'm balanced on both feet equally, being aware of my back, my head on top of my back, my arms at my sides, and I am going to push on one foot so that the body swings over onto the other foot. Now I have a slight swaying sensation. And I do this for a time with the eyes closed. Whilst standing, the awareness of my body and movement, the weight of my body, the balance, helps my body to let go; to relax. We are approaching the type of exercise that Aldous Huxley called dynamic relaxation: relaxation in movement. Now I'm going to open my eyes, and as I swing, with my eyes open, I am aware of a movement, in this case, of everybody in front of me. There is visual movement taking place. It is easier to see the movement if there is something in between, so why don't some people come and make a smaller circle in the middle, to provide some reference points. Now we have a point of reference and that will help you see a counter-movement between people nearer against people farther away. I am now seeing this counter-movement, and it is this counter-movement which stimulates the sight. It is the width of seeing which needs to expand. When the width of seeing improves in this way, there is a possibility of a change occurring in my field of perception.

It is important that there should be a whole-body movement, not just a part. It is a very slight movement. There is a merit in making very slight movements, because slight movements indicate a bigger movement taking place within the field of the sight itself. The field of seeing is activated more by small movements than big ones.

Seeing is also activated by thought, for example, I am looking at my finger, and I am wondering to myself: 'I wonder what is out over in that corner,' and as soon as I think out there, my eyes follow that thought. But if then my thinking changes to: 'I wonder what is going on in my finger,' my eyes have come back to focus on my finger; so that means that I can think out there, and my eyes can go out. I can think back here and the eyes will focus back here. This is an important point because, if this exercise is done as a muscular exercise, the stress which the eyes are labouring under may actually intensify. If, on the other hand, you use the thought, and you project your intention out there, the eye, quite naturally, by projecting the attention or the interest, is brought into the right form of visual motion.

Now I am going to finish on another note. If one is enabled to be connected to a more open way of seeing, which includes both myself and the external world, then it is possible to be aware that such an open seeing has a feeling of power. It has nothing to do with myself. Such seeing has a healing power on its own. It is as though, quite apart from myself, there is a seeing which exists in itself of which my own local seeing is part.

There is a thought to finish on.[2]

WORKSHOP 2:

Huxley and Practical Work with the Bates Method

We have some wonderful things to share together. Everybody knows that we cannot live without seeing, not as human beings. And although we depend, all of us, on our eyes and the sight, hardly anybody knows how to care for this precious faculty.

Aldous Huxley would have been in just the same position if he had not had the misfortune to suffer a very serious illness of his eyes, which meant that he was in danger of going blind. And if you can imagine what it would be like to go blind, then we can have some experience that, if somebody could turn the lights off, so there is no light on in this room here. Turn everything off. If everybody would like to start to read now what they have in front of them and, if anybody wears glasses, with their glasses off, you will now begin to understand what Aldous Huxley was going through. I invite anybody to read in just this light and, although it's actually still quite light, if anybody is having difficulty in reading it won't be so easy. Most people find that, when the reading becomes difficult, they need more and more light in order to identify the letters in the reading. So this is giving a very brief feeling of what a man who is going blind might be experiencing.

Now we have done that, we can perhaps draw the blinds back so we can have some more suitable light. If anybody wants to read again, in this light, you'll see it's much easier, because the windows are big, and the room is not very large. Something like that would happen, if somebody starts regaining their sight, there would be a feeling of there being more light. And in fact, if I read something of what Huxley says, this will show you: "At sixteen I had a violent attack of *keratitis punctata*, which left me (after eighteen months of near-blindness, during which I had to depend on Braille for my reading and a guide for my walking) with one eye just capable of light perception and the other with enough vision to permit of my detecting the two-hundred-foot letter on the Snellen Chart at ten feet." The top letter on that chart on the wall is the 200ft letter—and he could only see that letter at ten feet, whereas it should be possible to see it at the back of the room, and indeed further. "My inability to see was mainly due to the presence of opacities in the cornea; but this condition was complicated by hyperopia [a sort of long sight] and astigmatism [a condition where the front of the eye is curved in an irregular way, which then means that the images projected on the retina are not focused on one spot but on many different spots]. For the first few years, my doctors advised me to do my reading with the aid of a powerful hand magnifying glass. But later on I was promoted to spectacles. With the aid of these I was able to recognize the seventy-foot line at ten feet and to read tolerably well— provided always that I kept my better pupil dilated with atropine, so that I might see round a particularly heavy patch of opacity in the centre of the cornea."

"[...] Things went on in this way until the year 1939, when, in spite of greatly strengthened glasses, I found the task of reading increasingly difficult and fatiguing. [...] my capacity to see was steadily and quite rapidly failing. But just as I was wondering apprehensively what on earth I should do if reading were to become impossible, I happened to hear of a method of visual re-education and of a teacher who was said to make use of this method with conspicuous success. Education sounded harmless enough and, since optical glass was no longer doing me any good, I decided to take the plunge. Within a couple of months I was reading without spectacles and, what was better still, without strain and fatigue. The chronic tensions, and the occasional spells of complete exhaustion were things of the past. Moreover, there were definite signs that the opacity in the cornea, which had remained unchanged for upwards of twenty-five years, was beginning to clear up. At the present time, my vision, though very far from normal, is about twice as good as it used to be when I wore spectacles, and before I had learnt the art of seeing; and the opacity has cleared sufficiently to permit the worse eye, which for years could do no more than distinguish light from darkness, to recognize the ten-foot line on the chart at one foot."

Now that in its own way is a remarkable story, that somebody who could not see learnt how to see again. But nevertheless it is important not to make the mistake of believing that very serious problems of sight can easily be cleared up. They can't. If anybody has got very poor sight, it needs very prolonged and extensive work, to not only heal the structures but to re-educate the poor habits and permit better seeing to take place. So one mustn't run away with the idea that I am going to wave a magic wand and everybody will miraculously see better. Although one perhaps has to say that sometimes, if somebody is innocent enough, such a thing, even that, could happen. So it's in some ways a challenge for innocence.

Now this is an important thing to say because one of the big difficulties in any learning, is the ingrained habits of judgement and criticism, which will inhibit the open reception of a new idea. And many of the exercises which we will be trying will be to avoid, to bypass, these ingrained stresses of trying, of criticising, of judging. We are not aiming for immediate success; we are aiming to learn something. We are aiming to come to better terms with the experience, now, of what it is to see.

Now on this basis I would like to hand round so that everybody has copies of this pamphlet, "Helping the Eyes to Become Ready for Seeing."

This particular pamphlet is a very simple guide. I am going to run through this for a very simple reason, because I understand many of you people here today will be teaching, and you will come across difficulties with young children, and it is easy to understand that many children dislike very much being cooped up inside four walls all day long for the major years of their childhood. And they need to be helped in order that they can cope with the stresses of education, which, in the western world, is excessively intellectual. The first item says, 'Drink water.' The importance of water cannot be over-estimated, because water doesn't just moisten the body, it also produces energy, it produces energy in the brain. It helps the nervous system be filled with water so that the electrical impulses can be conducted. And it is water that is needed; not tea, not coffee, not coca cola, not fruit juices—water. In England water is drunk relatively little in comparison to other fluids. So to help children drink water is enormously useful. It is especially important to have water available in the classroom as it may well help any child focus their mind and their eyes better.

The next item says, 'Run central vessel.' The central vessel is an acupuncture meridian (or line). The body is covered in lines of energy. These lines conduct energy from one part to another. One of these lines, the central vessel, which runs up the front of the body, is a channel for the supply of energy to the brain. So simply to run the hand like that, up the front of the body, will help to supply a brief enhancement of energy up into the nervous system, will help you to maintain your energy.

Now again in order to help you to listen, to permit you to orient yourself in space, I am going to uncurl the outside ring of the ears from top to bottom. And you will feel that the ears take on a more active sensation. It is a comfortable feeling, uncurling the ears.

Then we speak a lot, and the voice can get tense. There are ten muscles or so in the front of the throat which can get very tight, and so to tweak the muscles all round in the front of the throat can help relax that part of the body.

If you feel behind the top of the ears with your fingertips, you'll find there are two small indentations behind the ears which appear to be connected to the eyes. It frequently happens that the eyes get locked, so there is strain looking in one position or the other. However, if I rub these points whilst looking in any particular direction, any residual tension that is held in this direction is released, and likewise, looking around the clock or the compass points, I'm looking

up to my right, back to the middle

to my right, back to the middle
down to my right, back to the middle
looking down, back to the middle
down to my left, back to the middle
to my left, back to the middle
up to my left, back to the middle
looking straight up, back to the middle, whilst rubbing these two points behind the ears.

This will help to free the tensions held in the different directions through the outside muscles of the eyes.

It has also been found that the muscles on the top of the shoulders have a connection with both hearing and seeing. People often walk around with their shoulders held up in tension. As these muscles need to be loose, we can free them by squeezing them, whilst letting the head turn easily from side to side at the same time, a bit like kneading dough. And with the head turning from side to side you'll start to pick up different things by noticing that, on the one hand there's a view through the window, to the trees and buildings, and, on the other hand, a map of Italy on the other wall. An interesting contrast.

Generally now people are not aware of their jaw, but there is an enormous amount of tension held in there. 50% of the motor nerves in the brain manage the jaw. 50% of sensory nerves go to this area. If there is tension in the jaw, any other part of the body, including the eyes, can become stressed or tense. So therefore we can yawn and rub around the jaw looking for tight or tense points and rub them. This will help to loosen the jaw, and will help it work better, and may help release tensions in the eyes.

The eyes also need to be helped to rest, and one way they rest is by blinking. When the eyes blink, they are given a brief moment of rest, the circulation is enhanced, and the tear fluid is washed over the surface of the eye and will clear off little specks of dust and so on. So to blink the eyes and squeeze the eyes shut from time to time, and even turn the head again from side to side, is a reminder to the eyelids that their job is to blink. Frequently, when they get tense, they will not blink any more.

Now, this figure here, the figure 8 on its side, is a symbol to help the re-integration of both sides of the brain—left side and right side—which frequently become dissociated. We can make a symbol for that by running the figure 8 around the eyes, with two fingers, or even with both hands. One can feel it's relaxing. It helps the eyes feel more comfortable. And likewise just turning the head like this in a figure 8 on its side when it gets so tight and tense, and this can help to loosen the head and the neck. So when you get bored waiting for the bus or the tram to come, or you don't know what to do when you're on a journey, you can practice these things, and people will think: " Oh well, they're doing something interesting."

However, if you get stressed because you imagine people are wondering what on earth you are getting up to, you could touch these two points on the forehead, which have a connection with the emotions. If you have a particular stressed moment, for example you are going for an oral test or examination and you don't know how you are going to manage, then you visualize what you are going to be going through, whilst touching these points. Or if you've had a terrible time and you've had an awful interview and you are not going to get the job after all, then you just run through in your mind the memory of it when holding these points, and it will help to release the stress. This is enormously important for the eyes, because the eyes are very sensitive. They pick up all these stresses. Anything which will help to release emotional stress can be a material help for the eyes to see more easily and indeed better.

It clearly cannot be denied that breathing is also important, and often when we get tense we forget to breathe. So therefore with the eyes closed, let the lungs breathe in and, with the eyes open, breathe out. So close the eyes to breathe in, and open the eyes to breathe out. Again a relief may come briefly for a moment of seeing.

The eye is very much like a camera. It takes pictures. But ordinarily we don't notice this, so that if we cover the eyes with the hands like this, and the hands then form, in effect, the shutter of the camera. I can uncover and open the eyes and there is a brief moment of seeing, and then, when the eyes are closed and covered again, an after image is left behind, a snapshot. It lasts for about a second, and then it fades. This effect is more easily noticed if I look out of the window towards the light, where the contrast of light will exaggerate this after image. This is one of the most useful ways of resting the eyes. You can also perform the same thing by simply closing the eyes and then opening them briefly. Closing the eyes, and opening. And if you want to rest the eyes when you are in movement, or when you are listening to somebody, then this is a very convenient way to do it, because nobody will ever notice you practicing this exercise.

Another way to help rest the eyes is to cover the eyes with the hands and leave a gap between the little finger and the ring finger. So I'm covering my eyes, but now I'm only looking through a slit. If I turn my head, I am getting an almost stroboscopic view of the world. It's encouraging the eyes (1) to be rested and (2) to focus on a small spot, which is how the eyes work best. You can look at everybody, but not all at once. You will find that you are looking at people moment by moment. This is called gap palming.

Very often people have eyes which are not the same. One eye works better than the other. Sometimes people do not even know that. So therefore it's important that each eye will work separately by itself as well as together with its friend on the other side of the nose. So if I cover one eye like this, we now have the experience of looking out with one eye, and then changing over, and you will then see immediately if there is any difference (there may not be) between each eye. You see, walking down the road like this may be extremely interesting.

Now going on, I'm just going to very lightly stroke outwards over the top of the eyelid—a very, very light stroke indeed. And coming in, from the outside in, a very, very light stroke underneath. Not hard, so that I pull the skin. Light enough so that it's just a very gentle sensation of touch. This can help bring the blood circulation to the eye so that it again will work better.

The next item says, 'Run lazy 8s.' Well, I don't mean running with the legs. I just mean running a shape with the fingers, or a pencil on paper, like this. Now, you're sitting down, so you can do it like that, and just let your eyes follow this movement of a figure 8 on its side, and this will help to integrate both eyes together, and help to bring both sides of the brain into harmonization with each other.

Our head is supported by the neck, and the neck is extremely important, in the sense that it supports the head but frequently itself gets tense. Moreover, the muscles in the neck are connected to the stomach acupuncture meridian, which starts underneath the eye, and is strongly connected to the functioning of the eye. If you close your eyes and let your head turn very easily from right to left and back again with the eyes closed, you'll notice how easy it is to make the movement without friction. For some people, when they turn their head like this, it feels as though there is a collection of rocks in the back of the neck, grinding over each other. Actually, the movement should be smooth and easy.

And then I'm going to open my eyes whilst continuing to turn the head, and just look around with the eyes open. That means I'm not fixing my look. The look is moving easily across the field of vision. Then if I hold my finger up, I'm going to look at my finger and do the same thing. And I'll notice that there's a movement of the background behind the finger in the opposite direction to the movement of my finger.

Now I'll take a brief diversion to explain something about this. The eye is a very interesting structure. The retina is filled with light-sensing cells to the number of 125 million. That is about twice the population of the United Kingdom. Of that 125 million, a few thousand are connected to the clear point of seeing situated in the middle of the retina; the concentration of very sensitive cells which pick up sharp details. All the rest of the cells are occupied only with general seeing. In the world we live in, there is an emphasis upon concentrating on what I'm reading, and my head is buried, so my sight gets narrowed down, and what happens is the eyes become over focused, and then a tension appears. In principle, what is needed when reading is to maintain an awareness of the width of view, and this will straight away bring a feeling of protest. How can I be aware of everything in the room when I'm trying to read? Isn't that very distracting? Usually the answer would be, 'Yes.' I can't split my attention in two parts; at least I believe I can't.

However, there's a difference between this small spot in the middle of the retina and the rest of the retina, because it has got a different electronic circuit which controls it. The middle part is a circuit connected in series. That is to say, the impressions come in one at a time, but very, very fast. The outside cells are in a circuit connected in parallel. Everything comes all at once, but nothing has any sharp intensity, and it's much slower. There needs to be a subliminal awareness of everything around in order to free my attention to focus easily on what I wish to read or do, and the more awareness there is, passive awareness in relation to active focusing, the better the focusing will work.

For example, everybody here in Latvia is much better at learning languages than people where I come from, in England. And so, when you want to learn another language, whatever it might be, let's say for the moment, Japanese, if you go to a busy place, like for example a railway station or a very busy restaurant, and you then learn the words of this new language in such a busy environment, curiously enough, you will remember better. It sounds odd, but you can make the experiment. Because of the awareness coming in, there are many more markers in the memory to which you can attach the memories you wish to maintain. And the struggle to keep your focus in the hustle and bustle going on around on the outside can actually assist the memory. So likewise, when you are reading, and you make sure there is an awareness of the whole field, you'll read better and remember better. Don't believe what I'm saying. Try it out.

So with this exercise here, I'm now focusing on my finger, all the direct seeing is on this point. Because of the counter movement when I move the finger across the field of view, I now have an awareness of what I have been describing, that everything in the background is moving, but I'm not concentrating or focusing on it. But nevertheless it's still present as a movement, a background movement. So I can continue like this for a moment, and that will again rest the eyes very nicely.

Because we have two eyes, we will be aware there's a left side and a right side in my world. Most of the time, we are stuck in the middle, but to be aware of what's on my left as well as on my right again is good, helping the eyes to remain relaxed and at ease.

Then you come to the bottom item on this page, No. 26, called, 'Finger Flex.' Finger flexing is done as follows. I am going to cover one eye and look at my finger going out and in. Change hands, and look at the other eye going right and in. Make sure the finger coming in comes right up to your nose. Don't *try* to see it. Simply allow the sight to follow, easily, without stress. And then both eyes, both fingers. So this is bringing a flexibility into the focus.

Now when people reach a certain age, and it differs according to the individual, they find they have to make their arms get increasingly long. They have not got arms long enough to read. They need an arm that is 10/20 foot, even the end of the room, before they can be able to read. This is not at all desirable. It is much better to continue with this exercise. So even though you may not be able to read at the near point, this very near distance (4"–12") is extremely important because this is the part that gets lost, it silts up, it becomes stiff through lack of use. In yoga it's considered that the body will start to age once the joints become stiff. Why do they become stiff? It seems because people do not stretch them. It is the same with the eyes. The eyes will get stiff if the flexibility is not maintained. So, to look at my finger coming in like this, I am exercising the flexibility, and there's a very easy adaptation of this when you are eating. Of course everybody gets hungry. We eat, how many times a day? One, two, three, four, five, six times a day? Whatever it is. Every time I pick something up in my hand, a piece of toast, a biscuit, whatever, it doesn't matter, I bring it up to my mouth, I can watch the food until it enters my mouth. That means that during that activity this flexibility is being exercised. If I do that, I might even notice there's a caterpillar on my piece of lettuce, then I don't have to eat it. So it pays sometimes to look at what you eat, rather than just eat at what you look. [Laughter]

The next exercise is, 'Finger near and far.' That means: I look at my finger, and I then look out. But we are looking at the mind, because the eye and the mind are linked because the retina is brain tissue. The body of the eye is body tissue, but the retina is brain tissue an extension of the brain, almost to the outside world. I am looking at my finger, and then, if I am looking facing the window, I am wondering what is out there. I am thinking out there. And as soon as I think, "I wonder what is out through the window," my eyes will look out and then focus out there. But I am keeping my finger held here, so I'm wondering what am I holding my finger here for, and straight away I'm looking at it. So the moment you think out, the eyes will follow. The moment you think in, the eyes will follow. So by thinking out, the eyes look out; by thinking in, the eyes look in; and in that way the flexibility is exercised and, moreover, in a more relaxed way. If, on the other hand, I do it as a muscular exercise, I look out physically, any tension in the eyes is going to be set in more strongly. So in order to help the muscular parts relax, it is better to think out and think in. Then the eyes will work better.

For the next exercise, running string, I am holding a string out, stretched from my nose to my outstretched fingers. I am running my finger out along the string and I am looking out along the string and back again, and anybody can do this, and you can see that you can let your eyes run out and in along the string. What will happen if you have both eyes that work together well, and you look out beyond the finger stretched out? What will happen is that the finger will become double. There will be two of them. When you look in to your finger, there is only one. When you look out, when both eyes are working together, there will be, and there must be, two fingers. Not one, not three, not four, but two. Likewise, when you look at your finger, it will take more time to notice this, but everything on the background is doubled. There will be two trees, or two windows. So there is an alternate singling and doubling. And again it is helpful to understand the eyes are both separate and they work together as a team.

Now we move on. The next one is called, 'Nose drawing.' This is when we want to think of ourselves being little children again, because some of these things are quite silly. And this is a very good thing because the eyes, if one was to personalize them, they are in some ways, like children. They like playing. So when you want the eyes to improve, you let them play. This means I am going to pretend that I have got a very long pencil on the end of my nose, and I'm now going to trace with my nose outlines of everything that I see. I'm making a slight movement with my head as I imagine drawing outlines around objects of vision, in order to bring movement into the sight. So that a mobility appears. The sight always gives the impression of stillness from the point of view of focus, but the focus itself is in constant motion when the eye is healthy. When the eye is not healthy any more, this movement stops, and then the eye becomes less able to see. The field of vision, on the other hand, is static. It doesn't move. And there's an odd contradiction here that, although the point of focus is in movement, it appears to be still, and although the field of vision appears to be still, it actually gives the impression of movement. So, when I'm running my imaginary pencil over everything, there can be a certain sense of movement as this pencil runs over everything I see.

The next item is called, 'Holes and gaps.' If the eyes are tending to become tense, to try to see something you want to look at will make them clench up, become very tight, become rigid. In order to free that, I want to look at something without definition, and that means the gaps or the holes between objects. So if I'm looking at you, the audience, I look between people's heads and shoulders. I'm looking at the spaces and gaps in between, and giving my eyes a rest. But if I look at people's features, then I might become a bit more tense. So to give my eyes a rest, I'm going to look out at spaces and gaps in between, and that is very quick and very useful.

And again, to avoid stress and tension, I'm going to look for something. One of the very first things I can ask people to do when they want to learn how to improve their sight is to look for a colour. Choose a colour, like red. In the modern world it's a very common colour. And I look everywhere. I let my whole body participate. I'm looking now for different patches of red. The recognition of red does not depend on outline, it depends upon quality. So it's very easy to recognize colours, and is restful for the eyes.

Now I'm going to hold my fingers to the side of my head, and I'm going to let the fingers flicker like this because, when I'm looking for a colour, I would like nevertheless to be aware of everything else in my field of vision. So we are now all doing something very nicely silly—flickering fingers. By flickering them I'm reminding myself my hands exist. So the sense of movement is now supporting the sense of sight, and I can even allow my hands to go out and support the sense of movement.

Now the next item, No. 34, is, 'Awareness of movement when looking for,' as I said, looking for a colour. So if I look from a patch of orange on the wall there, and I look to a patch of orange on the building over the other side of the park, then a movement has taken place. Everything else in the field of vision has moved back that way, and if I move from there to here, there is a visual movement back the other way. Being aware of this visual movement is a great help for the relaxation of the eyes and the seeing.

Any type of activity with a ball is very helpful, but, in principle, I can use anything comfortable enough to throw, for example, a handkerchief. I am going to throw something from one hand to the other. Even just passing from one hand to the other like this will help to stimulate a movement, and both the movement in myself, in my sight, and of the visual field outside. So throwing something from side to side, even your notebook, can be very helpful. After all, what is paper worth?

All the senses connect together. The sense of hearing, the sense of movement, the sense of touch on the skin, the sense of smell. Allowing all of these other senses to enter and to be aware of them will also support the sight. All the sensory system, the whole sensory system, works together. There is no reason for the sense of sight to be separated from anything else. So, I reach out to pick the glass up. If there is no co-ordination between my sight and my movement and the sense of the movement, and also the implicit sense of balance when I am standing up, then this simple movement of drinking will not be possible. It is interesting to watch an infant that is learning how to move, learning how to walk, to see the intense effort that this infant makes, as we all of us made when we were infants, to learn what we take now for granted, that learning how to walk is a very complex business. It takes the infant a very long time. But the infant learns through playing. It is not trying and failing. It does not get upset because it falls down again. It just tries again. Isn't that exactly how we should approach it?

Next, 'Comparing.' In the modern world, and indeed at any time, people have always compared things. I can compare what you've got to what I've got and I get very jealous because you seem to have more than I've got. I am not meaning that sort of comparison. I'm really meaning a comparison whereby I compare that side of the room with this side of the room. I can compare that picture with this picture. And by making a comparison a movement is brought in and a change of focus so that something is made more easy. Comparing, consciously comparing, two different things, is a good way to help the sight to relax.

Likewise edging. So many things have edges. By running the point of my sight over edges, it helps to sharpen the focus. It is making a differentiation between a small item to be focussed on and a large area to be seen generally. So running a point of focus around an edge is extremely useful.

And then, leading on to that, looking at angles. Angles help to bring the focus to a point. An angle comes to a point. So when I look at angles I'm helping my focus to become active. And likewise making it even smaller, I think of putting the point of a pin into what I want to look at, as though I want to go and visit Rome, and I put a pin in the middle of Rome (on the map on the wall), on the top of St Peter's basilica. I can do that from distance. I am putting a point where Rome is situated in order to help me focus. But I don't have to do it on a map of Italy. I can put a point on anything I wish to look at.

The next item seems very strange: 'Seeing worse.' That's exactly what I don't want to do. I want to see better. The explanation of this is very simple. You look at this chart out here, and you think, "Oh dear, I can't look at those letters. They are too small." However, if you look to one side of that chart, you will be aware of the chart, but you will notice that you cannot focus on it at all and so consequently, from the point of view of focus, it is seeing worse. This 'seeing worse' is a technical term. So by looking away from something, the point I want to see is seen worse. That means then I can look a little bit nearer but still see it worse, so then, if I look at this letter here, that one is worse. If I look at this one, this one is worse. So it is like a reverse way of helping the sight to improve, by looking away from something I keep the awareness, and it's quite clear it cannot be so clear or sharp as if I look at it directly. This can help take the attention away from desperately trying to focus.

Touch. Sight and touch are very strongly connected. So if you close your eyes and you run your fingers over some surfaces, some textures, you will find that you will be seeing, you will be noticing, you can even form a picture of what the surfaces are in some case. Now equally if I was to say to you, if you look at this wall here, and I was to say to you, "Is that wall made of wool?" you would say, "That's absurd. Of course the wall is not made of wool. How could it be made of wool? It would fall down. And, in any case, it doesn't look anything like wool." And I am making this ridiculous comparison in order to show that, through long experience, we have all of us a very extensive knowledge of what things are made of by looking. This means that, if I then imagine I can reach out an invisible hand to touch and experience the texture through my imagination, this will help my eyes to focus more easily. So that, as I was saying before, by fixing an imaginary pencil on the end of the nose and drawing what you see with the nose, you can also fix an imaginary finger to your nose, or let your nose grow out very, very long, so the tip of your nose runs over things and touches them just like a finger. And you can have this sensation of reaching right out over the view of the town and touching what you see at a very long distance, and it will be seen much better.

The next item: 'Triangulation,' also refers to a mental aspect. Two eyes, and when they focus together, the points of focus, the line of vision make a triangle, like that. So if I am looking at a point that is close, the triangle is like this, short and squat. If, on the other hand, I am looking far out, it is a very long, narrow triangle, so I can help to bring an equal seeing to both eyes by looking out as though I can project a beam from one eye, and project a beam from the other eye. I can imagine the point of this triangle coming at what I am looking at directly. This needs a little bit of mental concentration to manage this, but it can be very restful for bringing both eyes together.

When you are looking at a chart of letters like that, it can be discouraging because of the imagined pressure to read them off accurately. But I do not have to do that, I can make a game, so this now is a ski slope, and I am imagining I am running with my skis, I am slaloming down past letters. I'm avoiding them. I'm running down, in my mind's eye through the white spaces. I can even come back up in the same way. Or I could imagine that these are like branches of a tree, and that there is some imaginary bird which is perching on one letter, and is flying off to perch on another letter. I can invent all sorts of visual games, because there is no reason why I should not bring in a childlike aspect to what I am doing. The eyes are like children, and they certainly appreciate being played with.

The next one sounds even funnier: 'Whizzing.' For this, either I can use a comb, or I can use my fingers. By holding the fingers splayed out like this, and then waving them sideways, so the hands go one way, the head swings the other, and if I'm looking out through the fingers as they splay a visual flickering experience then takes place. This is a most important exercise, because it helps to free the point of focus from getting stuck, and allows it to re-focus again. The eye is then helped to take up its natural what are called saccadic movements, because the eye, when it is seeing normally, it is making a flickering movement quite naturally. And this exercise is almost the best one for helping this natural movement take place again.

Earlier on we practised 'looking for' something. Now we are going to make use of this 'looking for' to explore a colour. So that means, if I am looking at a colour, take the blue on the sky up there, I can say to myself, "Of how many different blues is that blue made?" Now that particular colour is not so interesting because it is a relatively simple colour, but other colours are more complex, and if you look at them, and that's even true if you look at somebody's face, and you wonder how many different colours you see in the tones of the skin, you will see almost every colour in the spectrum in somebody's face. And it is indeed interesting to look at people's faces from the point of view of colour. It tells you an awful lot about that person and what type they are and naturally enough how healthy they are, and so on and so forth. So to explore colour is one way of attracting interest quite easily, and of helping the sight to become more subtly engaged in what we are seeing because of the way that in the world we live in, the sight is just an instrument, it's like a throwaway instrument. You can throw it away once you have finished with it. However, if you want to keep the sight healthy and at ease, the best way is to awaken a real interest in the process and experience of seeing.

Now coming back to touching what we see, it is possible, therefore, to look out at a distance, and sense directly how far away something is. It's almost as though there is a tactile experience when I look at something, and I can detect directly how far away it is. I don't make a measurement of that and say, "It's that far, about 6ft, 10ft, 12ft, 30ft, whatever." No, no. I just know it's *that* distance." So that means I can know how to cross the road in the field of busy traffic and I know when to cross so that the car does not hit me. So there is constant sensing of distances taking place always, but we can become more aware of this, so that it works more directly for us as an aid to seeing.

The next item to consider is, 'Looking alternately between light and dark.' The eyes are not accustomed any more to seeing darkness. We live in an electronic world where, at the slightest hint of darkness, on go the lights. This is a mistake. One of the very best things anybody can do is to go for a walk in the countryside at sunset time. And make sure you are quite a long way away from home when the sun goes down, and then walk back in the increasing darkness, so that, by the time you get home, it is completely dark. You will be surprised, you can still see an awful lot in what appears to other people inside the house as being complete and total darkness. It is not dark at all. It is amazing how much you can see. But in these conditions here, where it is not easy to make that alternation, to look at something very dark and something very light, something out of the window, and something that is underneath the table, I'm helping the iris of the eye to open and close and become accustomed to different levels of lighting. And I should also say, contrary to what is said, to read in conditions of semi-darkness can be very healthy for the sight, even though it is not good to do that all the time.

Now if we take this pamphlet here, you see, on the left hand side, there is a reproduction of the chart on the wall. Now we can try what Bates tried in schools in America for a short period. To place a chart on the wall of a class room, in fact for each of the four walls to have a chart, so that young people would learn by heart, the whole sequence of letters on that chart and, because they knew them by heart, they were, therefore, much easier to see and recognize. Therefore, cheating is extremely good for eyesight. The more you cheat in seeing, the better you will see. So, if you know what you are going to look at, you will see it better. But do not try this please when you take academic exams because you will not be popular.

If you look alternately between one letter at the near point and the other out there on the chart, you are helping exercise the easy changing of focus and the recognition of letters out there, it helps to take the stress away from reading letters out there on the wall because I know what they are like here on the pamphlet. And so it is very helpful to make the comparison with the reproduction of such a chart which you can hold in your hand. This pamphlet can also be folded up for convenience, so you have a threefold leaflet, which means you can carry it with you and use it when you are on the train, for example.

Likewise, on the right hand side of the page, the text is printed in larger type at the top progressing to smaller at the bottom, and you can read down sequentially from 1 through to 11 and you can read as far as you can easily. If you start from the bigger print and you carry on reading down, you may find that, because you are reading from bigger to smaller, you may be surprised that you are reading a much smaller print than you had expected. Also, the text itself tells you something about the way the eyes work. When you look at the text in the centrefold, this print is actually quite tiny, and people will say: "I couldn't possibly read that!" But I am not so sure. Because, if you look at it without trying to read it and in fact you run your attention through the white lines, you do not try and read it at all, you run your attention through the white lines between the print, this will help take the stress away, and you may find that, in a way that you cannot explain, it is easier to read.

When reading, if you come to the end of a line, as when you're reading paragraph one on the right hand side, you close the eyes at the end of the paragraph and you remember what you have just read, then open the eyes and either read it again or read the next one. To read, and close the eyes at the end of a sentence or the end of a paragraph and remember is extremely helpful. To look out of the window is very helpful, and to be aware of the whole space of the room when you are reading is very helpful.

And to look from the right hand text to the middle text is helpful. So what I am trying to show you is that to vary the sight, to vary what you are looking at, not to stay in any one thing for too long, is very important. And indeed people have found that in, for example, learning languages. There was a man who could speak, I don't know how many, maybe it was 14, languages perfectly. He said: "Never spend more than 20 minutes on any one language at any one time." And there was another man who also spoke a number of languages and worked in London in the British Library. He travelled on the bus to work every day and it took about 20 minutes. The only time when he would study a language was when he went to work on the bus, and when he came home again in the evening. In this way he learnt a great deal. So to occupy the focus or concentrate your attention for a short time and to change and again change is much better for the sight and will be more beneficial than doing it for a long time continuously.[3]

WORKSHOP 3:
Huxley's Interest in Hypnotism
and his Collaboration with Milton Erickson

Amongst Aldous Huxley's many interests was the practical study of hypnotism. He collaborated with Milton Erickson, the foremost hypnotherapist of the twentieth century, in the use of hypnotism and trance in making an enquiry into various states of consciousness. The article by Milton Erickson on the results of this collaboration is the subject of this workshop.

I don't know if any of you know or have experience of what is called trance or hypnosis. I don't know whether you know, and I don't know whether or not you want to experience it. Only you can know that. Maybe even you don't know that. Maybe it is your unconscious that knows that and your conscious mind may not know anything about it at all. And indeed be sure that you are completely awake. Whatever you do, pay attention to what I say without the least deviation in your mind. Whatever you do, don't let your mind stray for one fraction of a second to ensure that you remain totally awake. Then, of course, you won't miss anything interesting that I am going to say.

There are, between Aldous Huxley and Milton Erickson, one or two striking similarities. Both worked with language as their primary tools. Both suffered crippling illnesses when they were seventeen years old. In Milton Erickson's case it was a severe attack of polio which left him totally paralysed. The attack was so bad that the doctor did not expect him to live. But he did live. And then he had the extraordinary self-task of finding himself in a body that could no longer move, and of relearning how to move again as would befit a young man of seventeen. Well, he indeed did learn this almost impossible achievement, and this was one of his beginnings in being interested in hypnotism.

His family were farmers, and after this attack he recognized that he would not any longer have the strength to run a farm, and so he decided therefore to become a doctor, and it was in the course of studying to become a doctor that his interest in hypnotism was awakened. Until that time the practice of hypnotism or hypnotherapy had been either of the stage type, demonstrating startling effects in the form of entertainment, or it had been directive from the point of view of clinical hypnotism. After Milton Erickson all this changed. Languaging became the chief mode for the induction of trance. Languaging means not just the words and their meanings, but the way the language is spoken, and how it is spoken, and to listen to a tape of Milton Erickson speaking shows a way of speaking which is completely outside the conventions of ordinary conversation.

I would like to introduce you to the first beginnings of this way of speaking, as recounted by Erickson when he was a boy on his father's farm: "It was not uncommon for my father to say to me: 'Do you want to feed the chickens first or the hogs?' or 'Do you want to fill the wood box or pump the water for the cows first?' What I realised then was that my father had given me a choice. I, as a person, had the primary privilege of deciding which task I was to do first. I did not fully realise at the time that this primary privilege rested entirely upon my secondary acceptance of all the tasks mentioned. I was unwittingly committed to the performance of all the tasks which had to be done by being given the primary privilege of determining their order. I did not recognize that I was accepting the position of being placed in a double bind."

A double bind is a very important hypnotic move. You might like to go into a trance in a minute's time, or perhaps you would prefer in five minutes'. And you certainly don't have to let you stop yourself going into trance, if that is what you want to do. You might even find it very enjoyable to let yourself relax more and more, and in so doing you might be interested in paying attention to the vase of flowers on the table there, and noticing what colour the flowers are, and noticing the scent of the flowers. If you are an innocent, naive person, which is what you should be, you would have hallucinated the flowers there, and by so doing you would be going nicely into trance. But of course there are no flowers there, are there? [Laughter]

It is not generally recognized how common trance states are. Few of us are aware of living through ultradian rhythms throughout the day, that is to say, every ninety minutes or so spontaneously going nearer into trance, and then coming further out of trance. And for any of you now who are near that point of going further into trance, where it can be so very comfortable to sit here, and allow your breathing to flow, it is so nice and warm, and there is this very smooth voice speaking, and you know you will very nicely go off into trance, and in so doing you will be paying attention to what I am trying to tell you in relation to what you want to know. You may not know you want to know anything, but the very fact you are in this circle means that you do want to know something. We don't yet know what that is. And we might find out, or you might each find out for yourself.

On that particular basis, I would like to read you some more of Milton Erickson's words: "Of course you can be interested consciously in what I say. But even though you may be intensely interested consciously, I would like to have you appreciate the fact that you are infinitely more interested on an unconscious level. And consciously you can just relax, you can close your eyes, and let your mind wander at will, from my words, to thoughts of what took place earlier on today, to thoughts of what we are going to eat later on when we get so very hungry. Despite every wandering thought that comes into your mind, there should be no effort on your part to try to listen to me. No effort whatsoever." And: "Just as you watch a flower open, you can sit and

watch without making any effort of your own. In exactly the same way you let
your unconscious mind open, and do its own thinking, its own feeling,
without any effort whatsoever on your part. All you need to know is that your
unconscious mind does exist. It is within you. It is part of you. Part of you that
you do not really know, but which knows a tremendous amount about you.
You are being watched all the time by your unconscious. That means you are
being taken care of so very nicely. It is so comforting to feel that there is
inside you this mind that is caring for you, and allowing you to relax and be at
peace."

"Now I want you to go deeply into trance, and very deeply. Not
necessarily deeply as you consciously understand it, but deeply as your
unconscious mind can understand it. And I think it should be interesting to
you consciously to discover many things that your unconscious mind already
knows and is willing to share with you. Consciously you can get bored,
indifferent, relaxed, curious, resentful, antagonistic in any way, and that is
entertaining to you as the conscious personality. You may go into a sleep
consciously if that is interesting to you, but I think you should recognize that I
want to talk primarily to your unconscious and that I will try and talk in such a
way that your unconscious understands a great deal more than your conscious
mind does. Because your unconscious mind should have many secrets from
me and many secrets from you consciously in order to get you to function
more adequately. And there we are, you may not have understood a single
word of that, but why should you, if you are going so nicely and deeply into
trance because then you don't need to understand, not consciously, and will
take it in so very nicely."

Early in 1950, Milton Erickson and Aldous Huxley met together to make
an enquiry into various states of consciousness, and the results of this enquiry
are evident in Huxley's last novel *Island*, from which I will read the following
extract: "'I hear you are from England. [...] I was in England just after the
war [...] as a student. [...] There was a girl in my psychology class, [...] her
people lived at Wells. She asked me to stay with them for the first month of
the summer vacation. Do you know Wells? [...] I used to love walking there
by the water, [...] looking across the moat at the cathedral [...]. How lovely it
was [...] and how marvellously peaceful! [...] Such an extraordinary sense of
peace. *Shanti, shanti, shanti*. The peace that passes understanding. [...] I can
shut my eyes. I can shut my eyes, [...] can shut my eyes and see it all so
clearly. Can see the church—and it's enormous, much taller than the huge
trees round the bishop's palace. Can see the green grass and the water and the
golden sunlight on the stones, and the slanting shadows between the
buttresses. And listen! I can hear the bells. The bells and the jackdaws. The
jackdaws in the tower—can you hear the jackdaws? [...] And there are white
clouds, [...] and the blue sky between them is so pale, so delicate, so
exquisitely tender. [...] And the swans, [...] the swans... [...] like the

inventions of heraldry. Romantic, impossibly beautiful. And yet there they are—real birds in a real place. So near to me now that I can almost touch them—and yet so far away, thousands of miles away. Far away on that smooth water, moving as if by magic, softly, majestically... [...] Effortlessly floating [...]. Effortlessly floating. [...] I'd sit there, [...] I'd sit there looking and looking, and in a little while I'd be floating too. I'd be floating with the swans on that smooth surface between the darkness below and the pale tender sky above. Floating at the same time on that other surface between here and far away, between then and now. [...] Floating [...] on the surface between the real and the imagined, between what comes to us from the outside and what comes to us from within, from deep, deep down in here. [...] Floating, [...] floating like a white bird on water. Floating on the great river of life—a great smooth silent river that flows so still, so still, you might almost think it was asleep. A sleeping river. But it flows irresistibly, [...] life flowing silently and irresistibly into ever fuller life, into a living peace all the more profound, all the richer and stronger and more complete because it knows all your pain and unhappiness, knows them and takes them into itself and makes them one with its own substance. And it's into that peace that you're floating now, floating on this smooth silent river that sleeps and is yet irresistible, and is irresistible precisely because it's sleeping. And I am floating with it. [...] Effortlessly floating. Not having to do anything at all. Just letting go, just allowing myself to be carried along, just asking for this irresistible sleeping river of life to take me where it's going—and knowing all the time that where it's going is where I want to go, where I want to go: into more life, into living peace. Along the sleeping river, irresistibly, into the wholeness of reconciliation. [...] Asleep on the sleeping river, [...] and above the river, in the pale sky, there are huge white clouds. And, as you look at them, you begin to float upwards towards them. Yes, you begin to float upwards towards them, and the river now is a river in the air, an invisible river that carries you on, carries you up, higher and higher. [...] Out of the hot plain, [...] effortlessly, into the freshness of the mountains. [...] How fresh the air feels as you breathe it. Fresh, pure, charged with life! [...] Coolness. Coolness and sleep. Through coolness into more life. Through sleep into reconciliation, into wholeness, into living peace.'"

That is from Huxley. But I read it as an induction, not as a novel. I have left out all the novel constructs because you would not have felt the trance induction feeling if I had read it out straight from the book, so I extracted just the induction because, when I read it like that myself, I was struck by the Ericksonian inductive quality of it. Now, I wonder if you would like me to go through Milton Erickson's article describing the enquiry he made with Aldous Huxley. They apparently worked together for a period of a year, planning this joint enquiry. The article is entitled "A Special Inquiry with Aldous Huxley into the Nature and Character of Various States of Consciousness." To prepare for the proposed study, they met in Huxley's home in Los Angeles early in 1950. However, the project could not be completed due to the destruction of Huxley's home and its contents by a brush fire in 1961. Erickson's article was written, from his own notes, after Huxley's death. They started off by Huxley describing his own practice of what he called "Deep Reflection":

"He described this state [...] as one marked by physical relaxation with bowed head and closed eyes, a profound, progressive, psychological withdrawal from externalities but without any actual loss of physical realities nor any amnesias or loss of orientation, a 'setting aside' of everything not pertinent, and then a state of complete mental absorption in matters of interest to him. Yet in that state of complete withdrawal and mental absorption, Huxley stated that he was free to pick up a fresh pencil to replace a dulled one, to make notations on his thoughts 'automatically,' and to do all this without a recognizable realization on his part of what physical act he was performing. 'It was as if the physical act were 'not an integral part of my thinking.' In no way did such physical activity seem to impinge upon, to slow, or impede 'the train of thought so exclusively occupying my interest. It is associated but completely peripheral activity.' [...] Huxley explained that he believed he could develop a state of Deep Reflection in about five minutes, but that in doing so he 'simply cast aside all anchors' of any type of awareness. Just what he meant and sensed he could not describe. 'It is a subjective experience quite' in which he apparently achieved a state of 'orderly mental arrangement' permitting an orderly free flowing of his thoughts as he wrote."

He was given signals to arouse at various times. "He became 'lost,' ... 'quite utterly involved in it,' ... 'one can sense it but not describe it,' ... ' I say, it's an utterly amazing, fascinating state of finding yourself a pleasant part of an endless vista of color that is soft and gentle and yielding and all absorbing. Utterly extraordinary, most extraordinary.' He had no recollection of my verbal insistences nor of the other physical stimuli. He remembered the agreed-upon signal but did not know if it had been given. He found himself only in a position of assuming that it had been given since he was again in a state of ordinary awareness. [...] One added statement was that entering a state of Deep Reflection by absorbing himself in a sense of color was in a fashion comparable to, but not identical with, his psychedelic experiences. [...] When he aroused, he had a vague recollection of having reviewed a previous psychedelic experience, but what he had experienced then or on the immediate occasion he could not recall. Nor did he recall speaking aloud or making notations. When shown these, he found they were so poorly written that they could not be read. I read mine to him without eliciting any memory traces. [...] A repetition yielded similar results with one exception. This was an amazed expression of astonishment by Huxley suddenly declaring, 'I say,

Milton, this is quite utterly amazing, most extraordinary. I use Deep Reflection to summon my memories, to put into order all of my thinking, to explore the range, the extent of my mental existence, but I do it solely to let those realizations, the thinking, the understandings, the memories seep into the work I'm planning to do without my conscious awareness of them. Fascinating ... never stopped to realize that my Deep Reflection always preceded a period of intensive work wherein I was completely absorbed. ... I say, no wonder I have an amnesia.' [...]"

"Huxley then suggested that an investigation be made of hypnotic states of awareness by employing him as a subject [first by induction of a light trance]. He found several repetitions of the light trance interesting but 'too easily conceptualised.' It is, he explained, 'A simple withdrawal of interest from the outside to the inside.' That is, one gives less and less attention to externalities and directs more and more attention to inner subjective sensations. [...]"

"In experimenting with medium-deep trances Huxley, like other subjects with whom I have worked, experienced much more difficulty in reacting to and maintaining a fairly constant trance level. He found that he had a subjective need to go deeper in the trance and an intellectual need to stay at a medium level. The result was he found himself repeatedly 'reaching out for awareness' of his environment, and this would initiate a light trance. He would then direct his attention to subjective comfort and find himself developing a deep trance. Finally, after repeated experiments, he was given both posthypnotic and direct hypnotic suggestion to remain in a medium-deep trance."

He then went into all sorts of hallucinations of sensations, and "from gustatory sensations [that is, sensations of taste] "he branched out to olfactory hallucinations [that is, sensations of smell] both pleasant and unpleasant, [though] he did not realize that he betrayed this by the flaring of his nostrils. His thinking at the time, so he subsequently explained, was that he had the 'feeling' that hallucinations of a completely 'inner type of process'—that is, occurring within the body itself—would be easier than those in which the hallucination appeared to be external to the body. From olfactory hallucinations he progressed to kinesthetic, proprioceptive, and finally tactile sensations. In the kinesthetic hallucinatory sensation experience he hallucinated taking a long walk but remained constantly aware that I was present in some vaguely sensed room. Momentarily he would forget about me, and his hallucinated walking would become most vivid. He recognized this as an indication of the momentary development of a deeper trance state, which he felt obligated to remember to report to me during the discussion after his arousal. [...]"

He then "proceeded to visual hallucinations. An attempt to open his eyes nearly aroused him from this trance state. Thereafter he kept his eyes closed for both light and medium-deep trance activities. His first visual hallucination was a vivid flooding of his mind with an intense sense of pastel colors of changing hues and with a wavelike motion. He related this experience to his Deep Reflection experiences with me and also to his previous psychedelic experiences. He did not consider this experience sufficiently valid for his purposes of the moment because he felt that vivid memories were playing too large a part. Hence he deliberately decided to visualise a flower, but the thought occurred that even as a sense of movement played a part in auditory hallucinations, he might employ a similar measure to develop visual hallucinations. At the moment, so he recalled after arousing from the trance and while discussing his experience, he wondered if I had ever built up hallucinations in my subjects by combining various sensory fields of experience. I told him that that was a standard procedure for me. He proceeded with this visual hallucination by 'feeling' his head turn from side to side and up and down to follow a barely visible, questionably visible, rhythmically moving object. Very shortly the object became increasingly more visible until he saw a giant rose, possibly three feet in diameter. This he did not expect, and thus he was certain at once that it was not a vivified memory but a satisfactory hallucination. With this realization came the insight that he might very well add to the hallucination by adding olfactory hallucinations of an intense, 'un-rose like,' sickeningly sweet odor. This effort was also most successful. After experimenting with various hallucinations, Huxley aroused from his trance and discussed extensively what he had accomplished. [...] This discussion raised the question of anaesthesia, amnesia, dissociation, depersonalization, regression, time distortion [and] hypermnesia."

Incidentally, amnesia is used to help people be free from pain. For example, you don't have to be in intense pain up here. In your head, for example, you might suggest to somebody, there is this strange itch that you might find developing at the bottom of your foot, and that itch is such a strange itch, and then the rest of your body is progressively becoming more and more numb, and as that becomes numb, of course, the pain disappears, but the itch is left slightly in place, because if you take everything away, there is no point of focus, and then the pain might come back. If you've got focus, in the sense of an itch, maybe the pain will not come back. And as to amnesia, well, you don't have to remember the things you don't need to, which are going to interfere with what you need to accomplish. So you might forget where you are, or what you were doing just a moment ago.

Also, it is useful to be able to make use of time distortion. A woman came to Milton Erickson who was a dental nurse. She was a very good nurse, but she had one difficulty. Whenever she saw blood, she fainted, she passed out! This was difficult for the dentist, because the nurse was no longer available to help him mop up the blood after extractions. So she went to see Milton Erickson and described the problem, and he said, very casually: "You don't mind if I smoke a cigarette do you?" and she said, no she didn't mind. He said: "And whilst I smoke a cigarette perhaps you could review all the times in your life when you remember seeing blood," and after about two minutes he roused her up out of that, thanked her very much for letting him smoke a cigarette—of course he had not smoked any cigarette whatsoever—and said: "And this is my bill." And she said: "Well, that's a bit steep, isn't it? You haven't done anything." And he said: "Yes, it is a bit steep, isn't it?" But he still presented his bill. She went home and was obviously not very happy, and went back to work the next day, and when the dentist was at one time engaged in pulling out a tooth, and there was blood and she very quickly mopped it all up, and he said: "But you didn't faint," she said: "I didn't faint!" So she went back to see Milton Erickson and she said: "But you must have done something." He said: "Yes, I must have done, mustn't I?"

And this is a very good example of time distortion. In a space of two minutes she had, in her subconscious, without her realising consciously, unconsciously reviewed every experience of blood and in so doing depotentiated her fear, or her reaction towards blood, so that her behaviour became normal. But I have to say that it takes a very experienced practitioner to get a result like that, because somebody who was just beginning wouldn't know, wouldn't get the feeling, wouldn't have the magnetic characteristic in himself to see that this could be done, to feel it, and to know that this would be the approach to pursue with that particular person, because it wouldn't work with anybody else. A similar thing would work, but not that thing.

And this is so very extraordinary. It is why it is not possible to put everybody into trance in an identical way, because there are too many personalities, sitting here, too many personalities… [Laughter] You see everybody is listening and attentive but Huxley has gone off.

"Hypermnesia [which is the opposite of amnesia, that is to say, total recall], so difficult to test [with Aldous Huxley] because of his extreme capacity to recall past events, was tested upon my suggestion by asking him in the light trance to state promptly upon request on what page of various of his books certain paragraphs could be found. At the first request Huxley roused from the light trance and explained, 'Really now, Milton, I can't do that. I can with effort recite most of that book, but the page number for a paragraph is not exactly cricket.' Nevertheless, he went back into a light trance, the name of the volume was given, a few lines of a paragraph were read aloud to him, whereupon he was to give the page number on which it appeared. He succeeded in identifying better than 65 percent in an amazingly prompt fashion. Upon awakening from the light trance, he was instructed to remain in the state of conscious awareness and to execute the same task. To his immense astonishment he found that, whilst the page number 'flashed' into his mind in the light trance state, in the waking state he had to follow a methodical procedure."

And so he evidently showed phenomenal states of memory when he was in that trance state.

"We then turned to the question of deep hypnosis. Huxley developed easily a profound somnambulistic trance in which he was completely disoriented spontaneously for time and place. He was able to open his eyes but described his field of vision as being 'a well of light' which included me, the chair on which I sat, himself, and his chair. He remarked at once upon the remarkable spontaneous restriction of his vision and disclosed an awareness that, for some reason unknown to him, he was obligated to 'explain things' to me. Careful questioning disclosed him to have an amnesia about what had been done previously, nor did he have any awareness of our joint venture. His feeling that he must explain things became a casual willingness as soon as he verbalized it. One of his first statements was, 'Really, you know, I can't understand my situation or why you are here, wherever that may be [he was in his own home], but I must explain things to you.' He was assured that I understood the situation and that I was interested in receiving any explanation he wished to give me and told that I might make requests of him. Most casually, indifferently he acceded, but it was obvious that he was enjoying a state of physical comfort in a contented passive manner. He answered questions simply and briefly, giving literally and precisely no more and no less than the literal significance of the question implied. [...] He was asked, 'What is to my right?' His answer was simply, 'I don't know.' 'Why?' 'I haven't looked.' 'Will you do so?' 'Yes.' 'Now!' 'How far do you want me to look?'"

"This was not an unexpected inquiry, since I have encountered it innumerable times. Huxley was simply manifesting a characteristic phenomenon of the deep somnambulistic trance in which visual awareness is restricted in some inexplicable manner to those items pertinent to the trance situation. For each chair, couch, footstool I wished him to see specific instructions were required. As Huxley explained later, 'I had to look around until gradually it [the specified object] slowly came into view, not all at once, but slowly, as if it were materializing. I really believe I felt completely at ease without any trace of wonderment as I watched things materialize.' [...]"

"With Huxley I tested this by enthusiastically asking, 'What, tell me now, is that which is just about 15 feet in front of you?' The correct answer should have been, 'A table.' Instead the answer received was, 'A table with a book and vase on it.' Both the book and vase were on the table but on the far side of the table and hence more than 15 feet away. Later the same inquiry was made in a casual, indifferent fashion, 'Tell me now, what is that is just about 15 feet in front of you?' He replied, despite his previous answer, 'A table.' 'Anything else?' 'Yes.' 'What else?' 'A book.' [This was nearer than the vase.] 'Anything else?' 'Yes.' 'Tell me now.' 'A vase.' 'Anything else?' 'Yes.' 'Tell me now.' 'A spot.' 'Anything else?' 'No.'"

"Huxley was then gently and indirectly awakened from the trance. [...] Huxley's response was an immediate arousal, and he promptly stated he was all set to enter deep hypnosis. While this statement in itself indicated profound posthypnotic amnesia, delaying tactics were employed in the guise of discussion of what might possibly be done. [...] There followed more deep trances [and, amongst other experiences,] he also developed catalepsy, tested by 'arranging' him comfortably in a chair [so he then became unable to move]. [...] Hence he sat helplessly, unable to stand and unable to recognize why."

So it was as though to say, right now, everybody in this room, they are sitting comfortably and there is no reason to move at all, and, in some strange way, if I were to ask Robin [Hull] to change places with Bernfried [Nugel], perhaps Robin would find that for some reason he could not move. That for some reason he has forgotten how to get out of the chair, and is sitting immobilized. Well of course I haven't done that to him so in fact if he decided to do so he could do so. Nevertheless he didn't actually do so. [Laughter]

"Further experimentation in deep trance investigated visual, auditory and other types of ideosensory hallucinations. One of the measures employed was to pantomime hearing a door open and then to appear to see someone entering a room, to arise in courtesy, and to indicate a chair, then turn to Huxley and to express the hope that he was comfortable. He replied that he was, and he expressed surprise at his wife's unexpected return, since he expected her to be absent the entire day. (The chair I had indicated was one I knew his wife liked to occupy.) He conversed with her and apparently hallucinated replies. He was interrupted with the question of how he knew that it was his wife and not a hypnotic hallucination. He examined the question thoughtfully, then explained that I had not given him any suggestion to hallucinate his wife, that I had been as much surprised by her arrival as he had been, and that she was dressed as she had been before her departure and not as I had seen her earlier. Hence it was reasonable to assume that she was a reality. After a brief, thoughtful pause he returned to his 'conversation' with her, apparently continuing to hallucinate replies. Finally I attracted his attention and made a hand gesture suggestive of a disappearance towards the chair in which he 'saw' his wife. To his complete astonishment he saw her slowly fade away. [...]"

"In a deep trance, with his eyes closed, Huxley listened intently as I opened the book at random and read a half-dozen lines from a selected paragraph. For some, he identified the page number almost at once, and then he would hallucinate the page and 'read' it from the point where I had stopped. Additionally he identified the occasion on which he had read the book. Two of the books he recalled consulting 15 years previously. Another two he found it difficult to give the correct page number, and then only approximating the page number. [...] In the post-trance discussion, [he] was most amazed by his performance as a memory feat but commented upon the experience as primarily intellectual, with recovered memories lacking in any emotional significances of belonging to him as a person. This led to a general discussion of hypnosis and Deep Reflection, with a general feeling of inadequacy on Huxley's part concerning proper conceptualization of his experiences for comparison of values. While Huxley was most delighted with his hypnotic experiences for their interest and the new understandings they offered him, he was also somewhat at a loss. He felt that as a purely personal experience he derived certain unidentifiable subjective values from Deep Reflection not actually obtainable from hypnosis, which offered only a wealth of new points of view. Deep Reflection, he declared, gave him certain inner enduring feelings that seemed to play some significant part in his pattern of living. During this discussion he suddenly asked if hypnosis could be employed to permit him to explore his psychedelic experiences."

Then he wanted to go further into more deep hypnosis "to permit him to explore himself more adequately as a person. [...] The best way to do this, I felt, would be by a confusion technique. [...] This decision to employ a confusion technique was influenced in a large part by the author's awareness of Huxley's unlimited intellectual capacity and curiosity, which would aid greatly by leading Huxley to add to the confusion technique verbalizations other possible elaborate meanings and significances and associations, thereby actually supplementing in effect my own efforts. [...] The actual suggestions [...] were to the effect that Huxley go ever deeper and deeper into a trance until 'the depth was a part and apart' from him, that before him would appear in 'utter clarity, in living reality, in impossible actuality, that which once was, but which now in the depths of trance, will, in bewildering confrontation challenge all of your memories and understandings.' This was a purposefully vague yet permissively comprehensive suggestion, and I simply relied upon Huxley's intelligence to elaborate it with an extensive meaningfulness for himself [...]. What I had in mind was not a defined situation but a setting of the stage so that Huxley himself would be led to define the task. [...]"

"It became obvious that Huxley was making an intensive hypnotic response during the prolonged, repetitious suggestions I was offering, when suddenly he raised his hand and said rather loudly and most urgently, 'I say, Milton, do you mind hushing up there? This is most extraordinarily interesting down here, and your constant talking is frightfully distracting and annoying.' [...] The play of expression on his face was most rapid and bewildering. His heart rate and respiratory rate were observed to change suddenly and inexplicably and repeatedly at irregular intervals. Each time that the author attempted to speak to him, Huxley would raise his hand, perhaps lift his head, and speak as if the author were at some height above him, frequently he would annoyedly request silence. After well over two hours he suddenly looked up towards the ceiling and remarked with puzzled emphasis, 'I say,

Milton, this is an extraordinary contretemps. We don't know you. You do not belong here. You are sitting on the edge of a ravine watching both of us, and neither of us knows which one is talking to you; and we are in the vestibule looking at each other with most extraordinary interest. We know that you are someone who can determine our identity, and most extraordinarily we are both sure we know it and that the other is not really so, but merely a mental image of the past or the future. But you must resolve it despite time and distances and even though we do not know you. I say, this is an extraordinarily fascinating predicament: Am I he or is he me? Come, Milton, whoever you are.' There were other similar remarks of comparable meaning which could not be recorded, and Huxley's tone of voice suddenly became most urgent. The whole situation was most confusing to me, but temporal and other types of dissociation seemed to be definitely involved in the situation."

"Wonderingly, but with outward calm, I undertook to arouse Huxley from the trance state by accepting the partial clues given and by saying in essence, 'Wherever you are, whatever you are doing, listen closely to what is being said, and slowly, gradually, comfortably begin to act upon it. Feel rested and comfortable, feel a need to establish an increasing contact with my voice, with me, with the situation I represent, a need of returning to matters in hand with me not so long ago, in the not so long ago belonging to me, *and leave behind* but AVAILABLE UPON REQUEST *practically everything of importance*, KNOWING BUT NOT KNOWING *that it is* AVAILABLE UPON REQUEST. And now, let us see, that's right, you are sitting there, wide awake, rested, comfortable and *ready for discussion of what little there is*.'"

"Huxley aroused, rubbed his eyes, and remarked, 'I have a most extraordinary feeling that I have been in a profound trance, but it has been a most sterile experience. I recall you suggesting that I go deeper in a trance, and I felt myself to be most compliant, and though I feel much time has elapsed, I truly believe a state of Deep Reflection would have been more fruitful.'"

So he was in an amnesia about what had happened. "After still further desultory conversation he was asked [apparently] *a propos* of nothing, 'In what vestibule would you place that chair?' (indicating a nearby armchair.) His reply was remarkable, 'Really, Milton, that is a most extraordinary question. Frightfully so! It is quite without meaning, but that word "vestibule" has a strange feeling of immense, anxious warmth about it. Most extraordinarily fascinating!'"

"He lapsed into a puzzled thought for some minutes and finally stated that if there were any significance, it was undoubtedly some fleeting esoteric association. After further casual conversation, I remarked, 'As for the edge where I was sitting, I wonder how deep the ravine was.' To this Huxley replied, 'Really Milton, you can be most frightfully cryptic. Those words, "vestibule," "edge," "ravine" have an extraordinary effect upon me. It is most indescribable. Let me see if I can associate some meaning with them.'"

"For nearly fifteen minutes, Huxley struggled vainly to secure some meaningful associations with those words, now and then stating that my apparently purposive but unrevealing use of them constituted a full assurance that there was a meaningful significance which should be apparent to him. Finally he disclosed with elation, 'I have it now. Most extraordinary how it escaped me. I am fully aware that you had me in a trance, and unquestionably those words had something to do with the deep trance which seemed to be so sterile to me. I wonder if I can recover my associations.'"

There followed twenty minutes of silence, obviously in thought, and "after some time I commented with quiet emphasis, 'Well, perhaps now matters will *become available.*' From his lounging, comfortable position in his chair Huxley straightened up in a startled amazed fashion and then poured forth a torrent of words too rapid to recall except for occasional notes. In essence his account was that the word 'available' had the effect of drawing back an amnestic curtain, laying bare a most astonishing subjective experience that had miraculously been 'wiped out' by the words 'leave behind' and had been recovered *in toto* by virtue of the cue words 'become available.' He explained that he now realized that he had developed a 'deep trance,' a psychological state far different from his state of Deep Reflection, that in Deep Reflection there was an attenuated but unconcerned and unimportant awareness of external reality, a feeling of being in a known sensed state of subjective awareness, of a feeling of control and a desire to utilize capabilities and in which past memories, learnings, and experiences flowed freely and easily. Along with this flow there would be a continuing sense in the self that these memories, learnings, experiences, and understandings, however vivid, were no more than just such an orderly, meaningful alignment of psychological experiences out of which to form a foundation for a profound, pleasing, subjective, emotional state from which would flow comprehensive understandings to be utilized immediately and with little conscious effort."

"The deep trance state, he asserted, he now knew to be another and entirely different category of experience. External reality could enter, but it acquired a new kind of subjective reality, a special reality of a new and different significance entirely. For example, while I had been included in part in his deep trance state, it was not as a specific person with a specific identity. Instead I was known only as someone whom he (Huxley) knew in some vague and unimportant and completely unidentified relationship. [...]"

"In his deep trance, Huxley found himself in a deep, wide ravine, high up on the steep side of which, on the very edge, I sat, identifiable only by name and as annoyingly verbose."

"Before him in a wide expanse of soft, dry sand was a nude infant lying on its stomach. Acceptingly, unquestioning of its actuality, Huxley gazed at the infant, vastly curious about its behaviour, vastly intent on trying to understand its flailing movements with its hands and creeping movements of its legs. To his amazement he felt himself experiencing a vague, curious sense of wonderment as if he himself were the infant and looking at the soft sand and trying to understand what it was."

"As he watched, he became annoyed with me since I was apparently trying to talk to him, and he experienced a wave of impatience and requested that I be silent. He turned back and noticed that the infant was growing before his eyes, was creeping, sitting, standing, toddling, walking, playing, talking. In utter fascination he watched this growing child, sensed its subjective experiences of learning, of wanting, of feeling. He followed it in distorted time through a multitude of experiences as it passed from infancy to childhood to schooldays to early youth to teenage. He watched the child's physical development, sensed its physical and subjective mental experiences, sympathised with it, empathised with it, rejoiced with it, thought and wondered and learnt with it. He felt as one with it, as if it were he himself, and continued to watch it until finally he realized he had watched that infant grow to the maturity of 23 years. He stepped closer to see what the young man was looking at, and suddenly realized that the young man was Aldous Huxley himself, and that this Aldous Huxley was looking at another Aldous Huxley, obviously in his early 50's, just across the vestibule in which they both were standing; and that he, aged 52, was looking at himself, Aldous, aged 23. Then Aldous aged 23 and Aldous aged 52 apparently realized simultaneously that they were looking at each other, and the curious questions at once arose in the mind of each of them. For one the question was, 'Is that my idea of what I'll be like when I am 52?' and, 'Is that really the way I appeared when I was 23?' Each was aware of the question in the other's mind. Each found the question of 'extraordinarily fascinating interest,' and each tried to determine what was the 'actual reality,' and which was the 'mere subjective experience outwardly projected in hallucinatory form.'"

"To each the past 23 years was an open book, all memories and events were clear, and they recognized that they shared those memories in common, and to each only wondering speculation offered a possible explanation of any of the years between 23 and 52."

"They looked across the vestibule (this 'vestibule' was not defined) and up at the edge of the ravine where I was sitting. Both knew that that person sitting there had some undefined significance, was named Milton, and could be spoken to by both. The thought came to both, could he hear both of them, but the test failed because they found that they spoke simultaneously, nor could they speak separately."

"Slowly, thoughtfully, they studied each other. One had to be real. One had to be a memory image or a projection of a self-image. Should not Aldous aged 52 have all the memories of the years from 23 to 52? But if he did, how could he then see Aldous aged 23 without the shadings and colorations of the years that had passed since that youthful age? If he were to view Aldous aged 23 clearly, he would have to blot out all the subsequent memories in order to see that youthful Aldous clearly and as then he was. But if he were actually Aldous aged 23, why could he not speculatively fabricate memories for the years between 23 and 52 instead of merely seeing Aldous aged 52 and nothing more? What manner of psychological blocking could exist to reflect this peculiar state of affairs? Each found himself fully cognizant of the thinking and reasoning of the 'other.' Each doubted 'the reality of the other,' and each found reasonable explanations for such contrasting subjective experiences. The questions arose repeatedly, by what measure could the truth be established, and how did that unidentifiable person possessing only a name sitting on the edge of a ravine on the other side of the vestibule fit into the total situation? Could that vague person have an answer? Why not call to him and see?"

"With much pleasure and interest Huxley detailed his total subjective experience, speculating upon the years of time distortion experienced and the memory blockages creating the insoluble problems of actual identity. Finally, experimentally, the author remarked casually, 'Of course, all that could be *left behind to become* AVAILABLE *at some later time.*'"

"Immediately there occurred the reestablishment of the original posthypnotic amnesia. Efforts were made to disrupt this reinduced hypnotic amnesia by veiled remarks, by frank, open statements, by a narration of what had occurred. Huxley found my narrative statements about an infant on the sand, a deep ravine, a vestibule 'curiously interesting,' simply cryptic remarks for which Huxley judged I had a purpose. But they were not evocative of anything more. Each statement I made was itself actually uninformative and intended only to arouse associations. Yet no results were forthcoming until again the word 'AVAILABLE' resulted in the same effect as previously. The whole account was related by Huxley a second time but without his realization that he was repeating his account. Appropriate suggestions when he had finished his second narration resulted in a full recollection of his first account. His reaction, after his immediate astonishment, was to compare the two accounts item by item. Their identity amazed him. He noted only minor changes in the order of narration and the choice of words."

And this was all done a third time, and "this discussion was continued until preparations for scheduled activities for that evening intervened, but not before an agreement on a subsequent preparation of the material for publication. Huxley planned to use both Deep Reflection and additional self-induced trances to aid in writng the article but the unfortunate holocaust precluded this."

So that's the essence of the collaboration which they made, and I felt that I had to go through the first part, but it's that last part which is so extraordinary;

this part where there are two people who are the same. And apparently Milton Erickson had worked with other people who had had strikingly similar experiences of finding themselves in deep trance looking at a double of themselves, and it does raise a strange question, a very strange question as to the nature of reality. Are we, in this room now, in any form of reality whatsoever? Because it may be that we are all a figment in Aldous Huxley's mind. We are all suggestions in Aldous Huxley's mind. How can we possibly prove that this is not so? Because the state of trance and amnesia make it so deep that all we have is the feelings of being in this room, believing it to be the total reality when in fact it may only be taking place in somebody's mind, and, at the snap of fingers, Aldous Huxley himself switches off and we will evaporate into the place from where we have come, without any remembrance of having been in this room at all. On the other hand, it might be said that how do we know that Aldous Huxley himself existed? We only have certain pieces of printed paper. That's no proof that a man existed. It is just a story that Aldous Huxley existed, lived. It is just a story that I am reading out—this all might be a fabrication.[4]

---

[1] Editors' note: The following three texts are transcripts of workshops presented at the Third International Aldous Huxley Symposium, Riga, 25–28 July 2004. To retain the lively workshop style, the editors have decided not to interrrupt the text by single page references but rather to give summary references in the endnotes.

[2] The quotations read out in Workshop 1 were taken from: W.H. Bates, *Better Eyesight Without Glasses* (London, 1979; first published as *The Cure of Imperfect Sight by Treatment Without Glasses* [New York, 1919]); Jacques Lusseyran, *The Blind in Society*, Proceedings No. 27, The Myrin Institute for Adult Education (New York, 1973); Flora Courtois, *An Experience of Enlightenment* (Wheaton, IL: The Theosophical Publishing Co., 1986).

[3] The quotations read out in Workshop 2 were taken from: Aldous Huxley, *The Art of Seeing* (New York, 1942).

[4] The quotations read out in Workshop 3 were taken from: Aldous Huxley, *Island* (London, 1962), 31-35; Milton H. Erickson, "A Special Inquiry with Aldous Huxley Into the Nature and Character of Various States of Consciousness," *The American Journal of Clinical Hypnosis*, 8.1 (July 1965), 14-33; *The Collected Papers of Milton H. Erickson on Hypnosis*, ed. E. L. Rossi (New York, 1980), I, 83–107, 413; *The Seminars, Workshops and Lectures of Milton H. Erickson*, ed. E.L. Rossi, M. Ryan and F. Sharp (London, 1988), I, 141, 147, 405; II, 67, 103, 183, 225, 245.

Robin Hull

(Hull's School, Zürich)

FRAGMENTS OF AN EVOLUTIONARY PSYCHOLOGY

This essay will endeavour to take a look at Huxley's notion of the Perennial Philosophy from the point of view of practice. The Perennial Philosophy, rather than being a rigorously logical system, is more like a collection of fragments forming part of an ancient psychology which sets out to show how man may evolve.

Huxley is often associated with the novel of ideas, and it seems too easy to picture him as a scholar who divided up his time between reading and writing, with brief spells in the garden or at the easel. We are surprisingly quick to edit out of our picture of Huxley a fact which is given prominence both in Sybille Bedford's biography[1] and *Aldous Huxley, Representative Man* by James Hull,[2] namely that Huxley's mysticism came about gradually as the result of many decades of practical inner work and that his novels and his non-fiction testify to this.

In a recent article Marvin Barrett, one of the senior editors of *Parabola*, a journal exploring the practice of the Perennial Philosophy, made a number of interesting remarks on Huxley.[3] He starts his essay by stating that he wishes to reconsider Huxley not as a writer but as a man. "Huxley," Barrett continues, "is responsible for the fact that at eighty-three I still invest an essential portion of each day in meditation, prayer, and devotional reading. The hope that Huxley gave me in my early twenties, in a world every bit as daunting as the one in which we live now, is still with me into my ninth decade" (Barrett, 90). Later on in his essay Barrett says:

> If it was Gerald Heard, the 'crackpot English polymath,' who eventually took on my spiritual direction, Huxley, Heard's most famous convert, was the one who set me on the path. If it was Heard, a formidable persuader in his own right, who on the eve of my departure for active duty at an unknown destination, handed me a week's worth of mimeographed meditations to channel my thoughts into prayer, it was Huxley who wrote them. Huxley's simple, eloquent paragraphs on being, beauty, grace, holiness, peace, joy, and mortification helped fuel me through the next four years of playing the naval officer—who incidentally was praying six hours a day. (Barrett, 91–92)

A bit further on Barrett paints a portrait of Huxley at Trabuco:

> Huxley was not only compelling on the page; his person, when I finally met him at Trabuco, Heard's commune for would-be saints in the foothills of southern California, was unique. [...] Nowhere in his behaviour was there the slightest assumption of privilege or

> superiority. He helped with table-setting and washing up, went on
> expeditions into the surrounding hills in search of cow pies for the
> compost heap, and sang at my twenty-sixth birthday celebration.
> [...] In the end he terrified me by soliciting my advice as to
> techniques of prayer. (Barrett, 92)

Sybille Bedford describes a number of instances when Huxley's presence
made a dramatic impression both on her and many others.

In his anthology *The Perennial Philosophy* [4] Huxley stresses that mysticism is entirely practical and based solely on experience. He also points out
that any progress in the realm of mysticism is normally—at least according to
the source texts of the major spiritual traditions—the result of a persistent act
of will over a long period of time. The implications for readers of Huxley's
texts would seem to be manifold. If we accept that Huxley had any real
mystical experiences, we may only hope to understand part of his writings in
our ordinary state; this part may be smaller than we at first imagine:

—there are levels of meaning in Huxley's works which are accessible to
  people who live exclusively in everyday life and take a purely theoretical
  interest in, say, the Perennial Philosophy;
—there are levels of meaning in Huxley's works which are coloured by his
  own inner growth, whatever this may have been, and demand of the reader
  that he share the corresponding experiences in order to follow; on this level
  Huxley is writing for the practitioner of the Perennial Philosophy;
—the Perennial Philosophy may also be viewed as a Perennial Psychology
  and a Perennial Physiology, as it is not concerned so much with ideas as
  with immediate reality as it may be sensed by the mind and the body;
—in order to benefit more fully from Huxley's works we seem to be invited to
  consider the practical implications for ourselves.

In the following I will draw primarily on Huxley's anthology *The
Perennial Philosophy* and a number of essays included in *The Human
Situation*[5] in an attempt to study some of the basic constituent elements of the
psychology of *metanoia*, in the hope that this may serve as a contribution to
an exchange about Huxley the practitioner.

Ordinary man in ordinary life

The Perennial Philosophy suggests that we are born far from perfect. We live
in a very small part of ourselves and die unaware of the extraordinary
potential we have been endowed with. The vast majority of mankind go
through life in a state of what is quite wrongly believed to be waking
consciousness, a state which is neither awake nor conscious in any deeper
sense.

We are born tripartite beings each with our peculiar form of imbalance, be
it emotional, intellectual or physical. Huxley frequently expresses this in
terms of the Sheldonian typology. Imbalance is one of the more permanent

features of the human being and constitutes the basis for psychophysical types.

Humans are never the same at any given moment, they are made up of what the early Buddhists call 'skandhas' or complexes of different features and behavioural patterns which keep recurring in the same body whenever they are triggered, to the point where the notion of an undivided and permanent self has to be abandoned. Man is a multiplicity with many people living in the same body.

Man lives in his personality, not in his Atman or real I. This personality blinds him to his potential and keeps him in a state of mechanicity or automatic behaviour. It represents a tiny part of man's mind. Huxley calls the degree to which personality distorts our true hidden selves the "'Bovaric angle'" (HS, 68). To make matters worse, this ordinary personality tends to be neurotic and to have suffered all sorts of damage due to upbringing, education and the effects of society.

Man's inner life is cut off from the present moment, from life, and happens in a dream world of memories and speculations about the future. Man lives in a distorted form of time and prefers this to the extraordinary possibilities offered at any given moment. Man's inner life is obscured by his love of day-dreams and his passion for negative emotions. He spends much of his day replaying negative memories involving other people, arguing with them internally and settling accounts with them. In *The Human Situation* Huxley calls our inner lives a "morass of non-actuality" (HS, 232). Huxley points to the "tragic fact that we get a bigger kick out of hate" (HS, 238) than out of placid virtues such as tolerance.

The prison

A relatively unflattering picture of ordinary man emerges from these considerations. They suggest that man is as a rule incapable of intentional activities and that he lacks real will. He has only the self-will—or surface will—of a particular moment which pulls him in different directions depending on his likes and dislikes. In his ordinary state man is largely incapable of ethical behaviour as he changes far too much from one moment to the next. The ordinary waking state is pathological and the root of all evil, it deprives man of his capacity for real feelings. Though he likes to dream of sensitivity, he is in reality quite insensitive to other people. Real sensitivity to other people depends upon our making contact with the corresponding faculties inside, which are part of the deeper self. Man is a complete egotist living in an illusory private world. Violence and negativity are unnecessary traits which derive from this egotism and account for all atrocities of human history. Unregenerate man is subhuman, living in hell and mostly evil. Huxley invokes Jallal Uddin Rumi at this point: "If thou hast not seen the devil, look at thine own self" (PP, 212). Without knowing it, unregenerate man forfeits any chances he might have of surviving physical death. In his later works, such as *The Genius and the Goddess*,[6] Huxley is quite explicit about this. For as long as man remains in his ordinary state there is little hope of any meaningful progress.

Why we make ourselves comfortable in the prison

Much as unregenerate man may find himself in the most undesirable condition, it involves less discomfort than the situation of man in transition. As a result, the interest in practice is not as great as it might be. Huxley mentions a number of factors preventing man from becoming a contemplative.

Many do not believe that they are quite as unfortunate in their ordinary selves as the Perennial Philosophy contends. The belief is widespread that what the Perennial Philosophy promises after decades of desperate struggle, namely humanity, consciousness, morality, individuality and immortality, is in fact common property and readily available to everyone. Human graces, the fulfilment in everyday life, are so enticing that the rewards of contemplation seem uninteresting. Huxley calls this self-willed ignorance, stressing that it is our responsibility to overcome it.

The escape route—characteristics of inner work

From Huxley's *The Perennial Philosophy* we may infer that there are at least three stages of man's possible inner development:

1. The state of unregenerate man, governed by the imbalance of his makeup. The majority of the characters in Huxley's fiction fall into this category.
2. The state of man in transition engaged in inner work who experiences moments of varying degrees of freedom and long periods of struggle, but has not yet achieved more permanent contact with the deeper levels. Most of Huxley's leading characters are at varying stages of transition reflecting certain changes in their author, as James Hull shows in *Aldous Huxley, Representative Man*.
3. The state of liberated man who has achieved more permanence in the realisation of his deeper self and is able to help others; in Huxley's later novels there are a number of characters who act as guides or teachers.

Interestingly, Huxley points out that the transitional stage between the two basic states is perhaps the most uncomfortable and accordingly cites the author of the *Theologia Germanica* :

> When a man is in one of these two states (beatitude or dark night of the soul) all is right with him, and he is as safe in hell as in heaven. And so long as a man is on earth, it is possible for him to pass often-times from one to the other—nay, even within the space of a day and night, and all without his own doing. But when a man is in neither of these two states, he holds converse with the creatures, and wavereth hither and thither, and knoweth not what manner of a man he is. (*PP*, 249)

The eightfold path of Buddhism, showing us the way from ordinary life to enlightenment, is evidently riddlcd with potholes.

The wish to overcome the self-willed ignorance we find ourselves in may originate in glimpses of reality. In our ordinary state we may on rare occasions catch glimpses of a different level of reality. Huxley uses the term 'gratuituous graces.' These are invitations to strive for what Huxley calls 'spiritual graces,' which result from inner work. The more our ordinary selves become passive or 'mortified,' the more this appears likely to happen. The higher faculties we are endowed with according to the Perennial Philosophy are gradually awakened. There would seem to be instances of this in Huxley's later novels. In order to renew such contacts we need to engage in what Huxley calls a persistent effort. If a certain effort is made over many years, a mysterious change may occur in us, bringing with it ever-increasing glimpses of a different, more real level of existence. This gradual change brought about by inner work goes beyond ordinary language and cannot be talked about without a dramatic loss in meaning. Here we are faced with Huxley's distinction between knowledge and understanding.[7] Knowledge happens primarily in the head while understanding relates theory to our being. *The Perennial Philosophy* uses language which mirrors our being and the level we are at. Huxley points out that knowledge is a function of being and that we cannot go further in this domain without starting to gain our own experiences.

The main focus of inner work according to *The Perennial Philosophy* seems to be connected with self-knowledge. The knowledge in question transcends the intellect and embraces the entire psychophysical organism. It becomes available gradually as the contemplative discovers ways of experiencing himself at any given moment. A mysterious form of inner detachment or 'non-attachment,' as Huxley tends to call it, is required which separates man into something which observes—again practically, not just intellectually—and something which is observed. A subtle form of effort seems to be essential to the practice of contemplation.

Huxley suggests that as we observe ourselves we become more aware of our true state and the many removes we are from reality. This, according to Huxley, we need to bear and it may cause us to become humbler. Much help can be derived from various forms of self-denial and the recognition of how strong the appetites are which rule supreme. Physical relaxation, the focussing of attention and extended periods of silence seem to play an important part.

Over time, right contemplation may lead to a gradual dissolution of our ordinary selves and ultimately the 'death' of our ordinary selves.

The struggle to wake up

The fundamental problem facing anyone who attempts inner work is that undivided attention is scarce and cannot normally be sustained. In *The Art of Seeing*[8] Huxley shows that it is a natural feature of attention to be in perpetual motion, focussing therefore goes against its natural tendency to become dissipated.

In *The Human Situation*, Huxley identifies the main obstacle to self-knowledge as being neurosis. Neurosis mars our everyday lives and makes any inner work more difficult, distorting our perception of ourselves and others. The more our personalities are divorced from our inner selves—i.e., the greater our Bovaric angle—the more difficult it is to engage in contemplation. Egotism is a quality which asserts itself as inner work begins. Huxley suggests that it continues to haunt the contemplative in a number of guises which may even appear spiritual, such as the excessive love of a certain spiritual exercise, say, of fasting.

Habits and routines, though they may help us to make a persistent effort over a longer period of time, may blind us to the present and destroy any chances of awareness. This would suggest that spiritual exercises lose their force and give no results if they are continued for too long without sufficient variation. There is also the illusion that self-reproach leads to salvation. Whoever starts working on himself will be tempted to indulge in self-reproach without noticing that this diverts attention to the ego and away from that which transcends it (see *PP*, 306). Spiritual pride poses a threat whenever we catch a tiny glimpse of something and feel superior to the 'unregenerate,' yet another powerful illusion which may beset the contemplative.

Lacking true will and changing from one moment to the next we are at first unable to make any sustained effort. Huxley points out that we need to attempt contemplation with what little will we have. He maintains that the surface will needs to be trained (see *HS*, 233), attaching great importance to the observation of failure and to the attitude with which the impossible is attempted.

Huxley suggests that our preoccupation with daydreams and negative emotions continues despite attempts at contemplation and even though they may have been identified as an obstacle to awareness. Contemplation may very easily become daydreaming about contemplation, just as the love of negativity may pretend to disappear only to resurface as puritanical obsession.

Huxley warns that when we attempt inner work we try in the way which is easiest for our type. The intellectual, for instance, will be happy to read many volumes about contemplation rather than try it in practice.

Liberation

In *The Perennial Philosophy*, Huxley quotes from a number of sources and paints a picture of the final state we may aspire to. We learn that the highest form of grace is a complete and permanent contact with our deeper self, our real I or Atman, to the point where we go beyond ourselves and become part of a larger sphere of consciousness, the Divine Ground or Brahman. In this state our inner world is related to the outer world, and we become open, peaceful and do not require words. Pure consciousness is characterised by charity, a sacred form of love which is different from the 'love' of ordinary life.

Even if we do struggle with ourselves, Huxley leaves no doubt about the fact that only relatively few people succeed in complete liberation. This would in itself not appear to be very motivating if it were not equally evident in Huxley's *The Perennial Philosophy* that the benefits of more modest spiritual progress are also considerable. Man has every reason to avail himself of any help he can get.

We need help

Contemplatives may derive much support from right teaching. Huxley's *The Perennial Philosophy* is an attempt to make the best spiritual teachings of all the major traditions available. It contains many useful hints about the practice of contemplation, in particular about how to work with spiritual exercises.

Huxley is anxious to point out that there is no simple technique—or patent medicine, as he puts it—and that what may work for a person of one type may not work for someone of a different type. The need for different approaches is illustrated by the three ancient traditions of Yoga: Karma (body), Bhakti (devotion, emotion) and Jnana (knowledge, head). Huxley stresses the need for experimentation. In *The Human Situation* he mentions a number of more recent developments including, for instance, Gestalt exercises in awareness, work with the body as in the F. M. Alexander Technique, and visualisation as in the case of Herbert Read's *Education through Art*.[9]

Spiritual exercises are a challenge to our intelligence and to our integrity:

> What ritual is to public worship, spiritual exercises are to private devotion. They are devices to be used by the solitary individual when he enters into his closet, shuts the door and prays to his Father which is in secret. Like all other devices [...] spiritual exercises can be used either well or badly. Some of those who use spiritual exercises make progress in the life of the spirit, others using the same exercises, make no progress. To believe that their use either constitutes enlightenment or guarantees it, is mere idolatry and superstition. To neglect them altogether, to refuse to find out whether and in what way they can help in the achievement of our

final end, is nothing but self-opinionatedness and stubborn obscur-
antism. (*PP*, 332)

Everyday life may serve as a source for practical exercises. Much is
achieved by "the acceptance of what happens to us in the course of daily
living" (*PP*, 120). Huxley recommends:

> If specific exercises in self-denial are undertaken, they should be
> inconspicuous, non-competitive and uninjurious to health. Thus in
> the matter of diet, most people will find it sufficiently mortifying to
> refrain from eating all the things which the experts in nutrition
> condemn as unwholesome. And where social relations are
> concerned, self-denial should take the form, not of showy acts of
> would-be humility, but of control of the tongue and the moods—in
> refraining from saying anything uncharitable or merely frivolous
> (which means, in practice, refraining from about fifty per cent of
> ordinary conversation), and in behaving calmly and with quiet
> cheerfulness when external circumstances or the state of our bodies
> predisposes us to anxiety, gloom or an excessive elation. (*PP*, 120)

Huxley's novels are unique in that they show what help there may be in
practical terms. In the novels an important part is played by characters acting
as guides and in his last major work—*Island*—the community becomes an
essential factor in awakening the individual.

The role of guides in the novels cannot be understated. Many of the
leading characters depend upon their partners for guidance while others
mutually assist each other. Elinor Quarles in *Point Counter Point*, Radha and
Ranga or the MacPhails in *Island* spring to mind. Outsiders act as guides,
such as Bruno (in relation to Sebastian) in *Time Must Have a Stop* or Dr
Miller in *Eyeless in Gaza*.

Perhaps one of the most convincing of the spiritual guides is Bruno in
Time Must Have a Stop. In *Aldous Huxley, Representative Man* it is suggested
that Huxley was trying to describe what he expected the enlightened
individual to be like:

> There were so many things one could mention. That candour, for
> example, that extraordinary truthfulness. Or his simplicity, the
> absence in him of all pretensions. Or that tenderness of his, so
> intense and yet so completely unsentimental and even impersonal—
> but impersonal, in some sort, above the level of personality, not
> below it, as his own sensuality had been impersonal. Or else there
> was the fact that, at the end, Bruno had been no more than a kind of
> thin transparent shell, enclosing something incommensurably other
> than himself—an unearthly beauty of peace and power and
> knowledge.[10]

Bruno seems to have achieved a degree of liberation where he no longer has
to obey his personality. It may come as a surprise that Bruno feels no
inclination to preach. What distinguishes him from others is a quality which

goes beyond personality and teaches through its mere presence. Paradoxically, this different mode of being seems far more human. By meeting Bruno Sebastian grows more aware of his own inner teacher and the need for a search.

Island is remarkable in that it includes an extraordinary range of further means which may be useful to practical inner work. Sex is transformed into maithuna, a yoga of sensuality inspired by the Oneida Community and the notion of male continence. Group meditation is a feature of everyday life and a natural element of inner work together with other forms of search. Systematic use is made of the moksha-medicine, a hallucinogenic, to enable teenagers to experience pure awareness. *Island* might be regarded as an enormous mystical school, an entire society dedicated to the fostering of awareness.

Whichever form of practice we choose, we can be sure that "undivided attention is with difficulty sustained for long periods at a stretch" (*PP*, 347). There will always have to be intervals when we return to ordinary waking consiousness. Activities like sweeping a floor lend themselves more to attempts at undivided attention than activities involving what seems to be one of the most hypnotic parts of life, the use of language. Huxley suggests that it is better to try to practise contemplation in the breaks between periods of linguistic activity (or similarly distracting undertakings), doubtless a point of great interest to Huxley scholars.

The chapter on spiritual exercises in *The Perennial Philosophy* arranges a number of different types of meditation in what would seem to be a hierarchic order implying that there are lower and higher forms of contemplation culminating in the Way of Tranquillity and the Way of Wisdom. While lower forms of contemplation make use of images and words, higher forms of contemplation become increasingly image- and wordless. This would seem to contain a number of interesting implications for anyone interested in a spiritual way.

A postscript and many questions

There is reason to believe that there may be unpublished texts by Huxley addressing a number of practical questions related to contemplation. It would doubtless be of great interest if such texts could be found and made available.

The novels highlight the importance of a guide. Sybille Bedford mentions a number of guides which Huxley met and maintained contact with over many years (F. M. Alexander, Gerald Heard, Krishnamurti, to mention but a few). A great number of texts in *The Perennial Philosophy* involve dialogues between teachers and students and nearly all sources derive from mystical schools. Interestingly, neither *The Perennial Philosophy* nor *The Human Situation* explicitly address the question of the school or even the teacher. There is no chapter in *The Perennial Philosophy* on finding a guide or even on the desirability of this.

Island broaches the matter of group meditation. We recall that Huxley spent some time with a number of communities without—it would seem—committing himself to either of them (The Peace Pledge Union, Trabuco, Vedanta, one of Ouspensky's groups, to mention but a few). A major role is assigned to hallucinogenics, which Huxley experimented with extensively and availed himself on his deathbed. However, neither *The Perennial Philosophy* nor *The Human Situation* mention either of these possibilities. Does Huxley give this question further thought in other writings?

Many questions of this kind could be added, but we should not neglect to add the most fundamental question: how to make *The Perennial Philosophy* a starting point for a practical enquiry. This potentiality would seem to be at the heart of what is unique about the works of Aldous Huxley.

---

[1] Sybille Bedford, *Aldous Huxley: A Biography* (2 vols., London, 1973–1974).

[2] James Hull, *Aldous Huxley, Representative Man,* ed. Gerhard Wagner, "Human Potentialities", 5 (Münster, 2004).

[3] See Marvin Barrett, "Touched by Aldous Huxley," *Parabola*, 28.4 (2003), 90–94.

[4] Aldous Huxley, *The Perennial Philosophy* (London, 1994). Hereafter, *PP*.

[5] Aldous Huxley, *The Human Situation*, ed. Piero Ferrucci (London, 1994). Hereafter, *HH*.

[6] Aldous Huxley, *The Genius and the Goddess* (London, 1955). Hereafter, *GG*.

[7] See Aldous Huxley, "Knowledge and Understanding," *Adonis and the Alphabet* (London, 1956), 39–72.

[8] Aldous Huxley, *The Art of Seeing* (New York, 1942).

[9] Herbert Read, *Education through Art* (London, 1943).

[10] Aldous Huxley, *Time Must Have a Stop* (London, 1946), 304–305.

INDEX

"Human Potentialities"
Studien zu Aldous Huxley & zeitgenössischer Kultur
Studies in Aldous Huxley & Contemporary Culture
hrsg. von / edited by
Prof. Dr. Bernfried Nugel (Universität Münster)
und Prof. Dr. Lothar Fietz (Universität Tübingen)

Ulrike Kretschmer
Der Mensch – Affe oder gottähnliches Wesen?
Philosophisch-anthropologische Vorstellungen im Werk Aldous Huxleys
"The proper study of Mankind is Man." Immer wieder hat sich der moderne englische Schriftsteller und Denker Aldous Huxley von dieser Prämisse aus Alexander Popes *Essay on Man* leiten lassen. Von den frühen Gedichten, Essays und Romanen bis hin zu seiner letzten positiven Utopie *Island* setzte Huxley sich mit der Frage nach dem Wesen und den Entfaltungsmöglichkeiten des Menschen auseinander. In diesem Sinne verfolgt die vorliegende Arbeit die philosophisch-anthropologischen Vorstellungen Huxleys, die über die kritische Analyse der in unlösbaren Konflikten gefangenen menschlichen Natur hinaus auch die systematische Klassifizierung seiner Modellvorstellungen vom Menschen umfassen. Als Synthese der deskriptiven Bestandsaufnahme der menschlichen Grundkonflikte und der sowohl autorspezifisch als auch generell anthropologischen Kategorien ergibt sich der Entwurf eines idealen Menschen, der fähig ist, die eigene Zeitgebundenheit zu überschreiten und sein ganzes menschliches Potential auszuschöpfen.
Bd. 1, 1998, 288 S., 25,90 €, br., ISBN 3-8258-3708-4

Sabine Menninghaus
Vorstellungsweisen künstlerischer Transformation
Naturwissenschaftliche Analogien bei Aldous Huxley, James Joyce und Virginia Woolf
Die klassische Moderne, die literarische Bewegung, die zur Jahrhundertwende ihren Anfang nahm, ist durch fundamentale ästhetische Innovationen gekennzeichnet. Zugleich prägen naturwissenschaftliche Revolutionen diese Zeit. Angefangen beim evolutionären Wandel aller Lebewesen, über die Stoffumwandlungen in der Chemie, bis hin zu den physikalischen Umwandlungen von Materie in Energie – das Prinzip der Transformation bestimmt die modernen Naturwissenschaften. Es vollzieht sich ein Paradigmenwechsel vom statischen, mechanistischen Weltbild zu einem dynamischen. Für die Beziehungen zwischen Literatur und Naturwissenschaften wird Transformation so zum zentralen Begriff, der die Erkenntnisse der Natur, das Weltbild und die Ästhetik durchdringt. Die literaturtheoretischen Positionen von Aldous Huxley, der sich selbst als "Brückenbauer" zwischen Naturwissenschaft und Literatur bezeichnet, sowie von James Joyce und Virginia Woolf, den ästhetisch innovativsten Autoren der Moderne, sind bislang kaum in Verbindung mit der naturwissenschaftlichen Revolution gebracht worden. Die Analyse konzentriert sich auf die naturwissenschaftliche Herkunft der Analogien, Bilder und Begriffe, die vom Transformationsgedanken getragen werden, und untersucht systematisch den geistesgeschichtlichen Zusammenhang zwischen künstlerischen Vorstellungen und naturwissenschaftlichen Erkenntnissen.
Bd. 2, 2000, 344 S., 25,90 €, br., ISBN 3-8258-4424-2

LIT Verlag Berlin – Hamburg – London – Münster – Wien – Zürich
Fresnostr. 2 48159 Münster
Tel.: 0251 / 620 32 22 – Fax: 0251 / 922 60 99
e-Mail: vertrieb@lit-verlag.de – http://www.lit-verlag.de

Gerhard Wagner
The 'Beauty-Truths' of Literature
Elemente einer Dichtungstheorie in Aldous Huxleys Essayistik
Aldous Huxley hat zwar keine systematische Literarästhetik verfaßt, doch spielen dichtungs-
theoretische Fragestellungen in seinem umfangreichen essayistischen Werk eine ausgespro-
chen wichtige Rolle. Seine Überlegungen zum Sinn und Zweck sowie zu den Grenzen und
Möglichkeiten der Literatur sind fester Bestandteil seines philosophischen Denkens und
geprägt von seiner Auffassung der besonderen Erfahrungs- und Ausdrucksfähigkeiten des
wahren Dichters. Für ihn ist höhere Dichtung Träger von Erkenntnis, nämlich in Form von
"beauty-truths". Die vorliegende Studie analysiert und systematisiert Huxleys literartheoreti-
sche Vorstellungen und gelangt dabei zu einem heuristischen Denkmodell, das weit ausführ-
licher und kohärenter ist, als bislang angenommen wurde. Idealziel der Dichtung ist demnach
ein Gesamtentwurf, der die unmittelbar-gefühlsmäßige Erlebenswelt des Menschen wie auch
sein rational-wissenschaftliches Denken und darüber hinaus die Welt des aus menschlicher
Perspektive Nebensächlichen und Unbedeutenden erfaßt. Indem die Untersuchung Huxleys
graduelle Wendung von einer betont skeptischen hin zu einer mystischen Weltperspektive
berücksichtigt, gibt sie außerdem Aufschluß über Konstanten und Entwicklungen seines dich-
tungstheoretischen Denkens.
Bd. 3, 2001, 280 S., 30,90 €, br., ISBN 3-8258-5358-6

Peter Edgerly Firchow
Reluctant Modernists: Aldous Huxley and Some Contemporaries
A Collection of Essays edited by Evelyn S. Firchow and Bernfried Nugel. With an
Introduction by Jerome Meckier and a Personal Memoir by Janice Rossen. Presented
on the Occasion of his 65th Birthday December 16, 2002
The essays collected here deal with modernist writers who, on the whole, felt 'reluctant' about
their modernist status because they believed that it was just as important to look backward as it
was to look forward. Indeed, for most of them looking backward was more important because
it was only through the past that one could understand one's proper place in the present and
in the future. That is why in Huxley's *Brave New World* it is the rejection of the past in the
future – and by implication in the present – that makes its satire so penetrating. Modernism, in
other words, means for these writers not a radical break with the past but a continuing search
for what still connects them (and us) vitally with it.
Bd. 4, 2003, 352 S., 30,90 €, br., ISBN 3-8258-5962-2

James Hull
Aldous Huxley, Representative Man
Edited by Gerhard Wagner
This psychological reading of Huxley's oeuvre as a whole traces Huxley's self-transformation
in his books and aims to do justice to the artist and the person who was Aldous Huxley. It is
safe to regard as basic to his entire work the unfolding of the conflict we find so clearly de-
lineated in his early short story "Farcical History of Richard Greenow" (*Limbo*, 1920), with
Pearl Bellairs representing the emotional tradition that threatens the synthetic philosopher.
Huxley's own story is plainly visible even in *Limbo* and *Crome Yellow* (1921), but it is in *Antic Hay* (1923) that the pattern of the future assumes a solid foundation. There we encounter
in full force the tensions that follow him throughout his life: on the one hand an extreme of
sensuality and on the other a longing for the "chaste pleasures," for a quiet and mystical worid
completely different from that in which he found himself. The question of the relations between body and mind as well as the mystery of human consciousness haunt him to the very

LIT Verlag Berlin – Hamburg – London – Münster – Wien – Zürich
Fresnostr. 2 48159 Münster
Tel.: 0251 / 620 32 22 – Fax: 0251 / 922 60 99
e-Mail: vertrieb@lit-verlag.de – http://www.lit-verlag.de

last, but after his mid-life crisis, depicted in *Eyeless in Gaza* (1936), a strong faith in the reality of a spiritual world is obvions. In the end he even manages to reinstate the body in his scheme of things.

Bd. 5, 2004, 624 S., 49,90 €, br., ISBN 3-8258-7663-2

Lothar Fietz
Aldous Huxley – Prätexte und Kontexte
Lothar Fietz hatte bis zu seiner Emeritierung einen Lehrstuhl für Anglistik an der Universität Tübingen inne. Schwerpunkte seiner wissenschaftlichen Publikationen sind der Strukturwandel in der englischen Literatur seit der Renaissance, die Literaturtheorie und die Theoriegeschichte. Im 6. Band von „Human Potentialities" sind fünfzehn Artikel versammelt, in denen er das Werk Aldous Huxleys vor dem Hintergrund literarischer und philosophischer Prätexte historisch kontextualisiert. Die Arbeiten zu Huxleys Weltanschauung und Weltanschauungskritik kreisen um Fragestellungen von Mythos und Geschichte sowie von Geschichte als Verfallsprozeß und Utopie. Der Verfasser verfolgt die Denkstruktur vom Verlust und der Rückgewinnung mythischer Ganzheit durch verschiedene Kontexte von der kontinentalen Renaissance bis ins 20. Jahrhundert. Weitere Arbeiten eruieren den Wandel der literarischen und philosophischen Fiktionsbegriffe seit dem 18. Jahrhundert, den Verhältniswandel von literarischer und szientifischer Kultur seit dem 17. Jahrhundert und strukturelle Analogien in Romanen Manns, Hesses, Brochs und Kasacks zum Spätwerk Huxleys.

Bd. 6, 2005, 256 S., 34,90 €, br., ISBN 3-8258-8497-x

Hermann Josef Real; Peter Firchow (eds.)
The Perennial Satirist
Essays in Honour of Bernfried Nugel
The present collection of essays primarily honours Bernfried Nugel the teacher and scholar, but it also pays homage to Bernfried Nugel the indefatigable worker in the cause of Aldous Huxley studies. It is due to this latter manifestation that many of the contribu- tors to this volume know each other personally, having met at one or more of the international conferences that Professor Nugel organized and either hosted or co-hosted. At Munster, his home university, he has been instrumental in establishing and heading a Centre for admirers of Huxley's work, along with a fine library of Huxley materials, including manuscripts and numerous first editions.

Bd. 7, 2005, 400 S., 29,90 €, br., ISBN 3-8258-8339-6

LIT Verlag Berlin – Hamburg – London – Münster – Wien – Zürich
Fresnostr. 2 48159 Münster
Tel.: 0251 / 620 32 22 – Fax: 0251 / 922 60 99
e-Mail: vertrieb@lit-verlag.de – http://www.lit-verlag.de

Jerome Meckier

Aldous Huxley: Modern Satirical Novelist of Ideas

A Collection of Essays edited by
Peter E. Firchow and Bernfried Nugel

"Human Potentialities"
Studien zu Aldous Huxley & zeitgenössischer Kultur
Studies in Aldous Huxley & Contemporary Culture

LIT

Jerome Meckier
Aldous Huxley: Modern Satirical Novelist of Ideas
Edited by Peter Firchow and Bernfried Nugel
The essays on Aldous Huxley collected here were written between 1966 and 2005 and have been arranged by their author in such a way that they approximate a book on Huxley as a modern satirical novelist of ideas. In this capacity, Huxley assessed the intellectual condition of his era, always excoriating folly but never losing sight of human potentialities, especially his own. Huxley's ingrained skepticism persisted into his later fictions, even after his conception of the nature of things improved. The amused and highly amusing Pyrrhonic aesthete turned into a Swiftian Prospero. Detached yet totally committed to bettering the human condition, Huxley epitomized the dedicated craftsman. This lifelong aesthetician, always a philosopher, continues to command attention as thinker, critic, and artist: both satirist and sage.
Bd. 8, 2006, 408 S., 34,90 €, br., ISBN 3-8258-9668-4

LIT Verlag Berlin – Hamburg – London – Münster – Wien – Zürich
Fresnostr. 2 48159 Münster
Tel.: 0251 / 620 32 22 – Fax: 0251 / 922 60 99
e-Mail: vertrieb@lit-verlag.de – http://www.lit-verlag.de

Aldous Huxley Annual
A Journal of Twentieth-Century Thought and Beyond

Jerome Meckier; Bernfried Nugel (eds.)
Volume 1 (2001)
Aldous Huxley Annual is the official organ of the Aldous Huxley Society at the Centre for Aldous Huxley Studies in Münster, Germany (see AHS homepage on the Internet via <www.anglistik.uni-muenster.de/Huxley>). It publishes essays on the life, times, and interests of Aldous Huxley and his circle. It aspires to be the sort of periodical that Huxley would have wanted to read and to which he might have contributed.

2001, 248 S., 34,90 €, br., ISBN 3-8258-4370-x

Jerome Meckier; Bernfried Nugel (eds.)
Volume 2 (2002)
Aldous Huxley Annual is the official organ of the Aldous Huxley Society at the Centre for Aldous Huxley Studies in Münster, Germany (see AHS homepage on the Internet via <www.anglistik.uni-muenster.de/Huxley>). It publishes essays on the life, times, and interests of Aldous Huxley and his circle. It aspires to be the sort of periodical that Huxley would have wanted to read and to which he might have contributed. Volume 3 will feature Huxley's typescript for Brave New World: A Musical Comedy N.B.: The submission deadline for volume 3 of Aldous Huxley Annual is 15 April 2003. For further details see inside front cover.

2003, 256 S., 34,90 €, br., ISBN 3-8258-6280-1

Jerome Meckier; Bernfried Nugel (eds.)
Volume 3 (2003)
Background to *Brave New World*: Five Essays by Huxley
Brave New World: A Musical Comedy by Aldous Huxley
F. H. Cushing: A Source for Huxley's Brave Old World
Onomastic Satire: Names and Naming in *Brave New World*
Crome Yellow Revisited
Aldous Huxley and Anti-Semitism Aldous Huxley Annual is the official organ of the Aldous Huxley Society at the Centre for Aldous Huxley Studies in Münster, Germany. It publishes essays on the life, times, and interests of Aldous Huxley and his circle. It aspires to be the sort of periodical that Huxley would have wanted to read and to which he might have contributed.

Bd. 3, 2003, 248 S., 34,90 €, br., ISBN 3-8258-7137-1

Jerome Meckier; Bernfried Nugel (eds.)
Volume 4 (2004)
Aldous Huxley Annual is the official organ of the Aldous Huxley Society at the Centre for Aldous Huxley Studies in Münster, Germany (see AHS homepage on the Internet via <www.anglistik.uni-muenster.de/Huxley>). It publishes essays on the life, times, and interests of Aldous Huxley and his circle. It aspires to be the sort of periodical that Huxley would have wanted to read and to which he might have contributed. This issue features Aldous Huxley's and Beth Wendel's drama-tization of The Genius and the Goddess never before published. It also includes several rather unknown travel essays by Aldous Hux-ley as well as Peter E. Firchow's opening lecture at the Third International Aldous Huxley Symposium held in Riga in July 2004.

Bd. 4, 2005, 240 S., 34,90 €, br., ISBN 3-8258-8272-1

LIT Verlag Berlin – Hamburg – London – Münster – Wien – Zürich
Fresnostr. 2 48159 Münster
Tel.: 0251 / 620 32 22 – Fax: 0251 / 922 60 99
e-Mail: vertrieb@lit-verlag.de – http://www.lit-verlag.de

Aldous Huxley Annual
A Journal of Twentieth-Century Thought and Beyond

Contents

Aldous Huxley's
Condé Nast Essays on Painting

edited by
James Sexton

Aldous Huxley aka Condé Nast's "Staff of Experts" (I)   James Sexton
Crome Yellow: The Georgian Poet Orders His Tomb   Jerome Meckier
Nancy, Carrington, and Aldous: Fact and Fiction   Peter E. Firchow
On Religion: Huxley's Reading of Whitehead   Michel Weber
Freud's Beyond the Pleasure Principle and Brave New World   Samantha Vibbert
Eyeless in Gaza: Mystical Means and Socio-Political Ends   Anna Deters
Premonitions of the Postmodern: After Many a Summer   Michael Snyder
Witches and the Devil in Salem and Loudun   Irina Golovacheva
Aldous Huxley and Russia: Brief History of a Dialogue   Valery Rabinovitch

Volume 5 (2005)

LIT

Bernfried Nugel, Jerome Meckier (Eds.)
Aldous Huxley Annual
Volume 5 (2005)
This and the next *Annual* feature a collection of Aldous Huxley's early essays in art criticism, for the most part published anonymously. The present issue focuses on Huxley's critical approach to painting, particularly to Modernist works (Part I); *AHA* 6 will concentrate on Huxley's appraisal of architecture, applied arts and sculpture in the 1920s (Part II).
Bd. 5, 2006, 232 S., 34,90 €, br., ISBN 3-8258-9292-1

LIT Verlag Berlin – Hamburg – London – Münster – Wien – Zürich
Fresnostr. 2 48159 Münster
Tel.: 0251 / 620 32 22 – Fax: 0251 / 922 60 99
e-Mail: vertrieb@lit-verlag.de – http://www.lit-verlag.de